Security Council Sanctions Governance

Little is known about how far-reaching decisions in UN Security Council sanctions committees are made. Developing a novel committee governance concept and using examples drawn from sanctions imposed on Iraq, Al-Qaida, Congo, Sudan and Iran, this book shows that Council members tend to follow the will of the powerful, whereas sanctions committee members often decide according to the rules. This is surprising since both Council and committees are staffed by the same member states.

Offering a fascinating account of Security Council micro-politics and decision-making processes on sanctions, this rigorous comparative and theory-driven analysis treats the Council and its sanctions committees as distinguishable entities that may differ in decision practice despite having the same members. Drawing extensively on primary documents, diplomatic cables, well-informed press coverage, reports by close observers and extensive interviews with committee members, Council diplomats and sanctions experts, it contrasts with the conventional wisdom on decision-making within these bodies, which suggests that the powerful permanent members would not accept rule-based decisions against their interests.

This book will be of interest to policy practitioners and scholars working in the broad field of international organizations and international relations theory as well as those specializing in sanctions, international law, the Security Council and counter-terrorism.

Thomas Dörfler holds a PhD in Political Science from the University of Bamberg, Germany, and a Master's Degree from Leiden University, The Netherlands. He has been a Japan Society for the Promotion of Science (JSPS)-UNU Postdoctoral Research Fellow with the UNU Centre for Policy Research, a visiting scholar at John-Jay College of Criminal Justice (City University of New York) and a consultant for the Security Council Affairs Division of the UN Secretariat. Most recently, he held a post-doctoral position at the Technical University Munich, Germany, TUM School of Governance and will shortly be taking up a research fellow position at the University of Potsdam, Germany. Thomas has published in academic journals including Regulation & Governance, Global Governance, Journal of International Relations and Development, Terrorism & Political Violence, Journal of Economic Policy Reform, as well as several chapters in edited volumes and policy-relevant articles. For his work on UN sanctions, he has received the 2018 Hans-Löwel-Prize and the 2017 Award of the UN Association of Germany.

Routledge Research on the United Nations

1 **Chairing Multilateral Negotiations**
The Case of the United Nations
Spyros Blavoukos and Dimitris Bourantonis

2 **Individual Agency and Policy Change at the United Nations**
The People of the United Nations
Ingvild Bode

3 **Reforming UN Decision-Making Procedures**
Promoting a Deliberative System for Global Peace and Security
Daniel Niemetz Martin

3 **The UN International Criminal Tribunals**
Transition without Justice?
Klaus Bachmann and Aleksandar Fatić

4 **Norm Change in International Relations**
Linked Ecologies in UN Peacekeeping Operations
John Karlsrud

5 **Security Council Sanctions Governance**
The Power and Limits of Rules
Thomas Dörfler

Security Council Sanctions Governance

The Power and Limits of Rules

Thomas Dörfler

Routledge
Taylor & Francis Group
LONDON AND NEW YORK

First published 2019
by Routledge
2 Park Square, Milton Park, Abingdon, Oxon OX14 4RN

and by Routledge
605 Third Avenue, New York, NY 10017

First issued in paperback 2020

Routledge is an imprint of the Taylor & Francis Group, an informa business

British Library Cataloguing-in-Publication Data
A catalogue record for this book is available from the British Library

Library of Congress Cataloging-in-Publication Data
A catalog record has been requested for this book

ISBN 13: 978-0-367-73173-1 (pbk)
ISBN 13: 978-1-138-33749-7 (hbk)

Typeset in Times New Roman
by Wearset Ltd, Boldon, Tyne and Wear

Contents

Figures

Tables

Acknowledgments

This book on committee governance in the Security Council would not have been possible without the tremendous financial and institutional support I have received in Bamberg, New York and Tokyo over the course of this project. This includes the Bamberg Graduate School of Social Sciences (German Excellence Initiative), to which I owe my doctoral education in research design and methods. The German Foundation for Peace Research provided invaluable support through their funding of a pilot study "The Al-Qaida/Taliban Sanctions Committees" (KA001/12-Nr.13/50-2011) and a research project "Rule-based Decision-making through Complex Governance Structures?" (PA003/13-Nr.02/12-2012). I would also like to thank the University of Bayern e.V. and the Elite Network Bavaria for supporting my research with a full PhD scholarship. I am grateful for the German Academic Exchange Service travel grant in support of my field research. I also kindly acknowledge the generous financial support of the Japan Society for the Promotion of Science as a JSPS-UNU Postdoctoral Fellow.

This book would also not have been published without the dedicated support of many individuals. First and foremost, I would very much like to thank the members of my dissertation committee, Thomas Gehring, Monika Heupel and Thomas Rixen, who have been truly inspiring but challenging supervisors. Your commentary, ideas and advice were integral for improving the manuscript and shaping it in ways that I could not have imagined. I would also like to thank Thomas Saalfeld, and Miriam Schneider of the BAGSS for their invaluable support. I owe much to Peter Romaniuk, Charles Strozier and Hammad Sheikh of the Center on Terrorism at John Jay College of Criminal Justice for hosting me during my field research. I am indebted to my former colleagues at UNU-CPR, David Malone, Sebastian von Einsiedel, Rebecca Brubaker, Lee Schrader, and Basilio Valdehuesa, who greatly supported this endeavor and gave me the autonomy I needed to complete the project. I very much appreciate the huge support and encouragement of Anita Mathur, Thomas Heimgartner, and Dana Baikenzhina at the UN Secretariat, who hosted me at the Security Council Practices and Charter Research Branch and opened a new perspective on committee governance without which the book would have been quite different. I am grateful for the support of Yasuhiro Ueki of Sophia University for being an inspiring and patient host researcher and Mari Otaki for her outstanding administrative support. I would also like to thank the discussants and commentators at various conferences and workshops where I presented parts of this book project, including, but not limited to Thomas Biersteker, Michael Brzoska, Tine Hanrieder, George Lopez, Clara Portela, Kimberly Prost, Bob Reinalda, Christian von Soest, Etel Solingen, Marcos Tourinho, Peter Wallensteen, and Oliver Westerwinter. I would also like to thank the numerous interviewees, government and international organization officials, who provided indispensable insights into Security Council committee governance, conducted in three trips to New York in 2012, 2013 and 2016.

It has certainly been a pleasure to work with Routledge. I would like to thank Rob Sorsby and Claire Maloney for seeing value in the project and guiding me meticulously through the process of finalizing my manuscript. Two anonymous reviewers have provided excellent comments, which helped tremendously in improving the text. I would like to thank Roland Parr for your comments and advice on style and language. This work also benefited enormously from the feedback, support and encouragement given by many colleagues and friends: Frank Bandau, Manuel Becker, Julia Dinkel, Christian Dorsch, Simon Fink, Axel Obermeier, Daniel Odinius, Len-Ole Schaefer, Diana Schacht, Eric Stollenwerk, Kevin Urbanski, Florian Weiler as well as Mareen Esmeier and Dennis Kleinert. All remaining errors are solely my responsibility.

Abbreviations

ADF	Allied Democratic Forces – National Army for the Liberation of Uganda, Rebel group operating in the DRC
AMIS	African Union Mission in Sudan
ASSMT	Analytical Support and Sanctions Monitoring Team, Panel of Experts associated with the Al-Qaida and Taliban sanctions regimes
CPA	Comprehensive Peace Agreement
DPA	Darfur Peace Agreement
E10	Elected non-permanent members of the UN Security Council
EU	European Union
FAO	Food and Agricultural Organization
FARDC	Forces Armées de la République Démocratique du Congo
FDLR	Forces démocratiques de libération du Rwanda, rebel group operating in the DRC
FNI	Front des Nationalistes et Intégrationnistes, rebel group operating in the DRC
G-7	Group of Seven
G-19	Group of 19, rebel group operating in Sudan
IAEA	International Atomic Energy Agency
ICC	International Criminal Court
ICRC	International Committee of the Red Cross
ICTY	International Criminal Tribunal for the former Yugoslavia
IO	International Organization
IRISL	Islamic Republic of Iran Shipping Lines
ISIL	Islamic State of Iraq and the Levant
JEM	Justice and Equality Movement, rebel group operating in Sudan
LRA	Lord Resistance Army, rebel group operating in the DRC
M23	Mouvement du 23 Mars, rebel group operating in the DRC
MONUC	Mission des Nations Unies en République démocratique du Congo
MONUSCO	Mission de l'Organisation des Nations Unies pour la stabilisation en République démocratique du Congo
MTCR	Missile Technology Control Regime
M/V	Motor Vessel
NSG	Nuclear Suppliers Group

ONUC	Organisation des Nations Unies au Congo
P3	Security Council Permanent Members (France, United Kingdom, United States)
P5	Security Council Permanent Members (China, France, Russian Federation, United Kingdom, United States)
P5+1	P5 plus Germany
SAF	Sudanese Armed Forces
SCR	Security Council Report, non-profit organization documenting Security Council activity
SITC	UN Standard International Trade Classification
SLA	Sudan Liberation Army, rebel group operating in Sudan
UK	United Kingdom of Great Britain and Northern Ireland
UNAMID	African Union/United Nations Hybrid operation in Darfur
UNAMIS	United Nations Advance Mission in Sudan
UNDP	United Nations Development Programme
UNMIS	United Nations Missions in Sudan
UNSC	United Nations Security Council
UNSCR	United Nations Security Council Resolution
US	United States of America

1 Security Council sanctions governance

The power and limits of rules

The United Nations Security Council increasingly delegates a broad range of decisions to specially created sanctions committees in the context of its sanctions regimes. These committees, which consist of the same 15 Council members, often decide about a large number of vital issues including, for instance, which "humanitarian" goods are exempted from a complete trade embargo or which individuals and entities are subject to assets freezes and travel bans. Remarkably, the early Yugoslavia Sanctions Committee adopted almost 35,000 decisions in just 1 year. Contemporary targeted sanctions committees together took almost 450 listing and delisting decisions in the last 5 years, and a total of almost 620 individuals and 300 entities found themselves on various Council sanctions lists in 2017. All of these decisions resulted from the past and present activities of specifically created sanctions committees, the activities of which often go unnoticed. Sanctions committee decisions can have grave humanitarian consequences or breach the fundamental human rights of sanctioned individuals. These decisions are legally binding and substantially enhance or strain the effectiveness and legitimacy of a key tool for conflict resolution. The question of how the Security Council's sanctions committees (should) work has triggered a fierce and critical debate over not only the Council's legal limits, but also the political feasibility of sanctions and their effectiveness among sanctions practitioners and Security Council commentators, as well as human rights activists.

To explore Security Council sanctions' governance, I present here a theoretical concept to answer a research question relevant to academics and policy practitioners alike: How and with what consequences does the creation of sanctions committees within the Security Council composed of member states' representatives affect the behavior of Council members and the content of their decisions? This subsumes four aspects: How are the tasks divided between Council and committee? How does delegation affect the Council? How does it change the committees' work? Additionally, how does this impact on the content of decisions? These questions refer to a fascinating theoretical and empirical puzzle. The delegation of tasks from the Council to its committees seems to affect the decisions taken, despite the fact that the same states are involved in taking all the decisions. Former sanctions committee members have noted that states' behavior in the committees is different from that in the Council. The sanctions committees often take decisions based on rules or precedents, thus in a more consistent and predictable manner. Looking back, David Malone asserted that:

> [t]he evolution of the Security Council's role on Iraq points to one significant shift – from a mainly politico-military approach to international peace and security to a greater reliance on a legal-regulatory approach. In its legal-regulatory approach, the Council establishes detailed rules governing the behavior of states or other entities and devolves power to implement and monitor those rules to administrative delegates.
>
> (Malone and Chitalkar 2016, p. 557, also Malone 2006)

Paul Conlon further affirmed that "[d]elegates frequently asked the secretariat for information on previous practice, precedents and similar cases in the past. Occasionally delegates consented to decisions they had originally opposed in order not to upset previously established patterns and practices" (Conlon 1996b, p. 280). Former Yugoslavia Committee delegates asserted that "(…) the record (*sic.*) of the Sanctions Committee's deliberations are full of references to previous cases which the Committee Members considered to constitute precedent (…)" (Scharf and Dorosin 1993, pp. 823–824). Other Council diplomats and close observers have made similar comments (van Walsum 2004; Koskenniemi 1991). How can we grasp the phenomenon that Security Council sanctions committees tend to take decisions in accordance with rules and precedents, although the same powerful member states are known to follow purely political interests in the Council chamber?

Sanctions form one of the few tools at the Security Council's disposal to maintain international peace and security below the level of military enforcement action. They are frequently imposed as a substitute for the use of force, alongside enforcement and peacekeeping, or as a first step which may ultimately lead to military intervention. While there were only 2 sanctions regimes during the Cold War, thereafter the Security Council has created almost 30 (Farrall 2007). Over the years, the Council has been most inventive in designing different sanctions measures. While relying on comprehensive trade embargoes as a means of coercing behavioral change in Iraq, Yugoslavia and Haiti, the extreme humanitarian consequences resulting from these types of sanctions subsequently led the Council to impose measures on specific individuals and entities, often referred to as "smart sanctions" because they are supposed to target those directly responsible for transgressions (Brzoska 2003). The Council has applied sanctions in a variety of situations, for instance to prevent Al-Qaida and ISIL terrorist activities as well as nuclear weapons programs in Iran and North Korea, to resolve internal armed conflicts in the Congo, and to avert gross human rights violations in Libya (Biersteker *et al.* 2016a).

For an organization steeped in great power politics and dealing with often contested issues of preserving world peace, Security Council sanctions regimes exhibit a remarkable design for implementing a variety of sanctions measures. Since the first sanctions regime, committees have been created that mirror

Council membership and decide on the implementation of sanctions by consensus. It was intended that the Council should be relieved of dealing with all questions considered too detailed and technical, while at the same time having a machinery ready to take on these issues at a later stage (Sievers and Daws 2014, pp. 519–543). Hence, sanctions regimes, although they are temporary arrangements, require significant regulatory decision-making, often over extended periods of time. Effectively, the Council detached broader political questions on why, when, how, how long and when to lift sanctions on a target state or target group from many small, technical follow-up questions: Who should be added to a sanctions list? Who should be removed from such a list and under which circumstances? Can a sanctioned individual travel to receive medical treatment? Which items have "dual-use" potential for a nuclear weapons program? What will be the response to a reported sanctions violation? Notably, such issues were already being faced in the first post-Cold War sanctions case on Iraq: "Were beer or cigarettes foodstuffs? Could surgical clamps be deemed supplies intended strictly for medical purposes? Could an Iraqi diplomat sell his car before returning home?" (Conlon 2000, p. 45). In essence, the overall impact of Council sanctions regimes depends on a plethora of small decisions taken in committees, while each such decision in isolation has quite limited impact. However, in high politics, member states, particularly the powerful permanent members, bargain hard over these decisions, which are politically sensitive and often controversial.

Despite the frequently observed implications of committee governance, the scholarly literature lacks a convincing account dealing with its effects in the Security Council. Accordingly, in this book I present a theoretical argument that explains why and how the transfer of decisions from Council to committee systematically pushes states toward a form of rule-based governance, even though the same group of states takes all relevant decisions. I explore why states are incentivized to align their decision proposals with pre-defined rules, and investigate the effects of committee governance with empirical evidence from the Council's Iraq, Al-Qaida/Taliban, Democratic Republic of the Congo, Sudan and Iran sanctions regimes. Using in-depth case studies, I highlight the consequences of delegating tasks to a committee, even among the same group of states. While each of the case studies is revealing in its own right, a structured comparison facilitates the drawing of conclusions beyond each case's particularities.

The Security Council presents a demanding case for a theory of committee governance in international organizations (IO). It is an almost purely intergovernmental organization whose secretariat has little or no influence over its decisions. Dominating the Council are the five great powers that serve as permanent members with rights of veto and often conflicting agendas. These great powers are well-resourced and hold comparatively high stakes in security matters. The Council's purview of maintaining international peace and security is often regarded as being least prone to institutionalized cooperation. Hence, the member states seek to remain in full control of all its decisions (including those taken in committees). Furthermore, the scholarly literature presents rather statist, obvious, and widely-shared alternative explanations for Council decision-making

(Bosco 2009). Accordingly, finding that sanctions committee members use rules and precedents to guide their behavior would strongly support the theoretical claim, even though these members have strong incentives to avoid the implications of such rules and precedents.

This book provides a rare systematic and comparative analysis of decision-making within Council sanctions regimes that exceeds the prevailing case studies of single sanctions regimes. I find substantial evidence that delegation to committees commits even the great powers to a form of rule-based sanctions governance, while the Sudan sanctions regime demonstrates its limitations. Although findings from the five case studies cannot be broadly generalized, the theoretical concept explicates the fundamental sources of a development that practitioners have suspected since the first post-Cold War sanctions regime. This book also contributes to intellectual debate about International Relations (IR). Despite contention regarding Council sanctions, member states have developed a remarkable governance system that may produce consistent and rule-based decisions founded on abstract criteria and evidence that one would not expect to witness in a "high politics" setting. Such delegation of regulatory tasks to consensus-based "committees of the whole" is a prevalent feature in international politics. Should these effects hold true for the Security Council, this institutional design would be a means of credibly committing IOs' member states to rule-based decision-making without losing their discretion to adopt explicit political decisions or even delegate decisions to an autonomous secretariat, court or regulatory network.

The argument: How committee governance triggers rule-based politics

I look at committee governance within the Security Council by exploring how divided labor among different member state bodies, the Council, and its committee affects their decision-making. Drawing from existing rational institutionalist accounts of international organizations in IR, I develop a theory that explains why, how and under which conditions the transfer of decisions to sanctions committees might drive the same member states toward rule-based governance. I regard rule-based politics as decision-making on separate implementation issues that follow formal rules, informal rules or precedents, even when those outcomes contradict the interests of powerful committee members. At the outset, I outline a concept of IOs that identifies their most basic function by continually adopting collective decisions for their members. IOs, including the Security Council, affect collective decision-making insofar as they structure negotiations. A group of self-interested states in the Security Council, which refers tasks to a committee, will, therefore, create an entirely different setting in both the Council and the committee, even if the same group of states decides on all issues.

The core argument developed throughout this book revolves around the idea that Council members profoundly affect decision-making if they separate broader political questions from many follow-up decisions of a similar nature.

Typically, the Council splits a sanctions regime into two stages. In a first the Council defines certain criteria; for instance, what kind of behavior merits sanctions. In a subsequent stage the committee then decides about many follow-up issues, which may for instance concern specific individuals to be added to a sanctions list in view of these criteria. This form of regulatory politics is quite different from the usual Council decision-making, where its members link many different issues into complex Council resolutions.

I argue that Council members create an incomplete contract if they entrust implementation decisions to a committee. In such a case the Council members are immediately relieved from taking all necessary decisions and postpone technical implementation to a later committee stage. Instead, Council members define a broader framework according to which follow-up sanctions decisions are taken in committee. This might include a more or less specific committee mandate, together with decision criteria or procedures. However, negotiating an incomplete contract submits the Council members to certain constraints. Whereas a complete contract allows for trading-off different issues, Council members now focus on negotiating rules that promise to ensure acceptable outcomes on many future follow-up decisions at committee stage. Even though Council members might favor certain committee decisions over others, each member has to aggregate interests on a whole range of potential future request into a general rule. I argue that states take interest in adopting rules that promise to result in widely acceptable solutions on many follow-up decisions across time. Designing general rules will be particularly constraining when states prefer different cases and moreover are uncertain about their nature in the future.

Why should Security Council members tend toward rule-based politics and accept certain unfavorable decisions when deciding within a committee? At committee stage, the same group of Council members decides about many small, separate and technical implementation decisions, for instance about concrete proposals for adding individuals to a sanctions list. While Council members would certainly prefer to uphold the division of labor between Council and committee, they have established to relieve the Council from taking all these decisions, member state compliance with rules can hardly be enforced. If committee members deal with many such decisions at different points in time, they cannot be linked to package deals. Yet, states will not always agree on substance. A committee member clearly cannot simply reject every unfavorable request because other committee members would do the same. Committee members have to consider each proposal in ways that are acceptable even for those who dislike the outcome. In other words, some committee members must compromise, while others will prevail. By contrast, arm-twisting over single implementation requests in a consensus-based committee almost inevitably leads to a deadlock. This resembles a situation in which states advocate different solutions but prefer coordination in principle because non-coordination presents an unattractive alternative, given that without implementation sanctions can obviously not take effect. These situations create the demand for focal points (Schelling 1960).

Committee members have two potential sources of focal points to arrive at a coordinated solution in the committee stage. Primarily, existing Council rules present themselves as a solution. In the event of the Council determining a particular set of criteria, rules, and procedures, states in the committee stage take an interest in adopting these as a benchmark for their decision-making. Instead of a choice between solutions favored by different member states, members now have a choice between following or violating existing rules. Hence, rules favor those preferring a rule-conforming solution. Even powerful members are likely to follow existing rules, therefore, despite some who might dislike one specific decision, because above all rule adherence is better than stalemate. Accordingly, committee members are likely to follow existing rules not because they are unbiased, just or equally preferred by all members, but due to such rules providing solutions to regulatory problems. However, committee members can also adopt their own self-regulating rules under the same constraints of making generalized rules applicable to many future cases.

Alternatively, should there be no suitable rules, committee members can resort to informal rules in the form of precedents. Basing decisions on similar but earlier accepted or rejected proposals offers convenient solutions to coordination issues that would otherwise lead to stalemate. An earlier decision – regardless of how it came about – will inevitably provide a benchmark for later decisions of a similar kind because it reflects a collective choice having been made. Its members will find difficulty in selecting a more widely acceptable alternative over the precedent. Repeatedly accepted precedents are likely to create a committee practice. As with rules, an established precedent creates collective expectations in differentiating between acceptable and unacceptable proposals. The mechanism is quite powerful, as those members who have sacrificed their preferred solutions in favor of committee compromise will insist that others, who face unfavorable choices, should also adhere to accepted practice.

This logic explains why Council members, who delegate decisions to themselves in a later committee stage, will tend to follow rule-based governance in committee. With an alternative to committee deadlock in mind, member states may instead favor unwanted outcomes, because this preserves the sanctions regime's functioning. Overall, the concept of committee governance reveals that delegating decisions to a committee generates fundamentally different incentives for a group of states. In fact, egoistic states can accept a rule-conforming decision, even if it is not their preferred solution, as long as they prefer agreement over stalemate. The logic of committee governance also accounts for why states pursue rule-based sanctions governance, even though they initially might prefer individual flexibility over binding rules.

Let me extend the limits of this argument. My claim is not that committee governance is dissociated from power. To the contrary, sanctions regimes are a result of great power interests, which is reflected in the design of a sanctions regime. Neither are Council rules devoid of power nor necessarily fair or justifiable. Instead, my claim is that committee governance comes with constraints that even powerful members cannot escape if they delegate tasks to a committee.

In reality, rules become a means of power. Hence, the Council and committee framework's institutional constraints shape, but do not rule out the exercise of power in single cases. Additionally, I focus on instances where streams of decisions, for instance the listing of individuals subjected to targeted sanctions, are referred to a committee because the committee governance thesis is to do with rules that apply to a broader range of cases. While these implementation decisions take up a large share of committees' workloads, I would also expect to find that the great powers completely dominate larger, important and less-regularized decisions, such as appointing Panels of Experts which advise the sanctions committees.

I compare my concept of committee governance with a traditional model of power politics (Voeten 2005), where Council members negotiate about all relevant aspects of a sanctions regime without recourse to a committee stage. In this model, Council members would negotiate a complete contract. In the absence of a committee system, I expect them to trade-off certain elements of a sanctions regime against each other, for instance different sanctions measures *together with* a list of targets, and bundle them into larger package resolutions. In this case, the Council members are likely to use all available means of institutional and material power (Schneider 2011) to achieve a political compromise closest to their preferred policies (Dreher *et al.* 2015; Carter and Stone 2015). Members allot potential cooperation gains based on how powerful each of them is. In other words, decisions are set to reflect the veto powers' will. Without a committee stage, I expect to find that Council members will have no interest in decisions that follow abstract rules which run counter to their preferred policies unless they receive something in return from other members. Conversely, adherence to rules would be less relevant for Council members. The Council has been established as a political body with far-reaching freedoms (Hurd 2007, pp. 83–105) and the provisions of the UN Charter provide hardly any constraints (Peters 2012, pp. 765–771).

The Security Council context is ideally suited for studying the merits of the committee governance argument as it is possible to isolate the causal mechanism from other explanatory factors. These committees operate under Chapter VII mandates, implying that their sanctions decisions are legally binding on all states and consequently very contentious negotiations are often involved. Five great powers dominate the Council, states which exert tight control over all policies. For a long time now, the permanent members have resisted any form of outside review that may encroach on their prerogatives. These great powers avoid any other limitations to their Council policies aside from what their own power allows them to achieve. The Council Secretariat has very limited influence, and thus the Council is least amenable to experiencing the effects of committee governance. If committee governance affects the five great powers in this intergovernmental "high politics" organization, it might also be observable in more complex international organizations such as the European Union or the World Bank, provided that they fall within the scope of committee governance laid out in this book.

Committee governance and international organizations

Although institutionalist scholars in international relations have recently rediscovered international organizations, the available literature does not yet offer a convincing explanation as to how intra-organizational aspects of IOs influence member state behavior. In criticizing the pessimistic neorealist notions of institutions, the institutionalist scholarship has considered international institutions to be a central unit of analysis, but focused specifically on international regimes and less so on international organizations (Martin and Simmons 2013, pp. 330–331). From a theoretical perspective, the literature has only just started to grasp the implications of decision-making within IOs' institutional settings. Yet, the empirical consequences of committee governance in the Security Council are still largely unaccounted for.

Rationalist scholarship has taken a great deal of interest in IOs. The rationalist principal-agent delegation literature investigates why and with what consequences states as "principals" delegate tasks to IOs as "agents." This recent scholarship on international organizations ascribes secretariats a central role in IO decision-making processes. Ideally, principals want their agents to act as they would have done in the agents' place. However, any agent may of course deviate from the principal's intention (Hawkins *et al.* 2006; Nielson and Tierney 2003). These approaches assume that principals must dispense with the proper means of control, such as "police patrols" and "fire alarms," in order to secure their agents' functioning according to the principals' interest (McCubbins and Schwartz 1984; Pollack 1997). Such approaches have been used to study the discretion of IO bureaucracies in designing new international organizations (Johnson and Urpelainen 2014), delegation within the European Union (Pollack 1997; Pollack 2003), the World Bank (Nielson and Tierney 2003) or the World Trade Organization (Elsig and Pollack 2014; Stone 2011). Yet, the Security Council has an almost purely administrative secretariat, which is unlikely to cause the observed effects of committee governance.

Related to the delegation literature, other scholars argue that states could enhance the credibility of their commitment to a cooperation project by delegating to an *independent* agent (Majone 2001; Franchino 2002). Without being credibly committed to the long-term cooperation goal, a state might use discretion in pursuing its short-term interest. This "time inconsistency" problem can be solved when the agent's incentives differ from those of the principal and thus commit the latter to a long-term interest in cooperation. The agent *must* be sufficiently independent to implement the desired policy freely. Such logic can be found in delegation to international courts (Alter 2006; Alter 2008), the International Criminal Court (Simmons and Danner 2010), and the European Central Bank (Majone 2001). However, the sanctions committees are first and foremost member state bodies mirroring Council membership.

Debate about the effect of committees and regulatory networks in the European Union also shares insights on IO committee governance. EU comitology literature has argued that delegation of decision competencies to executive committees affects the governance of a particular issue area (Joerges 2006; Joerges and Neyer 2001). Such approaches have maintained that functional differentiation forecloses states' abilities to achieve their preferred outcomes through power-based bargaining (Gehring 2004). Furthermore, this scholarship has shown that delegation to committees leads to problem-adequate, though "low-politics," governance in environmental politics (Gehring and Plocher 2009), protection of species (Gehring and Ruffing 2008), international development (Kerler 2010) and regulatory policies in the European Union (Gehring 2003; Gehring and Kerler 2008). Another strand argues that EU member state committees tend to move outcomes away from the EU Council's positions toward those of the Commission as agenda-setter (Ballmann *et al.* 2002). However, Security Council committees typically operate without such an agenda setter. A third strand claims that over time delegates in EU committees act in an increasingly consensus-oriented manner as a result of socialization (Quaglia *et al.* 2008). A fourth strand weighs the role of member states' regulatory networks in the EU polity (Coen and Thatcher 2008). However, as European networks are embedded within the firmly established European legal system and subject to European Court of Justice jurisdiction, neither similarly detailed administrative law nor judicial control are present in the Security Council (Kingsbury *et al.* 2005).

The turn to constructivist scholarship has contributed to understanding international organizations as bureaucracies with a view on IO secretariats. The bureaucratic culture approach highlights that the autonomous action of IO organs lies in the organization's ability, in this case the IO secretariat, to define its own bureaucratic rules (Reinalda 2013, pp. 17–18). Barnett and Finnemore conceptualize international organizations as bureaucracies, whose authority is exercised through the creation of impersonal rules. These rules can become problematic when they lead to "self-defeating outcomes" and organizational pathologies (1999; 2004, recently Salton 2017). Biermann and Siebenhüner maintain that secretariats are predominantly interested in problem-solving rather than maximizing their own mandate and power. Accordingly, differences in IO secretariats' autonomy can be attributed to differences in organizational culture (2009; 2013). However, this explanation is not transferable to Security Council sanctions because it lacks an influential secretariat.

The theory-driven Security Council literature has mainly focused on how external factors may affect the role of IOs in general and the Council in particular. Alexander Thompson looks at why and how great powers channel their potentially coercive activities through IOs, arguing that they serve a vital function of information transmission (2006; 2009). Vreeland and Dreher study how great powers may use external power resources, threats and bribes as incentives and disincentives to achieve their preferred outcomes in the Council (2014; see also, Dreher *et al.* 2009; Kuziemko and Werker 2006). Erik Voeten convincingly argues how credible and asymmetric outside options of great powers affect the bargaining room for Council decisions on the use of force (2001). While these perspectives have contributed to our understanding of IOs and the Security

Council, they do not tell us much about the impact of intra-organizational factors in shaping IO outcomes.

Both UN sanctions literature and international legal scholarship have critically engaged with the issue of targeted sanctions implemented through committees. However, there is a notable dearth of studies that capture decision-making on individual cases in Security Council committees, presumably because of data access restrictions. As a result, very few scholars have provided single-case studies featuring committees (Ward 2005; Scharf and Dorosin 1993; Conlon 2000). Besides the debate on sanctions' effectiveness (Biersteker *et al.* 2016a), a particular controversy has emerged around targeted sanctions against individuals suspected of supporting transnational terrorism (Biersteker 2004). Notably, the Watson report studied how Council's targeted sanctions regimes could more adequately be brought in line with the fundamental rights of listed individuals (Biersteker and Eckert 2006). Scholars of international law have devised normative standards for desirable due process protection (Hovell 2016), problematized the Security Council's rule of law deficiencies (Farrall and Charlesworth 2016), and explored how states can enforce such protection through massive disobedience (Tzanakopoulos 2011). The debate suggests that a sanctions committee serves power politics rationales and can hardly ensure due process, therefore, without an effective remedy outside the Council's purview (Sullivan and Goede 2013, p. 853). Accordingly, creating the remarkably strong Office of Ombudsperson has profoundly changed the situation within this sanctions regime (Eckert and Biersteker 2012, p. 36). These scholars almost entirely associate the increasing regulation with external pressure by member states or domestic courts within the Al-Qaida sanctions regime (Heupel 2013; Kanetake 2008). However, this can hardly explain why similar effects occurred before such external pressure emerged, as in the early Iraq sanctions regime or in the absence of such pressure in many other sanctions regimes.

The literature provides no convincing account of how committee governance affects IO decision-making, which is surprising because committees form a prevalent feature of IO policy-making. Both rationalist and constructivist strands of literature attribute the effects of international organizations to just *one* aspect, namely autonomous IO secretariats or courts. The IO literature either explicitly (Brown 2010, p. 142) or implicitly (Hooghe and Marks 2015; Haftel and Thompson 2006) excludes member state committees from the analysis of delegation relationships, principal-agent constellations or IO autonomy. Security Council committee governance does not trigger these channels of influence because the same group of states comprises both principal *and* agent; the secretariat has minimal influence. Yet, many scholars and practitioners seem to agree that Council *and* committee decision-making is inherently relevant (Kingsbury *et al.* 2005; Feinäugle 2010; Scharf and Dorosin 1993). In this book, I seek to explore systematically how committee governance in the Security Council structures its decision-making and the collective choice of its members. I adopt a fresh perspective that is deeply rooted in rationalism and bridges both rationalist and constructivist accounts of IO politics. The approach is embedded in existing research but makes it possible for different types of research questions to be posed. For instance, how can intra-organizational factors shape decision outcomes? How does the delegation of tasks to identical groups of states affect the behavior of rational states, including the great powers? What are the causal mechanisms that lead to these effects? And what is the role of rules and precedents in IO committee governance?

Methods and outline of the book

To investigate the causal mechanism behind committee governance, I take a primarily qualitative design and present five in-depth case studies: sanctions regimes concerning Iraq, Al-Qaida/Taliban, DRC, Sudan, and Iran. While each of these cases serves to underpin the book's theoretical claims, they combine the benefits of in-depth case-studies with the strengths of a systematic comparative design. Each chapter is based on a theory-testing process tracing of committee decision-making episodes (Beach and Pedersen 2013). My analysis draws extensively on details of decision-making in practice taken from primary documents, few of which have been accounted for in past research. The chapter on Iraq is based on original documents that contain all verbal interventions by committee members during the first 120 meetings of the committee. This also includes original records of all requests the committee received. Thereafter, chapters are based on diplomatic cables available online, which include detailed notes of committee meetings, proposals and decisions. I also rely heavily on press coverage of committee proceedings and reports by close observers, in particular from Security Council Report, a New York-based non-profit organization. At Council level, documents include resolutions, presidential statements, press statements, annual reports and verbatim records, while at committee level, analysis draws on various documentary bases including rules of procedures, sanctions lists, press releases and the committee annual reports. The Panel of Experts reports serve as another major data source. All material was complemented by three dozen expert interviews with sanctions committee members, Council diplomats, close observers and UN sanctions experts on the four current sanctions regimes conducted in New York. These interviews served mainly an exploratory function for selecting suitable cases, case-episodes and acquiring data. Yet, I have been careful to use interviews sparingly to confirm my data interpretation, so as to maintain confidentiality, objectivity and replicability; whenever it was possible I replaced interviews with written sources.

Since it is not feasible to study all of the more than 30 UN sanctions regimes to date, I have chosen 5 in particular for varying reasons. For each of these regimes the Council delegated streams of similar single cases to a committee, including, for instance, the listing of individuals subject to targeted sanctions or particular goods exempted from a trade embargo. While monitoring or reporting functions are of course politically important, they fall outside the scope of my theory. In cases where Council members do not intend to make decisions, clearly the effects cannot be observed, and hence the most recent sanctions regimes are excluded.

Cases have been chosen on the basis of being as different as possible from each other, because finding the same mechanism in similar cases will hardly increase our confidence in that specific mechanism. From a research design perspective, the Iraq sanctions regime's first five years form a great starting point. First, the US expressly rejected the idea of being bound by rules, yet had a strong position both in Council and committee, as any exemption to the embargo required its consent. Finding that committee governance triggers rule-based governance against the vocal opposition of the US in specific cases is compelling evidence for the book's thesis. Second, because of massive humanitarian consequences for the Iraqi population, the Council chose to introduce targeted rather than comprehensive sanctions. Finding rule-based governance in a sanctions regime prior to these sanctions reforms demonstrates that it was a consequence of committee governance, not collective learning. While much has been written about the Al-Qaida sanctions regime, and it is certainly the most advanced sanctions regime, possessing global reach and the largest sanctions list (e.g., Biersteker and Eckert 2006, p. 25), it is comparable to other regimes in as much as the Council transferred many single-case decisions to a committee. This case is crucial precisely *because* the literature suggests that a committee composed of member states simply follows a power politics rationale and cannot ensure rule-based due process standards. An independent review body outside the Council's control was, therefore, indispensable. The frequent reports that decision-making had been conforming with rules long before the Council created a review mechanism calls for investigating committee governance. Yet, because of the pressure for due process reforms by courts and member states, it represents a most likely case for committee governance.

I study committee governance for three additional targeted sanctions regimes. As the literature often claims that rule-based governance in the Al-Qaida case came about only in response to external pressure, finding rule-based governance in the DRC sanctions regime, which received almost no attention, would strengthen our confidence in this book's thesis. Furthermore, the DRC represents a case of noticeable conflict so far as the US, France and the UK were concerned (but not the P3, Russia and China). The Sudan case is probably the best to demonstrate the limits of committee governance. To impose sanctions on Sudan was highly contested, to the extent that China preferred a committee stalemate. To overcome this impasse, the Council sidelined its committee and subjected individuals to sanctions. I selected the Iran regime in particular because it makes possible a comparison of the differences in listing individuals via the Council versus listing individuals via a committee. Accordingly, it contrasts the committee governance thesis with the alternative arrangement without committee. It also offers another intriguing facet, namely the listing of dual-use goods subject to export restrictions, which do not raise due process issues as sanctions targeted on individuals. Discovering the effects of committee governance in the five different sanctions regimes may provide good reason to believe that they represent a broader phenomenon of committee governance across a range of different interest constellations or sanctions measures. Overall, the case selection rests on the falsifiable, but plausible assumption that different cases produce principally similar findings.

Beyond research design requirements, processes of committee decision-making in these key sanctions regimes are chiefly relevant to the wider academic and policy communities. The Security Council is perhaps the most important international organization in the area of international peace and security. Its decisions (or the lack thereof) are often controversial, contested and publicly scrutinized. Limited membership means that its legitimacy to a large extent depends on how much trust UN member states place in proper Council procedures. The sanctions tool is one of very few that fall below the use of force. For this reason, sanctions are likely to remain as one of the central policy tools for addressing what its members consider as threats to international peace and security, including violent conflict, terrorism and non-proliferation. This fresh theoretical approach might contribute an original perspective on committee governance in the Security Council. Paying analytical attention to early and current sanctions regimes could complement what we know so far about the Security Council and its sanctions committees. As Paul Conlon, an early UN Secretariat witness serving the Iraq Sanctions Committee, argued:

> If Council and subsidiary organ practice were more clearly distinguished from each other, the political discretion of the Council, with its often questionable sanctions decisions, might appear more legitimate. Member states would have to accept politically driven sanctions decisions of the Council, but once those decisions were adopted, member states would have a more predictable system of norms and practices to fall back upon within the sanctions committees.
>
> (2000, p. 9)

In the following Chapter 2, I develop in detail my theoretical argument and hypotheses, argue why the concept is applicable to the Security Council and operationalize core concepts. Chapter 3 then illuminates the broader dynamics of Security Council committee governance. This chapter explores the way in which Council sanctions regimes are more nuanced in design than the prevailing forum perspective on the Council would suggest. It reassesses how the Council divides various sanctions tasks between itself, the sanctions committees, and other relevant bodies including the UN Secretariat, the consultative expert panels, and a review body dealing with delisting petitions by sanctioned individuals. The chapter closes with a discussion on how each of these bodies works and how this might affect decision-making in favor of rule adherence.

In Chapter 4, I study committee governance in the Iraq sanctions regime, which the Council imposed in reaction to the Iraqi occupation of Kuwait in 1990. The sanctions committee's decisions were mainly to do with which UN member states' requests for humanitarian deliveries could be exempted from the trade embargo. At an early stage, rules and precedent helped to solve a conflict among committee members over the deliveries of food supplies to Iraq.

Following the Gulf War, this committee developed a fairly consistent practice based on categories which were termed "humanitarian items." A statistical analysis of 8,200 exemption requests from 1993–1995 reveals that the committee decided according to rules derived from item categories. Finally, an episode on flight exemptions shows how rule-based decision-making prevailed against the will of two Western permanent members. This chapter serves to provide an initial test for the committee governance hypothesis.

In Chapter 5, I cover committee governance in the Al-Qaida/Taliban sanctions regime. The Council had originally created this regime to curb Taliban support for terrorism, but transformed it into a global counter-terrorism regime after 9/11. The sanctions committee's key objective is to decide which individuals and entities suspected of supporting transnational terrorism should be subject to targeted sanctions. There being no conflict of interests among its members, the committee initially rubber-stamped requests for sanctions listings. Later, the Council adopted – and the committee refined – rules to address any lack of legitimacy and effectiveness. These in turn helped the committee to replace a laissez-faire approach with rule-based politics. The Council also created a separate Taliban sanctions regime to solve a committee deadlock over delisting Taliban members. Ultimately, the committee increasingly decided according to rules even before the Office of Ombudsperson was created. However, the potent mechanism for reviewing delisting petitions helped committee members abide by the rules and procedures. This chapter expands on the concept of committee governance to a targeted sanctions regime.

In Chapter 6, I study committee governance in the DRC sanctions regime, which targets individuals and entities that obstruct the peace process in eastern DRC. Initially, the absence of rules hampered the work of this particular committee, which ultimately solved the long-standing conflict over procedures by borrowing rules from another committee. In what followed, the Western permanent members resolved a conflict of interests over sanctions listings by appeal to abstract listing criteria. Finally, during its Council membership in 2013–2014, Rwanda halted the committee's work to shield from sanctions its allied rebel militias, which have been fighting other militias in opposition to the Kigali government in Eastern DRC. This chapter adds analytical depth by showing how committee governance also triggers increasing regulation in the absence of due process critique. It adds another facet in as much as the conflict of interests is among the P3 and does not fall along the usual "fault lines" between P3, Russia and China, while the biennial Rwandan episode points to the limits of the mechanism.

Chapter 7 explores how committee governance affected decision-making in the Sudan sanctions regime. The Council imposed sanctions on Sudan in response to the Darfur civil war, even though China had opposed Council sanctions for some time. This chapter illustrates why delegation to the Sudan Sanctions Committee did not lead to rule adherence. Because China rejected sanctions on Sudan for principled, economic and geopolitical reasons, Council members could not on this occasion resolve committee stalemate through rules. China rejected all committee initiatives, even those which the Council explicitly referred to the committee. After failed attempts to add individuals to a sanctions list in the committee, the Council sanctioned four individuals annexed to resolution 1672 (2006). Since then, China and Russia have threatened to veto any further initiatives. This chapter serves to illustrate the limitations of committee governance thesis.

Chapter 8 focuses on committee governance in the Iran sanctions regime, which addresses the conflict over Iran's nuclear program. This chapter shows that great power interests defined Council resolutions, whereas as mentioned earlier the same members tended to follow rules in committee. At first, Council members kept all key tasks in the Council and negotiated complex sanctions resolutions that also included those aspects usually delegated to a committee. These decisions mirrored trade-off agreements among the great powers. However, after 2012, Council members referred these tasks to the Iran sanctions committee. Committee members first developed rules on when to list sanctions violators. Eventually, even powerful committee members felt compelled to accept rule-conforming requests that they had originally sought to avoid. The goal of this chapter is to compare Council decision-making with committee governance systematically in the context of the same sanctions regime. This case also serves to expand the argument's reach to a case of non-proliferation sanctions.

The concluding Chapter 9 discusses implications resulting from the concept of committee governance and the empirical findings. Primarily, I reflect on our current understanding of international organizations in IR theory. I suggest that ongoing debate should accommodate and engage with the intra-organizational effects of international organizations. A group of states that delegates tasks effectively to themselves in a later committee stage significantly affects state behavior, even though no independent secretariat, bureaucracy or court is involved. This concept of an international organization incorporates influential agents but eschews a conceptual reduction to merely *one* factor, which may even lead to misperception: If there is no strong secretariat, the organization does not affect state behavior. Notably, the concept extends existing theoretical approaches toward international organizations without setting aside the pessimistic assumption of strategic state behavior.

Beyond the realm of international organizations in IR theory, I explore what we can learn about the Security Council and its sanctions regimes beyond great power politics. I discuss how the prevailing forum perspective may be extended and specified. This perspective seems to explain decision-making in the Council chamber well because it grasps the power dynamics among key constituents. Yet, I suggest that its reach does not fully extend to Council committees. I argue that based on the findings, small and medium-sized powers gain a tool to counter-balance P5 dominance through the strategic use of well-prepared proposals, possibly aligned to existing precedents and bolstered by criteria-based arguments. This is relevant insofar as their two-year terms allow them to grasp the committees' formal and informal rules. It also suggests that powerful members do not always have things their own way. In many instances, powerful members, including the United States, have failed to achieve their desired outcomes on committee decisions, because their policies violated established practice.

I conclude by discussing the policy implications of sanctions committee governance in the Security Council. I reason that the Security Council should systematically employ the built-in effects of separating broader political questions in the Council chamber from technical follow-up questions in a committee. This form of delegation seems to prompt rule-based governance and promises to make sanctions decisions more consistent and predictable, even though the main motivation would seem to be a reduction in workload rather than consistent decisions. The findings also suggest that rule adherence does not depend on the Council delegating technical sanctions decisions, such as listing and delisting of individuals, to an independent Ombudsperson beyond the influence of Council members. While this would ensure that committee members adhere to predefined rules in a more systematic and transparent fashion (the Ombudsperson is a case in point), this option is not politically feasible because it encroaches on Council privileges. Instead, committee governance provides a viable alternative that creates some form of *implicit* credible commitment to Council members' long-term interests. Contrary to what one might expect, the consensus procedure in committee may be particularly conducive to the emergence and subsequent application of rules because it creates the latent possibility of an inhibiting stalemate. Provided that all committee members prefer some solution over stalemate, pre-defined rules and rules gleaned from precedent suggest a way of overcoming deadlock, not because states particularly favor rules but because rules enable them to reap their long-term benefits in sanctions governance.

2 Committee governance, rules and precedents

In this chapter, based largely on rationalist assumptions, I develop a causal model of how committee governance affects decision-making and the decisions' content even if the same group of states decides about all major issues. This model is contrasted with the postulated effects of decision-making without recourse to a committee stage. I argue that separating into two stages, rule-making and subsequent rule-application, creates specifically different incentives. While states at the rule-making stage will face constraints of consistency and uncertainty, states at the committee stage are usually confronted with a stream of similar and separate requests, which preclude accumulating packages. At committee stage, therefore, states have incentives to decide according to rules, even if they have to accept some unfavorable single cases. Because states working as a committee are likely to prefer different solutions, they find themselves in coordination situations that create demand for focal points if states seek to avoid stalemate. Hence, states will turn to decision criteria, and if those are unavailable, adopt precedents that are applicable over a range of future cases as focal points.

I identify two decision-making ideal types, power politics and rule-based committee governance. Concerning the former, states could proceed in a unitary forum without recourse to a committee. This model provides almost no constraints and states will probably bargain over large politicized packages which are vital for cooperation. Hence, states will exert material and institutional power to move the negotiated solution closer toward their preferred options ("ideal points"). One would usually expect this simple *power politics* mode in an international organization. Concerning the latter, states could differentiate the decision-making process and retain rule-making in the main conference and refer subsequent rule-application to a committee. Thereby, a group of states would separate a grand political project into small increments, which individually are of only marginal importance, but taken together make up that whole political project. In this model, states may well be willing to accept some unfavorable, but small decisions as long as overall cooperation project yields in their terms positive outcomes. My key argument is that committee governance alters the dynamics among a group of states toward a logic of *rule-based governance.*

In the next section, I develop the foundations of an IO concept, showing that the primary function of an IO is to produce decisions collectively. In the second section, I argue that uniform decision processes provide little structure and incentivize decision-making purely by relying on situation-specific interests in all cases through negotiating package deals. Accordingly, decisions taken in a uniform decision process would reflect bargaining among powerful members. In the third section, a model of committee governance is developed. I maintain that separating rule-making from subsequent rule-application affects the decision situation at both stages in ways that favor rule-based decision-making. In the fourth section, I argue that the causal model is suitable for studying committee governance in the UN Security Council. Finally, I address questions of research design and operationalize key variables to close the chapter.

The foundations of international organizations

The foundations of an IO concept build upon the observation that formal IOs represent a particular form of cooperative arrangements in IR. Interested member states create a formal IO to realize one or several cooperation projects (Abbott and Snidal 1998, pp. 4–5). Thus, they are functional entities. This does not imply that the organizations' members or other actors do not have diverging particularistic interests. Indeed, creating a formal international organization rests upon a political compromise between states with a more or less heterogeneous preference constellation. In that sense, the instrumental or functional starting point for an IO concept is compatible with rationalist cooperation theory (Keohane 1984; Stein 1982). Consequently, IOs must at least achieve some cooperative gains for their constituents so as not to forfeit their legitimacy (Abbott and Snidal 1998, p. 5). Hence, the existence and decisions of IOs are conceptually closely tied to the interests of its membership.

In contrast to other cooperation-facilitating international institutions, the most basic function of IOs is to adopt collectively binding decisions (Koch 2009, p. 439). Whereas cooperation can also emerge from individual and uncoordinated behavior into "spontaneous institutions" without collective decision-making (Sugden 1989; Axelrod and Keohane 1985, p. 244) or international regimes in the form of treaties, an IO's structure makes it possible for decisions to be taken within a certain cooperation project as needed. The contracting parties do not need to negotiate about all decisions at once, but can focus on those decisions that are presently achievable and required. Otherwise, other more remote decisions can be deferred. IOs are created in fields with a frequent demand for decisions and allow for adapting to changing circumstances or reacting to external shocks. As such, IOs are incomplete contracts (Hawkins *et al.* 2006, pp. 16–17; Cooley and Spruyt 2009). The central elements of organizations are decisions: "[O]nce started, organizations do nothing else than decision making" (Koch 2009, p. 439). The concept contrasts with an "IO as forum" perspective and highlights IOs emergence from member state interaction, but can clearly be distinguished from members and their interaction (Dörfler and Gehring 2015, pp. 57–58).

IOs can be conceptualized as decision-making systems (Rittberger *et al.* 2012, pp. 71–75; Easton 1965, pp. 29–33). An IO forms a political system that converts inputs from its environment ("demands" and "support") into decisions, which may feed back into new input. Concerning the input, all interventions made by members or relevant actors can enter and affect decision-making. In the absence of signals from the environment, an organization is devoid of its key task, namely taking decisions. The organization is, therefore, totally dependent on input from its members. At the same time, as the systems theory strand of organization theory suggests, an IO processes incoming information and decisions solely in accordance with organizational rules. Consequently, even purely rational and self-interested members, who seek to pursue their interests within an IO, can do so only by taking rules into account (Koch 2009). Hence, it becomes evident that IOs structure the decision process and fundamentally shape rational IO members' opportunities to act. While actors may strive to follow, alter or replace such rules, they can hardly ignore them (Gehring 2009).

Even intergovernmental IOs, such as the Security Council, structure decision processes through rules on membership, scope and decision rules, often part of extensive pre-negotiations (Dörfler and Gehring 2015, p. 34). These basic organizational rules determine how decisions are taken going forward. First, the organization delineates its membership. While this may seem trivial, as a result it makes a considerable difference as to whether a member or a non-member makes an intervention in order to affect organizational decisions. Second, organizations restrict the scope of negotiable issues (Koremenos *et al.* 2001, pp. 770–771). States naturally seek to delimit the issues of concern to avoid overwhelming complexity. IO creators can opt for a rather broad scope and other seemingly unrelated issues might be linked to compromise (Sebenius 1983, pp. 292–300). However, the more actors are involved, the more incentives they have to limit the number of issues. Third, states need some principled mutual understanding on how future decisions will be taken (Koremenos *et al.* 2001, p. 772). In other words, members need to know how the input is transferred into organizational decisions. In principle, organizations can adopt decisions unanimously, by consensus or by any form of majority vote (Rittberger *et al.* 2012, pp. 78–79). Crucially, deciding on principled procedures defines which inputs become influential (Gehring 2002, pp. 94–98).

Organizational structuration effects can be traced back to two fundamental mechanisms. On the one hand, they result from the transfer of competencies to subsidiary bodies (Gehring 2003, pp. 93–97; Dörfler and Gehring 2015, p. 58; also Keohane and Martin 2003, pp. 102–104). Functional differentiation emerges "where the subsystems are defined by the coherence of particular types of activity and their differentiation from other types of activity" (Buzan and Albert 2010, p. 318). To increase efficiency, more complex IOs will comprise a series of different organs, each serving a different function (Rittberger *et al.* 2012, pp. 71–88). Functional differentiation can emerge even when a thematic working group focuses on a subset of issues or an expert committee appraises certain factual questions. Likewise, every transfer of authority to secretariats, international bureaucracies or courts creates a system of divided labor. Within the organization's decision process, such organs perform certain functions. Actors in every sub-process will eventually create a specific scientific, political or legal rationale, simply because it has a particular membership, scope and rules which affect how inputs are decided upon (Hawkins *et al.* 2006, pp. 12–20).

Essentially, in a functionally differentiated organization members can no longer affect an agreement's content by taking a single comprehensive decision, but can merely influence separate segments of the overall decision (Gehring 2002, p. 162). Functional differentiation often results in distributing authority among different organs all with their own procedures. For instance, the IO might establish a committee to focus on a specific issue area and operate under its own formal or informal procedures. Hence, the committee will have a significantly narrower scope than the main conference. However, the number of negotiated issues affects the preference constellation among members and hence also on the likelihood of cooperation (Sebenius 1983, pp. 292–300). In addition, committee procedures then determine who can influence decisions in practice. Moreover, this logic also applies if the same group of states processes two separated tasks, one after the other. If the overall decision is split into many separate but small decisions, which together produce the outcome, members can influence the outcomes of the portioned sub-processes only. As a result, separating the decision-making process into several sub-processes is likely to modify states' behavioral opportunities and thus the decision's content significantly (Gehring and Ruffing 2008, p. 125). Accordingly, which type of subsidiary body is selected for a task affects who can exert influence over decision-making (Schaefer 1996, p. 144).

On the other hand, IOs already structure decision-making through the mere fact that IO decision-making takes place against the background of all previous decisions (Gehring 2009, pp. 71–75; Keohane and Martin 2003, pp. 99–104). As a result, every new decision has to fit into the complex web of existing decisions. While courts, for instance, frequently settle disputes by recourse to earlier judgments as precedents (Koch 2009, pp. 440–444), this applies equally to non-juridical organizations. Feeding new decisions into a web of those already existing gives rise to a sequential decision-making process, whose subsequent decision-making is always structured by preceding decisions. Overall, organizational decision-making is typically characterized by path dependency insofar as previous decisions affect those taken later (Dörfler and Gehring 2015, p. 60).

This IO concept directs our attention to the fundamental sources of organizational autonomy. The concept does encompass agents, such as an influential secretariat, but does not reduce IO effects to just this one aspect. Instead, it shows that even entirely intergovernmental organizations such as the Security Council gain autonomy from their members. An IO will gain autonomy vis-à-vis its members as members opt for collective decisions, that they would not have chosen without organizational structuration. If the mere preference constellation of members can no longer explain IO decisions without taking modified decision processes into account, then the organization must have at least some autonomy. While IOs obviously vary in their degree of autonomy (Rittberger *et al.* 2012, pp. 15–34), this degree of autonomy depends on the extent to which the organization interferes between the interest constellation of members and the organization's decisions. The exact degree of IO autonomy is then a matter of empirical investigation and can be regarded as the gap between a decision's content and what we can would expect to see in the absence of structured decision-making processes. Hence, the more an organization interferes between member state interests and collective decisions, the more autonomy it has. However, while collective decision-making is one aspect of autonomy, to become an autonomous entity, the organization must also dispose of relevant governance resources, so as to make a difference for its addressees (Dörfler and Gehring 2015). This pooling of resources (Abbott and Snidal 1998) and granting an IO the right to dispose of these collectively (Coleman 1974) include, for instance, setting binding international law (EU), granting funds (World Bank) or using military assets (NATO).

Power politics

As a baseline for assessing the committee governance effect, to solve a cooperation problem a group of states can resort to power politics without recourse to a committee stage. The cooperation project must produce favorable outcomes for its members on a sizable scale, which in turn rests upon the members' ability to agree on grand political bargains. In this process, members have incentives to invest heavily in give-and-take bargaining to move the final settlement closer to their preferred solution. Hence, bargaining power becomes the major means of influence. Such negotiations would be subject to the logic of coordination within uniform negotiation settings. Accordingly, powerful actors will not accept unfavorable decisions unless costs are compensated for through linkages.

In the event of a group of states favoring decision-taking about certain issues without recourse to a committee stage, I expect to find that states will bargain hard over the decisions' contents. Conceptually, bargaining refers to a negotiation where states exchange demands reinforced by promises, threats and more or less credible exit options to achieve their objectives and maximize their utility (Risse 2000, p. 8; Elster 1989, pp. 50–96). Negotiators will seek to produce additional welfare beyond the status quo. In addition, they have to bargain over the exact distribution of gains along the "pareto frontier" (Scharpf 1997, pp. 118–124; Odell 2013, p. 387). Under these circumstances, states will enter with maximalist positions and subsequently seek to negotiate a solution by means of threats and step-wise offers. In this scenario, states have to make concessions because others have bargaining power, but seek to make as few concessions as possible (Elster 1989, pp. 68–74). The extent of bargaining power thereby depends on how credible a selective exit from the negotiations is. States with a credible exit option (also "outside option") can threaten to leave the negotiation table if the costs associated with the exit are small. In turn, with increasing bargaining power, an actor has to make fewer concessions (Elster 1989, pp. 69–82; Voeten 2001).

When member state interests diverge, members will try to nest single issues, which each benefit certain parties to the agreement ("asymmetric distributive effect") into a grand package. In contrast to considering implementation issues separately, which are each marginally important, the entire package of issues is in turn quite important to its members. Thus states will bargain seriously over distributing costs and benefits of the packaged agreement (Koremenos *et al.* 2001, pp. 770–771). A negative payoff for one party on one issue can be compensated for through a positive payoff on another issue. Hence, accumulating entirely unrelated issues into packages provides a viable means of ensuring a negotiated settlement in spite of contradicting interests (Sebenius 1983). Thus, while many decisions might be unfavorable for one party and hence accepting these on their own would be irrational, it may be completely rational if the whole package is beneficial (Scharpf 1997, pp. 116–150).

States might employ institutional and material power resources to push through proposals of egoistic interest and move the outcome closer to what they prefer (Schneider 2011). Concerning the former, member states may apply power originating from membership and voting rules. If some members enjoy permanent veto privileges over a group of non-permanent members without veto, as in the case of the Security Council, such members might dominate decision-making. The permanency of their membership enables them to gain institutional memory and control the decision process better than other states (Sievers and Daws 2014, pp. 125–126). However, even a non-permanent member enjoys a privileged position vis-à-vis all other IO members. Concerning the latter, states could use their economic or military resources to incentivize less powerful members to support solutions, which the powerful prefer (Vreeland and Dreher 2014). They might try to buy votes (Carter and Stone 2015), for instance, by paying off less powerful members through supporting their World Bank loan applications (Dreher *et al.* 2009), or pressuring them otherwise (Vreeland and Dreher 2014, pp. 67–69).

As a result, without committee, the decisions' content resulting from these grand bargains are characterized by the fact that potential cooperation gains are distributed in accordance with the constellation of bargaining power (Moravcsik 1998, pp. 60–67). In fact, these decisions will reproduce the power distribution and thus neglect the interests of less powerful actors (Scharpf 1997, pp. 122–123). The bargaining power of members will depend on their position relative to the status quo, and to what extent credible outside options are available. In the event of their position being close or equal to the status quo, a veto member has high bargaining power and can demand considerable concessions or linkages to compensate for losses. The decisive criterion for a successful negotiation is the achievement of a solution that is beneficial to all members. Consequently, a uniform decision process provides little incentives to forego exerting all material and institutional power available. Even in situations of uncertainty, when additional information is required, once such information is made available, members will pursue their interests with all power resources available (Gehring 2003, pp. 84–90; Odell 2013), because only through bargaining will the outcome be shifted in a desired direction. Thus, we cannot expect members not to bargain in a uniform decision process without committee, given that bargaining produces better outcomes for IO members (Gehring 2003, p. 86).

Conversely, as regards contents, we cannot expect that decisions taken according to the logic of power politics are particularly wise or efficient in implementation. While they might reflect problem-solving considerations or withstand criteria-based judgment, there is a stronger probability that they will not. Bargaining processes are not suitable for producing justifiable solutions as problem-solving requires members to forgo pursuit of those alternatives that they favor, but instead weigh alternatives against a given standard to find those that best fit the standard. Bargaining processes substantially inhibit problem-adequate processes and members will not accept arguments as relevant information, because they cannot expect others to be changing their preferences based on arguments. States will not engage in argument exchanges if they believe their interests will be better served in a simple bargaining process (Gehring and Ruffing 2008, pp. 125–128).

Power politics, therefore, serves as a baseline model that I expect to observe in an undifferentiated decision process and against which the effects of committee governance will be assessed. Hence, if members pursue decisions solely in one stage without recourse to a committee, I expect that decisions will mirror bargains, which reflect the interest constellation and relative power among members. These decisions will accumulate any relevant aspects of the cooperation project, including implementation decisions, into large political bargains. In this scenario, powerful actors will not accept unfavorable outcomes unless their costs are compensated for through linkages. Consequently, the decisions' contents will entirely reflect the power distribution among the group of states. Using the success rate of state submitted requests as an indicator, the power politics confounder suggests that more powerful states generally do better than those with less power.

Committee governance and the power of rules

A group of states alters the decision situation significantly and provides incentives for rule-based governance if the negotiation over a package deal is divided into two separate stages of making rules, which are subsequently applied to many single cases. This form of an incomplete contract is the case when the group of states refers implementation decisions to a committee. Accordingly, these states chop a larger political project into small increments, which are each of limited importance. However, the cooperation project's political utility rests with the IO's ability to produce favorable outcomes on a larger scale. In this process, members have to trade-off the cooperation project's overall utility against the investment of power resources to avoid every small implementation decision that runs counter to their interests. States may, therefore, simply accept some unfavorable decisions, provided that the organization largely produces reasonable decisions.

In contrast to power politics without committee, functionally differentiated decision-making affects the ability of rational states to push through their situation-specific interests systematically and incentivizes members to submit well-founded requests aligned to established rules (Gehring and Ruffing 2008, p. 126). In fact, IOs which are characterized by a high degree of functional differentiation can limit the desire of rational states to bargain for distributive gains and instead assess the merits of single-case requests vis-à-vis substantive criteria. Organization theory suggests that these structuring effects result from splitting formerly uniform decision-making into sub-processes with specific but limited functions. While separating tasks, for instance between a main conference and a committee, is a viable strategy, we would even expect to observe such effects if the same group of states processes all aspects of a cooperation project, since these effects stem from structuring decision-making and not from the body's composition (Dörfler and Gehring 2015, p. 62).

The structuration effect rests upon separating rule-making from rule-application (Becker *et al.* 2018). Members' behavioral options will be altered significantly when rule-making and subsequent rule-application are referred to two different stages, even if both are processed by the same group of states. Initially, this will defer a range of possibly contentious aspects including those dealing with implementing the cooperation problem and will instantly reduce the number of currently unresolved issues (Gehring 2003, pp. 95–96). As a consequence, when the group of states mandates a committee with solving a cooperation problem, they will almost automatically delimit a level on which states define the cooperation goal and a level on which the project is implemented. In such a differentiated setting, states at both stages will specialize on certain aspects. This will create a modified form of "institutional bargaining" (Young 1994, pp. 98–106), which changes decision-makers' calculus significantly (Gehring and Ruffing 2008, p. 126).

The constraints of rule-making

By separating rule-making from rule-application, states at the first stage circumscribe their own scope of functions so as to adopt the overarching framework for later decisions; this subjects IO members either entirely or partially to the constraints associated with adopting abstract rules. Particularly in the rule-making stage, members forfeit the possibility of overcoming conflicts of interests by means of package solutions, simply because single cases are no longer decided on at this stage. Instead, states have to concentrate on guiding subsequent implementation decisions through criteria, rules and procedures. As a result, this subverts the IO members who negotiate a general institutional framework from a logic of adopting balanced package deals to a logic of rule-making.

In a situation that requires negotiating generally applicable rules, IO members operate under systemic constraints that limit their ability to pursue case-specific interests while bargaining over rules. Rather, they gain an interest in negotiating over a set of *general* criteria, rules and procedures that will guide decision-making in the implementation stage (Gehring 2009, p. 77). As Brennan and Buchanan stress, there is a "categorical difference" (1985, p. 28) between choosing among different sets of rules and choosing among different options within the previously established rules. Unlike case-specific decisions, decisions about institutional rules apply across a broader range of contexts and longer timeframes (Young 1989, pp. 361–362; Brennan and Buchanan 1985, p. 29). At the same time, achieving the cooperation goal rests upon both stages being set up so as to adopt a sufficient number of small-scale implementation decisions. Specifically, when a committee decides about small implementation issues by consensus, the latent danger of committee deadlock threatens to achieve the cooperation goal. As a result, even rational utility-maximizers skeptical of rules become interested in guiding the rule-application stage through rules (Gehring and Ruffing 2008, pp. 126–127; Gehring and Dörfler 2013, pp. 569–571).

Negotiating criteria, rules and procedures subjects IO members to two pivotal constraints. First, because states bargain over criteria and rules without being able to know their preferences on all future cases the rules will apply to, they operate under a "veil of uncertainty" (Rawls 1971, pp. 136–142; Young 1989). At the time of rule-making, IO members do not yet know which of the potential options would best serve their interests because they have to define rules, which apply to as yet unknown cases. Brennan and Buchanan argue that "[a]s both the generality and the permanence of rules are increased, the individual who faces choice alternatives becomes more uncertain about the effects of alternatives on his own position" (Brennan and Buchanan 1985, pp. 29–30). As long as states are uncertain about their future preferences, they will be subject to the veil of uncertainty, which makes it difficult, if not impossible, to identify rules which promise an advantageous position vis-à-vis other states in the future. Hence, IO members cannot simply apply their bargaining power because they are uncertain about which specific option out of a number of available options would best match their particularistic interest (Gehring 2003, p. 104). Hence, rational IO members will try to reduce the probability that rules will have negative consequences in the future. If states have difficulties in estimating which consequences a particular rule will have on a range of unknown cases, they gain an interest in elaborating rules that will generally produce acceptable decisions in implementing the political project (Brennan and Buchanan 1985, pp. 29–30; Young 1989, p. 362). With increasing uncertainty, we can expect that IO members are increasingly deprived of pursing a bargaining strategy effectively, as long as they do not have similar preferences across single cases (Becker *et al.* 2018, p. 5). Although Brennan and Buchanan make this argument for individual citizens facing a constitutional choice, Young argues that the mechanism applies equally to collective state actors (1989, p. 362).

Second, even if IO members who bargain over rules know their future interests well, they will be constrained into making consistent rules. Should states know their preferences in every single case to be decided and should they have different preferences in these cases, they will barely be able to pursue and realize all those case-specific interests with one rule set. As a consequence, criteria, rules and procedures must apply to a whole range of single cases, because rule-making based on opportunistic interests in a single case is virtually impossible (Brennan and Buchanan 1985, pp. 28–31). IO members who merely negotiate sets of rules cannot pursue their case-specific interests, because such single cases are no longer decided at this stage. Instead, they have to represent a position that aggregates numerous single-cases (Gehring 2003, p. 105). Each member, therefore, is forced to aggregate all these case-specific interests into one consistent bargaining position. If states operate under such constrains, they will naturally have to sort out opportunistic case-specific considerations (Brennan and Buchanan 1985, pp. 29–31). This shows that even rational, powerful states will gain an interest in representing a position that reflects a median case and produces an acceptable outcome across a whole range of single cases (Gehring 2004, pp. 689–690). This rule-making effect increases with preference heterogeneity among veto players (Tsebelis 2000, p. 467), with every member's preference heterogeneity across cases, and with uncertainty about future cases.

My claim is not that rule-making is dissociated from power. Quite to the contrary, political projects of IOs, such as sanctions regimes, are a result of major power interests and their design will reflect the constellation of power. Also, the rules provided are not devoid of power, nor are they necessarily fair or just because they materialize from decision-making among powerful states that bargain to achieve rules most favorable to them at the committee stage. Instead, my claim is that committee governance comes with constraints that even powerful members cannot escape; no generalized rule will satisfy all a state's case-specific preferences. Due to these constrains, even powerful states cannot have all their specific opportunistic interests reflected in a collective set of rules. Accordingly, a member's influence is reduced to affecting just one set of rules, which will guide decision-making on many single cases at the committee stage.

These constraints apply to rule-making in the main conference and committee alike. The effects are also likely to occur if a group of states first decides about criteria, rules and procedures, thereafter processing single cases according to such criteria within the same IO organ. In essence, the group of states would first decide about the broader undertaking to adopt rules and would only then address the individual case-specific decisions at a second stage. Thus, it would first act as a main political body responsible for rule-making and then act as a committee responsible for rule-implementation.

The constraints of rule implementation

The committee stage differs substantially from the rule-making stage in as much as committee members now concentrate on implementing the given rules in many single cases. The committee is usually confronted with a steady-stream of requests and so exists in a "continuous decisional context" (Sartori 1987, p. 228). Furthermore, these requests are usually of a similar nature, such as adding individuals and entities to a sanctions list, and can either be accepted or rejected. In addition, requests will be relatively separated from each other so that they also have to be processed separately. Moreover, not every member will equally benefit from a single-case, which typically favor only some but not all members, while each of these implementation decisions is of limited importance. Simultaneously, committee members decide in light of a set of criteria provided earlier. Even if these rules were previously made by the same group of states, such criteria are likely to affect decision-making, unless the committee members are prepared to ignore these criteria and undermine the previously established separation of rule-making and rule-application.

At the committee stage, there is a pertinent danger that members insist on rejecting or accepting a specific case against the collective will of all other committee members, in particular because the rule-making constraints no longer apply. As members decide about single cases, they can define their interests well and thus are able to assess costs and associated benefits (Brennan and Buchanan 1985, p. 29). At the committee stage, rational actors will seek to maximize their individual utility in every case presented to them. In addition, enforcing rule compliance will be problematic if actors prefer conflicting solutions to the cooperation problem.

The logic of coordination situations at the committee stage

The IO members' decision-making calculus within the committee stage under consensus will entail the constant danger of a deadlock (Rittberger *et al.* 2012, pp. 101–102). Since the distributive effects of a single decision will most likely be asymmetrical, a single decision will hardly ever be of equal advantage for all committee members alike. Since not all members can realize their preferred outcome for each of the decisions taken, the effectiveness of the committee stage is compromised if actors seek to pursue their situation-specific interests in all cases. An obvious solution to this problem would be to balance an individual member's costs and benefits associated with a single case by accumulating larger packages. If single cases within the committee stage are small, well-separated and of a dichotomous nature so as to preclude putting them into packages, the decision situation at the committee stage will create the pertinent danger of deadlock if all actors pursue their situation-specific interests equally on decisions that will likely disadvantage some committee members over others (Gehring and Ruffing 2008, p. 127).

Let us assume that the committee faces only one isolated request, not a stream of requests. Committee members who strive to maximize their utility will unrestrictedly decide whether or not they want to support this proposal. Members will calculate the payoff of every possible outcome and decide according to what serves their interests best. In this case, they would ignore any available criteria or rules if these do not promise to increase their utility in this single decision. As not all members will benefit equally from a single decision, this situation resembles a "prisoner's dilemma" constellation, characterized by free-riding, which would result in a pareto-inferior collective outcome. If committee members follow their situation-specific interests strictly, they will not be able to coordinate their behavior and, as a consequence, endanger the realization of cooperative gains (Gehring 2002, pp. 176–177).

The members' calculus at committee stage will be altered significantly if they process an entire chain of single cases (Gehring and Ruffing 2008, pp. 126–127). In such a situation, which exhibits an iterated game structure, members will face many discrete single decisions across time. Members will have to consider that they are not deciding solely about a single case, but that every decision is part of a chain of decisions to be taken in the future. Consequently, achieving the overall cooperation goal depends on continually adopting separate decisions at different points in time. A member's overall gains, therefore, depend on each of the single cases including the expected utility of future cases. When deciding about a single case, states must take into account how their choices today affect choices in future. Members have to expect that their defecting in one game will be sanctioned by other actors in the following games. However, actors can also expect that their cooperation will be honored with cooperation in the future (Tit-for-tat, see Axelrod 1984).

Now, a committee member has two alternatives. On the one hand, a state can still support or object to a single case to maximize its payoff. However, the member also has to face costs associated with its short-term gains in the single case as the overall cooperation goal may be undermined. The state can no longer expect other members to be cooperative in the future. Achieving short-term gains in one case will result in losses of many cases longer term. On the other hand, the member can decide to accept a single-case decision, even if it runs counter to its own interests in the case. Despite incurring some losses in the short-term, it promises to increase the likelihood that member states will cooperate in the long run. We can expect that committee members facing such a decision situation will favor cooperation if the "shadow of the future" is large (Axelrod 1984).

This constellation resembles a mixed-motive coordination situation ("battle of the sexes," Stein 1982, pp. 309–311; Snidal 1985, pp. 931–936): Committee members have a common interest in cooperating and prefer agreement over stalemate, but prefer different solutions. Hence, members collectively have to select one solution from a range of equal solutions. These situations exhibit "multiple equilibria" and are characterized by the fact that they do not structurally emphasize *one* particular solution to the coordination problem (Schelling 1960, pp. 57–58; Garrett and Weingast 1993, pp. 181–187). At the same time, because each request presents a coordination problem, realizing the cooperation project depends on finding a solution to every single case. Because not all members can always achieve their case-specific interests at committee stage, a member ultimately has to accept some decisions that violates its preferences, unless the member prefers deadlock over coordination. In effect, assuming that preferences differ, some states will win, while others will have to compromise. However, a tremendous challenge then lies in determining, which of the equally plausible solutions to pick.

Coordination situations at committee stage create demand for focal points

At committee stage, multiple equilibria in coordination situations with diverging interests creates demand for focal points (Schelling 1960; Garrett and Weingast 1993), which indicate when members have to compromise and when they can pursue their situation-specific interests. Committee members will accept short-term losses only when they can reasonably expect that other members will accept future decisions, which are unfavorable to them. Without a focal point, a member will have no incentives to yield and consequently will eventually endanger the entire cooperation project. Accordingly, the situation creates the demand for criteria, rules and procedures that guide decision-making at committee stage. This issue is aggravated when decision-makers face a steady stream of decisions to be taken which will result in pressure for routinization and standardization of procedures (Gehring and Ruffing 2008, pp. 127–128).

The major point of interest in the study of focal points is how actors solve coordination situations with multiple equilibria (Martin and Simmons 2013, p. 331; Garrett and Weingast 1993, pp. 181–185). Members favoring agreement over stalemate require a mutually accepted focal point, which denotes a specific solution from several potential solutions. Since coordination situations exhibit two or more equally plausible solutions (Nash equilibria), a focal point indicates one specific solution that is "salient" (Mehta *et al.* 1994, pp. 661–662; Schelling 1960) or "sufficiently obvious" from other possible solutions (Sugden and Zamarrón 2006, pp. 615–617). It is the essence of cultural traditions such as etiquette to solve simple coordination problems (out of many possible solutions) by mutual expectation: Everyone expects everyone else to adhere to agreed rules (Schelling 1960, p. 91). This logic also applies to mixed-motive games, where individuals have a common interest in avoiding an uncoordinated solution but prefer different solutions. Take for instance an experiment where two players must divide 100 dollars between themselves and each player wishes to increase his/her individual share. When the players cannot communicate, both will likely choose to split the amount in half. Hence, even though all other solutions are equally possible, the 50:50 solution is unique and serves as a focal point, thereby solving the coordination problem (Schelling 1960, pp. 61–63).

Committee members can coordinate by consulting additional information, which help to converge expectations (Schelling 1960, p. 57). Which type of information is taken depends on the situation's context. Significantly, a focal point is taken from beyond the present situation precisely because coordination situations are indeterminate and do not naturally offer a point of reference as to when members are expected to compromise (Ringe 2005, p. 733; Sugden and Zamarrón 2006). Because of the information consulted, the members' perceived game structure is different from its formal structure. Focal points enable the members to pick one solution out of an amorphous range of possible options, precisely because of a certain special feature present in the chosen solution. Accepting the focal point becomes a rational choice (Schelling 1960, pp. 68–69).

It is a perfect method for making an "equilibrium selection." A focal point narrows the available range of identifiable solutions (Huth *et al.* 2013, pp. 92–93). Focal points translate an abstract cooperation problem into specific expectations in a given situation, even when members' interests diverge. The role of focal points is crucial under circumstances of complexity and uncertainty, where appropriate ideas are "pivotal mechanisms" in coordinating mutual expectations (Garrett and Weingast 1993, pp. 176–179).

At committee stage, actors can resort to two sources of focal points. First, external criteria, rules and procedures can act as focal points (Huth *et al.* 2013, p. 93; Martin and Simmons 2013, p. 331), even if the identical group of states has previously elaborated them. When the members have determined a set of criteria, rules and procedures at a previous stage, the same members gain a strong interest in accepting these rules as focal points to guide their decision-making in committee. In fact, these rules are easily available and produce no additional transaction costs. Essentially, these rules which have been adopted under the constraints of rule-making reflect precisely the long-term cooperation goal. However, as a prerequisite, all committee members, especially those that would otherwise obstruct the decision process, must accept a focal point. Alternatively, actors could simply agree to sideline the established criteria and accept other information as a focal point. Yet, this presupposes finding an alternative formal or informal rule, on which all members can agree. However, committee members logically have to agree on "how to take decisions" before they can do so, similarly to pre-negotiations in simple settings (Brennan and Buchanan 1985, p. 6; Gross Stein 1989). In addition, re-negotiating rules incurs additional transaction costs (Gehring and Dörfler 2013, p. 570). Accordingly, it is likely that members at the committee stage follow external rules not because they are unbiased, just or equally preferred by all members, but because these rules solve an otherwise intractable coordination problem.

Second, if there are no sufficiently precise criteria available, committee members can resort to precedents as equivalent, but internal focal points. In the absence of criteria, members will need other focal points to address a coordination problem that would lead to deadlock if unsolved. Resting decisions on similar but earlier accepted or rejected requests solves a coordination problem easily and meaningfully (March and Olsen 1989, pp. 21–38; Schelling 1960, pp. 67–68). An earlier decision – regardless of how it came about – will inevitably provide a yardstick for later decisions of a similar kind, because it reflects the collective choice by the same group of states in the same setting (Schelling 1960, p. 135). Members will find it difficult to select an alternative solution that is more widely acceptable than the precedent. The repeated application of a precedent to a number of similar single-cases will create a practice and increase the pressures for consistency (Snidal 1985, p. 936). Repeatedly accepted precedents are likely to create lasting expectations, which are determined by what the committee usually does in such a case (Schelling 1960, pp. 57–64; Young 1989, pp. 359–366). The mechanism will become increasingly self-sustaining as those who have accepted unfavorable decisions in favor of realizing the long-term cooperation goal will insist that others, who face unfavorable decisions, will also adhere to accepted practice (Gehring 2003, p. 109). Indeed, as with rules, an established precedent creates collective expectations about acceptable follow-up decisions both positively (i.e., "what is an acceptable proposal?") and negatively (i.e., "what is an unacceptable proposal?"). In addition, processing proposals in line with established precedents promises to reduce the transaction costs associated with deciding large numbers of cases that are complex but each has limited importance (Coleman 1988, p. 213).

As a result, the committee stage generates substantial constraints and strong incentives for rule-based governance. Existing rules and precedents will favor those actors that submit rule-conforming decision proposals and disadvantage actors that submit non-conforming requests. Members, who advocate a rule-conforming solution will expose deviant behavior as arbitrary, whereas those who favor a non-conforming solution will struggle to draw on a similarly persuasive account (Stone Sweet and Sandholtz 2004, p. 259; Huth *et al.* 2013, p. 94; on the similar concept of "rhetorical entrapment," see Schimmelfennig 2001). To the contrary, members will refuse to accept a collective solution that violates existing rules unless this is absolutely necessary, for instance because the type of case is unprecedented or because the proposal falls short of established preconditions. However, in the event of deviating preferences, a disadvantaged group of actors is unlikely to accept a solution that is not in conformity with the rules. Members without stakes will favor options that will be justifiable in light of criteria because they have no incentives to violate the established rules permanently (Gehring and Kerler 2008, p. 1007). While committee members might prefer power politics over rule adherence, rules serve as a means of overcoming stalemate in coordination situations, because rule violation in one case is likely to trigger retaliatory objections. Because power politics is likely to elicit deadlock, rule-based governance provides a viable alternative. Consequently, if committee members have an interest in avoiding non-coordination, they will tend to accept some unfavorable outcomes provided that the costs are small compared to the benefits of the entire cooperation project. Thus, even rational utility maximizers have incentives to accept a solution following a focal point as long as they favor agreement over stalemate.

Rule-application constraints inherent to committee governance imply a certain behavior of committee members submitting single-case requests. While proponents of a request have incentives to align their proposal with established criteria, rules and procedures emerging from a particular precedent, opponents will instead try to argue why the proposal is substantially different vis-à-vis the established practice and hence the rule/precedent was not applicable. The costs of obstruction will increase if the request is very similar to previously accepted cases. Repeatedly accepted decisions will trigger a stream of similar proposals insofar as states are aware of such committee practice. States will tend to submit proposals that they can reasonably expect will enable them to succeed and will tend to avoid submitting proposals that have little chance of success. This way, emerging mutually accepted criteria encourage submission of proposals that can be justified in light of the criteria, whereas they discourage the submission of unjustifiable proposals (Huth *et al.* 2013, p. 93). Furthermore, proponents of a certain proposal will seek to expand committee practice incrementally by aligning new but similar proposals to those previously accepted (Gerhardt 2005). Proposals are likely to be slightly different from one another. As such, members of the committee have to decide whether a proposal sufficiently resembles existing criteria and informal rules or whether differences in degree justify setting a new precedent. Members will seek to set new precedents deliberately so as to increase the chances of achieving their expected utility.

Applying rules to many cases at committee stage also affects committee members' options. Committee members have incentives to align their decisions to criteria, rules and procedures including those emerging from precedent. When deciding about a case, members have an interest in applying the same criteria across cases, so as not to provoke reciprocal shifting of criteria on their own decision requests in the future. Crucially, the situation provides incentives to accept all those requests, which are justifiable in light of criteria, even if a state favors a different outcome in these cases, provided that the IO produces favorable decisions overall. As a result, one could expect that a request's fit to the criteria becomes a decisive factor in explaining committee decision-making, not the interests of powerful members in all cases.

Alternatively, actors in the committee stage could confront the danger of stalemate by simply rubber-stamping all requests in a laissez-faire mode (Gehring and Dörfler 2013, pp. 570–571). This is likely to occur if committee members have little interest in the cases and thus no incentives to challenge proposals that have been submitted. Accordingly, committee members are not in a situation where they must coordinate among plausible solutions, which then prompts the danger of deadlock and, therefore, the associated willingness to engage in rule-based governance. Thus, the constraining effects of rule-application will occur only if actors are concerned about decisions at committee stage, which could give rise to a certain conflict of interests among members. Accordingly, committee rule adherence depends on a conflict of interests among members and their willingness to scrutinize, challenge and eventually block non-conforming requests.

These considerations can be summarized in the following two hypotheses:

> Hypothesis 1: If a committee of states processes separate and asymmetric proposals of limited scope that preclude accumulation into packages, committee members are expected to abide by given criteria, rules and procedures, even if these contradict situation-specific preferences of some committee members.

> Hypothesis 2: If a committee of states processes separate and asymmetric proposals of limited scope that preclude accumulation into packages, with criteria, rules and procedures being absent or ambiguous, committee members are expected to abide by rules derived from precedents, even if such rules contradict situation-specific preferences of some committee members.

This committee governance model is subject to three scope conditions. First, committee governance effects will occur only if proposals are entered separately. Otherwise, these could be accumulated into packages until negative payoffs have been sufficiently compensated. Second, committee governance effects will occur only if the states have to process a stream of single-cases that are each of relatively limited importance to decision-makers. Without such a stream of decisions there are no suitable rules or precedents because decisions are not similar in kind. On the contrary, if decisions are singular and isolate issues – whether technical or not – that are of vital interest to actors, they will invest heavily in bargaining to realize favorable distributive effects. Third, committee governance effects occur only if members find themselves in a coordination situation, which gives rise to the influence of focal points. In case a single member favors stalemate over rule-based governance, rules and precedents lose their ability to serve as focal points because focal points no longer signify a mutually acceptable solution. In this case, any coordinated solution would then be beyond the range of acceptable outcomes for the member ("win-set") and thus this member will likely stall. In all three cases, I would expect to observe power politics.

The logic of committee governance in the Security Council

The outlined causal model of committee governance applies to a multitude of IOs and is neither specific to a particular procedure nor to a certain organization. I would expect the causal mechanism to be present in circumstances where a committee of member states processes a stream of separate implementation decisions with limited scope, regardless of whether or not the organization operates in high or low politics and independent of the policy area. Moreover, rule-making and rule-application do not need to be separated between two bodies, but can equally be processed, albeit separately, by the same group of states within the same organ. The causal model relates to a multitude of organizations regardless of whether or not states intend to produce the effects of committee governance or simply delegate decision competencies to reduce the workload and increase efficiency.

The Security Council conforms to the fundamental IO concept outlined above. Apart from being a UN principal organ, the Security Council can be regarded as an IO in its own right, even though it lacks institutional features usually linked with organizational autonomy, such as a strong secretariat (Barnett and Finnemore 2004; Biermann and Siebenhüner 2013). The Council has a defined membership (UN Charter art. 23) and serves as a cooperation project with "primary responsibility for the maintenance of international peace and security." As an organization, the Security Council has the major task of continually adopting collectively binding decisions for all UN members (UN Charter art. 24–25). The UN Charter also outlines specific rules on how to take substantive and procedural decisions, including the veto power for permanent members (UN Charter art. 27). Due to its rights in adopting legally-binding international law, imposing sanctions, sending peacekeepers to conflict zones, or authorizing the use of force, the Council disposes of far-reaching action capabilities, which have the potential to affects its decisions' addressees.

The Security Council also matches the baseline model of power politics in cases where its members decide without recourse to a committee. The UN Charter provides no substantive limits to the Council's action (Peters 2012, pp. 765–771), and hence very few constraints on what it might do to address a conflict. The Security Council is not subject to any form of judicial oversight and the UN Secretariat serves primarily an administrative, rather than substantive role. Accordingly, Council member states retain *all* decisions for themselves. The permanent members possess both great material and institutional power. Being five great powers, they can employ vast resources to pressurize or otherwise incentivize less powerful members to support their proposals. They also possess a great deal of institutional power, by means of their right to veto. Their status as "permanent" members gives them access to institutional memory and domination over Council decision processes (Sievers and Daws 2014, 125–126). The non-permanent members, in turn, are less powerful, but still advantaged over all other UN member states. As a result, I would expect to observe Council decisions in the form of package deals following the interests of the most powerful members.

The Security Council equally conforms to the committee governance model. The Council serves as a suitable test case for the causal mechanism, according to which the transfer of competencies to committee fundamentally alters member state behavior and the decisions' contents. Typically we find committee governance within the Security Council's sanctions regimes. The Security Council frequently delegates streams of implementation decisions to its sanctions committees, which have identical membership to that of the main Council. These decisions are submitted separately and independently of each other and are mostly of a small scope, such as listing and delisting of individuals and entities subject to assets freezes and travel bans. Consequently, I expect to observe the effects of committee governance, if the Security Council within in its sanctions regimes delegates streams of single-case decisions of limited scope to its sanctions committees.

Let me proceed by taking the perspective of a Security Council member to situate committee governance. In what follows, I primarily focus on the P5, because these members have strong incentives to resist being affected by committee governance; hence, to find them experiencing these effects will provide strong support for my hypotheses. Figure 2.1 below provides a decision tree. This outlines the individual choices of permanent Council members that yield collective outcomes when the Council is confronted with a crisis and decides about whether or not to impose a sanctions regime.

When permanent Council members decide about whether or not to impose sanctions in a particular crisis, they can either do so or alternatively could veto the resolution establishing the sanctions regime (Choice I). In the former case, the Council institutes a sanctions regime if all permanent members prefer cooperation over non-cooperation. A skeptical permanent member will have to

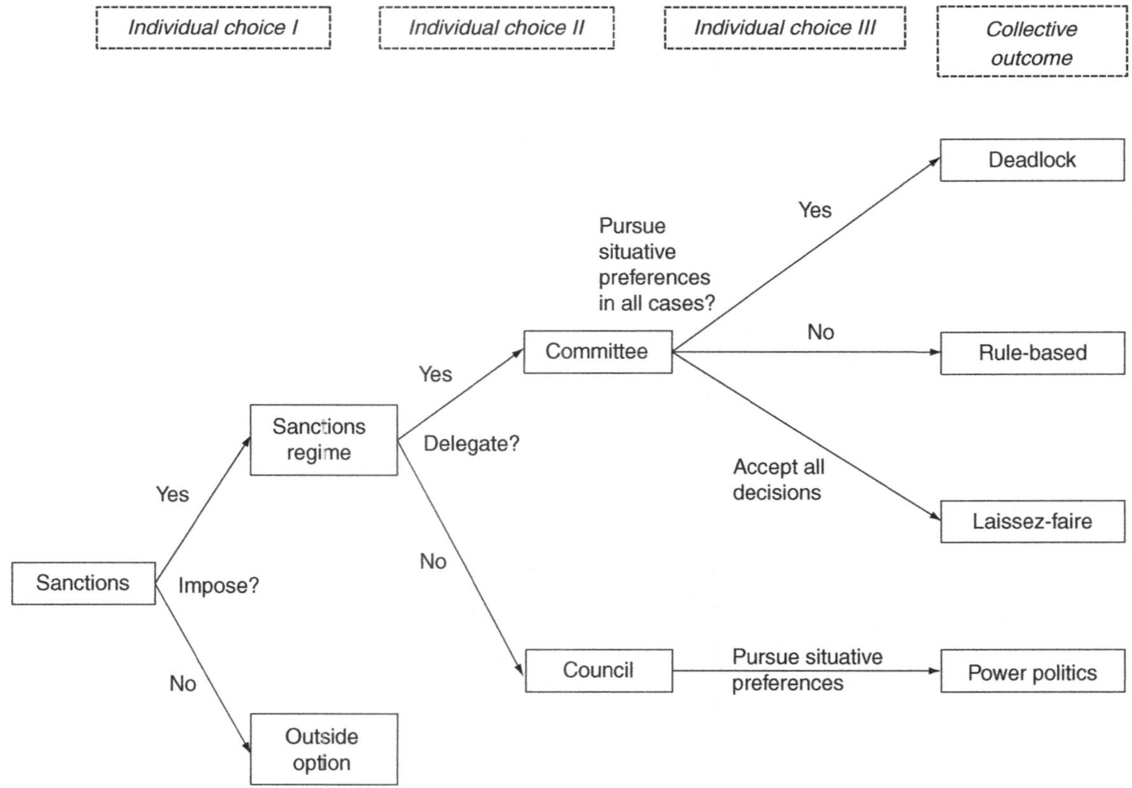

Figure 2.1 Decision tree: Security Council sanctions regimes.

Source: author's illustration.

weigh costs and benefits of cooperation vis-à-vis those of obstruction. On the one hand, P5 members may have an interest in how to address a particular crisis situation. These interests may derive from various sources including long standing political alliances, economic interests, geostrategic interests or principled objection to outside intervention. On the other hand, while the P5 veto may seriously impede Council action, the permanent members may often opt for some Council action over obstruction. Skeptical permanent members can employ the Council to control the far-reaching initiatives of proactive members (Contessi 2010). Proactive permanent members may use the Council as a tool for information transmission (Thompson 2006; Thompson 2009) or to legitimize their actions (Voeten 2005; Hurd 2007). In many cases, therefore, the P5 may have a diffuse shared interest in agreement and avoiding the veto (Krisch 2008, pp. 141–142). The costs and benefits depend on the relative position toward the status quo and whether credible outside options are available (Voeten 2001). A skeptical permanent member with a credible veto threat can extract concessions from proactive members provided that those members cannot fall back on a credible outside option, for instance, a unilateral military intervention. If a skeptical member can credibly draw on an outside option as the alternative to imposing a sanctions regime, that member is likely to veto the sanctions resolution. The extent of costs and benefits is then to the subject of empirical investigation and may vary from case to case.

As a second step, if the P5 have collectively created a sanctions regime, they can either delegate tasks to a sanctions committee or retain all sanctions regime aspects within the Council (Choice II). In the former case, members may profit from creating a committee, for instance by taking implementation decisions as necessary over a period of time and thereby reducing the Council's immediate workload. In the latter case, retaining important decisions within the Council enables members to pursue their preferences immediately, which will normally yield package deals. For instance, the P5 can opt for a unitary Council decision process if they are interested in a package deal, are under time constraints or wish to raise the decision's public profile. The decision's content is likely to be entirely determined by powerful Council members.

As a third step, if the permanent Council members prefer delegation to committee, its members' collective choices on single-cases can potentially yield three outcomes (Choice III). In a first scenario, if members decide to pursue their preferences for all single cases, the collective outcome is likely to be deadlock. A stalemate is also expected to occur if at least one committee member prefers blocking all requests. This route provides an alternative to a simple Council veto of a resolution imposing sanctions and can be beneficial for a skeptical permanent member because it similarly prevents meaningful decisions. However, committee deliberations are less visible than those of the Council. Non-permanent members can equally choose deadlock, but they could be outvoted in the Council and have a finite, "non-permanent" Council tenure. In a situation, where one committee member has an interest in deadlock, rules will be irrelevant because rules will probably point to solutions situated outside the skeptical permanent or non-permanent member's win-set. In a second scenario, if members decide *not* to pursue their preferences in all single cases, the collective outcome is likely to be rule-based. Should all committee members have some common interest in the sanctions regime's functionality but prefer different solutions, they will face a mixed-motive coordination situation. If decisions are taken at different points in time and thus cannot be accumulated into packages, states gain an interest in accepting some unfavorable decisions. Formal rules and those derived from precedents thus provide suitable focal points, which lead to acceptable coordinated solutions. Hence, the committee is expected to operate according to a logic of rule-based governance, if all members prefer a coordinated solution over deadlock. As a third scenario, if members simply accept all requests because they have a negligible interest in those single-case decisions, the collective outcome is likely to be laissez-faire decision-making. Hence, committee members have no impetus to challenge any of the requests. However, a certain conflict of interests is necessary to create coordination situations and the risk of stalemate, which ultimately provides incentives for rule-based governance.

Consequently, the aggregated preferences of Council members point to four distinct outcomes: deadlock, rule-based, laissez-faire, power politics. Accordingly, rule-based governance is only one potential outcome and will be expected to occur, when Council members delegate to a committee and have an interest in the implementation so that they both eschew laissez-faire and stalemate outcomes. Hence, the committee governance mechanism applies only if none of the permanent members prefers committee stalemate. As a result, I expect to observe committee governance effects, if the Security Council delegates implementation decisions of limited scope to a sanctions committee, while I expect power politics in the Council chamber without committee.

Research design and observable implications

Owing to the research interest testing whether or not the committee governance mechanism works as postulated under demanding circumstances, the analysis necessarily has to focus on the Council's powerful permanent members. For a solid test, the analysis has to demonstrate that committee governance binds even the great powers to formal and informal rules. These states would otherwise have abundant resources to invalidate rules. However, finding them following rules even if this means that they must accept some unfavorable single-case decisions, then one can infer that rules were decisive at committee stage.

Following the committee governance proposition, we should observe the following evidence: (1) Rule-based governance occurs when a committee systematically accepts decisions that are unfavorable to at least one member. This requires having three sorts of evidence. First, we observe the committee accepting rule-conforming decisions. Second, we observe the committee rejecting decisions, which did not conform to rules. Third, because the first two would not yet provide strong inferences, we should observe that powerful members accept decisions even if they prefer a different outcome. (2) Deadlock occurs when a committee produces no decisions in spite of having proposals before it. We should observe that the committee has received proposals, but all of these have been rejected. Alternatively, we should observe that even powerful members do not submit requests because they expect deadlock. (3) Laissez-faire occurs when a committee accepts all decision proposals across the board. We should observe that proposals are submitted to committee, and at the same time, that all of these are granted irrespective of requestor or content. (4) Power politics occurs when the Council or the committee accept decisions, which are in line with powerful members' interests, irrespective of the request's content. We should observe package deals and linkages compensating for losses of competing powerful members. Less powerful states' proposals would be rejected while powerful states' requests would be accepted.

The mechanism rests on the proposition that delegation to committee triggers rule-based governance, either by means of formal rules (hypothesis 1) or precedents (hypothesis 2). The consequences of rule-making can be observed only indirectly because data covering the entire negotiation process is difficult to obtain. Hence, I seek to assemble counter-evidence. In cases where we can observe specially crafted clauses for particular Council members, we have reasons to believe that the consistency requirement is not at work. I seek to assess, whether or not Council members create rules that benefit only a few powerful members. Thereby, it is not the rule's wording which is decisive, but rather its (intended) effect. As concerns rule-application, I would expect that members align proposals to rules in order to increase the likelihood of their adoption. I also seek to observe whether or not members refrain from submitting rule non-conforming proposals. Then, we need to establish whether or not the committee treats each proposal separately and also applies the same criteria to every proposal. We should find evidence that committee members comply with rules. Strong indicators are proposals, which do not fit rules and are therefore collectively dismissed. In addition, we should not be able to document cases where rules are violated. However, critical cases for establishing committee governance are those, where powerful members accept the rules, even in cases in which they have high stakes and prefer a different outcome. Conversely, finding less powerful states successfully submitting rule-conforming proposals even against the will of a permanent member provides strong evidence for committee governance.

The theoretical proposition of committee governance is quite demanding for empirical investigation, not least because uncovering single-cases in secretive Council committees is extremely challenging. From a research design perspective, only detailed "within case" analysis (Gerring 2004) promises to uncover empirical evidence of a type that enables making causal process observations linking the cause to the outcome, using the method of "theory-testing process tracing" (Beach and Pedersen 2013). To establish the relevance of committee governance, we need to look at many specific cases in committee, and the motivations behind them. We need to focus on how states solve decision-making issues, how they tailor specific requests, and what this means for their chances of succeeding. By establishing a temporal sequence, we can uncover the interplay between Council and committee. In addition, the focus on episodes and single cases systematically increases the number of observations (George and Bennett 2005, pp. 151–179). To that effect, in-depth case studies also make it possible to describe, and assess counterfactual claims of power politics (see Levy 2010).

The strength of individual case studies is complemented with a comparative analysis of five sanctions regimes. Selecting cases that share committee governance characteristics is crucial, because similar findings in similar cases are hardly likely to increase our confidence in the committee governance mechanism. These characteristics include delegation of many implementation decisions to a committee consisting of the same group of states, but differ in other respects, for instance the political constellation, the position of powerful members, the sanctions measures, the presence of an Ombudsperson, or dominance in the literature. Hence, I combine the in-depth assessment of committee decision-making in single cases, together with macro-level effects within each sanctions regime as well as modest generalizations across other sanctions regimes. In this way, finding committee governance within a diverse set of cases, we may assume that it speaks for an abstract mechanism, which is also observable elsewhere. Accordingly, the book departs from the literature's focus on single-case studies and macro-level studies of sanctions' effectiveness. It explores the Security Council as an exemplary case to draw conclusions for both IO theory and sanctions policy, which the following empirical chapters uncover in detail.

3 Security Council sanctions regimes

Complex governance entities

Security Council sanctions regimes are considerably differentiated, dividing tasks among various bodies, including the Security Council, sanctions committees, Panels of Experts and the UN Secretariat. In fact, the Council creates a "complex, multilayered governance system" for sanctions administration (Farrall 2009, p. 203). Each of these bodies performs a specific function, has a distinct composition and operates under criteria, rules and procedures either assigned by another superior body or emerging from its own practice. Within their mandates, decision-makers face constraints that affect the viability of preferred choices. As a consequence, in contrast to usual Council decision-making, the decisions adopted in Council sanctions regimes are the result of a complex interplay between various bodies.

In this chapter, I analyze how Council sanctions regimes are organized, focusing on scrutinizing the exact division of labor between the various bodies. In particular, I clarify which tasks the Security Council retains and which it transfers to other subsidiary bodies, how this affects decision-making within the entire governance system, and how Council members adapt the division of labor between the various organs over time. Additionally, I elucidate how the organization of sanctions regimes possibly affects Council members to align decisions with rules. I argue that while the UN Charter leaves Security Council members with wide-ranging discretion on how to administer its sanctions regimes, committee governance constrains decision-makers, thereby creating demand for rules and precedents to avoid stalemate.

The following sections consider how dividing specific tasks among five different bodies might cause such effects (see Figure 3.1). At its core, the Security Council creates and designs the sanctions regime and guides subsidiary bodies through the provision of criteria, rules and procedures. Next, the sanctions committees primarily focus on day-to-day activities including listing and delisting individuals or granting exemptions from trade embargoes. In addition, the Council usually establishes a Panel of Experts who review committee activities, monitor member states implementation and provide information for the sanctions committees' operations. In sanctions regimes which deal with internal armed conflicts, peacekeeping operations may coordinate with sanctions Panels of Experts and supply information on sanctions violations. The UN Secretariat Sanctions

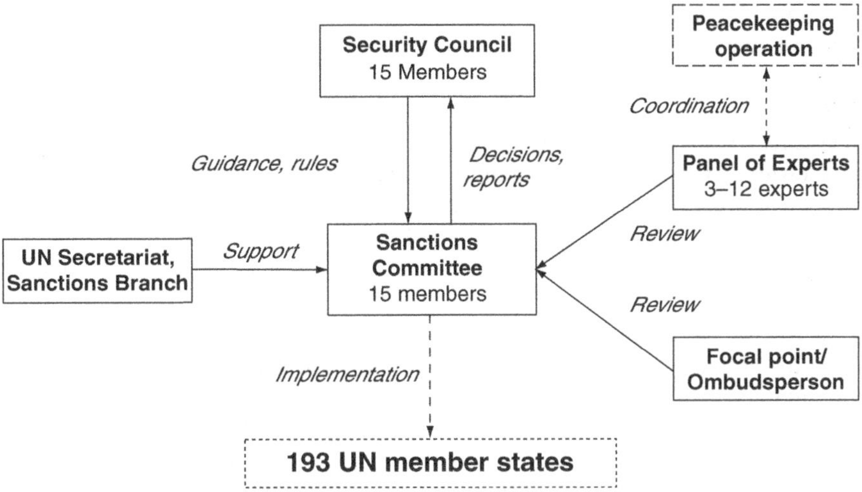

Figure 3.1 The governance structure of Security Council sanctions regimes.

Source: author's illustration.

Branch provides administrative support. Moreover, the Council has complemented the sanctions regimes with a mechanism for reviewing listing decisions (Focal Point/Ombudsperson). Finally, UN member states need to implement binding sanctions decisions collectively for sanctions to become effective.

The Security Council as master of its sanctions regimes

The Security Council as the central body within the governance system provides the framework for all other bodies and decides about the political direction of its sanctions regimes. The Council consists of 15 members, 5 of which are permanent (P5): China, France, the Russian Federation, the United Kingdom, and the United States. The General Assembly elects 10 non-permanent members for 2-year, non-consecutive terms. Decisions on substantive issues including resolutions are taken by nine affirmative votes with none of the permanent members voting against (veto).

Within sanctions regimes, four functions are served by the Security Council, as the "(…) parent body which exercises both authority and control (…)" (Paulus 2012, p. 989) in overall terms while leaving the day-to-day activities to its sanctions committees. Initially, the Security Council defines the scope, type and duration of sanctions measures adopted under Article 41 of the UN Charter. The Council is empowered to:

> decide what measures not involving the use of armed force are to be employed to give effect to its decisions (…). These may include complete or

> partial interruption of economic relations and of rail, sea, air, postal, telegraphic, radio, and other means of communication, and the severance of diplomatic relations.
>
> (UN Charter art. 41)

In essence, the Security Council enjoys wide discretion on how to "give effect to its decisions" when it decides about the scope and duration of sanctions measures. Over time, the quantity and quality of such measures has evolved considerably. The Council has markedly increased the frequency of sanctions' adoption from 2 cold-war cases to more than 30 in the period following 1990 (Farrall 2007).

Sanctions serve three broad purposes: to coerce behavioral change, to constrain the activities of a target or to signal to the international community that a particular behavior is unacceptable (Biersteker *et al.* 2016a, pp. 21–23). The Council applies sanctions to achieve a variety of objectives, including conflict resolution in interstate and internal conflicts, restoring democracy, nuclear non-proliferation, protection of civilians and human rights as well as counter-terrorism (Security Council Report 2013, pp. 3–5). Initially, as a matter of policy the Council imposed comprehensive sanctions, i.e., a ban on imports and exports of all goods with the target country while allowing for certain humanitarian exemptions. These involved Southern Rhodesia during the Cold War, and thereafter Iraq, Yugoslavia together with Haiti during the 1990s. However, massive humanitarian consequences for civilians of the latter three countries, prompted a growing criticism of sanctions and a reform initiative (Biersteker *et al.* 2005) toward more selective sanctions ("smart sanctions," Brzoska 2003). The idea of targeted sanctions is to direct measures toward those responsible for an undesired policy, while at the same time reducing unintended consequences for the general population. Since the 1990s, the Council has been targeting economic sectors with for instance embargoes on petroleum products, financial services, dual-use goods or specific commodities (e.g., timber, diamonds, charcoal, or wildlife products). While the Council has in the past also imposed aviation and diplomatic sanctions, today it most frequently imposes sanctions on distinct groups and individuals, often applying assets freezes, travel bans and arms embargoes (Biersteker *et al.* 2016a).[1] Yet, in order to "give them life," both comprehensive and targeted sanctions typically come with the ongoing need for many technical decisions. These for instance involve exempting certain goods from a trade embargo, listing individuals subject to assets freezes and travel bans or selecting goods as dual-use items banned from export to the target.

Council members can decide directly about sanctions implementation, such as listing targeted individuals (without recourse to a committee). Under certain circumstances, sanctions proponents may direct implementation decisions to the Council in the form of draft resolutions. Such situations could include: committee deadlock, anticipated committee deadlock, whenever an urgent decision is warranted, and raising a decision's public profile. For instance, during hasty negotiations over the Libya sanctions regime (resolutions 1970 (2011), 1973

(2011) and 2009 (2011)), and within the politicized Iran sanctions regime (resolutions 1737 (2006), 1747 (2007), 1803 (2008) and 1929 (2010)) Council members adopted listings in packages annexed to the resolution. Similarly, while the Council had tasked a sanctions committee with listing individuals and entities in the Sudan sanctions regime (resolution 1591 (2005)), proactive Council members circumvented a committee stalemate (Holslag 2008, pp. 81–82) and successfully listed four individuals in resolution 1672 (2006). In 2014, the Council added individuals to the Al-Qaida/Taliban sanctions list to increase public awareness about the threat posed by the Islamic State (ISIL) and the Al Nusrah Front (resolution 2170 (2014)). It is a widely held view that Council decisions are the result of bargaining between members accumulating individual listing requests for amendments to packages (e.g., Bosco 2009; McKibben and Western 2014). For instance, this could mean that a drafter drops one or more entries from the list of targets, but in return obtains a sanctions measure or other language in the operative paragraphs (interview with P5 member, December 2013, also Chapter 9). Such packages may also include additional parts of the same sanctions regime or even aspects taken from other sanctions regimes.

As an alternative to taking implementation decisions at Council level, its members almost always refer these to a designated sanctions committee. For instance, the Council has long delegated such tasks that would require independent expertise from courts, commissions or the UN Secretariat. The adjudicative Yugoslavia and Rwanda criminal tribunals, the UN Compensation Commission or the peace-keeping missions are cases in point. However, the core reason for delegating to sanctions committees is to relieve the Council's "heavy workload" of secondary decision-making on comprehensive and targeted sanctions (Sievers and Daws 2014, pp. 520–521), while at the same time keeping in full control over those decisions in a member state committee. Because the Security Council cannot perform all tasks on its own, indeed, "(...) subsidiary organs have become an indispensable tool for SC governance" (Paulus 2012, p. 987). In the absence of specific UN Charter provisions, the Security Council enjoys considerable discretion as to the design of its subsidiary bodies. Article 29 provides few substantive limits to the Council's discretion (Paulus 2012, p. 987). In fact, the Security Council's wide-ranging discretion is manifested in rule 28 from its provisional rules of procedure, which states that the Council "may appoint a commission or committee or a rapporteur for a specified question" (Paulus 2012, p. 993). Accordingly, through adopting a resolution, the Council is empowered to establish and dissolve subsidiary organs, including sanctions committees, albeit many subsidiary organs have sunset clauses.

Following the logic of an incomplete contract, once the Council has delegated implementation to a sanctions committee, it has a primarily political function in guiding and preventing any potential deviation by the committee, while determining its discretion via Council resolutions. In fact, resolutions become the major "legislative instruments" to guide sanctions regimes (Conlon 1996a, p. 75). While doing so, there are four options. (1) The Council may strictly regulate an issue area of subsequent committee activity to commit its members in the committee stage to pre-defined implementation rules. Strict regulation is a strong ex-ante control mechanism (Hawkins *et al.* 2006, pp. 19–20). This could be included in a major Council package agreement on a sanctions case. Strict regulation could ensure that a compromise at the time of its adoption is frozen to preserve the current committee practice and avoid any deviation in practice over time. Yet, the downside is that it also strictly limits division of labor benefits if the Council already predetermines all subsequent committee decisions. (2) The Council may limit committee discretion by defining decision criteria and procedures as to how the committee should implement an issue area. This will be useful when decisions differ in some respects (as, for instance, requests for listing different individuals). Hence, the Council can reap the benefits from division of labor and incomplete contracting, without having to predetermine all decisions completely. (3) The Council may require a committee to adopt or amend its own internal rules because Council members prefer rule-based governance to overreaching discretion in the committee stage, at a time when the details of such rules are not yet fully determined. The frequent adoption of resolutions that make such prescriptions illustrates that the Council uses its oversight function to govern its subsidiary bodies, even though the same group of actors is present in the Council and the committee. It also suggests that Council members intend to shift from completely unconstrained power politics toward a more regulated committee stage, though not all member states may prefer rule-based governance to an equal extent. (4) The Council may not regulate the committee stage, for instance, because the powerful permanent members seek to avoid being bound by rules or because the Council as a whole disagrees over sets of rules.

The Council often combines these options in the same sanctions regime: It may strictly prescribe committee action on one aspect, assign rule-making functions to the committee on another issue and leave a third aspect completely unregulated. Because the number of increasingly complex agenda items requires the Council to organize work efficiently, its activity will naturally shift toward steering the committee stage through resolutions. While the Council deals with issues of a political nature, sanctions committees take a much narrower perspective within the framework of Council guidance.

The sanctions committees as implementing agents

Sanctions committees constitute the main subsidiary organs which take numerous small implementation decisions. All major sanctions measures including both comprehensive and targeted sanctions require substantial follow-up decisions in order to implement a regime meaningfully. With rare exceptions, the Council has transferred these to separate and specifically established sanctions committees (Farrall 2007, p. 147). Besides adopting implementation decisions, a sanctions committee also has a role as secondary rule-maker. Both functions provide distinct incentives for committee members which are different from those in the Council.

Sanctions committees share three core characteristics. First, the Council has an established practice of duplicating Council membership in its sanctions committees, thus forming a "committee of the whole," although from the outset other design options would have been possible (Sievers and Daws 2014, p. 520). This composition follows a precedent established by the first sanctions committee on Southern Rhodesia in 1969. Thereafter, all sanctions committees have followed this model (Farrall 2007, pp. 147–148). The committees are staffed with career diplomats of a mid and low-rank, below the level of deputy permanent representative (van Walsum 2004, p. 183; Comras 2010, p. 88). Usually, these diplomats are generalists who have served in different functions before and not necessarily familiar with the specific matter at hand; however, more recently there is a trend toward specialization. Typically, diplomats serve in bilateral rather than multilateral settings (Scharf and Dorosin 1993, p. 821). Depending on mission size, different diplomats serve in different committees and increasingly so as the number of committees and workloads increase. Committees are chaired at the level of ambassador, with each chairperson selected from the E10 members rotating on an annual or biannual basis and serving in his/her personal capacity (Security Council Report 2013, p. 7).

Second, sanctions committees meet in private session (Sievers and Daws 2014, p. 520). Consequently, not only are deliberations secret, but also decisions, informal rules and justifications for decisions are not made public unless there is a need to provide such information exceptionally, as for example in the case of sanctions lists' publication. Essentially, there are two meeting formats, formal and informal. Regarding the former, a summary record of proceedings and verbal interventions are prepared by the Secretariat for limited distribution, i.e., not as a public document. Conversely, for the latter no such service is provided (Sievers and Daws 2014, p. 520). The major difference is that the committee can take decisions in formal meetings which it cannot do in informal meetings. However, organizing a formal committee meeting is more effort for little additional benefit. A committee can easily and effectively decide by using the written no-objection procedure and, accordingly, practice has over time not surprisingly shifted more toward informal meetings. It should be noted though, that in practice even informal sessions are very formal. The chairperson reads out from "Notes for the Chair" prepared by the Secretariat. Delegates often read out statements, exercise caution in sticking carefully to statements previously cleared by their capital and rarely speak "off the cuff" (Sievers and Daws 2014, pp. 485–486).

Third, sanctions committees decide by consensus and as a result all 15 committee members have a de facto veto. This is the most obvious difference between the Council and committees, with even a small state, therefore, having the power to block any decision. This consensus rule stems from the Southern Rhodesia Sanctions Committee. However, the literature does describe why this rule was chosen (Gowlland-Debbas 1990, p. 609; Farrall 2007, p. 156; Sievers and Daws 2014, p. 530). For practical considerations, all types of decisions including listing and delisting, exemptions, adoption of press releases or Panel of Expert reports, are usually taken in a written no-objection procedure (also: silence procedure). This procedure provides an efficient means of decision-making, particularly in committees with high workloads (Conlon 1995b, p. 647; interview with UN member state official, New York, March 2012). Accordingly, the committee Chair circulates decision proposals in writing among committee members, who have three options. First, they can do nothing and accept the decision. Second, they can place a technical hold; they may not wish to object, but do not yet agree so usually want to consult with the capital or request more information. Third, they can object to the proposal. For a decision to be adopted, no members must object or place a hold within the specified timeframe, which varies across committees and types of decisions (Farrall 2007, pp. 156–157). Hence, objecting to a proposal requires action, while acceptance occurs tacitly.

The Council designed sanctions committees to relieve it from having to deal with numerous issues of small scope (interview with UN member state official, New York, January, 2016). While rule-based governance may well be in the interests of powerful members, the Council members usually seek to stay in close control over how sanctions are implemented. As a standard Council practice, a separate committee is established for each sanctions regime, sole exceptions being the terrorism-related Sudan and the Somalia/Eritrea sanctions regimes (Paulus 2012, pp. 998–999). The Council does so, despite other organizational designs being plausible (Farrall 2007, p. 156). However, it is easy to understand the practical effect of existing practice. In a unitary organ, member states would be forced to develop a coherent sanctions management guided by overarching principles, whereas the creation of separate sanctions committees limits the constraints of adopting consistent decisions that would arise out of an alternate organizational design. For instance, the non-aligned Council members, mostly with majority Muslim populations, demanded a more lenient sanctions policy within the Iraq Committee while pushing for a more aggressive approach toward Serbia in the Yugoslavia Committee (Conlon 1995a, p. 329). This form of organization also allows for forum shopping. For example, one individual, who was delisted from the Al-Qaida list in anticipation of an Ombudsperson delisting, was instantly relisted in the Somalia Committee (Eckert and Biersteker 2012, p. 19).

Sanctions committees primarily serve to adopt small, separate case-specific decisions in the "day-to-day operation of the regime" (Krisch 2004, p. 886), which the Council delegates to the committee. As such, sanctions committees perform mostly an "administrative function" (Conlon 1995b, p. 646) for "(…) matters of the type that in Western societies are handled by regulatory bodies" (Conlon 2000, p. 31), but Council members want to keep under tight control. Different sanctions measures require different types of case-specific decisions. Whereas the administration of comprehensive sanctions requires decisions about exemptions from a trade embargo, targeted sanctions regimes require the listing as well as delisting of individuals and entities together with the granting of humanitarian exemptions from sanctions measures. In addition, arms embargoes require decisions about exemptions for peacekeeping operations or governmental forces. Other tasks include evaluating reports by member states or the Panels of Experts, investigating cases of sanctions evasion or non-compliance, reporting to the Council on its work through briefings and written reports as well as other tasks the Council assigned (Carisch and Rickard-Martin 2011, p. 4; Security Council Report 2013). Although these types of decisions are different in substance, they have in common that they are single-case decisions, while each single case has only marginal importance on its own.

Delegation to committee creates a different decision situation for Council members. First, this form of delegation strikes a delicate balance between relieving the Council and implementing a sanctions regime under member state control. Because Council members have chosen to delegate, the member states treat the committee as a body embedded within, yet separate from, the Council despite identical composition (Conlon 1995b, p. 663). Delegation to the committee reflects Council members' broad agreement on a sanctions regime and has passed the high threshold for Council resolutions. Accordingly, members usually have a general interest in maintaining the division of labor as well as following Council criteria and rules, irrespective of potential disagreement on substantive issues. They do not want to obstruct the work of committees, provided that in general terms they support using sanctions for the case being considered (six interviews with UN member state officials, March–April 2012). Because committee decision-making is embedded within the Council framework, member states accept representation by low-level diplomats in the committees. In turn, low-level diplomats collectively have little motivation to challenge what their own ambassadors have decided in the Council.

Second, committee decision-making is subject to a dense set of criteria and rules. Binding committee decisions, such as listing or delisting of individuals, are based on formal delegation and the Council in most cases defines basic parameters for the committee. On the one hand, in contrast to the Council, the narrow committee mandate makes linkages within and across sanctions regimes difficult; indeed, many aspects of the sanctions regime are beyond committee control. On the other hand, due to the narrow mandate, committee members can devote more attention to the specificities of tasks compared with what they could do within the Council's broad agenda. Hence, the committees deal with each decision request separately without linking them to packages (as in the Council, two interviews with UN member state officials, New York, March 2012, see also Conlon Papers). Even for the contentious Sudan Sanctions Committee, a US diplomat pointed out that because "the Committee approves or rejects names individually, not on a slate" (US Permanent Mission to the UN 2008b) packages are not feasible.

The leverage of individual members over decisions depends on the sanctions regime's set-up and the decision procedure's design. In the Iraq sanctions regime, for instance, all trade with the country was banned, except for those deliveries exempted by committee consensus. Here, the proponents of strict sanctions could withhold consensus. However, in targeted sanctions regimes the sanctions proponents need the cooperation of skeptics to list individuals and entities, while the opposite is true for delisting requests. In addition, the ability of committee members to evaluate proposals depends on the time limit inherent within the no-objection procedure's logic. In cases of complex proposals, a short time frame can pose significant limitations on committee members' ability to respond (Kanetake 2008, p. 147). Many member states missions are limited in their ability to consult with their capitals quickly because of time-zone differences. In such circumstances, decisions are difficult to challenge and consequently incentives to block decisions are provided only in matters of vital national interest (Biersteker and Eckert 2006, pp. 29–30).

While in principle any committee member may refer any unresolved or contentious issue to the Council, all members have strong incentives to leave matters within the committee (three interviews with UN member state officials, New York, March–April 2012). The non-permanent member states have a de facto veto power in committee, whereas they have an inferior position in the Council. The permanent members enjoy a privileged position in the Council. However, they also have strong interests to leave single-case issues within the committee because they risk exposing their motivations and politicizing an issue of limited scope. Although Council decisions are likewise mainly prepared behind closed doors, proposals and decisions are far more transparent than they are in committee and accordingly subject to public scrutiny. In addition, this would undermine the division of labor between committee and Council, namely to relieve the latter from taking many single-case decisions. While the option to refer issues to the Council has been applied in a few sanctions regimes (for instance on Sudan, resolution 1672 (2006)), it is rarely used.

Besides implementation decisions, sanctions committees specify rules given by the Council and elaborate on new rules in response to Council's requests (see previous section). Hence, committees not only interpret and clarify Council resolutions, but also provide ongoing definitions while deciding about single cases (Scharf and Dorosin 1993). Furthermore, committees are empowered to engage in selective "self-regulation" in order to overcome issues associated with case-specific decision-making and thus resolve decision-making stalemates. Because of the differentiated nature of sanctions regimes, Security Council members have incentives to defer meaningful authority to the committee for clarification and application of its resolutions; otherwise the Council would have to take all technical decisions itself. The effective implementation of complex sanctions regimes requires more detailed instructions and oversight than the Council is capable of delivering (Conlon 1995b, p. 650). In negotiating sanctions regimes, Council members naturally take a much broader perspective. Resolution drafters cannot feasibly consider all the implications of "compromise language" or previously "agreed language" from earlier resolutions under changing circumstances. The Council adopts resolutions at a certain point and often under severe time constraints (Conlon 2000, p. 46), whereas implementing a sanctions regime requires many small decisions on a continuous and routine basis. Council members may exclude divisive details from negotiations so as to achieve the broadest possible support and intentional ambiguity provides a tool for building consensus. Thus, to reduce transaction costs, the Council may explicitly or implicitly request sanctions committees to clarify technical details and operational definitions. Separation of the two main functions of rule-making and rule-application is observable in sanctions regimes, although this does not materialize in a clear division between the different organs. While the committee gains a rule-making function, such transfer of authority is unproblematic for Council members as the same members are present both in the Council and the committee (Scharf and Dorosin 1993, p. 813).

Committee rule-making is associated with the same institutional constraints as Council rule-making. However, if Council transferred the interpretation task to a committee, that committee is then under pressure to provide an authoritative interpretation, otherwise individual UN member states would "interpret on their own" (Conlon 2000, p. 46; Conlon 1996b, p. 256). Yet, any collective committee decision about an issue at hand requires prior agreement on how such decisions are to be taken. Hence, in cases where the committee engages in rule-making, the decision-making process is sequenced into an initial stage for defining the rules which apply to specific types of cases, followed by a decision on one or more of these types of cases according to the rules. This transfers the committee into a logic of rule-making which subordinates committee members to the constraints usually associated with Council decision-making. As an alternative to formalized rules, the committee can establish a precedent on a new type of case, after which similar cases follow the precedent (see discussions in Iraq and Yugoslavia Sanctions Committee, Conlon Papers, on file with author).

Similarly to the Council, sanctions committees have wide-ranging discretion as to how they organize their work; thus they can adopt their own rules of procedure and develop an informal decision-making practice (Conlon 1996a, p. 77). As to the former, each sanctions committee adopts its own "guidelines of the committee for the conduct of its work," detailing committee working methods and giving procedural instructions to the committee secretariat (Farrall 2007, p. 156; Sievers and Daws 2014). Committee guidelines vary considerably in length and precision. For instance, the early Iraq Sanctions Committee's guidelines comprised merely 10 short paragraphs on a single-page, whereas the extremely detailed Al-Qaida Sanctions Committee guidelines cover 18 paragraphs with multiple subparagraphs extending to 26 pages. On occasions, the Council directs the committee to issue or amend its guidelines to accommodate new sanctions measures or to solve decision-making issues (Sievers and Daws 2014, pp. 542–543). These directives illustrate how Council members perceive the Council and the committee as distinct arenas. Such a Council directive may also transfer divisive issues to the committee. However, in this case the committee must ultimately regulate such a decision problem. It is also possible for committees to sidestep their own guidelines or informal rules. Yet, members must then agree on how to replace an old rule with a new, formal or informal, rule (three interviews with UN member state officials, December 2013). The sanctions committee, as implementation agent, almost automatically engages in formal and informal processes of rule-making; consequently, in general terms this also significantly increases the density of rules within a sanctions regime (Gehring and Dörfler 2013, p. 573).

The Panels of Experts as reflexive component

With the Panels of Experts (sometimes referred to as Group of Experts, Monitoring Group or Monitoring Team), sanctions regimes include a "reflexive arm" without formal decision-making powers (Krisch 2004, p. 886). Traditionally, sanctions committees had the task of monitoring sanctions implementation. However, for the Security Council and committee staffed by diplomats and based in New York, it is impractical if not impossible to monitor sanctions implementation meaningfully in complex conflict settings. Moreover, diplomatic politics often inhibits critical evaluation. As a result, the Security Council decided to create expert bodies for independent monitoring and information gathering on its behalf (Farrall 2009, p. 195). Panels of Experts monitor sanctions regimes, assess weaknesses in the sanctions mechanism for specific cases, provide evidence on sanctions violations, and recommend improvements (Krisch 2004, p. 886). It is now standard Council practice to establish a Panel of Experts as a subsidiary body whenever it imposes a new sanctions regime. The Security Council establishes each Panel of Experts in an individually dedicated resolution outlining its size, duration, location, and mandate (Farrall 2009, pp. 194–196).

Panels of Experts vary considerably in their size (from 2 to 12 members), duration (from few weeks to years), and are usually located within the conflict region (except for the Al-Qaida, Iran and DPRK panels). These Panels are staffed with experts usually chosen for their competence in a required field or area. For instance, the Sudan Panel of Experts comprises experts covering: aviation, arms, international humanitarian law, and regional knowledge. Additionally, a financial expert serves as the Panel's coordinator (S/2014/206). The Secretariat proposes a list of candidates which is circulated among the respective sanctions committee members under the no-objection procedure. If one member objects, the respective individual is substituted until no more objections are received. The UN Secretary-General formally appoints individuals on a consultancy basis (Farrall 2009, p. 203; Carisch and Rickard-Martin 2011, p. 5). The UN Secretariat's Sanctions Branch covers administrative aspects of the Panel's work and provides initial training and advice on how to interact with the committee. On occasions, the Sanctions Branch also contributes to background research, report-writing and field work (Farrall 2009, pp. 202–203).

The Panels of Experts serve as independent advisory bodies under the direction of respective sanctions committees but have no decision competence. The Council defines its panels as "(…) organs with different and distinct mandates, of independent, expert and non-judiciary character, with no subpoena powers, whose primary role is to provide sanctions-related information to the relevant committees" (S/2006/997, para. 19). Expert bodies provide real-time information about their investigation of sanctions violations or other developments on the ground to the committee (e.g., ASSMT on Al-Qaida/Taliban or the SEMG on charcoal ban in Somalia). They also assist committees in ongoing assignments such as providing information on the listing of individuals or updating information on the committee's sanctions list. Beyond real-time reporting, the Panels submit more detailed mid-term briefings and final reports at the end of their mandates. These reports elaborate findings relevant to sanctions regimes, often detailing evidence collected in the field, make suggestions on how to improve overall sanctions effectiveness, propose additional individuals or entities for listing (mostly in a confidential annex), recommend establishing, lifting or modifying certain sanctions measures and highlight other issues (Carisch and Rickard-Martin 2011, p. 5; Boucher and Holt 2009, pp. 45–54).

The Security Council defines the scope of expert bodies' mandates and the standards of evidence to be employed by such expert bodies. Panel of Experts' mandates vary considerably in extent and detail. For instance, the mandate for the Analytical Support and Sanctions Monitoring Team (ASSMT) assisting the Al-Qaida and Taliban Committees has 28 provisions on three pages (resolution 2083 (2012), Annex I), whereas the mandate for the Panel of Experts on Sudan has only three provisions (resolution 1591 (2005), para. 3b, as subsequently extended). During the sanctions reform debates, the Council recognized the importance of detailing mandates and methodological standards (Biersteker *et al.* 2005, p. 27). The Security Council has regularly adapted its approach to Panels of Experts and acknowledged that the "working methods of expert groups have developed through a system of trial and error" (S/2006/997, para. 9). It accepted the importance of "common methodological standards" for the Expert Panels' work, and the specific pertinence that expert bodies "(…) should rely on verified documents and, wherever possible, on first-hand, on-site observations by the experts themselves, including photographs" (S/2006/997, para. 22). However, the Council stopped short of providing clear guidance on evidentiary standards. Even though they are subsidiary bodies, Panels of Experts are relatively independent in the way they approach their work within Council mandate limitations. All Panels of Experts have to submit regular written reports including a final report with recommendations to the Council through the committee. As such, the expert bodies are independent in the sense that they are solely responsible for the contents of their reports (Carisch and Rickard-Martin 2011, p. 5). Although the Panel as a collective is independent in its own reporting, the individual members have to agree not only on the substance and wording of the reports, but also which standards of evidence should be employed. In the event of diverging opinions, the Panel has to aggregate this divergence within a final written report. Panels have adopted different mechanisms for preference aggregation, including applying tighter standards of evidence, package deals, majority voting or simply noting a dissenting member's opinion in reports. The coordinator serves as official contact for the committee and coordinates the group's work (Farrall 2009, p. 203; Boucher and Holt 2009, pp. 61–62).

The respective sanctions committee is regularly briefed by expert bodies, receiving and discussing the final reports. Consequently, committees more frequently deal with expert bodies than the Council (Farrall 2009, p. 202). Once a specific report detailing the Panel's activities, findings and recommendations (Boucher and Holt 2009, p. 45) has been received by the committee, it is given a briefing by Panel members, following which the findings are discussed. Thereafter, the committee usually adopts the report and refers it to Council, at which time it becomes a public document (except for confidential annexes). However, some members may want to impede a report's publication because it contains findings they find unacceptable. The ability of committee members to block or delay expert body reports including certain findings first and foremost depends on the procedure employed, which varies across sanctions regimes. While most committees receive reports and transmit them to the Council (which requires a consensus decision), some expert bodies are mandated to submit reports directly to the Council (Security Council Report 2013, p. 8). In the former case, committee members have a "take-it-or-leave-it" option. For the latter, a committee no longer possesses the competence to decide about publication. For instance, the Council amended the procedure for submission of the DRC expert body report requesting it to "submit to the Council its final report upon termination of the Group's mandate" (S/2014/2136, para. 5), presumably to prevent the blocking of reports by committee member Rwanda (see Chapter 6). The committee can take action on the report's findings by adopting specific decisions itself or by recommending sanctions regime adjustments to the Council (Farrall 2009, p. 203).

There are a few mediating factors in the interaction of Council, committee and expert bodies. Committee members, particularly the permanent members, have increasingly tried to control the panels and final reports' contents by lobbying the Secretariat to put their "own" nationals on the list of candidates. This politicizes a Panel of Experts, often involves horse-trading between committee members (Security Council Report 2013, pp. 6–7), and introduces an element of bargaining into the panel's information gathering process. Usually, governments that are susceptible to controlling one expert, pick a career diplomat or ministerial official to ensure loyalty. However, even if individual experts succeed in deleting certain unfavorable content for their government, the logic of bargaining does not allow them to eliminate all unfavorable contents, particularly if the investigated cases are bolstered with facts and are clearly documented. Moreover, the expert body has an incentive not to overstretch its mandate as it can be dissolved by the Council and it is also encouraged to submit recommendations bolstered with sufficient evidence that have some chance of succeeding. Neither Council nor committee can discard all expert body findings and recommendations if the Council as a collective has mandated the expert body to fulfill a specific task and does not want to undermine the sanctions regime as a whole.

The UN Secretariat's "Sanctions Branch" as administrative component

The Secretariat's Subsidiary Organs Branch (often referred to as "Sanctions Branch") is mainly tasked with providing administrative support to the committee; however, it has no formal decision-making powers and at best serves an agenda setting role. The Sanctions Branch is situated in the Security Council Affairs Division (SCAD) within the Department of Political Affairs. As the number of sanctions committees grew, so did the number of servicing staff, from 18 in 1993 (internal Secretariat document, Conlon Papers) to 33 professional and general service staff over the ensuing 20 years (internal Secretariat document, as of October 2013).

The Secretariat's main function is to service committees through meeting organization and document distribution. Its staff, in cooperation with the Chair, prepare meeting documents such as the provisional agenda, "Notes for the Chair" (i.e., Chairman's script to guide the committee though the agenda during formal and informal sessions), as well as other relevant documents. Each committee is served by a Committee Secretary, the main contact point for committee members and non-Council member states, and the respective Panel of Experts. Each Secretary is assigned to another sanctions committee as back-up. Besides the Secretary, each committee is serviced by a team of additional staff (Carisch and Rickard-Martin 2011, p. 5), usually three, but subject to requirements this can increase to six as happened during the labor-intensive Yugoslavia Sanctions Committee (internal Secretariat document, Conlon Papers). As chairing a sanctions committee is quite labor-intensive, the Chairing delegation and committee Secretary usually work closely together (Boucher and Holt 2009, p. 58). In addition, the Secretariat maintains the "Committee eRooms," where documents including incoming and outgoing correspondence are electronically stored for internal committee use.

The Secretariat circulates incoming communications or decision proposals and often drafts the sanctions committee's annual reports, depending on the committee's workload and chairing delegation's capacities. Concerning committee guidelines, the Secretariat, in cooperation with the Chairman, provides a draft version, usually based on committee guidelines from other committees familiar to the Secretary. On an annual basis, the Secretariat briefs incoming E10 delegations on the work of the sanctions committees and assists incoming chairing delegations. Regarding the Panel of Experts, the Secretariat maintains a roster and proposes a group's composition for committee approval. Once a Panel of Experts is established, the Secretariat briefs incoming panel members and supports the panel's work concerning administrative matters, travel arrangements and communication with the committee. In some instances, Secretariat staff provide substantive support in terms of research, report-writing or accompanying the Panel of Experts on country-visits (Boucher and Holt 2009, pp. 56–58).

Although some former members ascribe an influential role to the Secretariat (Carisch and Rickard-Martin 2011, p. 5; Conlon 2000, p. 18; Boucher and Holt

2009, p. 58), its powers are quite limited. In this context, it is telling that the UN Secretariat does not appear as a sanctions actor in much of the UN sanctions literature (Farrall 2007; Biersteker *et al.* 2016b). Indeed, the Secretariat does not take positions on substantive questions, but merely presents options on procedural questions as requested by the Chair (interview with UN Secretariat member, New York, March 2012). The Secretariat archives communications, decisions and other relevant committee documents, while also maintaining databases on sanctions provisions and mandates for sanctions bodies. The Secretariat also archives Panel of Experts reports and recommendations to provide for a smooth transition whenever Panels of Experts' composition changes (Cortright *et al.* 2010, p. 12). However, in regard to the drafting of committee guidelines or committee annual reports, the Secretariat has at best an agenda-setting role, while the sanctions committee has formal decision-making responsibilities. The degree of Secretariat discretion is determined by Council and committee guidance on how to handle incoming communications. The Secretariat could potentially use this discretion to change the informal practice of committee conduct. However, individual committee members could simply object. Only in very few instances do decisions require long-term institutional memory. For such eventualities, the proactive permanent members maintain their own documentation systems (interview with UN Secretariat member, New York, March 2012). In regard to selecting suitable Panels of Expert members, the Secretariat acts as agenda-setter and has an interest in selecting qualified members with specific levels of expertise in avoiding objections from Council members (Farrall 2009, p. 207). Thus, even though the UN Secretariat provides administrative and on occasions substantive support, it is bereft of any meaningful decision-making powers and can never take precedence over the sanctions committee within the established hierarchy (Conlon 2000, p. 28).

The Focal Point and the Office of the Ombudsperson as individual complaints mechanisms

The Security Council complemented its sanctions regimes with an individual complaints mechanism as part of the delisting procedure; however, only the Al-Qaida Sanctions Committee mechanism has significantly far-reaching decision powers. The Security Council created the Focal Point for Delisting (resolution 1730 (2006)) in 2006, and the Office of the Ombudsperson (resolution 1904 (2009)), as being specifically tailored to the needs of the Al-Qaida/Taliban sanctions regime in 2009. The mechanism enabled two new types of actors to access the sanctions regimes. First, private complainants, listed individuals and entities, could directly trigger a committee procedure to review whether or not continued listing of the petitioner was still justified. Second, the Council established two organs within the UN Secretariat to receive and process review petitions (Biersteker and Eckert 2009, pp. 12–14; Sievers and Daws 2014, pp. 542–544).

Initially, sanctions regimes' delisting procedures were highly restrictive and entirely inter-governmental; targeted sanctions regimes did not provide any delisting procedure. Later, in order to process first delisting petitions, Council members began introducing such procedures, but made sure that the entire process was under the sanctions committees' full control. Accordingly, delisting requests would require consensus or conversely, any committee member could prevent a delisting by withholding consensus (Cramér 2003, pp. 90–95; Kanetake 2008, pp. 157–158). Moreover, any listed individual could trigger a review of the case exclusively through his/her state of nationality and/or residence. While any state can submit a delisting request in any of the sanctions regimes, this procedure is problematic as an individual has to depend on the support of a state and thus the reliability of these states to forward individual petitions to the respective committee. However, a petitioned state might not be willing to support a delisting request, be it for political reasons, insufficient capacity or simply lack of interest. Ultimately, this would deny listed individuals and entities access to the review process. Because complaints might not have been forwarded due to the lack of support from petitioned governments, it is not known how many individuals and entities have unsuccessfully sought to initiate delisting (Biersteker and Eckert 2006, p. 2).

To remedy the access issue, primarily related to the Al-Qaida/Taliban regime, the purely inter-governmental delisting procedure was complemented by allowing listed individuals and entities to petition their listing via the central Focal Point for Delisting within the UN Secretariat (resolution 1730 (2006)). This development is remarkable as individuals and entities could directly access the respective sanctions committee, even if their state of nationality/residency had objected to such a request. The Focal Point informs sanctions committees about incoming petitions, forwards them to relevant states, such as designating states and states of nationality/residency, and informs the petitioner about relevant procedures, the case's status and the final decision (Biersteker and Eckert 2009, pp. 12–13; Security Council Report 2013, p. 8). The Focal Point relieves the Council of administrative and routine tasks with the investment of very few resources (Biersteker and Eckert 2006, pp. 40–41).

Nonetheless, following the permanent members' preferences for a process that would not restrict committee prerogatives and limit the number of states involved (US Embassy Paris 2006b; Comras 2010, pp. 100–101), the Focal Point does not have any decision-making authority. While the initiation phase of the delisting procedure has dramatically changed, the subsequent decision procedure was only slightly modified. For decisions to be taken, petitions still require formal delisting requests by petitioned states, designating states, states of nationality/residency or any other committee members. Ultimately, this preserves the inter-governmental de-listing procedure, because committees decide about delisting requests by consensus. In addition, committees do not have to provide reasons for their decisions, neither to petitioners nor the public. However, this procedure merely ensures that committees automatically consider delisting petitions, following which petitioners are informed about the outcomes (Kanetake 2008, pp. 161–164; Rosand 2010, p. 259). The Focal Point procedure has remained fairly unchanged over the years. The Focal Point now receives requests from listed individuals or entities regarding exemptions in the ISIL/ Da'esh/Al-Qaida and Taliban sanctions regimes and conveys decisions on those requests. It also forwards complaints by delisted individuals from the ISIL/ Da'esh/Al-Qaida sanctions list, who were subjected to sanctions resulting from mistaken identification or confusion with other individuals. However, the Council does not prescribe timeframes for the consideration of individual petitions and thus some requests might remain pending indefinitely. Even as it was being established, many states that had favored a stronger review mechanism expressed their disappointment (statements by Switzerland, Austria, S/PV. 5446, May 30, 2006; Kanetake 2008, pp. 161–164).

Since 2006, the Focal Point has received delisting requests from 73 individuals and 39 entities in total (see Table 3.1). With a success rate of about 35 percent, the respective committees delisted 21 individuals and 17 entities, but denied delisting requests from another 37 individuals and 20 entities, with the remaining petitions still outstanding. Overall, after more than 10 years and considering the high number of listings, individuals and entities can be said to have rarely used this tool. In addition, there are significant differences between the sanctions regimes in terms of how different individuals use the procedure. Most delisting requests have been made to the Al-Qaida/Taliban, Liberia and Iraq Committees, together comprising about three-quarters of all requests, while other committees with substantial lists, for instance Iran or Taliban, have yielded very few.

Table 3.1 Focal Point for Delisting statistics

Sanctions regime	*Requests*	*Delisting*	*Listing upheld*	*Success rate (%)*
Somalia/Eritrea	1 individual		1 individual	0
Al-Qaida/Taliban (as of 2009)	18 individuals 22 entities	3 individuals 17 entities	13 individuals 3 entities	50
Iraq	14 individuals 1 entity	2 individuals	1 individual 1 entity	50
Liberia	23 individuals 9 entities	14 individuals	9 individuals 9 entities	44
DRC	8 individuals 4 entities	1 individual	7 individuals 4 entities	9
Côte d'Ivoire	2 individuals		2 individuals	0
Iran	2 entities		2 entities	0
Libya	3 individuals		2 individuals	0
Taliban (since 2011)*	3 individuals	1 individual	2 individuals	0
Central African Republic	1 individual 1 entity		1 individual 1 entity	0
Total	**73 individuals** **39 entities**	**21 individuals** **17 entities**	**37 individuals** **20 entities**	34

Note
Data as of July 19, 2018, adapted from Focal Point statistics at www.un.org/sc/suborg/en/sanctions/delisting/de-listing-request-stats.

For the Al-Qaida regime specifically, the Council strengthened its individual complaints mechanism and created the Office of the Ombudsperson as an independent and impartial entity mandated to review delisting petitions (resolution 1904 (2009), see also Chapter 6). In the role's original form, the Ombudsperson was entitled to interact with the petitioner and collect information from relevant actors involved, judging whether or not there was sufficient evidence for upholding the listing. To that effect, the Ombudsperson provided a "comprehensive report" to the Al-Qaida/Taliban Committee reviewing the case. However, although the Ombudsperson did not have the right to make formal recommendations and her assessment did not have any direct consequences, she nevertheless had a potentially powerful agenda-setting function (Eckert and Biersteker 2012, pp. 14–25; Prost and Wilmshurst 2013).

In 2011, this role within the procedure was dramatically enhanced (resolution 1989 (2011)). The Ombudsperson was given powers to make formal recommendations and, strikingly, if the Ombudsperson now requests a delisting, the entry is deleted after 60 days unless the committee decides by consensus to uphold the listing or unless one member state refers the matter to the Council (resolution 1989 (2011), Annex II, para. 12). This procedural change significantly enhances the Ombudsperson's agenda-setting power and alters the decision-making rationale for committee members. A formal recommendation from the Ombudsperson is now difficult to overrule as the committee has to achieve consensus in maintaining the listing. A designating state intending to retain a listing despite an Ombudsperson's delisting recommendation would have to convince all other committee members for such a recommendation to be overturned. Provided that the Ombudsperson recommendation is convincing, this procedure then shifts the burden of proof to designating states. Moreover, the committee has to communicate and justify its decision to the petitioner via the Ombudsperson (guidelines November 2011, Annex II, para. 13), which increases the number of hurdles to be overcome in retaining a listing when facing a delisting recommendation (Eckert and Biersteker 2012, pp. 14–25; Prost 2012a).

Concluding thoughts

With its increasing resort to sanctions, the Council has created a governance structure that allocates distinct functions among its subsidiary organs and thereby moves away from a pure forum for power politics. The Council, sanctions committees and expert bodies perform distinct functions, have a distinct composition, operate under distinct procedures and serve distinct mandates. Decision-makers in each body face different types of decisions and different institutional constraints for deciding upon them. Because of the complex structure of sanctions regimes, the sanctions system's effective functioning creates demand for governing relationships through rules and integrating the various bodies.

Three messages can be distilled from the above. First, Security Council members have in principle two ways of implementing a sanctions regime. As the superior body, the Council can either adopt implementation decisions independently, usually by packing several decision requests into a formal resolution and then trading-off various aspects of the resolution until it reaches a majority. In practice, there have been a few sanctions regimes, including Iran and DPRK, when Council members have indeed preferred to keep implementation decisions within the Council at various stages during the process. Alternatively, Council members can collectively establish a sanctions regime, transfer decision competencies to its subsidiary organs and then guide those through the provision of rules. In this case, Council members deal with much broader political questions, because implementation decisions are no longer decided at this level. Rather, when the Council transfers technical decisions to the committee, it then has to focus on its role as a rule-maker when directing the sanctions committee through resolutions. In most sanctions regimes, Council members prefer to take advantage of establishing and transferring those decisions to a committee.

Second, provided that the Council does indeed delegate to a committee, it becomes clear that the decision-making ability within a sanctions committee is much narrower than that of the Council. When the Council decides to delegate decisions, the sanctions committees, which mirror Council membership and decide by consensus, are in turn tasked with taking the rather technical single-case decisions, such as listing and delisting of individuals or granting exemptions from trade embargoes. Accordingly, committee members decide about small decisions that are confined to the specific conflict at hand. At the same time, the Council often provides criteria before charging the committee with adoption of such decisions. As a secondary role, in order to overcome problems which can stem from diverging interests, sanctions committees adopt rules through their guidelines or practice. In that respect, committees serve as secondary rule-makers and implicitly separate rule-making from rule-application.

Third, Council sanctions regimes do not follow an envisioned, comprehensive design, but evolve reactively and step-wise over time (Biersteker and Eckert 2009, p. 12). The permanent members are skeptical toward limiting their discretion and moreover negotiating Security Council resolutions is time-consuming. As such, the Security Council remains as a political body and resolutions, therefore, mirror the political dynamics at the time of their adoption. Key decisions taken in Council resolutions are rather stable and rigid in nature, because they require extensive negotiations in order to be amended (Doxey 2000, pp. 10–11). Nevertheless, external and internal factors may trigger the Council to govern a sanctions regime. On the one hand, the Council may react to changes in the environment, such as new conflict actors' emergence, and modify a sanctions regime accordingly. In fact, sanctions regimes are "complex adventures" and sanctions targets or other players may adapt their behavior, thus leading to unintended consequences (Conlon 1995b, pp. 658–660). On the other hand, the Council may interpret its own resolutions to overcome regulatory issues or stalemates within a sanctions committee. For instance, resolution 1617 (2005) clarified a significant decision criterion of a potential listing "associated with" Al-Qaida to improve the listing process' quality. In this way, the Council may also standardize informal committee practice.

In the following chapters we will see how delegation to sanctions committees affects the behavior of their members, and decisions in practice. Each case study will first assess the sanctions measures' set-up, the political constellation among Council members and what that leads us to expect by way of committee governance. Taking a closer look at how single-cases are decided, the case studies do not just depart from the macro-focus of the literature, but shed light on how committee governance plays out in practice, how formal rules and precedents are devised, and how they affect the behavior of even the powerful permanent members in unfavorable situations. The five case studies reveal several facets that will be collected and discussed in the concluding section of the book.

Note

1 See http://sanctionsapp.com/ [last accessed July 13, 2018].

4 Disarming Iraq

Governing comprehensive sanctions under siege

Following the swift and unequivocal condemnation of Iraq's Kuwait invasion on August 6, 1990, the Security Council banned all trade with Iraq. This response marked a tremendous shift from the great power confrontation, which paralyzed the Council for much of the Cold War. As an early sign of what many hoped would be a "new world order," the Council was eager to use its sweeping powers to coerce Iraq into compliance with UN Charter principles. It was an initial test case to assess how this new spirit of cooperation between the great powers would change the Council's approach to violent conflict. The international community condemned the Iraqi invasion as a clear violation of international law. But a conflict over the trade embargo overshadowed the Council's dealings with Iraq right up to the point of the US-led invasion in 2003, which sidelined the Council and stymied its work thereafter. Whereas the US and UK placed the utmost pressure on Iraq, other non-aligned Council members, and later France, Russia and China, demanded an early lifting of or at least generous exemptions to the sanctions regime that was bringing hardship to countless ordinary Iraqis.

Council members essentially transferred to themselves in the form of a sanctions committee all regulatory tasks, including the political conflict over Iraq sanctions. Governing the trade ban on Iraq proved to be a tremendous challenge. The committee had to make constant decisions on literally hundreds of UN member state requests regarding a broad range of humanitarian supplies to Iraq. Each decision was insignificant in its own right, but taken together they could cripple the Iraqi economy and create a humanitarian catastrophe for the country's population. Consequently, committee members with diametrically opposed views fought fiercely over these politically-charged decisions; one side wanted all requests exempted, whereas the other wanted as few exemptions as possible. In the Iraq Sanctions Committee, Council members were not bound to follow any rules or precedents. Yet, Paul Conlon observed that the committee created an astoundingly consistent practice as "delegates consented to decisions they had originally opposed in order not to upset previously established patterns and practices" (Conlon 1996b, p. 280).

To date, those interested in Security Council sanctions have struggled to understand why the Iraq Committee should have followed rules emerging from its practice. How exactly did the Council's transfer of decisions to the same group of states in committee affect the dynamics of decision-making? What did this do to the quality of decisions? The concept of committee governance helps us to explore these issues more carefully, accounting not only for why rules did matter, but also why they were followed even by the powerful permanent members.

The early Iraq sanctions regime is an ideal case for examining Security Council committee governance and presents a fascinating puzzle. Because we find the US and UK equipped with Council and committee vetoes, it is not easy to understand why they would accept a precedent to alter their stances on any single request. These members could use a plethora of material and institutional resources to influence decisions in their favor and had the most to lose from rules, namely the right to object to any waivers that might ease pressure on Iraq. From a realist perspective, it is hard to imagine how a great power could maneuver itself into a situation where it has to abide by committee practice because it is so enmeshed with institutional rules. Finding that the great powers develop and follow rules, even though they are in stronger positions than all other states, is a vivid illustration of committee governance at work. Yet, the Iraq sanctions regime is far from being a special case. In fact, the committee confronted decision problems strikingly similar to those of other sanctions committees. However, I do not intend to provide a complete historical account of the Iraq sanctions regime here; instead I want to focus on a theory-driven analysis of major variables.

This chapter's analysis uses authentic primary documents contained in the publicly available Paul Conlon United Nations Sanctions Papers, exceptional, but rarely accessed records covering the Iraq Sanctions Committee proceedings which were collected by a former UN Secretariat member who was responsible for servicing the committee. The roughly 6,000-page archive includes detailed, complete and original files from all 120 Iraq Sanctions Committee meetings between August 1990 and February 1995. These include primarily the "summary records" (short "SR.x"), which document all verbal interventions made in the committee. Also included are original committee records of all requests received and decisions taken. From a research design perspective, this is about as close as a researcher could come to observing the private meetings directly without actually having been present at the time. Its "status of communications" lists provided the basis for the Iraq Sanctions Committee Decisions Dataset containing 8,200 committee decisions from 1993 to 1995. These documents have been complemented with news articles, available public Council and committee documents as well as secondary literature.

The next section explores the Iraq sanctions regime's political origins, how the ideological conflict about sanctions on Iraq emerged, and what is implied for committee governance. To evaluate the viability of my committee governance hypotheses, I then trace four case episodes detailing how the committee dealt with exemption requests to the sanctions regime. In a first episode, I study the early conflict over committee practice on foodstuff shipments to Iraq. Second, I examine how the committee developed its practice on humanitarian waivers, exempting medicines, foodstuffs and many other items after the Gulf War. In a third episode, I take a quantitative perspective on how the committee decided about the high number of requests received from 1993–1995, using the Iraq Sanctions Committee Decisions Dataset. Finally, I focus on the committee conflict over requests for waiving humanitarian flights to Iraq.

The political origins of the Iraq sanctions regime

Iraq's invasion and annexation of Kuwait constituted a blatant challenge to the existing global order. In contrast to the first Gulf War, when Saddam Hussein was not challenged about his waging war against Iran, on this occasion 10 years later the Iraqi dictator wholly miscalculated the international community's resolve. On August 6, 1990, despite abstentions from Cuba and Yemen, with 13 votes in favor the Security Council imposed a comprehensive ban on all imports from and exports to Iraq and Kuwait, as well as a complete financial embargo (resolution 661 (1990)). The Council further tightened its sanctions regime, enacted a coalition-enforced naval blockade and restricted flights to and from Iraq (resolutions 665 (1990) and 670 (1990)). When Saddam Hussein refused to withdraw, the Western powers pushed the Council to authorize the use of force in restoring the territorial integrity of Kuwait (resolution 678 (1990)). Following the Gulf War, the Council upheld the sanctions regime for a further 13 years even though its initial objective had been achieved (resolution 687 (1991)).

The Iraq Sanctions Committee delegates were confronted with an entirely different task from that which had faced them in the Council. Diplomats were now charged with deciding about whether or not to grant numerous small-scale requests from UN member states or how otherwise to respond in light of the Council's resolutions on Iraq (Gordon 2010, p. 23; Conlon 2000, 45–46, 59–60). In practice, the committee had to involve itself in granting exemptions, without which a full trade embargo would have ensued. However, such waiver requests included a very broad range of issues on which committee members often strongly disagreed. David Bosco neatly summarized this task: "Medicines clearly fell outside the sanctions regime. But what about books, clothes, construction materials, and agricultural equipment? And how should the Council respond to requests for sanctions exemptions from states heavily dependent on Iraqi oil?" (2009, p. 164).

Committee members were in constant disagreement over the Council's sanctions policy on Iraq, which presented a serious prospect of committee stalemate under the consensus rule (Koskenniemi 1991, pp. 126–127). This political conflict occurred between three, more or less homogenous, groups of states. The US and UK, supported initially by France and later on occasions by Germany and Japan, formed one extreme pole (Graham-Brown 1999, pp. 71–72). To enforce Iraqi compliance, the US and UK were determined to prevent any weakening of the sanctions regime. Accordingly, they favored a highly restrictive approach, which translated into granting as few exemptions as possible. Their stance on sanctions had been fairly stable, although over time their policy goal might have changed from regime change to dual-containment (Gordon 2010, p. 2). Rules were to be avoided and decisions taken purely on a case-by-case basis. Despite concessions agreed to in Council resolutions, once the same members had taken on their committee responsibilities, any decisions that led to the easing of pressure on Iraq had to be avoided. As permanent members, the US and UK had dominant positions within the Council. Because sanctions resolutions had no sunset clauses, the sanctions enforcers could veto or threaten to veto any draft resolution which would effectively ease the pressure on Iraq. Moreover, under the consensus rule within committee, any exemptions to the embargo required their consent.

An extremely vocal group of sanctions opponents formed the other extreme pole, consisting largely of elected members from the non-aligned caucus. This included Colombia, Cuba, Malaysia, Yemen, and later Djibouti, Ecuador, Morocco together with Oman. These members were ultimately seeking to lift all sanctions on Iraq entirely (Malone 2006, pp. 65–67). Because this would require a Council resolution which would very likely face a veto, their policy goal was the "maximum liberalization" of sanctions. In other words, "all sanctions measures were bad and thus all waivers were good" (Conlon 2000, p. 79). In the Council, these members were not equipped with a veto. Nevertheless, they determinedly tried to relax sanctions through the committee. By using committee practice, these states skillfully exploited humanitarian waivers, which they regarded as a "Trojan Horse" for exempting an increasing number of item categories from the all-encompassing embargo (Conlon 2000, p. 60).

Nonetheless, all committee members were staunchly intent on obtaining clearances for their own requests. As Conlon notes, the committee "was deciding on trade permits and trade policy in thousands of individual cases where the members of that body themselves had an interest in the outcome of their own decisions" (Conlon 2000, p. 80). Even the UK, which was championing as few exemptions as possible, was one of the largest requestors of waivers and actively promoted British exports to Iraq (Graham-Brown 1999, p. 73).

Despite these starkly differing agendas, the two camps shared a common interest in avoiding committee stalemate. Even though the sanctions drivers had the upper hand and could object to any undesired exemption, a sustained deadlock on waiver requests could carry the risk that states would "make unilateral findings of humanitarian circumstances" (Conlon 1995b, p. 652). The US and UK also depended on the cooperation of sanctions skeptics for effective monitoring and for following up on reports of non-compliance (Conlon 1995a, p. 329).

A third group, positioned between these two extreme poles, comprised states such as Belgium, Canada or the Chairing delegations from Finland, Austria and New Zealand who collectively adopted a moderate policy position. In the early stages, China and the Soviet Union silently supported the sanctions regime, while remaining members, including the African caucus, hardly ever took the floor.

Considering these disparate positions, I would fully expect to find that committee governance prompts rule-based decision-making in the Iraq sanctions regime. Committee members had an interest in avoiding stalemate and collectively interpreting Council provisions, while they strongly disagreed about the granting of requests. Thus, in line with hypotheses 1 and 2, I expect committee members to set focal points either through rules or informal precedents. Although the sanctions enforcers were in a better position, I nevertheless expect them to accept waiver requests akin to those that the committee has previously cleared. Otherwise, they would upset established committee practice and could expect the opposing members to cease cooperating on other issues. I expect the sanctions skeptics to align similar but slightly different exemption requests to past precedents so as to expand the range of permissible items.

As a result of the clashing interests, the Council defined overly vague basic terms and procedures for how the committee should interpret resolution 661 (1990) (Koskenniemi 1991, 122, 126–130). Iraq was subject to a complete trade embargo and only medicines were clearly exempted. Foodstuffs could be shipped only in "humanitarian circumstances," the meaning of which the committee was left to decide upon. There are two main reasons for this. To placate skeptical members, the Council intentionally left the embargo's exact nature undefined, in particular whether or not the blockade also applied to foodstuffs, and if so, under which conditions food aid would be permissible. Moreover, because the US and UK had serious reservations about creating rules that might later bind them, they "had little interest in formulating general rules for how the [Iraq Sanctions Committee] was to decide individual cases" (Conlon 2000, 50, also 45–53).

The beginnings: Setting and enforcing rules on the issue of foodstuffs in "humanitarian circumstances"

The episode immediately after resolution 661 (1990) shows that a committee stalemate on foodstuff shipments in "humanitarian circumstances" prompted Council rules and committee precedents to guide committee practice. While states opposing sanctions considered foodstuffs as generally exempted, the sanctions proponents preferred a literal interpretation. In other words, no such "humanitarian circumstances" had yet arisen (Koskenniemi 1991, pp. 126–127). Those states opposing sanctions closely aligned their waiver requests with earlier precedents and thereby widened the range of foodstuff beneficiaries, something that powerful members wanted to avoid.

Within the sanctions committee, the use of ambiguous language to describe "humanitarian circumstances" instantly led to contentious discourse about whether or not sanctions on foodstuffs were admissible; consequently, requests to ship foodstuffs to Iraq caused a deadlock. As early as the second meeting, Cuba and Yemen argued for a broader approach "which prohibited the use of hunger as a means of warfare" (SR.2). Although many committee members (Canada, Cuba, Yemen, UK, US, USSR) agreed that either the committee or the Council should clarify the nature of the foodstuffs' embargo, for instance through adopting "(…) general principles (…) of deliveries of foodstuffs"

(USSR, SR.5), committee members preferred different solutions. At one extreme, the US, the UK and Canada wanted to retain a complete economic embargo and advocated strict interpretation. Accordingly, it was suggested that the committee or the Council should first determine if humanitarian circumstances really existed and only then should the committee decide on how shipments should proceed (all SR.6). In fact, these sanctions proponents were opposed to such shipments because they feared that food shipped to foreign nationals "might fall into the wrong hands" (emphasis removed, Simons 1996, 45–46, 115–116). At the other extreme, Cuba, Yemen, Colombia, and Malaysia simply wanted all foodstuffs shipments to go ahead without question (SR.2, SR.5, SR.6).

Defining "humanitarian circumstances" assumed a greater sense of urgency when non-committee member India requested the shipping of foodstuffs to 160,000 Indian nationals residing in Iraq and Kuwait (Chair, India, SR.5). While the UK and US had an interest in providing clarification before UN member states could unilaterally apply a broad interpretation of the resolution, they delayed action and requested more information (SR.5, SR.7). Canada and Zaire followed later by the UK and US advocated consultation to agree on the wording of a general rule, while Cuba, Colombia and Yemen preferred immediate granting of the request (all SR.7). Significantly, committee members recognized that a decision on the Indian request would have repercussions on how the committee dealt with similar requests in future. One group suggested that the committee should adopt a general procedure (Canada, US, SR.7; US, UK, France SR.8), whereas other members believed that "the Committee might be setting a precedent by adopting the draft decision" (China, SR.8, also Ethiopia, SR.12) or that the Indian request was a "test case" (Canada, SR.12), which would guide decision-making in later cases (also Zaire on behalf of non-aligned caucus, Finland, SR.8, Canada, SR.14). Subsequently, the P5 circulated a draft rule under which foodstuffs were to be allowed "on the basis of impartial information" and only in emergency situations (France, SR.8) to satisfy the resolution's terms, namely to exempt foodstuffs but only for humanitarian circumstances. However, Zaire, on behalf of Cuba, Yemen, Colombia, and Ethiopia introduced a competing proposal to grant the Indian request, which led to a heated debate on how the committee should resolve the difficulty, given the following options: (1) adopt the Indian request as a precedent; (2) negotiate a general framework; or (3) seek a combination of both (SR.8).

Because the committee had persistently failed either to adopt a rule or to grant the Indian precedent (SR.7–8, 10), the issue "that had clearly become a matter which the Security Council alone could decide" (US, SR.10) was referred to the Council. Sanctions enforcers were determined to allow as few exemptions as possible because they feared that waiving the Indian shipment would "cause a deluge of requests" which could be difficult if not impossible to reject (Doyle 1990). On September 13, the Council adopted resolution 666 (1990) despite Cuba and Yemen voting against. Agreement to the resolution was coupled with a package deal to grant the Indian shipment "on the basis of the information provided (…) to be carried out as provided for in the relevant Security Council resolutions" (SR.11, also Cuba, SR.13). The US immediately stressed that the committee had authorized solely "one Indian ship" (Boucher 1990).

The Council negotiations on resolution 666 (1990) created the postulated consistency pressures of rule-making. The rule on foodstuffs shipments did not contain provisions that one-sidedly benefited powerful members. The Council requested the committee to determine if "circumstances (…) in which there is an urgent humanitarian need to supply foodstuffs" have arisen. However, the committee should decide only "after receiving the reports from the Secretary-General (…) on the availability of food" (paras. 3, 5). If the committee granted foodstuffs shipments, these "should be provided through the United Nations in co-operation with the International Committee of the Red Cross or other appropriate humanitarian agencies and distributed by them or under their supervision" (para. 6).

Immediately, other non-committee members, who had not yet evacuated all their nationals residing in Iraq or Kuwait filed foodstuffs shipment requests almost identical to the Indian precedent. Sri Lanka aligned its request to the precedent "hoping to send a ship under the same conditions as had applied to (…) India" (Sri Lanka, SR.15). Bulgaria, Yugoslavia and Vietnam pledged that their requests were "in compliance with the relevant Security Council resolutions" (Bulgaria) and that they "stood ready to comply with any conditions set by the Committee, including, (…) the dispatch of [Red Cross] personnel" (Yugoslavia, similarly Vietnam, SR.15). In fact, sanctions skeptics succeeded in "creating a precedent that they hope will allow for food relief shipments" (Hall *et al.* 1990). Although sanctions enforcers acknowledged that foodstuffs could be sent to third-country nationals, first distribution and supervision should be determined in the Indian case (US, SR.12), and for other cases more information on the precise need (Canada, SR.12) or dissemination would be necessary (US, SR.12; US, France, SR.13). Hence, these states deferred the pending requests and argued that as a consequence of evacuations, foodstuff surpluses from the Indian shipment would deprive requests of their legal basis because primarily "(…) it was important to determine the existence of humanitarian circumstances" (US, UK, SR.16, also US, France, SR.15). After a lengthy debate, the P3 ran out of arguments as to why foodstuffs, which they had accepted for Indian nationals, would be impermissible for Bulgarians, Sri Lankans and Vietnamese. Accordingly, the P3 ultimately authorized India, albeit grudgingly to coordinate bilaterally with those states wishing to supply surplus food to their nationals (SR.15, Chair, SR.16).

Because powerful members had acquiesced by allowing India to make surplus food available to third-country nationals on a bilateral basis, they reluctantly had to grant an identical Palestinian request (S/AC.25/1990/COMM.22[1]). This was problematic for the US and UK since the Palestinian Liberation Organization had publicly supported Iraq. It was feared, therefore, that the food could be diverted to Iraqi authorities or armed forces (Malone 2006, p. 10). In a heated committee debate, the US "felt bound to state that there was a difference between the situation of the nationals of [other states] (…) and the situation of the Palestinians, in Kuwait, a large resident population (…) [which were not] third-State nationals" and that in fact, foodstuffs were originally intended for "detainees and hostages" (SR.20). Additionally, in desperation the US challenged the claim that humanitarian circumstances really did exist (SR.20). However, the Chair, "in accordance with the Committee's practice," had already informed the Palestinian authorities of established procedure, namely that they should approach India bilaterally (SR.20). China, Cuba, Malaysia and Yemen fiercely refused to repeal this decision, stating that it "had already been taken (…) and (…) [Yemen] therefore regarded as unacceptable the repeated attempts to introduce new procedures for the sake of political expediency" (Yemen, SR.20). China regarded repealing the decision as a "mistake" (SR.20). The US delegation unwillingly gave in to a face-saving compromise that the decision would be on a "one-time basis" (US, SR.21), while the final decision was unrestricted and allowed to supply surplus foods to "all needy non-Iraqi groups" (Chair, SR.21).

Before the Gulf War, the committee had steadily expanded its range of foodstuff beneficiaries against the will of powerful members, and until early 1991 its sole acknowledgment was that humanitarian circumstances existed for third-country nationals in Iraq and Kuwait. Only in a few instances, after determining the existence of humanitarian circumstances and offering reassurances of national Red Cross supervision, did the committee approve foodstuff shipments. Notably, the committee granted a USSR application "to deliver foodstuffs, citing 'humanitarian circumstances,' to Soviet nationals in Iraq" without discussion (SR.20). Shortly afterwards, Pakistan put in a request "to airlift foodstuffs to their nationals on humanitarian grounds" (1990/COMM.156), which prompted a fierce committee exchange because the US and UK wanted to withhold approval. While both delegations agreed that the request was acceptable "in principle," they argued that more information about distribution was required (UK, US, SR.22). Other committee members entirely rejected this position. Cuba argued that "Pakistan's request was no different from other requests that had been granted" (SR.22). Malaysia complained that the committee could not discriminate "among different nationalities" (SR.22) and Yemen demanded that "the Committee should proceed with regard to Pakistan in the same manner as it had with regard to the Soviet Union, (…) which had been granted without difficulty" (similarly China, Colombia, Côte d'Ivoire, Ethiopia, France, all SR.22). Indeed, after the Chair had received assurances that Pakistani embassy employees would distribute the shipment to Pakistani nationals, the committee quietly granted the request (1990/COMM.169).

Non-committee members sought to broaden this "third-country nationals" practice by requesting shipments to the general population. In early 1991, Iran, Libya and Mauritania each requested shipments of foodstuffs to ordinary Iraqis (1991/COMM.42, COMM.43, COMM.53). The UK protested because the committee had not yet determined that humanitarian circumstances existed for Iraqis pending a Secretary-General report (SR.26). However, as information on the dire humanitarian situation was mounting, Iran carefully reformulated its request and closely aligned it to the committee practice on non-Iraqi beneficiaries. Iran now intended to ship foodstuffs to the "most vulnerable population groups as indicated in resolution 666 (1990)" (1991/COMM.68, COMM.69), outlining the items, beneficiaries, quantities and Iranian Red Crescent supervision (Chair, SR.30). The US grudgingly accepted the waiver but argued that this constituted "a specific case" so that "no general determination of circumstances of humanitarian need could yet be made" (SR.30). However, a precedent had been set. Thereafter, the committee approved similar requests from Belgium and Denmark under identical conditions (1991/COMM.70, 1991/COMM.72), which led to even further similar requests. When Yemen requested the supply of "20,000 tons of wheat intended for the most vulnerable population groups in Iraq," distributed by the Yemeni Red Crescent and the ICRC, it explicitly stated that the request was "identical to another that had already been dealt with by the Committee" (SR.33). Although sanctions enforcers again tried to delay a positive decision arguing that they had not yet received instructions (UK, SR.33), they gave in because the request clearly resembled earlier precedents. Thereafter, the committee systematically granted other foodstuffs requests detailing beneficiaries, quantities and distribution (Denmark, 1991/COMM.90/95; Germany, 1991/COMM.98; Jordan, 1991/COMM.105), while the committee granted incomplete requests only after receiving additional information (Mauretania, 1991/COMM.91; Turkey, 1991/COMM.93; Libya, 1991/COMM.94).

These events conform to the logic of committee governance and what hypothesis 2 postulates. Despite deeply antagonistic positions on the foodstuffs embargo, all committee members wanted to avoid stalemate. Even the powerful members slowly accepted that certain exemptions may be unavoidable. Sanctions skeptics and their non-committee allies skillfully aligned their requests to Council rules and earlier waivers. They set precedents enlarging the range of beneficiaries in humanitarian circumstances, first to third-country nationals, and ultimately even to ordinary Iraqis. Although powerful committee members were extremely uneasy about this escalatory pattern, they could no longer ignore that a precedent had been set and thus the committee would have to treat similar requests consistently.

After the Gulf War: The need for precedents on "no-objection items"

The Gulf War led to fundamental changes in the sanctions regime. With a massive bombing campaign and ground forces, the US-led coalition forced Iraqi occupiers to retreat and restored the territorial integrity of Kuwait. Even though the coalition's decisive victory had realized the Council's demands, the sanctions regime was far from being dismantled. To the contrary, the US insisted that despite the cessation of hostilities, the sanctions regime would still need to be upheld. The Council imposed far-reaching conditions and obligations on Iraq, including border demarcation, disarmament, weapons inspections, and compensation. In fact, resolution 687 (1991) transformed the sanctions regime into a long-term preventive effort to safeguard Iraqi compliance (Bosco 2009, p. 164).

The decisive military campaign coupled with almost eight months of economic isolation had created a bleak humanitarian situation in Iraq. Immediately after the war, the Secretary-General dispatched Finnish diplomat Martti Ahtisaari on a needs assessment mission (S/22322). Ahtisaari's report created a grim picture of ordinary Iraqis' humanitarian situation and the destruction of Iraq's basic infrastructure. He noted that "[t]he recent conflict has wrought near-apocalyptic results (…)" (S/22366, para. 8). He warned that an "imminent catastrophe" would ensue unless "massive life-supporting needs are (…) rapidly met" (para. 37). Ahtisaari urged removal of sanctions on foodstuffs and machinery for producing foodstuffs, in addition to water and sanitation equipment, as well as medicines on an "extended scale" including generators, emergency vehicles and incubators.

In light of these profound developments, on March 22, 1991 the committee reorganized its procedures, and made "a general determination that humanitarian circumstances apply with respect to the entire civilian population of Iraq" (S/22400, paras. 2, 3). Furthermore, the committee adopted three exemption procedures. First, it restated that the embargo excluded medical supplies. Second, a notification procedure for foodstuffs was enacted: A state exporting foodstuffs to Iraq need notify only the committee. From this point, the committee treated edible foodstuffs as mere notification items (1991/1992/1993 COMM.Log). Third, it established a "no-objection procedure" for all other "civilian and humanitarian imports to Iraq as identified in Mr. Ahtisaari's report" (para. 3). The committee would grant such a request unless at least one member objected. The Council formalized these procedures in resolution 687 (1990), which was adopted having 12 votes in favor, with Cuba voting against and Yemen and Ecuador abstaining. Criteria were slightly corrected to read "materials and supplies for essential civilian needs as identified in the [Ahtisaari] report (…) and in any further findings of humanitarian need by the Committee" (para. 20).

This episode sheds light on how the Iraq Sanctions Committee used informal rules derived from precedent to process waiver requests. The concept of committee governance helps to explore why the process of deciding within the sanctions committee provided incentives to create abstract criteria on what types of goods and end-users would be considered humanitarian. This committee practice prevailed even though powerful members rejected rule-based governance and wished to keep the committee as flexible as possible. Any judgment on an incoming request provided a precedent for how to deal with similar requests in the future.

Although the committee had adopted rules on a whole new range of items, its members faced the same regulatory problem. Delegates had to define whether or not any incoming request would fall under the vague criteria of humanitarian exemptions, the terms of which remained contested (Graham-Brown 1999, pp. 70–72). Numerous separate UN member states' requests for shipping a certain item in a certain quantity confronted the committee with a stream of applications. The content of such requests varied tremendously, ranging from "soap," "textiles," "cars," unspecified "spare parts," "steel sections," a "combine harvester" to a complete "water desalination plant." Although many goods would clearly be humanitarian or non-humanitarian, the provision left a large gray area (Conlon 1996b, p. 253). However, with each decision the committee implicitly defined which of these goods did indeed represent "civilian and humanitarian imports" and which were incompatible with Council resolutions.

Nevertheless, committee members fundamentally disagreed over the Council's Iraq sanctions policy, even though they wanted to avoid stalemate (Graham-Brown 1999, p. 71). On the one hand, the US and UK pledged to uphold the economic embargo unless Iraq would comply with all previous resolutions. The US argued against any "premature relaxation" of sanctions, not least to provoke regime change (Lewis 1991). Initially, the US had even disputed Ahtisaari's findings and only reluctantly agreed to the revised procedures (US, SR.36). Thus, the committee should grant exemptions only in tightly constricted circumstances, on a case-by-case basis and not expand the range of waivers. Any member should have the right to object, irrespective of previous decisions. On the other hand, those states opposing the sanctions regime continued to campaign for lifting all sanctions, and if that was not feasible, at least broadly extending the range of waivers (Johnstone 1994, p. 17). Moreover, exemptions presented the opportunity to trade with Iraq under the pretense of serving humanitarian requirements. A committee member had little intrinsic reason to refrain from promoting requests for political or economic reasons and demanding acceptance of any requests they may have submitted.

Since the Council rules only vaguely distinguished between "supplies intended strictly for medical purposes," "foodstuffs" and "civilian and humanitarian imports" as acceptable and all other items as unacceptable goods, the committee had to adopt precedents. Earlier requests were solely to do with ICRC and Red Cross societies' shipments (34 requests, 1991 COMM.Log); as a rule, the committee granted such requests without debate and regardless of the items concerned. The committee also expanded this logic to UN system agencies (30 requests, 1991 COMM.Log), and state requests on behalf of domestic humanitarian agencies (12 requests, 1991 COMM.Log). This remained consistent committee policy (Conlon 2000, pp. 68–69).

Simultaneously, UN member states began to request "no-objection items," which required the committee to determine the limits of acceptable categories based on humanitarian characteristics and the end-use of the goods collectively. Sweden submitted the first such request and sought a waiver for sending "spare parts for Dura/Taji silos and an electric engine for a grain silo" to Iraq, which the committee cleared (1991/COMM.133). But soon other requests followed in increasing numbers. The committee granted requests by Germany (spare parts for harvester threshers, 1991/COMM.175), Turkey (detergent and water pumps for tractors, 1991/COMM.179), Sweden (3 containers of Water Treatment Plants, 1991/COMM.198) and again Germany (50 harvester threshers, 1991/COMM.199). The committee regarded those as satisfying humanitarian need.

The committee took its first negative decision when Bulgaria sought an export clearance for Iraqi-owned "zinc oxide" (1991/COMM.209). When the Chair requested further information, Iraq confirmed it was indeed for the "manufacture of automobile tires and batteries" (1991/COMM.229). Thus, the shipment clearly fell into the category of embargoed items. Similarly, when Turkey requested a delivery of "clutches and other parts and accessories of motor vehicles" (1991/COMM.218), the US objected:

> According to the Ahtisaari report, parts for transport equipment fell into the category of essential items. (…) [The US] wished to receive an assurance that the export of the parts and accessories in question would actually facilitate the distribution of foodstuffs (…).
>
> (US, SR.44)

The Chair responded that "[i]t was his understanding that the parts would be used solely for humanitarian purposes (…), and if the Turkish authorities gave a satisfactory response the Committee would approve the request. If not, authorization would be denied" (Chair, SR.44). After Turkey clarified that the parts would be used to repair civilian vehicles, the committee rejected the request (SR.47).

Numerous cases illustrate that the committee gradually developed a consistent practice. It granted many requests for items considered as finished products, satisfying the essential civilian needs criterion and thus not constituting an input to the Iraqi economy (Turkey, mixed animal feed, 500 tons (1991/COMM.216); Denmark, equipment, spares for repair of the Sulalimaniya water supply (1991/COMM.239); Turkey, 16,200 tons of soap, 6,550 tons of detergent (1991/COMM.240); Denmark, 2,010 rolls of reinforced polyethylene film for erecting civilian shelters (1991/COMM.242); Germany, 800 stove pipes as steam baking oven spares (1991/COMM.245); Australia, aluminum hydroxide for drinking water purification, 3,000 tons (1991/COMM.251); Austria, chlorine and other materials for drinking water disinfection (1991/COMM.252); Turkey, steel water tubes, 50.4 tons (1991/COMM.255); Netherlands, milk sterilizer spare-parts (1991/COMM.257); France, quinoleate 15 fungicide, 400 tons (1991/COMM.258)).

The committee granted requests similar to earlier waivers. This included Turkey's request to export 5,000 tons of soap and 20,000 tons of detergent (1991/COMM.292) together with a Dutch request to ship 20,000 tons of planting material for potatoes (1991/COMM.306). Germany could ship used clothes, shoes, soap, detergent and books (1991/COMM.495). The committee also granted Japan's request for 12 small water treatment units (1991/COMM.528). A Brazilian request to export "four shipments of kraftliner and fluting paper," for packaging and storage of foodstuffs and medical supplies was cleared accordingly (1991/COMM.631). Turkey put in a request to provide "1,000 tons of soap, 105 tons of other ovens and 200 tons of detergent." The committee accepted soap and detergent, while the UK requested more information on "other ovens" (SR.47). After Turkey clarified that the items were "small electric ovens (…) for home use" (1991/COMM.316/Add.1), the UK withdrew its objection.

Requests that included more than one item or those without a clear humanitarian purpose illustrate that the committee carefully scrutinized requests against earlier precedents, taking end-use into account as the secondary rule. When Turkey tabled a request to deliver "angora goat hair, soap, glassware and calcium" (1991/COMM.270), the UK rejected 300 tons of industrial calcium as non-essential (UK, SR.47). The committee accepted calcium for water purification (US, 1992/COMM.210, France, 1992/COMM.961, Jordan, 1992/COMM.973), while denying it for other industrial uses (Turkey, 1992/COMM.486). As Japan requested provision of "radio communications equipment" for communicating between hospitals and local Iraqi Red Crescent offices (1991/COMM.284), the UK objected because the exact humanitarian need "had not been substantiated" (UK, SR.47). Sweden's bid to ship refrigeration equipment for use in beer brewing (1991/COMM.704) was rejected on grounds that this would clearly not fall within the "category of exports intended to meet essential civilian needs" (US, SR.62). When Turkey raised a request to ship "polypropylene bags, grate cooler plates (…), artificial leather, wheat bran for animal feed and printed metallized film for use in the packaging of confectionery goods," the committee accepted only animal feed (1991/COMM.430). While Turkey's request to export wooden spools for use in outdated weaving machines was rejected, it could ship jersey and used clothes (1991/COMM.625).

The committee even challenged and rejected permanent members' requests if they did not meet humanitarian purposes. When the USSR filed a request to trade "parts for grain elevators and for the installation of a drainage collection system, under contracts concluded with Iraq in 1986" (1991/COMM.289), the committee granted grain elevators parts, but the UK rejected "automobile and tractor equipment and road-building machinery," which the USSR representative criticized (SR.47). Further, the committee blocked a French request for approval of "spare parts for refinery process pumps and fire pumps" (1991/COMM.649; SR.58). When the UK sought clearance for "Gulley Emptiers/Sewerage Equipment" (1991/COMM.560), the committee granted the request only after four months and the UK having "[r]evised technical details" (SR.55). The US lifted its hold on a UK request shipping "various chemicals and equipment for water purification" (1992/COMM.745) only after the UK had specified items and end-use (SR.76). A UK request for "5,000 tons of polypropylene granules for the manufacture of flour bags" (1992/COMM.1062) also met resistance. Japan argued that while it did not object to flour bags it "did object to exporting polypropylene granules for their manufacture." The US "[e]ndorsed that objection" adding that polypropylene had "a variety of possible uses, and 5,000 tons was a very substantial amount. Moreover, since Iraq had always been authorized to import bags, there was no need for it to manufacture them" (SR.79). In anticipation of committee objections, the UK withdrew a request for shipping "500 tons of caustic soda for use in the manufacture of soap and detergent" (1992/COMM.1063) as this constituted an input to Iraqi economy and the committee had previously cleared only ready-made soap and detergent. As the UK sought to ship "hospital bedlinen, towels and (…) tobacco" (1993/COMM.665), Japan declared that it "would not have objected to the export of completed cigarettes, [but] did object to the export of tobacco as an input into Iraqi industry" (SR.93). The US even blocked a request by a US company to ship "5,000mt of water pipes" because civilian use assurances were lacking (SR.76).

Several members argued that goods, which the committee consistently cleared as a matter of practice, should be formally exempted, but sanctions enforcers objected. As a compromise, the Council requested the committee "to study immediately those materials and supplies for essential civilian and humanitarian needs (…) with the purpose of drawing up a list of items which may (…) be transferred from the "no-objection" procedure to a simple notification procedure" (S/23305). On behalf of the non-aligned caucus, Zimbabwe formally requested the transferring of such a list (SR.61). In support, India argued that the committee "had taken decisions which tended to be consistent with" the content of the proposed list of goods. The list would formalize committee practice "in accordance with previous decisions to clear items" (SR.61). For almost three months, the Chair conducted inconclusive consultations. The non-aligned countries favored "a straight transfer" of as many items as possible (Ecuador, Zimbabwe, India, Cape Verde, SR.66). However, the US favored keeping the committee "as flexible as possible," and argued against "any formal change in procedure (…) [restricting] the right of all delegations to raise objections where there was cause for concern" (US, SR.66). While the UK representative admitted that it "had not raised objections in the past to items in the categories indicated, (…) his delegation maintained the right to object to any items which might have a dual use or did not fall strictly within the categories indicated" (UK, SR.66).

Eventually, with a so-called "gentlemen's agreement," the committee agreed on an informal set of rules that had emerged from previous practice. The committee, in a diplomatically phrased formula (SR.66), recognized that the "members did seem to agree to look favourably upon requests" under the no-objection procedure for the following items: medical equipment and supplies, packaging material for foodstuffs, civilian clothing, supplies for babies and infants, soaps and detergents, animal feed and agricultural seeds, animals and eggs for breeding purposes, materials for education, materials for water treatment and sewage disposal plants as well as storage facilities for grain and foodstuffs (SR.66). Five categories that had been proposed in the non-aligned letter were not included: electrical supplies for civilian use; refrigeration, heating equipment; kitchen supplies; vehicles, spare parts for civilian use; and supplies for agricultural and cattle breeding sectors (Conlon 2000, p. 62). The gentlemen's agreement demonstrates that even states, which rejected formal rules could not avoid the constraining effects of informal rules "in practical terms" (Ecuador, SR.66).

Overall, the Iraq Sanctions Committee's practice provided a working definition of "essential humanitarian items," although the US and UK consistently rejected any formal rules. The committee would grant the provision of finished consumer goods with civilian or humanitarian end-use. This also included larger development projects such as water treatment facilities. Unfinished products, which could be further manufactured and thus were not intended for direct human consumption, would be rejected. This explains why caustic soda to produce soap was withdrawn but finished soap was granted. Arguments took place in the gray area between acceptable and unacceptable items. Elected members often faced precedents to which they had originally not consented. Yet, they either had to consent to an unwanted decision or risk compromising established practice. For instance, Japan perceived "cigarettes" as objectionable, but did not formally object to preserving established practice (SR.73).

The established practice is strikingly consistent. It allowed committee members and requesting states to prejudge the chances of a request based on the item type, end-user, supporting documents and justification. This practice created shared expectations of how other committee members would behave, so that committee decisions could essentially be predetermined (Kaul 1996, p. 101). Paul Conlon noted that "[b]ecause of its frequent dealings with the Committee in the past, the Jordanian Permanent Mission is very well able to predict which requests have some chance of being authorized" (United Nations Inter-office Memorandum by Paul Conlon, September 7, 1993). Even sanctions critics expressed concern about how imprecise some requests were. Yemen complained that requests were often too "vague" to make it possible for their merits to be judged (Yemen, SR.34, 48; US, SR.61, UK, SR.93, France, SR.94). Furthermore, the committee Chair noted that "[s]ome countries supplied a very brief description of the items they intended to export. Others, (…) provided more detail concerning the humanitarian justification for the shipments." Turkey, in particular, "should be asked to submit more detailed requests and explain the reasons for the export of various articles which, at first sight, did not seem justified" (SR.76). All this suggests that information was the major factor determining whether or not the committee either granted or rejected a waiver.

The logic of committee governance helps to explain why the committee, faced with a stream of requests, created precedents with earlier waiver requests that gradually developed into a practice on exemptible goods (hypothesis 2). This was clearly not intended, since several permanent members opposed the formalization of exemptions. However, with sharp disagreements among committee members, openly inconsistent choices would have risked committee deadlock, which none of its members wanted. Altogether, establishing a system of consistent practice following categories of acceptable and unacceptable items became "(…) the rational core of an attempt to define more clearly which sectors and activities should benefit from humanitarian mitigation considerations (…)" (Conlon 1996b, p. 259).

Quality of requests, not power determines committee decisions

The previous section revealed *how* the Iraq Sanctions Committee created a remarkably consistent practice on waivers, despite the political clash among supporters and opponents of sanctions. But does this hold true for the thousands of cases, sometimes up to 800 per meeting, decided on by the committee at a later stage? I demonstrate the merits of my committee governance thesis with descriptive statistics and regression models based on the *Iraq Sanctions Committee Decisions Dataset*. In line with hypothesis 2, which holds that committee members are expected to abide by precedents, even if such contradict preferences of powerful committee members, I would expect to find that the committee treats the same item consistently regardless of which state, no matter how powerful, applied for its clearance. Hence, the granting of a waiver should depend on whether or not the committee usually regarded this item as humanitarian.

In mid-1993, the UN Secretariat introduced the "status of communications" lists, documenting all requests received since a previous meeting. These lists named *country*, *item*, *decision* and *justification* for any objections. Unfortunately, the lists omit secondary factors such as end-use or quantities. Using these lists, I constructed a dataset that contains 8,189 requests over 17 meetings from June 1993 to January 1995.[2] I coded almost 3,700 different items into 69 item categories according to the UN Standard International Trade Classification (SITC Rev.4). Some 270 items could not be coded due to missing information on the material (e.g., "tubes"). In addition, I screened meeting records for released holds or lifted objections. On average, the committee approved about 43 percent of all requests. The number of requests varied considerably across states. From 60 states in total, only 14 filed more than 50 requests. Jordan (5,055) and Turkey (1,148) alone accounted for three-quarters of all requests. Non-committee members and humanitarian organizations submitted 7,478 requests (91.3 percent), non-permanent members 164 (2.0 percent), and permanent members 548 (6.6 percent). Among P5 nations, the UK filed 443 requests, followed by China (48), the US (28), France (15) and Russia (14). A substantial number of UK requests can be attributed to its policy of promoting exports to Iraq after thorough domestic vetting (Graham-Brown 1999, 73).

The committee processed requests in accordance with primary and secondary rules. First, the committee determined which decision procedure was to be followed (S/1996/700, paras. 38–44). Even though the embargo excluded *supplies intended strictly for medical purposes*, understood as drugs and supplies for end-use, the committee regarded precursors and devices such as x-ray appliances as no-objection items (Conlon 2000, 61). The committee also considered only "finished edible products" as *foodstuffs* and food production materials such seeds, emulsifier or bitter hops as no-objection items (internal memo, October 27, 1993). Even the P3 never challenged foodstuffs notifications (Conlon 2000, 127–129). For *no-objection items*, the committee applied a "modified categorical approach" and accepted or rejected requests based on the item belonging to an acceptable or unacceptable category, but also considered end-user, end-use, or quantity (Conlon 2000, p. 65).

Descriptive statistics show that the committee decided primarily on the basis of item type (see Table 4.1). The averaged approval rates of SITC item categories display tremendous variation. The committee accepted finished goods,

Table 4.1 Approval rates by Standard International Trade Classification categories

SITC Code	*Description*	*Approval rate (%)*	*Systematic exceptions*	*N*
0, 5, 8	Food and live animals	100.0		16
4, 9	Malt, hops, color, emulsifier	0.0	Food color pigment (+/1)	11
11	Beverages	100.0	Liquor, whisky, wine (–/3)	5
121	Raw tobacco	6.1		33
122	Tobacco manufactures	100.0		45
22	Oil-seeds, oleaginous fruits	100.0		4
23	Crude rubber	0.0		11
24	Cork, wood	1.6		61
25	Pulp, waste paper	0.0		5
26	Textile fibers	0.0		5
27	Crude fertilizers/minerals	0.0	Filter perlite (+/1)	7
29	Crude animal/vegetable materials	100.0		28
32	Coal, coke, briquettes	0.0	Charcoal (+/3)	8
33	Petroleum (products)	0.0		2
41	Animal oils/fats	0.0		2
42	Fixed animal/vegetable fats, oils (crude)	16.7		6
50	Chemicals	18.8		16
51	Organic chemicals	5.3		19
52	Inorganic chemicals	11.8		119
522	Caustic soda	30.9	*Contested*	113
53	Dyeing, tanning, colouring materials	0.0		68
54	Medicinal, pharmaceutical products	93.8	Raw materials for medicine production (–/4)	36
55	Essential oils, resinoids, perfume materials; toilet, polishing, cleansing preparations	98.4	Cosmetics, incense, shoe paint, shoe polish, shampoo elements, carnel olive oil (–/11)	381
56	Fertilizer	62.5	*Contested*	8
57	Plastics (primary form)	0.7		150
58	Plastics (non-primary form)	65.4	*Contested*	104
59	Chemical materials, products	1.0		198

591	Insecticides, rodenticides, fungicides, herbicides, anti-sprouting products, plant-growth regulators, disinfectants, in forms, packings for sale	68.4	*Contested*	19
61	Leather, leather manufactures	0.0		95
62	Rubber manufactures	0.8	Partially: tyres for bicycles, tyres for ambulances, tyres for agricultural vehicles (+/15)	497
63	Cork, wood manufactures (excl. furniture)	2.6		117
64	Paper, paperboard, articles of paper pulp	48.0	*Contested*	125
642	Paper, paperboard, cut to size/shape, articles of paper or paperboard [diapers, sanitary towels]	100.0		19
65	Textile yarn, fabrics, made-up articles	6.3	Coffin cloth, agricultural textiles, food packaging, school uniforms textile (+/19)	807
658	Made-up articles of textile materials [fishing nets, bed sheets, carpets, bedding]	95.7		140
66	Non-metallic mineral manufactures	9.3	Mill stones (+/3)	143
661	Lime, cement, fabricated construction materials [marble]	0.0		23
662	Refractory bricks	68.8	*Contested*	16
665	Glassware	98.1		206
666	Pottery [ceramic tableware]	100.0		59
67	Iron, steel	4.6		175
68	Non-ferrous metals	4.3	Aluminum for packaging (+/9)	78
69	Manufactures of metals	4.8		355
69(1)	Manufactures of metals for Iraqi end-user	86.0		221
71	Power generating machinery, equipment	35.0	*Contested*	20
72	Machinery specialized for particular industries	54.2	*Contested*	369
73	Metalworking machinery	50.0	*Contested*	2
74	General industrial machinery, equipment	60.4	*Contested* Valves (–/12)	268
75	Office machines, automatic data-processing machines	20.0		35
761, 762, 763	Monitors, projectors, sound-recording, reproducing apparatus	0.0		12

continued

Table 4.1 Continued

SITC Code	*Description*	*Approval rate (%)*	*Systematic exceptions*	*N*
764	Telecommunications equipment	80.0		10
77	Electrical machinery, apparatus, appliances	14.6	Electrical switches (+/20)	281
775	Household-type electrical, non-electrical equipment	82.0		189
78	Road vehicles	5.2		401
79	Other transport equipment	50.0	*Contested*	2
81	Prefabricated buildings; sanitary, plumbing, heating, lighting fixtures, fittings	88.4		285
8122	Ceramic sinks, wash-basins, wash-basin pedestals, baths, bidets, water-closet pans, flushing cisterns, urinals, similar sanitary fixtures	10.0		30
82	Furniture, parts thereof	52.9	*Contested*	17
83	Travel goods, handbags etc.	75.0	*Contested*	8
84	Apparel, clothing access	97.5		315
85	Footwear	97.2		72
8519	Parts of footwear	18.5		27
87	Professional, scientific, controlling instruments	94.7	Adhesive for medical use (–/4)	175
88	Photographic, equipment, supplies, optical goods; watches, clocks	57.9	*Contested*	19
89	Miscellaneous manufactured articles	81.9	Audio/video cassettes (–/13)	311
D	Diplomatic goods	100.0		19
99	Not categorized	51.9		270
Total				7,693

Notes
Excludes 251 requests rejected for secondary reasons (incomplete request, large quantities), 232 humanitarian organizations' requests, and missing values. Approval rate excludes systematic exceptions. Systematic exceptions column shows whether exception is positive "+" or negative "–" and the number of cases. I consider categories above 20 and below 80 percent approval as contested.

while it rejected pre-processed goods, which ran counter to the embargo. Most item categories have either a very high approval rating above 80 percent (22 categories with 2,536 requests) or a very low approval rating below 20 percent (33 categories with 3,797 requests). A request from any country in these categories has either a very high or a very low chance of approval. The remaining categories are contested (12 categories with 1,090 requests). In these cases, the committee used secondary rules such as end-user, which the dataset does not reveal.

Several examples highlight this logic. The committee rejected raw tobacco for producing cigarettes (6 percent approval), but consistently accepted finished cigarettes (100 percent). Similarly, the committee rejected textiles, yarn and fabrics for producing garments (6.8 percent) but cleared ready-made clothing (97.5 percent). Regarding manufactures of metals, the committee approved those items that were for human consumption such as razor blades, shavers or door locks (86.4 percent); however, it disagreed with those that would support Iraqi production such as nails, screws, welding bars or reinforcement steel (4.8 percent). Among the non-metallic mineral manufactures, the committee rejected raw glass sheets (9.3 percent) or luxury products such as marble (0 percent), whereas it accepted drinking glasses (98.1 percent) and household ceramic tableware (100 percent).

Some item groups exhibit specific secondary rules. The committee regarded raw textiles as permissible in circumscribed end-uses, including coffin cloth, agricultural textiles, food packaging or school uniforms. Likewise, the committee did not approve the supply of rubber manufactures, consisting mostly of car tires, but cleared tires for ambulances, tractors and bicycles. The committee accepted beverages but rejected hard liquors. Among essential oils, the committee accepted soaps and detergents, but objected to cosmetics, incense, and shoe polish. Finally, while the committee usually cleared "miscellaneous manufactured articles," audio and video cassettes were consistently regarded as non-essential. Even among contested categories, items with a humanitarian end-use such as "paper for school" or a "water purification plant" were admissible.

Committee members also respected the *gentlemen's agreement items*. The committee cleared almost 96 percent of such items regardless of requesting states with few exceptions (see Table 4.2). The committee rejected only unfinished products, for instance, raw materials for producing food packaging, and items considered non-essential or luxurious. The remaining variation could further be reduced if the dataset contained end-use and quantities. Only water and sewage treatment items were contested. While the category still fared well above the overall acceptance rate, it contained many dual-use items such as water treatment chemicals. For instance, caustic soda is usable in embargoed industry, but also as cleaning agent in food production, drug precursor or for sewage treatment. However, for such items the committee also rejected requests from a permanent member and other Western states.

The dataset shows that the P5 accepted this practice even if committee members challenged their own requests because of the item type or end-use.

Table 4.2 Gentlemen's agreement items approval rates

Item group	*Requests*	*Approval rate (%)*	*Exceptions*
Medical equipment, supplies, incl. packaging	202	91	*Bulgaria*: med. material; *Jordan*: adhesive, tape f. med. belts/use, hospital fabric, phenol, med. mould, raw materials, glycerine; *Netherlands*: cosmegenlyovac injections; *Turkey*: hematocrit centrifuges, pharmaceutical products; *India*: atenolol, cetrimide; *Pakistan*: med. supplies
Foodstuffs packaging material	70	97	*Jordan*: tin-plate sheets ghee packaging, polypropylene compound (food packaging)
Civilian clothing	387	98	*Jordan*: industrial gloves (2), carpenter outfits (2), steel shank pairs; *Korea*: ski gloves, leather jackets; *Spain*: children clothing (large request); *India*: children shoes
Baby, infant supplies	80*	94	*Jordan*: fluff pulp, treated pulp f. baby diapers, alum. seals f. babies' feeding cups; *India*: cotton garments, baby suits, underwear, socks, children's shoes; *Spain*: children's clothing (large request)
Soaps, detergents	373	98	*Egypt*: detergent; *Jordan*: carnel olive oil, dry-cleaning detergent, liquid soap, soap flakes/powder; *Turkey*: detergent, soap
Animal feed and agricultural seeds	40	100	
Animals and eggs for breeding or hatching	7**	100	

Books, materials, supplies for primary, secondary education	38	87	*Jordan*: cartons, cassettes, exercise books; *Turkey*: school bags; *Korea*: drawing boards
Water treatment, sewage plants spare parts	63	83	*Italy/Jordan/Lebanon*: Water treatment chemicals (7); *Finland*: water purification plant; *Italy*: water filtering, desalination, purification system, water treatment system; *Jordan*: water purification filters, pumping stations/water treatment plants' spare parts, water treatment spare parts, water treatment additives/material; *Lebanon*: water treatment equip.; *Sweden*: water treatment plants, water treatment plants pumps/electrical equip; *UK*: sewer cleaning equip.
Grain/foodstuffs storage facilities	24	100	
Total	**1,274**	**95.6**	

Notes
Excludes humanitarian organizations' requests and requests rejected for secondary reasons. Approval rate includes exceptions.
* Often submitted as "medical supplies" or "foodstuffs."
** Often submitted as "foodstuffs."

Indeed, the committee approved only 57 percent of Russian, 75 percent of American, 79 percent of Chinese, 80 percent of French and 98 percent of British requests. The committee objected to several P3 requests in line with established practice. This included UK requests to do with "paint for domestic use" or "hand tools" (SR.101/103), seven US requests for "generators" (SR.116/121) and French requests for "material for the manufacture of electric transformers," "concrete slabs of wood" and "textiles" (SR.112–4). Similarly, committee members argued that certain Russian and Chinese requests ("building material," "equipment and spare parts for power plants," "batteries," "generators' or "tires") were "non-essential," constituted "industrial input" or lacked information. Remarkably, the P5 did not question rejections during meetings (SR.101–2, 110–3, 116–7, 120–1).

Do those descriptive findings also withstand a statistical test? In line with the logic of committee governance, I would expect that the committee consistently decided on every request based on the criteria, namely the item type, regardless of which country had submitted it. Even though committee governance does not entail expectations on the exact goods categories, I expect to find that categories falling within the permissible practice would be exempted, whereas those running counter to the embargo would be rejected, continuing the committee's developing practice. Thus, the item categories should predict decision success particularly well. Conversely, the rival logic assumes that decision success and the requestor's institutional or material power resources are positively associated. Hence, this logic would predict inconsistent results across goods categories. Furthermore, committee members should fare better than non-committee members and permanent members should fare better than elected members.

Table 4.3 presents logistic regression results using a dichotomous dependent variable, *decision success*, which indicates whether a request was approved (1) or rejected (0). My primary independent variable for rule-based decision-making is the *item group*. To facilitate the statistical analysis, I assigned the 69 SITC goods categories used above to 11 broad item group dummy variables.[3] Non-coded requests serve as baseline model (52 percent approval). For the rival thesis, I used two sets of independent variables. As institutional power proxies, *P5-status* applies to a permanent Council member's request (1) and is (0) for any other country's request, accounting for P5 dominance. *E10-status* applies to a country's non-permanent membership at the time of a request (1) and is (0) for a non-Council member's request. The non-permanent members were privileged because they decided about their own claims and thus could potentially extract package deals. As material power proxies, I use the logged Gross Domestic Product (GDP) in billion US$ (current prices), as published by the IMF World Economic Outlook Database. As "Hard power" resources I took the logged Composite Index of National Capability of the Correlates of War Project. This index comprises military expenditure, military personnel, energy consumption, iron and steel production, urban population and total population (Singer 1987).

I control for a state's regulatory ability, using the World Bank *regulatory quality* index,[4] using it as a proxy for the degree of public and private entities' legal and administrative skills to create approvable drafts and submit substantiated requests. With country dummies, I also control for frequent requestors, including Jordan, the leading requestor with a low success rate (29 percent), and the UK as leading P5 requestor with an outstanding success rate (98 percent). Waiver requests were submitted by states and so the observations are not entirely independent. Hence, to account for the hierarchical data structure, I used clustered standard errors for states.

The logistic regression models show that item groups predict decision success exceptionally well, even without having information on end-use. Model 1, which assesses the effect of item groups on their own, finds that three groups affect decision success positively. This includes items for direct human consumption (odds ratio: 28.45), medical products such as precursors and medical supplies for non-end users (odds: 10.6) and finished items (odds: 5.35). Five goods categories affect decision success extremely negatively. These are electrical appliances (odds: 0.17), prefabricated items (odds: 0.11), chemicals (odds: 0.11), transportation items (odds: 0.06) and crude items (odds: 0.03). Three goods categories, food production, agrochemicals and machinery, show no significant effect on decision success. These variance patterns across goods categories would seem to make sense. The successful items groups consist of ready-made items intended for civilian end-use, which makes them a logical choice for exemption from the trade embargo. Yet, unsuccessful item groups comprise those pre-processed items that require further manufacturing and thus would fall under the trade ban.

Model 2 controls for the regulatory quality and reveals that the requesting state's regulatory capacity positively affects decision success. This suggests that an applicant state required a certain administrative capacity to prepare convincing requests. Model 3 further controls for Jordan and the UK. While Jordan has a strongly negative effect, the UK exhibits a strongly positive effect. In both control models, the product categories affect decision success in similar ways. All three rule-based models yield a considerable model fit for the variances in decision success.

The rival thesis receives far less support. Model 4, testing both the institutional and material power resources variables, shows that elected member status and greater material power do not translate into increased decision success. Yet, permanent member status (odds: 5.48) and higher economic resources (odds: 1.58) strongly increase decision success. This might suggest that power resources serve as instruments to influence committee decisions. However, when I control for regulatory quality again (model 5), or for Jordan and the UK (model 6), none of the power variables significantly affects decision success. These results demonstrate that decision success depends largely on skillfully formulating complete and documented requests, rather than a requestor's power resources. Compared with the rule-based models 1–3 (pseudo R^2 of 0.48 and above), the power-based model yields a considerably lower model fit (pseudo R^2 of 0.14 or less).

A combined model (model 7) further supports the claim that committee decisions were largely based on rules relating to item groups, not power. The goods

Table 4.3 Decision success of requests (logistic regression)

	(1)	*(2)*	*(3)*	*(4)*	*(5)*	*(6)*	*(7)*
Items for human consumption	28.45***	33.80***	28.62***				30.59***
	(10.71)	(12.89)	(12.15)				(12.34)
Precursors and medical supplies (non-end user)	10.67***	7.02***	7.44***				7.02***
	(5.01)	(3.46)	(2.93)				(3.05)
Finished items	5.35***	6.29***	5.86***				6.06***
	(1.88)	(2.36)	(2.34)				(2.35)
Food production raw materials	2.89	1.64	2.28				1.74
	(1.89)	(1.03)	(1.34)				(1.05)
Agrochemicals	2.00	2.24	1.89				1.53
	(1.61)	(2.18)	(1.60)				(1.50)
Machinery	1.26	1.15	1.32				1.21
	(0.44)	(0.53)	(0.44)				(0.46)
Non-essential electrical appliances	0.17*	0.13**	0.08***				0.07***
	(0.14)	(0.08)	(0.05)				(0.05)
Prefabricated items	0.11***	0.13***	0.12***				0.13***
	(0.05)	(0.06)	(0.06)				(0.06)
Chemicals	0.11***	0.12***	0.12***				0.13***
	(0.04)	(0.05)	(0.05)				(0.05)
Transport	0.06***	0.07***	0.07***				0.07***
	(0.01)	(0.04)	(0.03)				(0.03)
Crude items	0.03***	0.03***	0.03***				0.03***
	(0.02)	(0.02)	(0.02)				(0.02)

logGDP				1.58***	1.09	1.24	1.00
				(0.19)	(0.22)	(0.22)	(0.25)
logHardPower				0.90	1.39	0.96	1.10
				(0.18)	(0.33)	(0.17)	(0.20)
P5 status				5.48*	3.20	1.54	2.57*
				(3.68)	(2.15)	(0.60)	(1.17)
E10 status				0.34	0.35	0.35	0.64
				(0.41)	(0.46)	(0.36)	(0.50)
Regulatory quality		3.59***			1.91		1.80
		(1.10)			(0.84)		(0.65)
Jordan			0.43***			0.47	0.71
			(0.06)			(0.22)	(0.38)
UK			48.83***			14.49***	7.41***
			(8.96)			(4.74)	(4.15)
Constant	1.00	0.65	1.41	0.00*	1.86	0.10	1.56
	(0.58)	(0.33)	(0.54)	(0.01)	(6.06)	(0.29)	(5.57)
Log Likelihood	–2711.05	–2522.55	–2475.01	–4541.68	–4535.70	–4508.03	–2450.07
AIC	5446.1	5071.1	4976.0	9093.4	9083.4	9026.1	4934.1
Pseudo-R2 (McFadden)	0.481	0.517	0.526	0.131	0.131	0.1370	0.531
N/clusters	7662/48	7662/48	7662/48	7660/47	7660/47	7660/47	7660/47

Notes

Unstandardized Logistic Regression Results (odds ratios). Standard error clustered by country. $^{***}p \leq 0.001$; $^{**}p \leq 0.01$; $^{*}p \leq 0.05$. Excludes objections based on secondary reasons (e.g. “large quantities,” $n = 251$), humanitarian organizations’ requests ($n = 233$) and diplomatic goods ($n = 19$).

categories are superior predictors for decision success and explain much more of the variation. Above all, the effect sizes of the rule-based variables far exceed the level of those from the power-based variables, of which only P5 status is significant. Medical supplies, finished items, and items for direct human consumption strongly increase the odds of decision success, while crude items, transport, prefabricated items, chemicals, and non-essential electrical appliances strongly decrease the odds. Although the P5 variable is significant, it affects the probability of decision success less than most goods categories. Moreover, inclusion of the power variables in model 7 only slightly inflates the model fit of the rule-based model 1 (pseudo R^2 of 0.53 vs. 0.48). When one considers that the integrated model includes six additional variables, the model also becomes less parsimonious than the model using goods categories only.

Figure 4.1 presents the predicted approval probabilities of item groups obtained from model 1. Exemption requests had a high likelihood of approval if they related to items for human consumption (96 percent), precursors and medical supplies (91 percent), and finished items (84 percent). Exemption

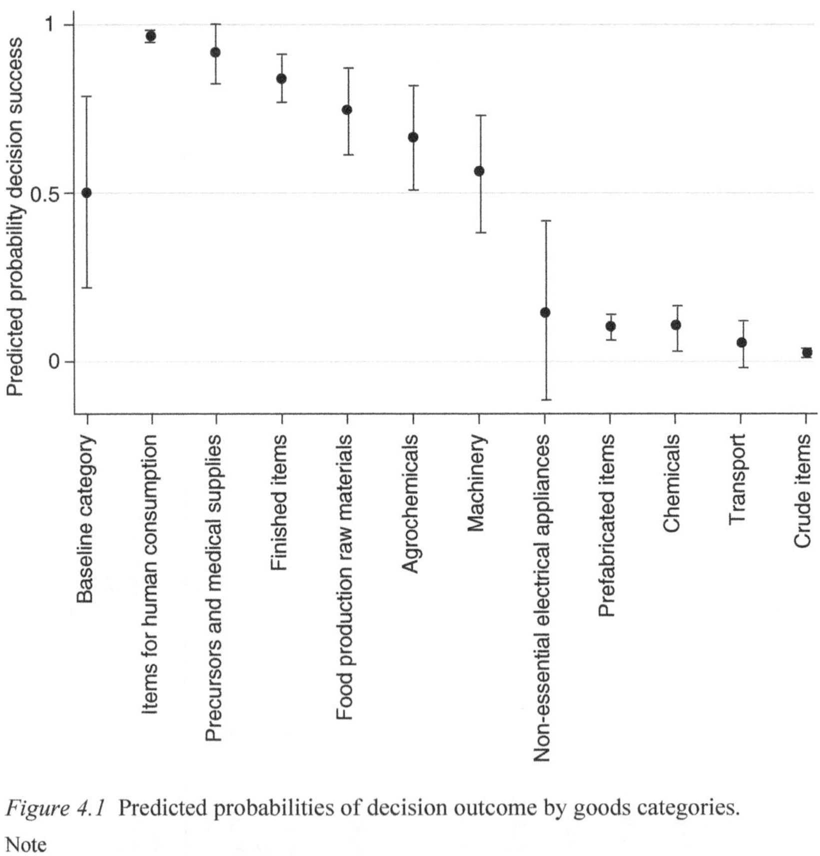

Figure 4.1 Predicted probabilities of decision outcome by goods categories.

Note
Probabilities obtained from model 1 of Table 4.3.

requests relating to electrical appliances (15 percent), chemicals (10 percent), prefabricated items (10 percent), transportation (5 percent) or crude items (2 percent) had a particularly low approval probability. This practice reflected a collective intent to exert pressure on the Iraqi state and economy, while ensuring the civilian population's survival. The remaining variance for statistically insignificant item groups, including food production (74 percent chance), agrochemicals (66 percent) or machinery (almost 56 percent) can be partially accounted for since the committee seems to have used secondary criteria here. The committee cleared three-quarters of the food production requests but denied waivers for those non-essential items excluded from the notification procedure, for instance, malt and hops for brewing or luxury items, including hard liquor. The Committee also used to grant agrochemicals and machinery requests after ascertaining end-users and quantities. It considered, for example, insecticides for pest control operations, combine harvesters, cold stores and water treatment facilities as serving humanitarian purposes. Yet, it rejected industrial end-use items, such as commercial weaving machines, or non-eligible purposes such as aluminum phosphate tablets, unspecified valves, or centrifuges, if they could be used in military-grade weapons programs (Conlon 2000, pp. 65–70). Hence, information on end-use could further reduce the remaining variance.

Findings support the committee governance thesis merits via precedents (hypothesis 2). This patterned approach of decision-making is remarkable and emerged even though the committee did not formally recognize any of these criteria. Indeed, this practice emerged despite the US and UK's opposition to formal rules, as well as the attendant pressure of conformity. Yet, it also illustrates how informal rules, set by precedent and repeated practice, impact regulatory decision-making in Council committees. The committee exempted exactly those items that were later formalized, (resolutions 1284 (1999) together with 1409 (2002)), and essentially removed from the committee agenda by positive and negative items lists (Malone 2006, pp. 119–120).

The power of rules and precedents in governing flight approvals

Two months after imposing sanctions on Iraq, the Security Council applied further restrictions by effectively banning "all means of transport, including aircraft" (resolution 670 (1990)). The Council tasked the sanctions committee with exempting flights from the aviation embargo as and when requested by states. The committee's dealings with flights demonstrate how rules and precedents made a difference despite the reluctance to accept constraining regulation. Committee governance illustrates how consistent Council rules emerge and how previous committee practice empowered less powerful states to submit successful requests and reduced powerful members' use of their discretion to object.

The Security Council adopted two sets of rules on flights. First, the Council tasked the committee with deciding about any flight exemptions subject to its consensus. Second, to guide committee decision-making, the Council stipulated that flights would be permissible only if they shipped items exempted from sanctions, including foodstuffs and medical supplies (Farrall 2007, p. 267).

This immediately led the committee into heated debate about flight bans. Many delegations felt that a case-by-case approach created considerable additional workload. Canada, supported by Colombia, the USSR and the Chair proposed that "the Committee should consider the first specific cases, from which parameters (…) for dealing with requests from other countries" could be derived (Canada, SR.15). Accordingly, the committee approved an Indian request for an evacuation flight as a precedent based on the prerequisite that appropriate inspections would commence (Chair, SR.15). Thereafter, slightly different requests broadened the scope of flight exemptions. The committee accepted a Belgian request for a flight "carrying only medical supplies to Baghdad and returning only with passengers" (1990/COMM.109) and a Vietnamese flight for its diplomatic personnel (1990/COMM.123). While the UN Disaster Relief Office merely provided notification about UN entities' flights, the committee approved UN member states flights without consideration. This included two UK flights for "medicines, personal effects of Irish citizens in Iraq" (1991/COMM.11) together with "food and medical supplies" (1991/COMM.116) plus two US flights to "evacuate United States Embassy staff and other foreign nationals from Iraq" (1991/COMM.18) as well as shipping "food, medicine, and supplies intended for medical purposes" (1991/COMM.115). The committee also accepted two Indian requests to "evacuate Indian nationals from Iraq" (1991/COMM.17 and 28) and ship "medicines, milk powder and biscuits for children" (1991/COMM.83) as well as MSF to send "foodstuffs and water treatment supplies, items required for medical purposes" (1991/COMM.108). As a secondary rule, the committee consistently rejected Iraqi flight requests (information for the Chairman, March 14, 1995). While singular flights using Iraqi aircraft were authorized as long as they were not requested by Iraq and returned to their departure location (US, 1991/COMM.18; India, 1991/COMM.28), a blanket approval of flights with Iraqi aircraft was rejected outright (1991/COMM.377, 1992/COMM.249).

A serious conflict over aviation sanctions emerged in July 1992 when Sudan notified the committee about a shipment comprising 20,000 tons of meat and requested the committee to approve 500–550 flights. The consignment of meat would be airlifted onboard a Sudan Airways aircraft en route from Khartoum to Bagdad (1992/COMM.602). At four flights per week, if granted, the committee would have given advance approval for cargo flights over a period of two-and a half years. According to Council rules on flights, "meat" clearly fell into the foodstuffs category and accordingly, "meat flights" would be permissible. Furthermore, committee members had never challenged any foodstuffs notifications (internal memo, October 27, 1993). The committee had also approved all flight requests carrying foodstuffs in the first half of 1992 without discussion (Algeria "baby formula," 1992/COMM.45, similarly 1992/COMM.464, Germany "milk powder," 1992/COMM.57).

However, the US and UK found Sudan's request to airlift meat to Iraq highly questionable. Out of principle, sanctions enforcers wanted to see the embargo implemented as strictly as possible (Johnstone 1994, p. 17). The Sudanese meat flights' commercial nature was obvious because the cargo airlifting of meat bore excessive unit costs and made the delivered meat a luxury item possibly to the benefit of Saddam's inner circle (Conlon 2000, p. 97). As an alternative, one single cargo vessel shipment would have sufficed. Several diplomats found Sudan's motivation "bizarre" since it depended on food aid (Rowe 1992). Close observers suspected "hidden functions" including illegally unfreezing Iraqi assets, kickback schemes, illicit passage of individuals or smuggling of arms or other items (Conlon 2000, p. 97). In addition, Sudan had supported Iraq during the Gulf War. The US also suspected Sudan to be a state-sponsor of terrorism (Schweid 1993). Consequently, the sanctions enforcers perceived the request as illegitimate. Even the neutral Austrian Chair publicly supported this view: "We had a bad feeling in the committee. (…) We didn't think it was intelligent. People are starving and they're exporting food" (Rowe 1992).

Within committee, the Sudanese request sparked an intense debate which continued over several meetings. Many committee members including Yemen, Zimbabwe and China immediately welcomed the request and demanded a quick positive decision in line with Council rules and previous committee decisions (SR.57). Even sanctions enforcers reluctantly acknowledged that the shipment of "meat" to Iraq clearly fell into the category of "foodstuffs" and was simply a "matter of notification" (UK, Chair, SR.57). Still, despite contention over the transport scheme, the committee would nevertheless need to consent to humanitarian flights. Because a positive decision would mean granting hundreds of commercial flights, the UK and US expressed serious concerns, noted that the flight scheme was simply "not acceptable," and suggested that Sudan should use different means of transport instead (SR.61). However, despite significant reservations and after delaying the decision by demanding detailed information from Sudan, ultimately the sanctions enforcers accepted the request because flights carrying "food in humanitarian circumstances" would clearly be acceptable (1992/COMM.602). Instead, they insisted on using non-Iraqi aircraft, cargo inspections and reporting after each flight (SR.74). When UNDP Khartoum, which supported the meat export scheme as a development project, assumed responsibility for cargo inspections, the sanctions enforcers found no further reason to reject the request (Chair, SR.76).

Even though it would have been reasonable not to approve Sudan's flight request, the Sudanese meat flights did receive a committee waiver. The US and UK could simply have objected to the request by withholding consensus. However, a rejection would have been against established practice. Yet, they were anxious that such rule violation would affect their own requests as other committee members could withhold consensus for future legitimate US or UK flight exemptions (e.g., US, 1991/COMM.168, 1992/COMM.174; UK, 1992/COMM.326, 338, 422, 505). In essence, "[b]ecause Sudan's proposal did not violate the terms of U.N. sanctions against Iraq (…), the committee could not block the request" (Rowe 1992). Only in late 1994, after evidence was mounting that Sudan had illegally unfrozen Iraqi assets, transported "passengers" for unknown purposes and diverted the flights to other locations through "bad weather" in violation of the approved scheme (1992/COMM.1280/Add.9; S/1996/700, paras. 49–50), did the P3 withhold consensus for further meat flights, which sanctions skeptics strongly criticized (SR.117).

It is difficult to explain these dynamics without recourse to the logic of committee governance, which helps to shed light on how and why the Iraq Sanctions Committee developed a rule-based practice on flight exemptions (hypothesis 1). In the "Sudan meat flights" case, consistent Council rules combined with committee practice enabled Sudan to submit a successful waiver aligned to established practice. Despite many concerns, the powerful members accepted this request because it conformed to previous permissible flights.

Concluding thoughts

Swift Council response to the Gulf crisis in 1990 set the scene for what David Malone termed the "legal-regulatory" approach to international peace and security (2006). Suddenly, diplomats in the Iraq Sanctions Committee had to shoulder a difficult regulatory task: They had to decide how to deal with thousands of requests to deliver a vast range of unrelated items to Iraq. The Iraq sanctions regime is a confirmatory case for committee governance. Internal committee documents show how committee decision-making repeatedly relied on precedents and practice in regular, systematic and consistent fashion.

The committee's rule adherence through precedents was spontaneous and unintended: a consequence of untying many different, but comparable cases from the political questions relating to Iraq. The Council could not agree on clear-cut rules determining how the committee should implement the sanctions because the US and UK resisted any constraining rules. The opposing positions among members created a situation in which all constituents preferred coordination over stalemate. Because committee members disagreed over rules, the committee took a step-by-step approach using previous practice as a yardstick. The Iraq Sanctions Committee is a striking example of how precedents created consistency pressures, because any precedent applies to similar cases which follow. This practice transformed decision-making toward consistent, but entirely informal, rule-adherence. Even the permanent members could not ignore this practice, although they struggled to avoid any constraints.

The Iraq Sanctions Committee provides systematic evidence in support of hypothesis 2 – that committee members are expected to abide by rules derived from precedents, even if such rules contradict what some committee members want. Before the Gulf War, as Council rules on foodstuffs in "humanitarian circumstances" were overly ambiguous, states in opposition to sanctions closely aligned their waiver requests to earlier decisions. Progressively, they could set precedents and enlarge the range of foodstuff beneficiaries from third-country nationals to ordinary Iraqi citizens, even against the will of powerful members. The episode after the Gulf War further confirms hypothesis 2. Though the Council had eased its trade ban, the committee still faced a coordination situation. The demand for rules on acceptable and non-acceptable categories of goods created a consistent decision-practice, although powerful members were opposed to issuing lists of acceptable goods. In the long run, the committee decided according to rules on item categories, end-use and quantities, even rejecting powerful members' requests that did not fall into acceptable categories. The statistical analysis further confirms hypothesis 2. The logistic regression models demonstrate that the committee decided upon requests based on earlier committee practice. In line with what former Iraq Sanctions Committee members observed, committee decisions are best explained by abstract item categories. The committee cleared those requests that included items falling into a previously exempted item category and rejected those belonging to a previously rejected item category. The committee rejected items it deemed would require further processing, either crude or pre-processed goods as well as transportation items and chemicals constituting dual-use concern.

Although committee delegates mostly relied on precedents, the Iraq sanctions regime also provides confirmatory evidence for hypothesis 1, which holds that committee members adhere to formal rules, even if these at times go against the interests of some members. The "Sudan meat flights" example shows how Sudan successfully proposed a series of foodstuffs flights to Iraq. Sudan's request conformed to Council resolutions, according to which such flights would be permissible. The US and UK fiercely objected, but grudgingly accepted this request because they feared that objecting to a legitimate request would backfire on their own flight clearances in the future.

Receiving little support is the rival thesis, according to which committee decisions are dictated by powerful states. Internal documents show that the committee treated each request as a separate matter. I find no evidence for package deals or side payments as a convincing alternative account to the committee governance thesis. The statistical test further supports this claim. It reveals that goods categories can predict the chances of any request well, while several measures of institutional and material power fail to predict the fate of a request. Notably, powerful members widely accepted that some of their requests were turned down when they fell into categories that the committee usually rejected.

Even though the Security Council has shifted to targeted sanctions over recent years – the subject of the next chapter – the Iraq sanctions regime is not a special case. However, it does demonstrate how committee governance produces similar decision-making effects in a sanctions regime based on a trade ban, in the absence of the due process criticism inherent to targeted sanctions. The effects are entirely comparable to those of modern sanctions regimes because the Iraq regime prompted an equivalent decision problem for committee members, namely processing many unrelated single-case requests in light of Council resolutions.

Notes

1 All Communications referenced in this chapter are from the "S/AC.25" Iraq Sanctions Committee and are denoted as "199x/COMM.x." For nomenclature, Sievers and Daws 2014, pp. 465–467.
2 Meetings 103, 106, 108, 114, 119 were missing.
3 *Food production raw materials* includes SITC categories 0, 4, 5, 8, 9, 11, 22, 29, 42 ($n = 70$). *Precursors and medical supplies (non-end user)* 54, 87 ($n = 211$). *Crude items* 23 to 27, 32, 33, 41, 57, 121 ($n = 284$). *Prefabricated items* 61 to 69, 77, 661, 662, 8122, 8519 ($n = 2768$). *Finished items* 58, 81 to 83, 88, 89, 665, 666, 691, 764, 775 ($n = 1430$). *Items for human consumption* 55, 84, 85, 122, 642, 658 ($n = 591$). *Chemicals* 50 to 53, 59 ($n = 335$). *Agrochemicals* 56, 591 ($n = 27$). *Transportation items* 78, 79 ($n = 403$). *Machinery items* 71 to 74 ($n = 659$). *Electrical appliances* 75, 76 ($n = 47$).
4 Data source: Worldwide Governance Indicators (WGI), available at: http://info.worldbank.org/governance/wgi/index.aspx#home. Data is for 1995.

5 Terrorist or scapegoat?

Targeted sanctions and the threat of Al-Qaida and the Taliban

The Security Council's sanctions regime against ISIL (Da'esh) Al-Qaida and associated individuals groups, undertakings and entities is a key effort in the global fight against terrorism. Back in October 1999, the Security Council imposed targeted sanctions on the Afghan Taliban in response to the blatant disregard of Council requests and, continued support for transnational terrorism and harboring Usama bin Laden, who was suspected of being responsible for major terrorist attacks including the horrendous 1998 US Embassy bombings in Nairobi and Darussalam (resolution 1267 (1999), paras. 1–2), which killed 224 people. Bin Laden had issued fatwas in 1996 and 1998 calling on all Muslims to "kill the Americans and their allies." The blatant refusal of Taliban leaders to comply with Council demands combined with terrorist plots such as an attack on the USS Cole in Aden during 2000 killing 17 US sailors attributed to Al-Qaida affiliates induced the Council to impose targeted sanctions against Usama bin Laden and Al-Qaida associates (resolution 1333 (2000)). Following the Al-Qaida masterminded 9/11 attacks on the World Trade Center and the Pentagon, which cost the lives of almost 3,000 people, the Council transformed the sanctions regime into a global counter-terrorism effort, shifting away from the focus on Afghanistan. Over time, the regime developed, as did transnational terrorism. The Council was aware of Al-Qaida's compartmentalization, which developed regional networks such as Al-Qaida in the Arabian Peninsula or Al-Qaida in the Islamic Maghreb, as well as affiliates in Southeast Asia, the Sahel and others. In 2011, the Council split the single sanctions regime into two separate regimes for Al-Qaida and the Taliban to support the Afghan peace process (resolutions 1988 and 1989 (2011)). The Council further tightened its measures with the rise of the Islamic State and associated foreign terrorist fighters.

The sanctions regime is infamous among human rights activists, scholars and states, who perceive the imposition of open-ended sanctions on individuals and entities without even minimum due process to be an infringement of fundamental human rights. Several listed individuals have subsequently brought cases in domestic and European courts against their placement on terrorist sanctions lists, freezing their assets and preventing their travel. The group of Like-Minded States on Targeted Sanctions, comprising mainly European states, has championed the provision of "fair and clear procedures" for targeted sanctions, with a focus on the Al-Qaida sanctions regime. It is the only sanctions regime which the Council equipped with a potent and independent review mechanism, the Office of the Ombudsperson, to review petitions and, if necessary, make recommendations which will subsequently be difficult to overturn for delisting individuals and entities who no longer meet the listing criteria.

The Al-Qaida/Taliban sanctions regime is an ideal case for examining Security Council committee governance and presents a fascinating puzzle, despite its prominence. In fact, it is central to my analysis precisely because the human rights and legal literature focuses only on this case among all sanctions regimes. So far, those interested in Security Council sanctions have predominantly ascribed transformation from the largely unconstrained Al-Qaida sanctions regime into a tightly regulated decision-making apparatus to the external pressure by courts, states, academics and human rights activists, not rules emerging from its practice. The highly vocal due process debate on targeted sanctions suggests that a sanctions committee composed of member states naturally follows a power politics rationale and cannot ensure rule-based due process standards. To cure these defects, an independent review mechanism (in the form of an Ombudsperson) outside the Council's control was indispensable. Such accounts also maintain that the remarkably strong Office of the Ombudsperson has changed the situation profoundly. In other words, before the Ombudsperson had been appointed, the situation was bleak. However, frequent reports that the Al-Qaida Committee had increasingly followed rules even before the creation of the Ombudsperson calls for an investigation of committee governance.

Being the most advanced sanctions committee in procedural terms, it is particularly well suited to making possible the studying of determinants and consequences from changes. So how exactly did the transfer of decisions by the Council to the same group of states in committee affect the decision-making dynamics in this case? How did this affect the quality of decisions? The concept of committee governance enables us to explore these issues more carefully, distinguish between committee governance and external pressure, accounting not only for why rules did matter, but why even the powerful permanent members followed them. Based on new material, including leaked diplomatic cables, finding out that the great powers followed rules even before establishment of an Ombudsperson would illustrate how much committee governance matters. However, the Al-Qaida Committee is not a unique case in regard to committee governance. It is entirely comparable with other cases because the Council transferred many single-case decisions (the listing and delisting of individuals) to a committee.

The next section explores the Al-Qaida sanctions regime's political origins, how consensus around counter-terrorism sanctions emerged, and what this means for committee governance. To evaluate my committee governance hypotheses, I then trace five episodes of committee decision-making. In a first episode, I examine how the committee – unusually compared with other regimes – developed a laissez-faire attitude toward sanctioning suspected supporters of terrorism, and how this undermined effectiveness. Next, I study how Council and the committee used rules to cure these defects even before establishing a review mechanism. Thereafter, I evaluate the approach to delisting and connected issues of committee governance. Then, I take a closer look at committee governance around the Taliban sanctions regime's splitting. Finally, I focus on how the Office of the Ombudsperson affected committee decision-making. The chapter concludes with a summary of the main findings.

The political origins of the Al-Qaida/Taliban sanctions regime

With its initial focus on the Afghan Taliban, the Council sanctioned Taliban controlled airlines and ordered the freezing of Taliban-held financial assets. Shifting to Al-Qaida, the targeted sanctions regime included an assets freeze, a travel ban as well as an arms embargo on designated individuals and entities to disrupt or at least constrain Al-Qaida terrorist activities. The Council strengthened the sanctions regime after 9/11 (resolution 1390 (2002)) and transformed it into a global, open-ended counter-terrorism effort (Comras 2010, pp. 59–85). Since then, the Council and its sanctions committee have advanced the sanctions regime significantly, providing for more detailed listing criteria, exemptions, delisting and review procedures. In addition, the Council mandated an Analytical Support and Sanctions Monitoring Team to serve as a Panel of Experts (resolution 1526 (2004)). With the shift to global counter-terrorism, the Council continued its targeted sanctions measures but expanded them to ISIL, Al-Qaida and associated individuals and entities (resolution 2253 (2015)). The Council also imposed a ban on recruiting, organizing, transporting, or equipping foreign terrorist fighters (resolution 2178 (2014)); furthermore, it banned trade in cultural property from Iraq and Syria as well as oil, petroleum products, and equipment, together with ransom payments and internet hosting for designated individuals and entities (resolution 2199 (2015), 2253 (2015)).

Members of the Al-Qaida/Taliban Sanctions Committee have faced a considerably different decision situation from that of the Council. The committee's main task has been to list and delist individuals as well as entities subject to targeted sanctions, review the accuracy of current listings, and decide about exemptions to the assets freeze (for foodstuffs, rent, or medical treatment) or travel ban (e.g., for religious obligation or judicial proceedings) (Comras 2010, pp. 94–95; Rosand 2004, p. 748). The committee has been facing a stream of technical decisions and "[t]o be effective, the sanctions committee must be continually up to date on the individuals and groups involved in al Qaeda (…)" (Boulden 2008, p. 614). While each individual decision is of marginal importance, the regime's viability depends on regularly adopting many reasonable decisions. At the same time, the Council has given committee members the responsibility for "determining who exactly should face economic sanctions" out of all requests submitted. This is tremendously challenging considering that "[b]ecause Al-Qaida is a disperse organization with a multitude of loosely connected affiliates, determining who exactly should be sanctioned is much more difficult than sanctioning state actors or particular armed forces" (Gutherie 2005, pp. 495–496).

Because terrorism can affect any UN member state and indeed has been affecting many, Council members and non-members have been widely supporting the sanctions regime as a viable counter-terrorism instrument at UN level (Doyle 2004, p. 86; Gutherie 2005, pp. 496–497; Romaniuk 2010, pp. 64–72). The area of counter-terrorism is one where Council member's fundamental interests largely converge (Einsiedel *et al.* 2016, p. 831), despite the possibility of targeted individuals' fundamental human rights being infringed. While interest in this regime was lower during its early days, states strongly supported it after 9/11. In response to increasing terrorist threat, a broad coalition of states pushed for imposing sanctions and the subsequent strengthening of measures. Usually three or four permanent members (US, UK, Russia and sometimes France) as well as non-permanent members from all regions and other states including Afghanistan's neighbors sponsored sanctions resolutions. Except for resolution 1333 (2000), where China and Malaysia abstained, the Council adopted all Al-Qaida/Taliban sanctions resolutions unanimously.

Simultaneously, states' interests in the sanctions regime diverged so far as maintaining the sanctions list was concerned, because of states' potential misuse for their own interests, be it to criminalize and constrain domestic opposition activities or to pursue other geopolitical interests (Rosand 2004, p. 752; US Embassy Paris 2005b). As a leading counter-terrorism expert puts it, the sanctions regime provided some governments "(…) with an opportunity to squelch their own local insurgencies, or to otherwise taint opposition groups, providing names that had nothing to do with either the Taliban or al Qaeda" (Comras 2010, p. 95). The Bush administration also saw merit in using additional listings as a means of demonstrating progress in the "war on terror" (Biersteker 2010, p. 88). After the Beslan terrorist attack, Russia continually insisted on a relationship between Chechen rebels and Al-Qaida, unsuccessfully pushing for transformation of the Al-Qaida/Taliban regime into a counter-terrorism regime beyond Al-Qaida affiliates (Rosand 2010, p. 264). Russia has been a staunch opponent of delisting Taliban members. Moreover, China tried using the sanctions regime for designating domestic separatists such as the East Turkestan Liberation Organization (US Permanent Mission to the UN 2006a). Consequently, a successful regulatory outcome depended on the sanctions committee's ability to scrutinize listing proposals vis-à-vis Council resolutions collectively and effectively.

Considering these positions, I would expect that committee governance prompts rule-based governance in the Al-Qaida/Taliban sanctions regime. Here, committee governance creates strong demand for criteria, rules and procedures, which in turn affects committee decision-making. While Council members share a collective interest in counter-terrorism, they are likely to prefer different outcomes on specific cases at hand. Hence, I expect committee members to set focal points either through rules or informal precedents in line with hypotheses 1 and 2. Committee decision-making will likely create coordination situations with diverging preferences. Hence, Council or committee criteria, rules and procedures as well as precedents could provide focal points on which to coordinate behavior. Because Council members have a pronounced interest in the regime (particularly after 9/11) and the numerous decisions provide substantial demand for rules, I expect the regulatory density to be comparatively high.

Initially, the Council did not apply strict regulation to the committee but instead allowed a wide degree of discretion in implementing the sanctions regime. The Council provided a vague set of criteria and quite rudimentary procedures, presumably because members expected few decision-making issues. The Council gave the committee a broad mandate to "designate the aircraft and funds or other financial resources (…) owned or controlled directly or indirectly by the Taliban" (resolution 1267 (1999), para. 6e). Later, the designation criteria were expanded to "Usama bin Laden and individuals and entities associated with him" (resolution 1333 (2000), para. 8c) and tasked the committee "[t]o establish and maintain updated lists (…) of individuals and entities designated as being associated with Usama bin Laden" (para. 16b). In regard to imposing a travel ban, the Council shifted the designation criteria to "Usama bin Laden, members of the Al-Qaida organization and the Taliban and other individuals, groups, undertakings and entities associated with them" (resolution 1390 (2002), para. 2), and requested the committee "to update regularly the list" (para. 5a). However, the overly discretionary criteria and rules created many of the issues and problems that the sanctions regime had to cope with in subsequent years.

Laissez-faire decision-making without criteria, rules and procedures

This episode illustrates how committee members can confront the decision problem of which sanctions targets to select by taking a laissez-faire attitude; they simply can accept all proposals regardless of their fit to the sanctions regime's objectives. Before 2005, committee members had enormous discretion on whom to list because there was no definition of who fell within the overly broad designation criteria, combined with there being little interest in challenging designations after 9/11. Designating states were not required to provide reasons for listing proposals. While the list grew substantially after 9/11, this laissez-faire attitude caused severe governance problems, undermining not only effectiveness, but also the UN membership's willingness to implement the sanctions regime (Gehring and Dörfler 2013, pp. 574–576).

Before 9/11, the listing process was not problematic. The case resembled a country-specific sanctions regime and the committee exclusively listed high-level and publicly known Taliban leaders. Not until six months after Council resolution 1267 (1999), did the committee issue a first sanctions list including the Taliban leader Mullar Omar, Ariana Airlines and four Afghan banks including the Afghan Central Bank (SC/6844, SC/6938, SC/6955). In 2001, the committee added 30 Taliban ministers and governors (SC/6998). The following March, the Council adopted resolution 1333 (2000), which allowed for designating "Usama bin Laden and individuals and entities associated with him" (resolution 1333 (2000), para. 8c). Yet, the committee still focused on Taliban leaders. Prior to 9/11, the list comprised of 152 Taliban including ministers, deputy ministers and governors, as well as 10 individuals and 1 entity associated with Usama bin Laden, including Aiman Al-Zawahiri and Usama bin Laden (SC/7028, SC/7124). However, shortly after 9/11 as the committee was used to targeting a swiftly increasing number of Al-Qaida associates, many unresolved issues became apparent. First, the Council left it open to interpretation, which individuals and entities the committee should regard as "associated with" Usama bin Laden, Al-Qaida and the Taliban. Second, neither the Council nor committee provided clear directives as to how the committee should process a listing proposal. It was left unclear, whether or not information should be provided and if so of what kind this should be to warrant a listing, which parties should be involved and what details should be made available to listed individuals and the public.

To confront the problem of which designation requests to accept, committee members navigated with an unexpectedly laissez-faire attitude before and immediately after 9/11, presuming that designations would be accurate (Gutherie 2005, p. 511). As a consequence, committee members accepted virtually all proposals "without much ado" and without scrutinizing or later reviewing these decisions (Comras 2010, p. 95). New listing requests contained only minimal information on the individual concerned and lacked evidence about the connection to Al-Qaida (Rosand 2004, pp. 748–749). In fact, a large majority of designations immediately after 9/11 to early 2002 stemmed directly from the US (Cramér 2003, p. 88). In essence, the committee adopted all US listings requests unchallenged assuming that the US "must have good reasons," even though the US regularly based them on classified material (Biersteker 2010, p. 88). During this phase, not even committee members could evaluate the evidence that led to a designation and requests for disclosing confidential information would be rejected (Hoffmann 2008, p. 546). In 2001 alone, the committee designated 123 individuals and entities allegedly associated with Al-Qaida (Cortright 2009, pp. 9–10).

The listing process placed the burden of proof on the states which objected (Biersteker and Eckert 2006, p. 29; Gehring and Dörfler 2013). Under the no-objection procedure that is applicable to all decisions, committee members have to object to a decision proposal actively while acceptance requires no action. However, committee members were in practice precluded from rejecting non-eligible proposals. Without reliable criteria and clear procedures, committee members could not distinguish acceptable from unacceptable proposals. The designation criterion was overly vague and provided wide-ranging discretion (Heupel 2009, pp. 310–311). Challenging a listing proposal immediately created a bilateral and politicized issue. Consequently, committee members felt that raising concerns about a proposal's appropriateness was costly and unwise, considering that no decision was particularly important to most members (Biersteker and Eckert 2006, p. 29). In addition, for the committee to consider a listing request, this required a member to take action in asking for the request to be included on the committee agenda. Furthermore, the short 48 hours timeframe for raising objections effectively excluded objections from states that did not have the capacity to acquire disconfirming information quickly. All this biased the process toward accepting decisions across the board (Kanetake 2008, p. 147; Biersteker and Eckert 2006, p. 29; see guidelines November 2002, para. 8b).

Two episodes illustrate the broad discretion of committee members in the absence of a reliable "associated with" standard, which led to what the Watson Report termed "toxic designations" (Biersteker and Eckert 2009, p. 24). Some governments designated domestic opposition members, separatist or rebel groups that had little connection to Al-Qaida, the Taliban or transnational terrorism to postmark them as terrorists and to legitimize counter-terrorism activities (Comras 2010, p. 95; Rosand 2004, p. 749). In one instance, the committee listed the Eastern Turkestan Islamic Movement, a Chinese separatist group on September 11, 2002. The listing was criticized for its lack of evidence on the groups association with Al-Qaida (Rosand 2004, p. 752; DeYoung 2002). Four states, including China, the US (allegedly to garner Chinese support for the Iraq war), Kyrgyzstan and Afghanistan had requested the listing, while European committee members "expressed concern" and requested "more evidence" from the US. The skeptical members, asserting that the US documentation merely resembled unproven Chinese allegations, admitted that they ultimately "acquiesced into the United Nations listing only to preserve unity" (Eckholm 2002).

In a second instance, the US along with Russia and other states requested the listing of three Chechen entities together with two individuals (SC/7676; SC/7803; SC/7842), allegedly to garner Russian support for the Iraq war. While the US previously considered Chechen rebels as separatists, Russia had for long claimed connections to Al-Qaida (Agence France Presse 2003). The literature notes other instances of political listings (Hoffmann 2008, p. 546; Schorlemer 2003, p. 275) and ASSMT statements also suggest that the committee made dubious listings to serve particular states' political interests (S/2004/679, para. 34). Frequent references in US cables termed many "early (pre-2006) listings" as "inappropriate designations" which needed to be cleared (US Permanent Mission to the UN 2009b); also mentioned were "errors on the 1267 Committee's List, including inappropriate listings that should have been removed a long time ago" (Rice 2009b), and warnings to do with being "careful about allowing governments to misuse the 1267 listing process for other internal purposes" (US Embassy Paris 2005b).

The laissez-faire approach caused three severe problems. Initially, the committee's attitude made the sanctions regime ineffective. Many UN member states reported

> a lack of clarity concerning the process and procedures for submitting to the Committee names to be added to the list (…). They also noted a lack of established guidelines or evidentiary criteria for determining which names should be added to the list.
>
> (S/2002/1050, para. 26)

As the ASSMT recognized, the "[p]rovision of a basic definition of terms by the Security Council or the Committee, particularly of 'associated with,' would provide States with a better understanding of when to propose names for listing, thereby encouraging new listings" (S/2005/572, para. 27). Second, UN member states also perceived the sanctions regime as illegitimate. The High-Level Panel on Threats, Challenges and Change acknowledged that the sanctions regime "suffers from lagging support and implementation" (A/59/565, para. 153). This manifested in more than 50 states that had expressed serious concerns about designating individuals in the absence of clear procedures and basic due process (S/2005/761, para. 37; Biersteker and Eckert 2006, p. 36). Until 2004, only:

> (…) 21 States have submitted names for inclusion on the List (…). The number of contributors to the List suggests that many States are reluctant to provide names. Issues of due process may be holding some States back, as may concerns over the definition of Taliban and Al-Qaida. In addition, the List has had to avoid accusations of political point scoring.
>
> (S/2004/679, para. 34)

This reflected member states reluctance to implement targeted sanctions against Al-Qaida (Biersteker 2010, p. 91). On the one hand, sanctions regimes depend on the UN member states forwarding names to the committee (Kanetake 2008, p. 134), without which any sanctions regime can be undermined. On the other hand, UN member states may have ceased to implement sanctions, willingly or unwillingly, which tarnished the effectiveness of constraining the transnational Al-Qaida network (Comras 2010, p. 90).

Third, the poor quality of identifiers provided by designating states posed obstacles for genuinely implementing targeted sanctions. In its first report, the Monitoring Team had already recognized the issue of "insufficient identifiers" and recommended provision of a list providing at least basic identifiers including date of birth and nationality (S/2002/541, paras. 8, 10–17; S/2002/1050, para. 29). For instance, the Monitoring Team documented that in 2003 there were still 34 listed individuals for whom no information on their first name(s) had been presented (S/2003/669, para. 74) and noted that lacking basic identifiers "makes enforcement action virtually impossible" (S/2004/679, para. 37). Thus, UN member states and banks could hardly identify funds to freeze and immigration officials could not enforce travel bans (S/2007/572, paras. 65, 121). Indeed, lacking identifiers posed the risk of targeting innocent individuals (S/2007/677, para. 29; S/2007/137, para. 9–10). A Council diplomat mocked that he knew instances of "an individual on the sanctions Committee list, which identified him as coming from a certain country and being between the ages of 32 and 35," which applied to "thousands of individuals in that particular country" (S/2007/137, pp. 9–10). Even the committee has recognized that "65 Member States have addressed the problem of sanctions not being implemented against certain entries (…) because there are insufficient identifiers" (S/2005/761, pp. 2–3).

This episode prior to and shortly after 9/11 shows that the unregulated listing process and overly broad committee discretion prompted serious governance issues. In the absence of meaningful designation criteria and a defined listing procedure, committee members confronted the decision problem with a laissez-faire attitude, simply adopting all proposals across the board without verifying their merits. While this is unexpected, it does not contradict the committee governance thesis. Rather, it shows that a laissez-faire attitude represents another option for overcoming the decision problem without rules while at the same time circumventing deadlock. However, it is also one that seriously undercuts the Council's long-term interest in sanctions governance. The quickly growing sanctions list posed substantial problems for member states' implementation and potentially sabotaged UN member states' willingness to cooperate. However, as the next episode shows the Council can also overcome these issues by means of committee governance.

Criteria, rules and procedures trigger rule-based governance on the listing of individuals and entities

This episode demonstrates that Council members can remedy the laissez-faire attitude by taking committee governance seriously and providing focal points to coordinate behavior. It highlights that effectively separating rule-making and rule-application provides incentives for rule-based governance. At Council level, despite the skepticism of permanent members to restrict their flexibility, decision-making on rules confirms the need for adopting consistent criteria. At committee level, the increased regulation not only profoundly transformed the situation toward rule-based decision-making, but also provided incentives to submit well-reasoned proposals, scrutinize decision requests vis-à-vis established committee practice and reject requests that fall short of established standards. Significantly, these effects occurred even before the Council created the Ombudsperson mechanism (Gehring and Dörfler 2013, pp. 576–579).

The Council had two alternatives for resolving these issues and restoring effectiveness. Council members could have pressured UN member states to comply with illegitimate sanctions decisions, which seemed impossible, though, as Council decisions can hardly be enforced among many UN member states simultaneously. However, the Council decided instead to restore UN member state cooperation by means of rule-making. It became clear that the sanctions regime required consistent criteria applicable for a range of cases, while not too narrowly limiting the committee's flexibility for effectively addressing the terrorist threat. Clear criteria would promote sanctions implementation and member states would know better whom to propose for listing to the committee. In this way, designation criteria would also provide a yardstick for sanctions targets as to what behavioral change would be required to achieve a lifting of sanctions (Biersteker and Eckert 2006, p. 38). Consequently, proactive states used a mix of Council rules and Council directives for the committee to make rules, as well as committee self-regulation in reaction to governance issues. They reluctantly laid out criteria and rules that made it possible to distinguish between acceptable and unacceptable proposals; the Council also restricted committee discretion, although the "US and Britain argued strongly against an evidence-based system (…), on the grounds it would compromise intelligence sources" (Doyle 2004, p. 86). Furthermore, the Council repeatedly directed the committee to review its guidelines to ensure that "fair and clear procedures exist for placing individuals and entities on the Consolidated List and for removing them as well as for granting humanitarian exemptions" (including 1617 (2005), para. 18, resolutions 1730 (2006), para. 2; 1735 (2006), para. 13).

In a first step, the Council overhauled listing criteria, despite a rift between European permanent members and the US over due process protections (Wadhams 2005a; Wadhams 2005b). For instance, France and the US argued against any rules that "would make it any harder to designate supporters of terrorism," while acknowledging the need "to be careful about allowing governments to misuse the 1267 listing process for other internal purposes" (US Embassy Paris 2005b). Some UN members advocated for strict designation criteria, whereas others argued for committee discretion (see S/PV.5529). In recognition of this issue, the Council had called upon designating states to supply sufficient identifiers and evidence on the association with Al-Qaida voluntarily (resolution 1526 (2004), para. 17). However, such calls went unheeded, and consequently listing requirements remained unchanged until 2005. Accordingly, it was left unclear which individuals and entities would be considered "associated with" Al-Qaida and the Taliban and which not. After several rounds of negotiations, Council members agreed on resolution 1617 (2005), which was adopted on July 29, 2005 and clarified that individuals and entities

> participating in the financing, planning, facilitating, preparing, or perpetrating of acts or activities by, in conjunction with, under the name of, on behalf of, or in support of; supplying, selling or transferring arms and related materiel to; recruiting for; or otherwise supporting acts or activities of Al-Qaida, Usama bin Laden or the Taliban, or any cell, affiliate, splinter group or derivative thereof (…) shall be eligible for designation.
>
> (Resolution 1617 (2005), paras. 2, 3)

This criterion is consistent and does not include any exceptions that one-sidedly favor a powerful member. Notably, the Council adopted criteria that would be applicable to all current and future cases. These criteria specify which acts of an individual or an entity would constitute an association with Al-Qaida and which not, though they still leave some "wiggle room" ("otherwise supporting acts of"). The committee incorporated this standard as the basis of a listing (guidelines November 2006, para. 6c). Thereby, the committee hoped that the definition of "associated with" would prospectively increase the number of listing requests (S/2006/22, para. 32).

As a second step, the Council substantially increased the evidentiary requirements for any listings regardless of the submitting state (Prost 2012a, p. 417).

In the early years, evidentiary requirements were unclear, and designations could be made just "on the basis of relevant information provided by Member States" (resolution 1390 (2002), para. 5a). Nowadays, designating states must provide a detailed "statement of case" (resolution 1617 (2005), paras. 4, 6). Initially, the Council did not define what such a statement would need to incorporate for the committee to come to a decision (S/2006/154, para. 27; S/2006/635, para. 6). In its November 2006 guidelines, the committee defined that the statement of case should incorporate

> as much detail as possible on the basis(es) for listing (...), including: (1) specific findings demonstrating the association or activities alleged; (2) the nature of the supporting evidence (...) and (3) supporting evidence (...). States should include details of any connection with a currently listed individual or entity.
>
> (Para. 6d)

The Council later formalized the evidentiary requirements for statements of cases (resolution 1735 (2006), para. 5). Redacted versions of these statements should be provided for the sanctions targets (para. 10). A later amendment by the committee required states to add information on "relevant court cases and proceedings" against the individuals and also declare which portions of the reasons are confidential rather than which portions could be released (guidelines July 2010, para. 6e). In addition, the designating states would need to supply sufficient identifying information including any names and aliases, date of birth, place of birth, gender, nationality, residence, addresses, occupation, and travel document numbers. The committee foresaw similar requirements for adding entities to the sanctions list (guidelines November 2006, para. 6e).

As a third step, the Council required the committee to issue publicly available reasons for listing ("narrative summaries") covering each current and future listed individual or entity. The narrative summary was to be based on the publicly releasable portions of the statement of case, outline how the individual or entity is associated with Al-Qaida and what specific acts gave rise to the listing decision. The ASSMT would be available to assist in preparation (resolution 1822 (2008), para. 13). The committee also adopted a rule that the narrative summaries must be issued at the time of listing, without which no listing could commence (guidelines July 2010, para. 6k).

Finally, as a fourth step the committee standardized the submission of listing proposals. Attached to its guidelines, it introduced a "Cover Sheet for Member State Submissions" to designate individuals or entities. The cover sheets required the designating state to list identifying information in accordance with the guidelines and listing reasons based on the "associated with"-standard (S/2006/750, Annex II, incorporated in guidelines November 2006, with minor revisions in resolution 1735 (2006), Annex I, Section II). The committee revised cover sheets following a Council request after the introduction of narrative summaries. For this, the ASSMT had proposed more fine-grained cover sheets, which were expanded for original script, physical details for Interpol-UNSC Special Notices and annexes for identification documents (resolution 1822 (2008), para. 14). Finally, resulting from a European initiative to allow more time for considering requests, the committee significantly extended the no-objection procedure's timeframe for raising objections, first from 2 working days (guidelines November 2002) to 5 working days (guidelines December 2005) and later to 10 working days (guidelines July 2010) (Biersteker 2010, p. 97).

The refined listing criteria and procedures constrained committee member behavior, even before the Council created the Office of the Ombudsperson in 2009. The committee was by now operating under a dense set of rules and every proposal had to pass a detailed procedure. Designating states had to provide substantial information on the proposed individual or entity, including detailed reasons for why they should be listed and what their association with Al-Qaida, Usama bin Laden or the Taliban were. Notably, the detailed criteria and procedures raised the threshold for a successful designation significantly. The criteria provide a point of reference for committee members to evaluate listing proposals against the so-called "associated with"-standard (interview with UN member state official, December 2012, also Comras 2010, pp. 95–96). The ASSMT noted that committee practice followed an evidence threshold for association with Al-Qaida that was needed for a successful listing. The Team recommended that the committee should reflect this threshold "commonly required for a successful listing request" in a cover sheet, including the "associated with"-standard when evaluating listing requests (S/2006/154, para. 27). States, which have not consulted the committee guidelines were unclear about how to submit a request or what information would be required, risked the rejection or significant – sometimes indefinite – delay of their listing proposal (S/2006/154, para. 25). As the ASSMT pointed out:

> (…) a successful listing is most often linked to a complete and thorough account of the basis for listing, including the nature of the subject's association with Al-Qaida or the Taliban. The Team believes that successful listings generally are factual, avoid unsupported allegations or broad assumptions and reference supporting evidence or documentation to the greatest extent possible.
>
> (S/2006/154, para. 27)

The ASSMT recognized these effects in a report outlining the listing procedure. Listing proposals from committee members, including the permanent members, and non-committee members were handled in the same manner (S/2007/132, paras. 42, 46). While the time to place a listing was previously only a few days, by 2005 and 2006 the committee needed about three weeks of consideration to complete most listings and thus longer than just the five working-days no-objection procedure. The time spent on listing decisions also depended on the "amount and quality of information provided" (para. 44). Listing proposals, including those from permanent members, were in fact held up and both permanent and elected members placed holds on submissions (para. 46). As an example, the report cites the listing requirements applied by Denmark during its 2005/2006 Council tenure. Domestic authorities would scrutinize the listing proposal against the "associated with"-standard and had set the standard of two reliable information sources corroborating the request's plausibility. Moreover, Denmark had placed "numerous" proposals on hold (p. 18, Box II).

Close observers also recognized these effects. The Watson report acknowledged that more detailed listing requirements would prevent further unwarranted listings (Biersteker and Eckert 2006, p. 7). Known cases illustrate this effect. The report cited three instances where the committee acceded to requests with above threshold information, while it rejected those requests that were lacking information. In a first case, the committee granted a listing request, presumably by Italy, for three individuals accompanied by one general paragraph and six detailed paragraphs on each individual. In another case, the committee accepted a listing request for 6 individuals bolstered with 70 pages of documentation including arrest warrants. To the contrary, the committee rejected a listing request, presumably by Libya, accompanied by a single-paragraph statement of case that included references to 74 names (Biersteker and Eckert 2006, p. 26; Secretary of State 2008a). The rules on identifying information similarly affected the amount of information provided for a successful listing (Biersteker *et al.* 2008, p. 235). Even though the committee had not adopted "minimum criteria for listing, it is unlikely that it would accept a new submission for the listing of an individual which lacked basic identifiers" (S/2008/324, para. 26). The committee had recognized that states required basic identifiers to implement sanctions effectively and had installed a listing procedure which now ensures that "a new listing with inadequate identifiers is virtually unthinkable" (S/2009/502, para. 14).

This episode is a confirmatory case for hypothesis 1 and shows that the early laissez-faire committee behavior prompted Council members to regulate committee decision-making substantially in accordance with the constraints of rule-making. The strengthened rules are strikingly consistent and do not favor any powerful member in particular. Within the committee, the increasingly dense set of criteria and rules allowed committee members to reject unsubstantiated listing requests and transformed the committee listing process toward rule-adherence.

Stalemate creates demand for delisting and review procedures

In the early phase of the sanctions regime, the absence of a delisting procedure coupled with the lack of criteria and evidentiary standards as to when a delisting should commence led to a deadlock. The existing no-objection procedure was biased against delisting decisions, which threatened the regime's functionality and provoked even skeptical members to adopt consistent delisting rules. Council and committee criteria, rules and procedures enabled its members to delist unwarranted designations, while additional rules reduced the discretion of committee members to prevent undesired delisting decisions by indefinitely delaying decisions.

The debate on delisting took its initiation as Sweden requested the removal of three Swedish citizens from the sanctions list in 2002. On November 9, 2001, the committee had listed these Swedish citizens and two associated entities after they had been added to the US sanctions list. The Swedish government, under public pressure, first bilaterally requested information from the US about the reasons leading to its decision. The US responded by supplying 27 pages of information, mostly comprising public news-releases (Comras 2010, p. 97). Swedish security officials established that this material could not confirm the accusations and the individuals were in any event not suspected of being criminals (Cramér 2003, pp. 90–91). However, the US authorities refused to provide additional evidence and disclose their intelligence (Doyle 2004, p. 86). To the contrary, when Sweden requested the committee to delist these individuals, the US objected arguing that the individuals had failed to present exonerating evidence (Miller 2003, p. 48). Further, Sweden as a non-Council member formally requested a review of the entire sanctions list together with the establishment of guidelines and criteria for targeted sanctions implementation according to the Council's call on the committee "to promulgate expeditiously such guidelines and criteria" (resolution 1390 (2002), para. 5d; Boustany 2002). France supported the Swedish initiative and submitted a proposal to establish "rules of the game," including more specific criteria and a regular review mechanism. However, the US refused to provide justifications and establish a threshold for listing in order not to compromise its intelligence sources (Schmemann 2002). After further Swedish initiatives remained unsuccessful, Sweden threatened unilaterally to unfreeze the accounts (Comras 2010, p. 97). Thereafter, when the Swedish authorities bilaterally supplied information to US counterparts, the US was at least willing to evaluate the case and ultimately removed two of the individuals from its domestic sanctions list (Cramér 2003, p. 94).

The effects of committee governance prompted the committee to make rules selectively. While this request concerned just one case, many committee members acknowledged that a decision would go beyond the case's scope and that a general rule was required (S/2002/1423, para. 11; Lederer 2002). On August 15, 2002, the Chair announced that the committee had established a new delisting procedure, negotiated over "several months of intensive consultations" (SC/7487; S/2002/1423, paras. 6, 15). This purely intergovernmental procedure stipulates that petitioners should request the state of citizenship or residence to negotiate bilaterally with designating states based on the justification provided in support of delisting. Both the petitioned state and the designating state could formally request a delisting decided by committee consensus (SC/7487). In effect, every committee member could reject the delisting without justification (Guthe-rie 2005, p. 514). Under the new provision, Sweden and the US submitted a delisting request, which the committee finally approved (SC/7490).

This Swedish initiative illustrates the distinctive feature of an unregulated committee process. First, the committee lacked a delisting procedure, detailing who could trigger such a procedure, who is to supply what information and how to take a decision (Eriksson 2010, p. 164). Without such procedure, committee members would enjoy wide-ranging discretion in dealing with such cases. Second, the initiative highlights that the burden of proof rested with the state requesting delisting. This state had to convince those committee members who favored a continued listing, why this would be inappropriate (Miller 2003, p. 48). In turn, any committee member could prevent the delisting without presenting additional information why the listing was still warranted. Third, committee members became subject to the constraints of rule-making as they sought to remedy this issue by negotiating a delisting procedure, even though the issue emanated from a single-case. That negotiations on a simple intergovernmental rule took eight months to complete implies that powerful members hesitated to adopt such a rule (Lynch 2002).

However, this intergovernmental delisting procedure still proved to be totally inadequate because the state of nationality and residency constituted gatekeepers. In fact, should the petitioned state have rejected support for a delisting request on behalf of the petitioner for any reason, this would have denied access to the review (S/2005/83, para. 56). It is not known how many individuals and entities actually requested a delisting via any of the states of nationality/residency as these petitions have never reached the committee stage and accordingly unsuccessful complaints were not registered (Biersteker and Eckert 2006, p. 36). Also the ASSMT emphasized that a reform would be in the committee's long-term interest:

> The Team recommends (…) to allow explicitly for the possibility of de-listing when a party demonstrates (…) that it no longer is associated with Al-Qaida or the Taliban (…). Such revisions to the process could help to reduce the possibility of one or more potentially negative court decisions (…). The establishment of this process would cost the Committee nothing. In the end, no de-listings will occur without the consent of all 15 Committee members. Therefore, the Committee would be able to ensure that parties linked to Al-Qaida and the Taliban are not removed from the List without sufficient evidence; (…) and States could propose names for listing with the assurance that, if circumstances change, a robust de-listing system is available.
>
> (S/2005/83, paras. 57–59)

Hesitantly, the committee and the Council tried to secure an effective sanctions regime; however, the negotiations were protracted because the P5 refused any outside review of designations. In resolution 1617 (2005), the Council had requested the committee to continue its work on listing and delisting issues (para. 18). Though the committee agreed to revise the listings provisions in November 2006, it still disagreed on a revised delisting provision (S/2007/59, para. 9), and consequently following a French-US initiative, the issue was referred back to the Council. These two permanent members had joined forces in opposition to other European countries' preference for an independent Ombudsperson. They wanted to ensure that a changed delisting process would not restrict committee prerogatives, limit the number of states involved and ensure that the mechanism would work merely as a "mailbox" (US Embassy Paris 2006b). As a result, the Council created the Focal Point for Delisting (resolution 1730 (2006)) as a UN Secretariat entity in 2006. The Focal Point procedure was innovative in that petitioners could gain access to the committee directly, trigger a delisting procedure, force the committee to consider their petition and circumvent their potentially unwilling states of nationality or residence. Nevertheless, for a request to be successful, a consensus committee decision was still required. The Focal Point transmitted petitions to relevant states and the committee then served as a means of communication between committee and petitioner. However, the Focal Point merely functioned as a registrar of petitions and had no independent review or decision-making capacity, a factor that was criticized (Denmark, Greece, Qatar, S/PV.5599; Kanetake 2008, pp. 162–163).

Despite the new arrangements, though, the intergovernmental procedure still continued to cause problems. On the one hand, even though new listings would have to meet the increased listing standards, this did not affect the existing entries. Of the 488 entries in 2008, around 270 stemmed from designations made in 2001, hence before the Council had established any requirements (Prost 2012a, p. 418), which also created problems in drafting narrative summaries for these listings (S/2009/502, para. 29). As the ASSMT has repeatedly noted, listings without proper justification and identifiers would undermine a sanctions list's credibility and inhibit sincere implementation. In early 2008, almost 90 entries lacked even basic identifiers, which diverted limited resources toward identifying assets with only having little information, risked targeting the wrong individuals or even made implementation completely impossible. These entries have "limited or no operational value" (S/2008/324, paras. 24–25; S/2009/502, para. 13). On the other hand, delistings were unlikely to occur. UN member states without their own designations or nationals on the list would have little interest in taking up a case. Those states that were concerned may have been hesitant to advocate delisting of an alleged terrorist. The reluctance of the committee to grant delistings discouraged member states to submit such requests with low chances of succeeding (S/2009/502, para. 16). As most designations stemmed from P5 members, these were gatekeepers to delisting any of their designations if there were no good reasons. An earlier rule according to which the committee circulated all listings not been updated for 4 years has resulted in merely 2 reviews of 115 entries eligible because a committee member had to actively pursue a review and provide justification, which posed a high hurdle for cases of limited importance (guidelines November 2006, para. 6i, S/2010/497, para. 13). Even the US recognized that the de-facto "life-sentence" for listed individuals undermined member states cooperation in submitting new names. Hence, the list was increasingly outdated and "irrelevant to global counter-terrorism actions," while delistings could enhance state cooperation (Khalizad 2008a).

These listings were useless and created the demand for guidance on how to review existing entries. In response, the Council requested the committee to undergo a "comprehensive review" of all 488 list entries separately by June 30, 2010 "to ensure the Consolidated List is as updated and accurate as possible" (resolution 1822 (2008), para. 25; S/2010/497, para. 1). The Council directed the committee to detail a procedure on how such reviews were conducted and ensure that each entry is reviewed at least every three years thereafter (resolution 1822 (2008), para. 25–26). In addition, the Council requested the committee to produce narrative summaries for those entries retained in the review process (para. 13).

After negotiating for more than five months, where the scope of narrative summaries especially was highly contentious "with the United States and European countries favoring summaries that were more expansive (…), while Russia preferred a much narrower scope" (US Permanent Mission to the UN 2009b), new committee guidelines outlined how the review should proceed (guidelines December 2008, para. 9a–e). Every trimester, the committee would circulate a subset of names to the designating states and the states of residence/nationality to provide any additional reasons for listing and identifying information. Subsequently, the cases and the information would be circulated to all committee members and the ASSMT for collecting further information. After this, each case was put on the committee's agenda following which the original entry would be amended. At every stage, any designating state, committee member, or other UN member state could file a delisting request if a listing was no longer warranted (guidelines para. 9a, e; Biersteker and Eckert 2009, pp. 16–17).

Committee practice further elaborated the review procedure and developed a "standard pattern" for each case (S/2010/497, para. 31). After the ASSMT presented the case together with new information, the committee would discuss it. In the case of no committee member or other reviewing state requested a delisting, the entry remained valid. Whenever a state including non-committee members filed a delisting request, the Chairman circulated such a request under the no-objection procedure. To evaluate a request, the committee applied the "associated with" standard and the Interpol–UNSC Special Notices requirements on identifiers. However, the committee retained a listing if at least one committee member objected to the name's removal (S/2010/497, paras. 29–34).

The comprehensive review reveals that the regulation has indeed affected committee behavior. On the one hand, the considerable number of delistings shows that individual cases were scrutinized during committee meetings and that the review has increased the hurdles that must be overcome to retain an entry. During the comprehensive review, the committee delisted 45 individuals and entities, amended 465 list entries (S/2010/497, para. 43) and significantly decreased the number with inadequate identifiers (S/2012/729, para. 38). On the other hand, the considerable number of rejected delisting requests demonstrates that committee members still had much discretion and that the procedure "tends to be biased against making changes to the list" (Biersteker and Eckert 2009, p. 22). Even the US acknowledged that

> Committee members, including the United States, may be reluctant to remove any names (…). Keeping a name on the list may be seen as the "safe" option (…). Nevertheless, a willingness to de-list weak designations will show that the Committee is serious about clearing away the inappropriate designations that have tarnished the legitimacy of the regime.
>
> (US Permanent Mission to the UN 2009b)

The committee rejected 39 out of 161 delisting requests, 14 were withdrawn and the remaining postponed. Notably, most of the rejected delisting requests stemmed from permanent members (S/2010/497, para. 25).

The usage of "holds" during the comprehensive review created another issue of committee governance (Biersteker 2010, pp. 98–99). Long before, some requests were kept on hold for many years (S/2012/805, 3.2.). For instance, the Swiss exemption request for an individual's assets was left pending for three years (S/2003/1070, para. 78). Without a time limit, committee members could dilute petitions and exemptions through placing holds. As a result, the excessive use of holds could undermine listings of potentially dangerous terrorists and delistings of innocent individuals alike (Biersteker and Eckert 2006, 32–42). Especially during the comprehensive review, the committee was unable to agree on a growing number of cases as members extensively put decisions on hold, not least to avoid delistings (interview with UN member state official, August 2012). In December 2009, 31 issues were indefinitely unresolved unless a hold would be voluntarily released (S/2010/497, para. 93). As a remedy, the Council directed the committee to resolve pending issues until the end of 2010 and ensure that members may place holds for no longer than six months unless the committee decides to extend the period (resolution 1904 (2009), paras. 41–42). Faced with a Council directive, the committee decided that a pending issue would be automatically deemed approved unless the committee extended the hold for three months (guidelines July 2010, para. 4c). Later, the committee expanded this rule to all (future) procedures where the Council had not provided a time limit (guidelines April 2013, para. 4j, k). Earlier, the committee decided that elected members' holds would cease to have effect after they had rotated off the Council (guidelines December 2005, para. 4c). As a result, these rules restricted the discretion of committee members. The rule guaranteed that pending issues would finally be resolved positively or negatively. Regulating holds ensured that a hold would now be useful only for its intended use, namely to request information, rather than dilute unfavorable decisions. It has reduced the number of holds during the remainder of the review (S/2010/497, para. 93) and ever since (interview with UN member state official, March 2012).

This episode of committee governance, as confirmatory evidence for hypothesis 1, illustrates that the initial deadlock on removing unwarranted designations created functional issues that incentivized even skeptical Council members to regulate committee decision-making. Under the constraints of rule-making, the Council devised delisting and review procedures, which enabled committee members to delist unwarranted listings and improve the substance of existing sanctions list entries, while additional committee self-regulation restricted its members' discretion to dilute decisions through excessive placing and maintaining of holds, sometimes indefinitely.

Deadlock on Taliban prompts division of the sanctions regime

The episode highlights that apart from symbolic value, the deadlock over potential removal of Taliban figures from the sanctions list prompted division of the sanctions regime and allowed for rule-based governance despite Russian objections. Political developments in Afghanistan had made it increasingly difficult to treat the Taliban and Al-Qaida sections differently under the same set of criteria. In June 2011, the Council decided to separate the Taliban from the Al-Qaida list and established a separate sanctions regime focused on the Afghan peace process including a separate sanctions committee. As evidence for hypothesis 1, new criteria solved committee deadlock and bound even powerful members of the Taliban Sanctions Committee to rules' adherence.

Council members had two motives for this fundamental change. First, the Council wanted to express symbolic and political support for the Afghan peace process by taking the changing situation in Afghanistan more into account. The Council's political focus shifted toward supporting the peace and reconciliation process as well as reaching a political solution to the conflict in Afghanistan. The new sanctions regime should "support and promote Afghan-led reconciliation" and shift the sanctions regime away from terrorism toward internationally endorsed reconciliation criteria (US, S/PV.6557). The new Taliban sanctions regime enhanced emphasis on the Afghan government to give more attention to its views, for instance through a mechanism for consultation prior to listing or delisting initiatives (see statements S/PV.6557). Second, and more importantly from the perspective of committee governance, the sanctions regime suffered from a functional problem: It became difficult to treat Al-Qaida and Taliban members differently under uniform decision criteria. Ideally, the Taliban would need to satisfy Afghanistan-focused delisting criteria, where renouncing terrorism is only one aspect among others to be considered, while a delisting in the Al-Qaida regime would require a renouncement of terrorism to be the key factor (three separate interviews with UN member state official, New York, March 2012, October 2013). In committee practice, this had created repeated necessity for justifying different treatment despite uniform criteria (interview with UN member state official, New York, March 2012). Statements from Germany, UK and France reflected these issues, noting that the "design of the regime may have to be further developed," favoring a split of the list and refined criteria for both groups, whereas Russia considered such a split to be "unwarranted" (S/PV.6536, pp. 6, 12, 22). The ASSMT noted an increasing discrepancy:

> (…) the Committee has, since November 2001, treated all listed persons in the same way. The Guidelines (…) make no distinction between the Taliban

> and Al-Qaida sections of the List. Some have argued that it is now time to treat listed Taliban (…) differently. (…) They argue that the criteria for the removal of Taliban names cannot be identical to those for Al-Qaida.
>
> (S/2011/245, para. 16)

This was hardly an academic issue as the committee faced a stream of delisting decisions that concerned the list's Taliban sections. In March 2011, the committee considered delisting requests for more than a third of the 137 Taliban names on the list. Furthermore, the Afghan Government increasingly complained "that the process of de-listing is too uncertain, too slow and too complicated; it is unsure what it has to do to persuade the Committee to agree to a de-listing" (S/2011/245, para. 20). The ASSMT further noted that the committee should first decide on some "basic criteria that would have to be met" before considering these requests; it should provide a check list to assist the Afghan government in its preparation of delisting details for those who fulfilled these criteria (para. 23).

The decision criteria's opacity led to a stalemated delisting process in regard to Taliban members. In 2006, Council resolution 1735 (2006) had already explicitly instructed the committee "to clean up the Taliban side of the sanctions list" and laid out "three distinct actions to improve the list: delist former Taliban, sanction new Taliban members, and update the biographic information" for Taliban continuing to be sanctioned (US Permanent Mission to the UN 2007b). Yet, the ASSMT noted that the committee had been highly reluctant to grant delisting requests for Taliban members:

> It is not easy to get off the List. Judging by its past decisions, the Committee will take a cautious approach to removing any Taliban name without clear indications, over a sustained period, that the individual concerned is fully committed to (…) the Afghan Constitution, has renounced violence, and has severed connection with Al-Qaida.
>
> (S/2011/245, para. 14)

Internal US sources reveal that the Taliban section had not changed since 2001 with some corrections in 2003, mainly because France, the UK and Russia, which had designated all Taliban entries in 2001, were gatekeepers. In fact, all 20 Afghan delisting requests for Taliban engaged in reconciliation in 2005 and 2006 had been put on hold for over two years. While France and UK were willing to review their stances, the Russian delegation's "instructions from Moscow are to oppose all Taliban delistings" (US Permanent Mission to the UN 2007b). China and India were also hesitant (US Permanent Mission to the UN 2007l; Riechmann 2011). When Russia continued to block the Afghan requests, the UK pleaded that "Moscow should not employ a higher burden of proof for de-listing than for listing" (US Permanent Mission to the UN 2007l). The ASSMT informally suggested overcoming Russian objections first by devising "criteria to delist reconciled Taliban" and in a second step "submit[ting] two or three names of people who met those criteria" to set a precedent and show that the mechanism actually works (US Embassy Kabul 2009). Western members advocated splitting the "consolidated list into two distinct lists, one dealing with the Taliban and one dealing with Al-Qaida [but] Russia argued strongly for retaining a unified consolidated list as currently exists (…) (SCR Forecast June 2011).

Ultimately, the Council split the sanctions list into two and created a new sanctions committee to manage the separate Taliban list (resolutions 1988 (2011) and 1989 (2011)). The Council recognized a need to treat the two groups differently and directed its new Taliban Sanctions Committee to "(…) remove expeditiously individuals and entities (…) that no longer meet the listing criteria (…)" (para. 18) and to relist those who have been reported as having returned to sanctionable behavior (para. 23). The Council also established delisting criteria tailored to the Taliban. The committee should

> (…) give due regard to requests for removal of individuals who meet the reconciliation conditions (…), which include the renunciation of violence, no links to international terrorist organizations, including Al-Qaida, (…), and respect for the Afghan Constitution, including the rights of women and persons belonging to minorities.
>
> (Resolution 1988 (2011), para. 18)

To align Afghan peace process objectives with those of the sanctions regime, the Council placed greater emphasis on the Afghan government's role so that it is regularly consulted, provides information on reconciled individuals and can trigger early review of individuals deemed to have relinquished terrorist activities (resolution 1988 (2011), paras. 18–29). Before adopting its own guidelines in November 2011, the committee had agreed provisionally to follow the guidelines of the Al-Qaida Committee (S/2012/543, paras. 10–11). These guidelines specified rules on delisting requests, not only for reconciled individuals to include a confirmatory statement by the Afghan High Peace Council, but also for former Taliban members to contain an Afghan government statement confirming the reconciled status (guidelines para 8i/j).

The split into two regimes had significant implications. The Council decreased the likelihood of making package deals across committee boundaries. The two groups could now be treated differently under tailored criteria and rules. This alleviated the previous need to justify why the decision criteria could be stretched in Taliban cases (interview with UN member state official, New York, March 2012). Whereas the Ombudsperson procedure was extended in scope (see Chapter 3), it remained restricted to the Al-Qaida regime because some permanent members were anxious about setting a precedent by having cases referred to the Ombudsperson outside the Al-Qaida context. This was possible at the time, simply because none of the Taliban was challenging the listing via the Ombudsperson (interview with UN member state Official, March 2012). As a result, the Focal Point would receive delisting petitions for the Taliban sanctions regime.

The new rules provided a focal point and restricted committee members' discretion to objecting if they did not accept warranted requests for removing Taliban members from the list. Before the split, states requesting delisting of Taliban had to provide sufficient evidence proving that the individuals had renounced terrorism (US Embassy Moscow 2008). Now, new criteria applied. Whereas the committee had removed only very few Taliban from the original list (Nordland 2011), within one month of the regime split, the 1988 committee delisted 15 individuals, all of whom were listed before 9/11 (SC/10306; SC/10328). Initially, the Afghan government had requested about 50 delistings before the split and committee members expected resistance from Russia, China and India (Agence France Presse 2011a; Nordland 2011). Because a high number of individuals were included, the committee extended consideration of the request (Lederer 2011). Since the split, the committee has delisted 32 individuals (S/2012/971, fn. 16; S/2014/402, para. 16), a quarter of all entries, despite the initial resistance of one permanent member to any delisting on the Taliban section of the formerly comprehensive list. The last delisting took place in 2017 (SC/12721).

This episode shows that a permanent member's obstruction on removing Taliban members could be alleviated through Council rule-making, namely, by splitting the sanctions regime. In fact, the Council developed two different sets of eligibility criteria, both of which confined decision-making within the respective committees to a restricted circle of sanctions targets. In effect, even powerful committee members abided by the delisting rules for Taliban members and associates. In line with committee governance hypothesis 1, the Taliban Sanctions Committee operated in the mode of rule-based decision-making.

The Ombudsperson as safeguard for rule-based governance

The creation of the Office of the Ombudsperson as a powerful and independent agenda-setter to review existing listings and its subsequent strengthening has been fostering committee members' adherence to existing rules. In contrast to the literature, though, I argue that while the Ombudsperson provides additional incentives for rule-adherence, the presence of this new role has not changed committee members' incentives systematically (Gehring and Dörfler 2013, pp. 579–582).

Although the Focal Point for Delisting had granted targeted individuals direct access to the committee, it proved inadequate to restore the regime's effectiveness (Biersteker and Eckert 2009, pp. 31–32). In the face of successful court challenges in the EU annulling the implementing directives, EU members were in a dilemma between either violating international law or ignoring their courts (Sievers and Daws 2014, p. 543). The Focal Point did nothing to relieve the pressure; between 2007 and 2009, it received delisting requests for 18 individuals and 22 entities but the committee removed only 3 individuals and 17 entities (Security Council Report 2013, p. 21). Sharp critique also came from other corners, including the Special Rapporteur on the

Protection of Human Rights while Countering Terrorism, the UN Office of Legal Affairs, academics and human rights activists. Even the ASSMT has called on the Council to restore the regime's effectiveness and proposed an independent review mechanism before courts imposed their own standards of review (S/2009/502, para. 42).

Reflecting the logic of committee governance and appealing to focus on long-term interests instead of short-term gains, even the US recognized that the existing procedure was dysfunctional:

> Bold U.S. action is needed to salvage an irreplaceable UN counter-terrorism tool (…). These measures, however, combined with a redoubling of U.S. efforts to scrub the 1267 List of inappropriate entries, would go far toward restoring confidence in the regime and heading off more radical and dangerous proposals. (…) New safeguards will probably make it harder to designate and/or retain on the list some individuals (…). This will be particularly true in cases where we lack recent and convincing declassified information to justify a designation. (…) Instead of viewing this consolidation as a failure to designate terrorists, the United States should welcome the emergence of a smaller – but much more credible and better implemented – List. The preservation of the tool, (…) is far more important than the designation of a handful of marginal figures (…).
>
> (Rice 2009b)

In 2009, the Council created the Office of the Ombudsperson as independent entity to review delisting petitions and adopted a detailed review procedure (resolution 1904 (2009)). In a two-months information gathering stage, the Ombudsperson forwarded the petition to committee, designating states, state of nationality/residency, other states or UN bodies (para. 2a,b), and the ASSMT to assemble information on the case (para. 3a–c). In a two-months dialogue' stage, the Ombudsperson interacted with the petitioner and communicated between petitioner and states involved (paras. 5, 6a–c). Afterwards, the Ombudsperson provided a "Comprehensive Report" to the committee which should "[b]ased on an analysis of all the information available (…), lay out for the Committee the principal arguments concerning the delisting request" (para. 7a–c). In the "decision" stage, the Ombudsperson presented the report to committee (paras. 8–9) after which the committee would decide by consensus (para. 10). Should there be a rejection, the committee should transmit the decision and "explanatory remarks" to the Ombudsperson, who would convey them to the petitioner (paras. 11–14). The Secretary-General appointed former ICTY judge, Kimberly Prost, to serve as the first Ombudsperson.

Although the Ombudsperson could not formally recommend delisting at this point, a fact that was widely criticized (S/PV.6247, p. 3), her presence did affect decision-making. The petition triggers an independent investigation, which the sanctions committee decides upon, so the petitioner is relieved from having to seek the support of any state. Crucially, the Ombudsperson relies on states willingness to share critical information. Yet, information requests are based on a Chapter VII authorization and s/he is mandated to report states, which have failed to cooperate. In a comprehensive report, gaps between requested and received information would become obvious. In the biannual reporting to the Security Council, the Ombudsperson would list non-cooperative states (Prost 2012a, p. 419). Only six delisting petitions were filed under this first Ombudsperson procedure, which resulted in four individuals being delisted, one petition being rejected, and one petitioner withdrawing (S/2012/49).

To remedy the imminent danger that domestic or regional parliaments or courts would partially suspend sanctions because there was a lack of due process and effective remedy, the Council revised the procedure in June 2011 and gave the Ombudsperson the right to issue recommendations (resolution 1989 (2011)). Since then, an Ombudsperson's delisting recommendation will lift the sanctions on a target after 60 days unless the committee overturns the recommendation by consensus or a committee member refers the case to the Council (so-called "trigger mechanism") (Prost and Wilmshurst 2013, p. 7). The heightened role of the Ombudsperson was contentious as it touched upon Council prerogatives, which the permanent members were keen to uphold (SCR Forecast June 2011). The administration in Washington opposed the idea, but the US Mission in New York saw the advantage of granting the Ombudsperson more power while retaining the right to refer any delisting request to the Council (interview with UN member state official, New York, December 2013).

This trigger mechanism placed the Ombudsperson in a strong agenda-setting role, by actively intervening and fostering committee members' rule adherence. In essence, the trigger mechanism substantially increased the number of hurdles to be cleared in seeking to overturn an Ombudsperson recommendation (Eckert and Biersteker 2012, p. 24). A dissenting committee member would now have to convince all other members that the Ombudsperson recommendation was inappropriate and why the listing was still warranted. As a result, the negative consensus procedure shifted the burden of proof onto the state that favors a continued listing. Hence, the Ombudsperson decision almost predetermined the outcome. The Council members "have recognized that in a case where the Ombudsperson recommends a delisting, it is extremely unlikely that the Committee will reject that conclusion by consensus" (S/2012/968, para. 12; Eckert and Biersteker 2012, p. 37). Thus, this procedure also incentivizes state cooperation, as states seeking to retain listing had to convince the Ombudsperson by supplying information during the process, otherwise delisting would ensue rapidly (S/2012/49, para. 41). Indeed, as a bi-product this procedure has increased the willingness to share such information (S/2012/968, 14).

The considerable number of successful delisting petitions signifies that committee members, including the P5, accepted the Ombudsperson procedure as it became consolidated and standardized (Eckert and Biersteker 2012, p. 15). Up to August 2018, 81 petitions had been filed, and 74 cases had been completed. Following the Ombudsperson's recommendation, the committee delisted 52 individuals and 28 entities (S/2018/579, para. 11). Moreover, the committee delisted three individuals before completion of the Ombudsperson process (S/2018/579, para. 11). While the successful delistings have attracted a flow of petitions (S/2012/729, para. 30), 17 delisting requests have been rejected (one under resolution 1904 (2009)), for all of which the Ombudsperson had recommended continued listing (S/2013/467, para. 34; S/2014/553). The Ombudsperson procedure has become an integral element so that it is "highly unlikely that the Security Council would abolish the Ombudsperson mechanism before it brought the regime as a whole to an end" (S/2012/968, para. 15). This resembles the proponent's view that it will be difficult to scrap a procedure from the regime, which is well-established and works in line with its original objective to ensure that a listing is still warranted (interview with UN member state official, August 2012). The Council restricted the timeframe for providing reasons after retaining a listing or acceding to an Ombudsperson recommendation (What's in Blue 2014c).

Three exemplary cases, which were almost overturned because powerful permanent members objected to the delisting, serve to illustrate the effect (S/2012/968, para. 12, also Eckert and Biersteker 2012). The Saudi Al-Faqih residing in the UK was delisted on July 1, 2012, as the UK, Germany, South Africa and Guatemala rejected overturning the Ombudsperson recommendation because the information provided would not warrant continued listing. According to a diplomat involved, he "may not be a saint but he doesn't belong on this list" (Charbonneau 2012a). This is remarkable as most committee members, including four permanent members, objected to his removal from the list. Reportedly, the non-member Saudi Arabia had exerted heavy pressure on committee members to overturn the recommendation (Eckert and Biersteker 2012, p. 20). Members who have requested additional information from Saudi Arabia had merely been supplied with six pages in Arabic language that showed little connection of Al-Faqih to Al-Qaida (interview with UN member state official, August 2012). After the decision, Al-Faqih was even maintained on the US domestic sanctions list, illustrating the US' opposing views (BBC 2012).

The "Kadi Case" also came very close to a Security Council referral (interview with UN Secretariat official, New York, December 2013). In the past, Kadi had challenged his listing in various countries, before the Al-Qaida Committee (interview with UN member state official, New York, March 2012), and finally petitioned his listing via the Ombudsperson. His listing dates to the time immediately after 9/11. After reviewing the case for more than 10 months, Kadi was delisted upon an Ombudsperson recommendation, because European members refused to overturn it (Charbonneau 2012b; Eckert and Biersteker 2012, p. 20; interview with UN member state official, New York, December 2013). However, a US court maintained that his "listing in the United States was 'amply supported' by both classified and unclassified materials" (S/2012/968, para. 7). Still, he was finally removed from the OFAC list in late 2014 (FR Doc. 2014-28598).

In the Jim'ale case, the committee did not overturn the Ombudsperson recommendation, but collectively listed the individual in the Somalia regime, which is not under the Ombudsperson's purview. The Somali national was listed directly after 9/11 and initiated an Ombudsperson procedure in March 2011. According to his narrative summary, he was "closely linked" to Usama bin Laden and allegedly responsible for the Barakaat network, which had channeled weapons to terrorist supporters and employed 1,000 fighters (on file with author). In February 2012, the committee delisted Jim'ale following a recommendation from the Ombudsperson (Prost 2012b, p. 5). However, on the same day he was re-listed in the Somalia sanctions regime, which employs identical sanctions measures (Eckert and Biersteker 2012, p. 19). In the justification for his re-listing, the Somalia Sanctions Committee stipulates that Jim'ale was the "chief financier" of Al-Shabaab (SC/10545). While Jim'ale allegedly had a relationship with Al-Shabaab, which had been listed on the Somalia sanctions list since 2010, the 1267 committee had not formally associated Al-Shabaab with Al-Qaida. Thus, Jim'ale was listed under the Somalia sanctions regime and, therefore, beyond the reach of the Ombudsperson (interview with UN member state official, August 2012). Even though the Ombudsperson had been circumvented, it shows that rules and committee governance matter.

None of the cases under the Ombudsperson procedure have been referred to the Council, although this option is explicitly provided for (S/2012/590, para. 30, S/2014/73, para. 32). Even though the Security Council retains its role as a political body, overturning the Ombudsperson's ruling via a resolution is unattractive. It is difficult to imagine a situation where a committee member would consider referring a case to the Council unless the member had assurances that it will receive nine votes on a resolution that would overturn the Ombudsperson's judgment. Such a move would politicize an issue of limited scope and reveal committee disagreements, while the member would have to convince the same group of (dissenting) members with sensitive information in a public setting (S/2012/968, para. 12; two separate interviews with UN member state officials, March 2012).

In the absence of delisting criteria, the Ombudsperson also engages in rule-making. Any review procedure presupposes criteria for how cases are to be reviewed and when delisting would ensue. Supporting evidence would then be considered in the light of accepted standards (Kanetake 2008, pp. 168–169). Since the Council has failed to provide criteria to the Ombudsperson, she developed her own negative listing criteria. Accordingly, the Ombudsperson would recommend a delisting if no reliable information could be generated that would warrant a listing at present. The listing request, therefore, has to pass the benchmark of "whether there is sufficient information to provide a reasonable and credible basis for the listing" (Prost and Wilmshurst 2013, pp. 4–5). This standard along with the increasing number of petitions received standardized the process, while the Ombudsperson still had discretion to take the specifics of cases into account (Eckert and Biersteker 2012, p. 15).

Beyond delisting, the Ombudsperson has raised the incentives to provide well-reasoned listing proposals in the first place. Because unreasonable decisions can easily be overturned, the trigger mechanism provides incentives to consider the listing criteria seriously, to offer as much information as possible on a case and to refrain from listing decisions based on political considerations (S/2012/49, para. 39; S/2012/590, paras. 12–13, 31; Prost and Wilmshurst 2013, p. 5). As an ex-ante effect, designating states began to submit listing requests that would withstand an Ombudsperson procedure (interview with UN member state official, March 2012). Designating states rely increasingly on unclassified material to bolster their cases, while keeping other sources confidential (interview with UN member state official, December 2013). Several states including the US, which had been reluctant to share confidential information, have made confidential information sharing "arrangements" with the Ombudsperson (Eckert and Biersteker 2012, pp. 20–21).

The Council–Ombudsperson relationship also exhibits the typical agency slack issues in principal-agent relationships. On the one hand, as the Ombudsperson delisting criteria are de-facto negative listing criteria, Council members have also gained an interest in developing listing criteria that are useful for the Ombudsperson review ex-post (S/2012/968, para. 13). The Ombudsperson has incentives to not overstretch her competences. The prerogative of every committee member to take any petition to the Council provides incentives to provide only well-reasoned recommendations. In addition, because the Council has to extend the mandate and the committee to appoint an Ombudsperson regularly, this provides incentives to align her activities to the long-term interests of committee members rather than the Ombudsperson's own interests. For instance, after the Secretary-General appointed the second Ombudsperson, Catherine Marchi-Uhel, former ICTY Head of Chambers (S/2015/459), as a Head of the Mechanism of the Syria crimes investigation mechanism in July 2017, the Ombudsperson position was vacant until filled by Daniel Kipfer Fasciati in May 2018, due to friction between Russia and other P5 members over the wide-ranging decisions of the Office (SCR Forecast May 2018).

The Ombudsperson review procedure is an intentional principal-agent mechanism and works, as the Council intended, as a strong agenda-setter. In practice, the Ombudsperson takes de-facto delisting decisions on behalf of the committee, even though these could be overturned. The Ombudsperson fosters committee members' adherence to rules without, though, radically shifting committee members' behavior. It complements a well-advanced governance system that commits even the powerful permanent members to their long-term interests in rule-based governance while preserving their principle privileges in decision-making.

Concluding thoughts

The Al-Qaida/Taliban Sanctions Committee is another confirmatory case for my committee governance thesis. While Council members widely supported the sanctions regime as a viable counter-terrorism tool, they disagreed as to who exactly should be added to the sanctions list, as states might misuse the sanctions regime either to criminalize domestic opposition groups or for other geopolitical interests. As a result of this coordination situation, Al-Qaida/Taliban Sanctions

Committee mainly followed the logic of rule-based governance and powerful committee members adhered to rules even if they preferred different outcomes on specific cases. The Al-Qaida sanctions regime, in contrast to the Iraq regime studied in the previous chapter, stands for a case where Council members *intended* to limit unconstrained committee behavior, albeit slowly and hesitantly.

This sanctions regime provides confirmatory evidence for the effects of rule-making; whenever the Council or committee elaborated rules to affect committee decision-making, both faced the expected constraints associated with negotiating a rule-set applicable over a range of cases. These findings are robust in three episodes detailed in this chapter. In the second episode, Council members regulated the committee designation process strictly to overcome the previous laissez-faire approach that had made the regime ineffective and illegitimate. The rules are strikingly consistent and did not favor any powerful member. In the third episode, a stalemate on delisting incentivized skeptical Council members to regulate committee decision-making by means of consistent rules. In a fourth episode, the Council intended to overcome a stalemate on delisting Taliban members by separating a Taliban sanctions regime and supplying a set of abstract reconciliation criteria despite one permanent member hesitating to delist Taliban members.

The Al-Qaida/Taliban sanctions regime strongly confirms hypothesis 1, which holds that if committee members process proposals of limited scope separately, they abide by criteria and rules, even if these contradict the short-term preferences of some members. The effect is robust in three episodes. The second episode shows that separately processing designation requests and the increasingly dense set of criteria allowed committee members to reject unsubstantiated requests and transformed the committee listing process toward rule-based governance. In the third episode, delisting criteria and procedures enabled committee members to delist unwarranted entries, while additional self-regulation restricted the committee member's discretion to dilute decisions through using holds excessively. Remarkably, the last episode on Taliban delisting decisions shows that even powerful committee members abided by Taliban delisting rules after splitting the committee.

The Al-Qaida/Taliban sanctions regime yields three additional and intriguing insights. First, the regime's early phase is a "rather unusual period" (Biersteker 2010, p. 88). After 9/11, the committee listed numerous suspected Al-Qaida associates neither prompting stalemate nor rule-based governance. Instead, committee members took a laissez-faire approach and adopted all requests regardless of their merits. However, the rapidly growing sanctions list without clear evidence tainted implementation and the willingness of non-committee members to cooperate. This finding demonstrates that sanctions committee members' adherence to rules relies on a conflict of interests among Council members and their willingness to scrutinize requests. Only such a conflict prompts the reasonable prospect of stalemate, which in turn incentivizes rule-based committee governance as an alternative. Indeed, this mutual control was then observed in later stages. Second, the splitting of the Taliban sanctions regime shows that the committee cannot treat two entirely different types of sanctions targets with the same set of criteria. As the Taliban disassociated from Al-Qaida over time, it became difficult for the committee to decide on the Taliban entries because rules regarded the Taliban as a terrorist organization, not a political actor in Afghanistan. Accordingly, the Council split the regime and provided separate reconciliation criteria for Taliban members. The episode illustrates that separating the Taliban from the Al-Qaida regime, both operating under specific rules, altered committee behavior completely, although the same group of states still takes all the decisions. Third, the effects of committee governance occurred even before the Council installed the Ombudsperson. Although being a strong agenda setter and eventually overturning committee decisions, the mechanism only slightly alters the committee situation. Instead of unwarranted decisions, which the Ombudsperson could easily overturn, committee members are incentivized to accept rule-conforming at the outset. From a theoretical perspective, the position of Ombudsperson demonstrates that an independent agent *can* foster rule-based governance, but this is hardly surprising given its role. As other episodes have shown, the effects of committee governance occur even if the same group of states takes all decisions; however, this does not rule out the possibility that committee members could use their committee veto. Hence, the Ombudsperson mechanism may be better understood as additionally safeguarding rule-based governance.

The Al-Qaida/Taliban sanctions regime case is well-suited for evaluating the due process debate's claims that a sanctions committee inevitably follows power politics or that only external review would affect decision-making systematically, from the perspective of committee governance. While the attention by states, courts and activists certainly highlighted the reform's urgency, the case is entirely comparable to other sanctions regimes as the Council separated rule-making from making numerous implementation decisions. The findings suggest that committee governance is a means of bringing Council rules, and committee behavior better in line with fundamental rule of law principles; following rules enables stalemate to be overcome, avoids laissez-faire, and eventually realizes the Council's long-term objectives. Empirical evidence does not support the rival thesis, which holds that the constellation among powerful states can explain all decisions taken. Neither do powerful members abuse rule-making to insert one-sided exceptions, and nor do I find evidence for package deals or side payments as an alternative account.

6 The Democratic Republic of the Congo

Targeted sanctions and civil war

Civil war in the Democratic Republic of the Congo (DRC) is one of the worst humanitarian crises in the modern era and has caused untold suffering. Since the end of the Cold War, the DRC has witnessed three wars that go back to the 1994 Rwandan genocide and the country continues to be plagued by conflict, mainly in the Eastern Kivu provinces. In the second Congo war ("Africa's World War," Prunier 2009), Rwanda, Burundi and Uganda, sought to replace president Kabila by backing Congolese rebel militias resulting in one of the deadliest African conflicts, prompting Angola, Namibia and Zimbabwe to intervene on the government's side. The conflict parties finally agreed to a peace deal, the Pretoria Agreement, in 2002. However, after foreign troops had withdrawn, many areas particularly in Eastern Congo were left in a power vacuum. This vacuum led to the onset of a conflict emerging from latent local, regional and international interlocking struggles, which the Congolese army and an entire range of non-state armed groups have been fighting over ever since. The Congolese military's inability to control the territory effectively and reintegrate former combatants has resulted in all sides contributing to massive displacement, looting, grave atrocities against civilians, rape, torture and the recruitment of child soldiers. Right up to the present time, DRC's richness in natural resources and their illegal exploitation continues to finance rebel groups and fuel the conflict. Furthermore, DRC's neighbors are guilty of constant intervention, mainly through supporting armed groups in their fight against the army or opposing other armed groups (Soderlund 2012, pp. 1–18; Carayannis 2013).

In response to the brutal civil war and atrocities, ahead of sanctions being included on the Security Council agenda, the Council's deployment of military observers (resolution 1258 (1999)) was later transformed into one of the largest UN peacekeeping missions to date (MONUC, later MONUSCO). In 2000, the Council established a Panel of Experts on natural resources, who suggested imposing targeted sanctions on those who maintained armed groups by illegally extracting revenue from natural resources (S/2001/1072, para. 160, S/2002/1146, para. 176). In July 2003, concerned about the massive violations of human rights and humanitarian law in Eastern DRC, the Council finally imposed an arms embargo on armed groups in Eastern DRC to support the peace process and the disarmament of militias (resolution 1493 (2003), paras. 20, 21). Months later, the Council created a sanctions committee to monitor the arms embargo and devise a way forward; it also set up a Group of Experts to track down arms embargo violations and determine who carried responsibility for arms trafficking (resolution 1533 (2004), paras. 8–10). However, these measures were ineffective. Thus, in April 2005, the Council expanded its arms embargo to the entire DRC, excluding UN peacekeepers and integrated DRC army units (resolution 1596 (2005), paras. 1–2), imposing a travel ban and assets freeze on individuals together with entities that violated the arms embargo as listed by the committee (paras. 13–16). Since then, the Council has regularly extended and refined the sanctions regime designed with a sunset clause.

To date, scholars dealing with Security Council sanctions regimes cannot account for why the DRC Committee should have followed rules instead of power politics. Indeed, the DRC Committee has largely been ignored in the sanctions (committee) literature, even though it is quite an active committee and a fascinating case. So how exactly did the transfer of decisions by the Council to the same group of states in committee affect the decision-making dynamics and quality of decisions? The concept of committee governance helps us to delve into these issues and account for why rules mattered, as well as explaining why the powerful permanent members followed them. Furthermore, Rwanda's Council membership in 2013–2014 is an example not only of how Council members anticipate a committee stalemate, but also how they deal with seemingly obstructionist members through rules and early decisions.

The DRC sanctions regime complements the analysis with a targeted sanctions regime that received almost no attention in the literature (in contrast to, for instance, Liberia or Côte d'Ivoire). This is surprising as it is an excellent research object because of its comparatively large sanctions list and the creation of substantial political conflict involving the US, France and the UK but not between the P3 and Russia and China. Even though the lack of attention complicates data generation, this case study is to a large degree based on diplomatic cables available online to illuminate committee effects. As key to this book's purpose, the DRC case provides an intriguing comparative perspective: It prevents us from prematurely concluding that the dense regulation of committee decision-making can be explained entirely by pressure from scholars, human rights activists, states, and courts to ensure due process, almost exclusively exerted in the Al-Qaida/Taliban sanctions regime's context. Because such public pressure was absent in the DRC sanctions regime, finding the effect of committee governance in this case underscores its merits in light of a widely-held alternative explanation.

The next section describes the political origins of the DRC sanctions regime, considers differences between France, the UK and the US, looks at who drives the sanctions regime and what this means for committee governance. To evaluate the merits of the committee governance thesis, I trace two case episodes detailing how the committee settled upon the sanctions implementation concerning its key task of deciding about which individuals and entities should be subjected to targeted sanctions. I also focus on how the committee solves clashes of interest and look at the impact of rules on committee decision-making. The third section, from the perspective of Rwanda as a country directly involved in the civil war in Eastern DRC, then examines how its Council membership in 2013–2014 affected the committee and how Council members preventively regulate committee procedures to overcome anticipated future deadlock. The last section summarizes the main findings in light of the committee governance thesis.

The political origins of the Democratic Republic of the Congo sanctions regime

The proliferation of non-state armed groups, local militias and their splinter groups, which fight over territory, natural resources and influence, features heavily in the DRC conflict. We can distinguish roughly four groups of conflict parties (though groups might appear, merge, split or vanish and allegiances may change over time). The first is made up of groups with an agenda vis-à-vis Rwanda. This includes the *Forces Démocratiques de Libération du Rwanda* (FDLR) and splinter groups (e.g., *Ralliement pour l'Unité et la Démocratie* (RUD-Urunana)), formed by Rwandan members of the government ousted in 1994 who seek regime change in Rwanda. However, the *Mouvement du 23 Mars* (M23) and the *l'Union des Patriotes Congolais* (UPC) seek to counter the FDLR presence in Eastern Congo. The second are groups with an origin in Uganda. For instance, the *Allied Democratic Forces* (ADF) began as a Uganda-focused rebel group with Islamist tendencies. The third group comprises a range of purely domestic groups, some with foreign lines of support, for instance the *Kamwina Nsapu* in the Kasaïs, the *Forces de Résistance Patriotique d'Ituri* (FRPI), or other *Mayi Mayi* in the Kivus. Many of these groups are genuinely interested in economic benefits from natural resource exploitation. Political agendas are heralded publicly, but are mostly of a secondary interest (the FDLR probably having the strongest political claim). The fourth conflict party is the Congolese military *Forces Armées de la République Démocratique du Congo* (FARDC) and its allies, some of which are also associated with armed groups, including FARDC officers indicted for collaborating with FDLR, and with ADF (For an overview of non-state armed groups, see Monusco 2018; Armed Conflict Location & Event Data Project 2014; Prunier 2009).

In contrast to the Council, members of the DRC Sanctions Committee found themselves to be regulatory decision-makers. Beyond its monitoring functions, the committee's major task has been to determine individuals and entities facing targeted sanctions, updating the list and deciding about exemptions when requested (Farrall 2007, pp. 416–417). At this point, instead of larger political questions surrounding the Congo conflict, committee members had to focus on many small decisions of a technical nature, without which the targeted sanctions would have little impact. The committee had to take an active role in listing individuals and entities by consensus, while inaction would have been tantamount to presenting a targeted sanctions regime without targets. But who exactly should be placed on the sanctions list to face sanctions and who should be omitted? Why should a certain individual be on the list (and not another)?

Council members' interests did not clash along usual lines, the P3 opposing Russia and China, but instead among France, the UK and US, all of which favored sanctions, albeit on different targets (interview with UN member state official, December 2013, New York). France, due to its historic commitment toward Francophone African countries, positioned itself as the leader on DRC, lobbied for stepping up Council efforts and drafted resolutions on DRC (Agence France Presse 2005; SCR Update Report 2005). Thus, the French had a strong geostrategic and ideological interest in the Francophone DRC, contributed military units to stabilize the country (Annan 2012, p. 117), and donated significant development aid aimed toward supporting the DRC government. With the Hutu regime's collapse in Kigali, France lost a French-speaking ally and as a result, experienced strained relations with the Rwandan leadership over accusations of supporting the previous government. Hence, eager to protect its zone of influence against Anglophone expansion, France was responsive to the DRC's government, and inclined to use sanctions against foreign-supported militias opposing the government (Gegout 2009, 236, 239–242; Doyle 2004, p. 89). However, following failure to stop the Rwandan genocide, the UK developed closer ties with the post-genocide Anglophone Rwandan government. It also tended to support its former colony Uganda. Accordingly, the UK was more sensitive toward Rwandan and Ugandan concerns and sanctioning the anti-Rwandan and anti-Ugandan groups, such as the FDLR or ADF. The US took a modest position in-between the two (Doyle 2004, p. 89; Gegout 2009, p. 236).

China and Russia were mostly indifferent or cautiously skeptical toward sanctions. Although China was largely dismissive of sanctions and interference in sovereign states' domestic affairs (for instance, SC/7057), it did nevertheless have stakes in the mining sector within the resource-rich but conflict-prone Eastern DRC. As Curtis notes, "China's economic involvement in Africa [made] it sensitive to instability" (2013, p. 559). Hence, China tended toward supporting the DRC government, which included provision of military aid and contributions to peacekeeping operations (Holslag 2009; US Embassy Kinshasa 2005b). Russia seemed fairly indifferent toward the DRC conflict, but cautioned against adopting "hasty decisions based on emotions" (SC/7057). Some elected European members, including Belgium as a former colonial power, have had traditional interests in the conflict and pushed for Council involvement, to the extent of authorizing EU missions (Gegout 2009, p. 236). Colombia and Mauritius as non-aligned members remained skeptical about imposing sanctions (SC/7057).

Even though the "Council has been divided over implementing targeted sanctions" (SCR Forecast November 2005a), and despite interest in this sanctions regime being less pronounced than others, committee members shared a common interest in avoiding committee stalemate. The Council members did have an interest in doing something about the DRC conflict, but at the same time they had no appetite for another military adventure after Afghanistan and Iraq, preferring a UN peacekeeping operation for managing the conflict (Carayannis 2013). The P5 agreed to keep the costs in check, opting for stability over interventionism. Thus, a working sanctions regime provided a means for the P3 and other interested states to address the conflict with limited costs (SCR Forecast June 2006a; SCR Forecast December 2006).

Due to the rotation of African non-permanent seats (Security Council Report 2014, pp. 6–7), the DRC Sanctions Committee repeatedly had to deal with members, which are also DRC's neighbors and economically, militarily or politically involved (Turner 2013, pp. 46–73). In this context, Rwanda is noteworthy as having direct security concerns in the DRC, linked to the Hutu rebels opposing the Kigali government (mainly the FDLR) and has been continually seeking to expand its influence in the DRC (SCR Update Report 2005). Rwanda served as a non-permanent member in 2013–2014 and its long-term, direct and "active role" in the conflict has been widely documented (Security Council Report 2012a, p. 5, Group of Experts reports e.g., S/2012/348.Add1; S/2012/843). Hence, it had great stakes not only in the conflict but accordingly also how the committee implemented the sanctions regime. Additionally, over recent times several other "problematic" member states have served on the committee: Angola in 2003–2004 and 2015–2016, Republic of Congo (*sic*!) in 2006–2007, both of which have been siding with the DRC government (Cassimon *et al.* 2013, p. 57), as well as Uganda in 2009–2010, which has been supporting DRC rebel militias since the second Congo war (Prunier 2009, pp. 293–294; S/2001/357; S/2012/843). Ugandan security concerns related to Lord's Resistance Army (LRA) activities and those of the ADF, which started in Uganda with some extremist tendencies (SCR Update Report 2005).

Due to the clash of political interests among the P3, I would expect that committee governance has a distinct effect on committee decision-making. While the P3 agreed on the virtue of a DRC sanction regime, China and Russia were at least indifferent about the proposal. Yet, France, the UK and the US preferred different outcomes within the sanctions regime and were thus likely to face coordination problems. Accordingly, recourse to rules or precedents as focal points could help coordinate and forge agreement among the P3 on how to implement sanctions in the committee. Indeed, this would lead us to expect that the committee followed rules; hence, committee decisions could hardly be explained by the logic of power politics.

With respect to targeted sanctions, the Council provided a first set of criteria, but fixed only rudimentary procedures for the committee and in broad terms mandated the committee to monitor the arms embargo and "take appropriate action on (…) alleged violations [thereof]" (resolution 1533 (2004), para. 8). As regards criteria, the Council delivered an initial designation criterion: individuals and entities "as acting in violation of the [arms embargo]" (resolution 1596 (2005), para. 13). Listed individuals could be exempted from the travel ban in case of "humanitarian need, including religious obligation, or where the Committee concludes that an exemption would further the objectives of the Council's resolutions" (para. 14). Assets freeze exemptions were foreseen for "basic expenses" in the absence of a negative committee decision and for "extraordinary expenses" subject to committee approval (para. 16). Concerning procedures, the Council simply mandated the committee to "designate persons and entities (…) and regularly to update its list" (para. 18a), decide upon exemptions (para. 18d), but left the specifics and required level of evidence up to the committee. To that end, the committee should adopt guidelines "as may be necessary to facilitate implementation [of sanctions measures]" (para. 18e).

Targeting individuals and entities: No listing without procedures

The first episode illustrates that, despite elaboration in another sanctions committee, procedures helped committee members to overcome a stalemate on initial listings. In effect, because the committee could not agree on its own guidelines, it could not list targets for the Council's travel ban and assets freeze. In response, the committee used an external focal point, namely a section of the Côte d'Ivoire guidelines, as a set of preliminary rules to process listing requests. Thereafter, proactive committee members aligned prospective designations to the criteria and procedures before deliberating about the viability of listing requests. With the necessary processes in place, the committee members then adopted a first set of individuals and entities that would be subject to sanctions in line with the listing criteria.

However, while the Council resolutions provided clear listing criteria, the exact listing procedure for the committee was left open. Resolution 1596 (2005) stipulated that "(…) all persons designated by the Committee as acting in violation of the [arms embargo] (…)" should be subject to a travel ban and assets freeze. This included the "financing and financial assistance related to military activities" (1596 (2005), para. 1) together with "provision of any assistance (…) to all foreign and Congolese armed groups and militias" (resolution 1493 (2004), para. 13). Previously, the Group of Experts had supplied abundant information on such alleged violations that would merit early designations (S/2004/551; S/2005/30; S/2005/436). However, precisely how a listing should commence in the committee had not yet been determined. In the meantime, after a final deadline for conflict parties to comply with demands had passed, the Council extended the sanctions regime by 12 months in July 2005 (resolution 1616 (2005)).

Although the P3 were gathering listing requests, the committee could not sanction any individuals because its members first had to negotiate a listing procedure (SCR Forecast November 2005a). However, the committee's adoption of such guidelines was problematic. Although the Council had created this committee in 2004, it took until 2010 finally to agree on internal procedures, but only after the Council had directed the committee "[t]o promulgate guidelines (…) within six months" (resolution 1896 (2009), para. 4a). The committee members discussed different draft versions of its guidelines over a number of years. Nevertheless, consensus was not forthcoming, with the result that eventually no guidelines could be adopted (S/2008/17, para. 28). Almost four months after targeted sanctions had been imposed, on August 9, 2005 during an informal meeting the committee considered a set of "draft procedures for establishing and maintaining a list of individuals and entities subject to [targeted sanctions]." However, as it was unable to agree on those draft procedures, the committee approved the "temporary use" of the Côte d'Ivoire Committee guidelines "for establishing its list" (S/2006/54, para. 12).

The Côte d'Ivoire sanctions committee rules of procedures proved to be a useful precedent for several reasons and acted as the focal point on issues of disagreement. The same group of Council members had decided about those rules, albeit in a different committee. The Côte d'Ivoire sanctions regime also addressed the matter of civil war in a Francophone West African state and thus applied similar sanctions measures (arms embargo, targeted sanctions, later diamond sanctions) (Farrall 2007, pp. 439–447). At the time, its guidelines were the most recent and elaborate of all committees.[1] While other sanctions committees' guidelines were outdated or nonexistent, the Côte d'Ivoire sanctions committee had only recently established its rules of procedures on June 13, 2005. These guidelines were even slightly more detailed than the Al-Qaida/Taliban Committee guidelines (on file with author). In fact, the Côte d'Ivoire guidelines themselves had also been quite contentious, mainly because of a disagreement among the P5 over the timing and suitability of sanctions (Security Council Report 2005; Security Council Report 2006). The guidelines had been adopted only after "extensive discussions during various Committee meetings" (S/2006/55, para. 13). Yet, the DRC Committee could simply accept as precedent these guidelines previously adopted by consensus among the same group of states, because they provided a way out of the disagreement which had hitherto been hampering committee action.

Criteria and procedures conform to the logic of rule-making in committee governance. The rules do not favor any party to the conflict and therefore any actor violating the arms embargo could be subject to targeted sanctions irrespective of allegiances. This included the exploitation of natural resources in rebel-held areas if it financed arms trafficking. In specific terms, the Côte d'Ivoire guidelines stipulated that the committee should decide by consensus on a listing proposal (para. 8a) under a no-objection procedure within two days of receiving a request (para. 9a). Concerning the format, the guidelines specified that UN member states must submit a listing proposal in writing (para. 9a) and should provide a "narrative description of the information that justifies how that individual or entity fits within the [decision criteria]" (para. 8b). Furthermore, designating states should provide "to the greatest extent possible, relevant, specific and up-to-date" identifying information (para. 8c). Finally, changes to the list should be published in a committee press release (para. 8e).

After the committee had agreed on draft procedures for listing, the P3 decided to propose a first list of designees (SCR Forecast November 2005a) and finally pursued those requests that best fitted the listing criteria. A US cable from its Kinshasa embassy shows that the P3 carefully scrutinized the lists and dropped at least one individual. The US was concerned about listing this particular person "unless there [was] viable evidence (...) demonstrating his involvement with illegal arms trafficking," in other words, the listing criterion. The US further noted that having "a government official on the list based on nothing more than rumors would risk undermining the credibility of the sanctions program" (US Embassy Kinshasa 2005a).

The P3 proposed to designate 15 individuals and one entity for the sanctions list, which the committee subsequently adopted by consensus on November 1, 2005. The individuals were all associated with major rebel groups operating in Eastern DRC, including Rwandan and/or Ugandan supported factions (Frank Bwambale, RCD-ML leader; Germain Katanga, FRPI chief, now General in FARDC; Jérôme Kakwavu, Former President of UCD/FAPC, now General in FARDC; Kawa Panga Mandro, PUSIC Ex-President; and Laurent Nkunda, Former RCD-G General), anti-Rwandan/anti-Ugandan militias (Bosco Ntaganda, UPC/L military commander; Thomas Lubanga, UPC/L President; Sylvestre Mudacumura, FDLR Commander; Ignace Murwanashyaka, FDLR President; Matthieu Ngudjolo, FNI Chief of Staff; and Floribert Ngabu, FNI President) and other individuals and entities implicated in arms embargo violations (Jules Mutebusi, Former FARDC Deputy Regional Commander; James Nyakuni, weapons trader; Ozia Mazio, President Fédération des Enterprises du Congo in Aru Territory, providing financial assistance to FAPC rebels; Douglas Mpano, Manager of Compagnie Aérienne des Grands Lacs, weapons airlifts; Tous pour la Paix et le Développment, supplying trucks to RCD-G for arms smuggling). The list includes mostly DRC, but also Rwandan and Ugandan nationals.

The successful requests provide reason to believe that committee members decided according to rules. While a package deal cannot be ruled out as an alternative explanation in principle, it is nevertheless unlikely. Each listing request makes an explicit link to the listing criterion: violation of the arms embargo. All designations also justify why the individuals have met the listing criteria. So the committee designated six individuals as having been involved with weapons transfers in violation of the arms embargo, seven individuals for commanding a rebel group violating the arms embargo and two individuals as well as one entity for "provision of assistance" in violating the arms embargo (SC/8546, BBC 2005). Furthermore, for seven individuals and the entity arms embargo violations had been documented by the Group of Experts (S/2004/551; S/2005/30, S/2005/436).

These events all conform to the logic of committee governance. Even though the Council supplied the committee with criteria, the members could not process listing requests without first adopting committee guidelines, which in itself produced a struggle. By way of a solution, the committee accepted the Côte d'Ivoire guidelines' relevant listing section as precedent on a temporary basis. Thereafter, committee members aligned their proposals to listing criteria in order to submit successful decision requests. At least one non-conforming request had previously been rejected. All designations resembled the listing criteria and justified how each met the criteria.

Decision rules provide focal points for listing requests among the P3

This episode of listing proposals following the 2006 DRC elections illustrates that new designation criteria served as a focal point in overcoming diverging interests among the powerful P3. At Council level, defining decision criteria was subject to a consistency requirement. On the committee level, the proactive members wishing to submit successful listing requests needed to assemble convincing listing proposals carefully. Although these states principally wanted sanctions imposed, they rigorously ensured that each individual being proposed not only separately conformed to the designation criteria, but also fulfilled informal evidentiary standards, usually two sources of evidence. Five batches of listing requests demonstrate that committee governance indeed prompts rule-based decisions. As part of a detailed screening process among proactive members, below-threshold requests were out-sorted and rejected, whereas above-threshold requests were accepted. Even powerful states had to provide convincing arguments to garner support for committee decisions.

At this stage, Council members widely supported the sanctions regime and new designations of commanders from non-state armed groups in the DRC (SCR Forecast July 2006); yet, there were some marked differences on the specifics. Whereas the UK was leaning toward supporting Rwanda, France tended to support the DRC government (see Doyle 2004). In this phase of proceedings, Council members France, the UK and Tanzania were particularly concerned about the lack of progress in disarming foreign militias. Accordingly, they suggested new targeted sanctions against political and military leaders of foreign armed groups (SCR Forecast June 2006a). Earlier, Burundi, the DRC, Uganda and Rwanda, despite tensions among them, had called upon the Council to impose sanctions on rebel leaders (Agence France Presse 2006b).

Even though sanctions had already been extended well into July 2006, seven months earlier the Council had adopted resolution 1649 (2005) to "tighten sanctions against those armed groups" and refined the designation criteria (SCR Update Report 2005; Deutsche Presse Agentur 2005). In the wake of a French-led Council mission to the Great Lakes region, the Council concluded that it "needs to take a firmer line against the remaining armed groups." The resolution was not particularly contentious, despite some Algerian, Chinese and Russian skepticism toward sanctions. The DRC together with Burundi, Uganda and Rwanda also supported this initiative, yet with different objectives in mind (SCR Update Report 2005). The Council unanimously extended the listing criteria to "political and military leaders of foreign armed groups" in the DRC "who impede the disarmament and the voluntary repatriation or resettlement of combatants belonging to those groups" and "political and military leaders of Congolese militias receiving support from outside" the DRC; in particular, the new listing included those "who impede (…) disarmament, demobilization and reintegration processes" (resolution 1649 (2005), para. 2ab).

Reflecting on the Council's thematic agendas to do with "Children and Armed Conflict" and the "Protection of Civilians in Armed Conflict," the Council also added human rights violations to the criteria that might warrant an individual being listed (Security Council Report 2016, pp. 13–14). In July 2006, Council members unanimously extended the sanctions and the listing criteria still further to include "[p]olitical and military leaders recruiting or using children in armed conflict" and "[i]ndividuals committing serious violations of international law involving the targeting of children in situations of armed conflict, including killing and maiming, sexual violence, abduction and forced displacement" (resolution 1698 (2006), para. 13). The Council tasked the committee with listing individuals who fulfilled these criteria (1649 (2005), para. 4, 1698 (2006), para. 14), and also directed the Group of Experts to assist committee members in designating individuals (1698 (2006), para. 5h). Additionally, more detailed recommendations on natural resources' exploitation were requested (para. 6). On March 13, 2008, responding to the ongoing violence from FDLR and other armed groups refusing to join the peace process, the Council adopted resolution 1804 (2008) on the FDLR. The Council demanded that all such groups disarm, stop recruiting children and cease all forms of gender-based violence. It reaffirmed that "leaders of the FDLR, ex-FAR/Interahamwe and other Rwandan armed groups" met the sanctions designation criteria (Agence France Presse 2008b).

As the committee governance thesis leads us to expect, the amended criteria confirm the expected consistency requirement. The listing criteria neither one-sidedly favor the French nor the British position on conflict parties. Hence, any political or military leader of any conflict party engaging in violations or refusing to disarm could be designated for inclusion on the sanctions list. This would include the FDLR, but also a range of other armed groups. Resolution 1807 (2008) consolidated previously existing listing criteria into one single paragraph shortly afterwards (para. 13).

All five subsequent listing initiatives until late 2012 demonstrate that proactive members aligned their proposals to rules as focal points to overcome coordination situations; the committee then ultimately decided according to those rules. As a first listing initiative following resolution 1649 (2005), the UK and France considered adding names based on the annexes from Groups of Experts' reports (S/2006/1048, para. 21; Bolton 2006b). In May 2006, the UK circulated a first rudimentary proposal of 35 potential targets belonging to several rebel militias: 24 individuals were associated with the anti-Rwandan FDLR, together with its splinters and off-shoots, 4 with the Congolese Revolutionary Movement (MRC) expelled from Uganda, 3 with the Mayi Mayi allegedly supporting the FDLR or the Burundi rebel group FNL, and 4 other combating MONUC and FARDC forces (Bolton 2006a).

However, the UK did not pursue this listing request further for two reasons. First, the proposal provided insufficient information to be successful. The listing request did not establish why particular individuals should be listed and also lacked enough identifying information on the large majority of those included

(Bolton 2006a). Second, because of the fragile situation surrounding the 2006 DRC elections, the P3 deferred their sanctions initiative until early 2007. For now, Council members focused on safeguarding the electoral process through MONUC and EUFOR missions, as well as managing post-electoral violence, allegations of rigging, and a post-electoral MONUC draw-down due to budgetary concerns (SCR Forecast July 2006; SCR Forecast September 2006).

Internally, the P3 continued to exchange detailed arguments about who should be listed and for what reasons. All such proposals were based on the understanding that a convincing P3 proposal, which fitted the designation criteria, would be elaborated to prevent blocking by other P3 members (Bolton 2006a; Bolton 2006b). Notably, the UK crafted a new, different and much shorter proposal based on listing recommendations in the Group of Experts report from June 2006. The UK considered that enough condemning evidence had been amassed on two individuals (Kambale Kisoni, Omar Oria), and two entities (Uganda Commercial Impex (UCI), Machanga Ltd.). The UK argued that Kisoni:

> is referred to in the Group's confidential annex as "an economic proxy of the FNI," and the Group had documented his role in militia-financing gold trading (buying from the FNI and selling to UCI) in their report S/2005/30 paras. 127–130.
>
> (Bolton 2006b)

In addition, the UK noted that the Human Rights Watch (HRW) report "Curse of Gold":

> supports these allegations, and also refers to the use of Kisoni's aeroplanes to fly in military supplies to the FNI. It is our view that Kisoni's support of the FNI constitutes "provision of assistance" to illegal armed groups, in breach of the arms embargo.
>
> (Bolton 2006b)

The UK also considered Omar Oria eligible for designation "for the same reasons as described above for Dr. Kisoni," but without any evidence to show how Omar Oria matched the listing criteria (Bolton 2006b).

The UK also believed:

> the Group of Experts' claim that UCI has bought from gold traders in the DRC who have financed illegal armed groups in the DRC is well-founded. This was well-documented in the Human Rights Watch (HRW) report "The Curse of Gold" (2005), as well as the Groups' own reports. We consider this to constitute "provision of assistance" to illegal armed groups, in breach of the arms embargo as per [paragraph] 18 of SCR 1493 and [paragraph] 1 of SCR 1596.
>
> (Bolton 2006b)

Concerning Machanga, the UK maintained that it:

> is documented as having bought from Ozia Mazio (now himself listed) in the Group of Experts report S/2005/30 (paras. 116–126) and from Omar Oria in the HRW "Curse of Gold" report. Both (…) are collaborators and financial backers of Commandant Jerome and his FAPC illegal armed group. Listing Machanga would not only be consistent with listing UCI; it would increase the effectiveness of the measures.
>
> (Bolton 2006b)

The UK immediately argued strongly against listing Modeste Makabuza and two entities, Hussar/Hussar Services, a British company, and Argor-Hereaus, a Swiss company. It was stressed that these entities had already changed their behavior as a result of public criticism and had cooperated with the Group of Experts (Bolton 2006b; see also Carisch 2014, p. 55). Regarding Modeste Makabuza, the UK considered his "provision of assistance to 'men from Nkunda's group' in December [20]05 to be in breach of the embargo to which targeted sanctions might be an appropriate response (…)." However, the UK argued against listing because:

> the Group of Experts quotes only one source (Colonel Kasikila) to support this allegation. We believe Kasikila is a fundamentally unreliable source, particularly since he is likely to view Makabuza as a rival in the mining business. We have not been able to confirm this allegation from any other sources ourselves.
>
> (Bolton 2006b)

To achieve consensus, the P3 dropped inadequately supported or outdated requests (Omar Oria, Modeste Makabuza, Hussar/Hussar and Argor-Hereaus), and further fleshed out reports on those who they considered best fitted the criteria as focal points and against whom they had convincing evidence. They also added three entities and an individual: Butembo Airlines, directed by Kisoni, was implicated in gold smuggling and financing arms embargo violations (S/2005/30, paras. 127–130); Congocom Tradinghouse is a gold trading entity owned by Kisoni (van Woudenberg 2005); The cargo airline Great Lakes Business Company, owned by the previously listed Douglas Mpano, was implicated for using its aircraft to transfer weapons in violation of the arms embargo (S/2005/30, para. 144, S/2006/53, paras. 154–155). In addition, the P3 added Straton Musoni, both because of his role as leader of FDLR, and for his association with the already listed Ignace Murwanashyaka, thus fulfilling the designation criteria of resolution 1649 (2005).

In December 2006, following DRC elections, the P3 presented these two individuals and five entities to the sanctions committee (US Permanent Mission to the UN 2007k; SCR Forecast December 2006). Before introducing these requests, the P3 asked for the support of other members arguing that the individuals and entities "(…) have been involved in violations of the weapons embargo, in gold trade with rebel groups and have otherwise played a role in undermining stability in the DROC," all sanctionable acts under the relevant resolutions (US Embassy Beijing 2007b). Accordingly, the committee added two individuals (Straton Musoni, FDLR leader; Kisoni Kambale, gold trading and financing of FNI illegal armed group) and five entities (UCI and Machanga Ltd., gold trade linked to militias constituting "provision of assistance" in violation of arms embargo; Butembo Airlines, gold and arms smuggling; Congocom Tradinghouse, owned by Kisoni, gold trade linked to militias constituting "provision of assistance" in violation of arms embargo; Great Lakes Business Company, transport of arms) to its sanctions list on March 29, 2007 (SC/8987).

The first listing initiative suggests that committee members decided in line with the listing criteria. Again, a package deal was unlikely. In fact, sanctions proponents explicitly aligned their requests to the designation criteria of resolutions 1596 (2004) and 1649 (2005). Furthermore, besides FDLR leader Musoni, all the designated individuals and entities had also been mentioned for violations in earlier Group of Experts reports (S/2005/30; S/2006/53). The P3 then dropped inadequately supported requests and ultimately pursued only those for which they had assembled well-documented evidence. Additionally, they provided arguments for why a particular individual or entity should be included and why others should be dropped.

As a second listing initiative on May 15, 2008, the conflict-party Rwanda sent a list of 19 individuals for designation to the committee (S/2010/93, p. 2). The list named solely certain individuals who were associated with the FDLR rebel group, an adversary of the Rwandan government which conflicted with its interests in Eastern DRC. Belgium, France and the US instantly placed holds on the Rwandan request "in order to evaluate the information available for each proposed target" (US State Department 2008d). Even the UK, which tended to be sympathetic to Rwandan concerns and had pursued FDLR sanctions before, placed a hold (SCR Forecast May 2010). The four Western states realized that the list lacked even basic identifiers such as date of birth, full (correct) names and aliases as well as additional essential information on location, nationality, passport numbers, among other details, which clearly did not conform with requirements set out in the committee guidelines (Côte d'Ivoire guidelines Apr 2007, para. 8c; US State Department 2008d). More importantly, the listing requests fell short of explaining how "each individual meets the listing criteria" (US State Department 2008a).

Although the P3 and Belgium supported new sanctions in principle, they carefully screened each suggestion to check whether or not the sanctions committee's requirements had been met both in informational and evidentiary respects (US Embassy Paris 2008). Early in August 2008, because the P3 did not support the listings in their current form, the US, together with France, UK and Belgium initiated new listings including some of the rudimentary Rwandan suggestions. While the UK welcomed this initiative, the French were hesitant. Because the US expected disagreements even among its "allies," it asked for potential designations to be kept within the group of "like-minded Council members" initially to avoid "public disagreements in the sanctions committees" (US State Department 2008d). On June 5, 2008, the US circulated a list of eight "primary" targets, for which the "preliminary assessment of the evidence available to the (…) [US Government] indicates that there may be sufficient available information to designate these individuals" (US State Department 2008a), inviting the allies to contribute information if possible. While dropping one entry, for which no information on any current involvement with FDLR was available, the US incorporated additional British, French, Belgium and Rwandan information within the seven remaining targets. The US also added eight other individuals as potential targets, for whom identifiers did not yet exist (US State Department 2008c). The State Department requested the US embassy in Kigali to seek provision of further information such as basic identifiers from the Rwandan authorities. The State Department highlighted that for successful designation "[p]ersons or entities proposed for listing must meet one or more of the listing criteria from operative paragraph 13 of UNSC resolution 1807 (2008)" (US State Department 2008c).

Following this information gathering phase, the proactive members decided to pursue only those listings, which best fulfilled the evidentiary standards and informational requirements as a focal point, so as to place successful requests. Belgium, France, the US and UK began exchanging arguments on who should be designated and for whom more information would be required to meet committee standards. After France had voiced concerns about listings that were backed up by only one information source, in this case Rwanda, the initial list was split into "two potential tiers": *Tier one* included six names "for which our governments have significant information," and *tier two* consisted of eight names, albeit with incomplete information (US State Department 2008d). While the UK signaled support for five *tier one* names (US Embassy London 2008), in October 2008 two names from *tier one* were transferred to *tier two*. The first entry on the listing, an individual, was removed as it had less information compared with other *tier one* requests. For the second individual, the UK and France requested more information and Belgium believed that "the information available on Hakizimana does not confirm that the individual currently meets the designation criteria" (US Permanent Mission to the UN 2008c). Based on discussions, the US created four listing requests from the information each carrying identifying details and a listing justification ("evidentiary package"). Before submission, the UK expressed a strong preference for inclusion of explicit references, linking respective individuals with the designation criteria; three of the four requests also needed to be bolstered with further material covering the recruitment of child soldiers, based on details contained in the Group of Experts reports (US Embassy London 2009; Secretary of State 2009). To finalize *tier one* listings, the US, France and UK (Belgium had by now rotated off the Council), invited Rwanda to re-submit these four names because "[n]on-western governments should be encouraged to propose listings (…)" (US State Department 2009). However, Rwanda refused to re-submit the four names in place of the 19 originally proposed. Accordingly, the US turned its "temporary 'hold' on

Rwanda's request into a permanent 'block' due to inadequate identifiers in the 2008 submission" and emphasized that "Rwanda will need to provide the required information for any subsequent submissions" (Secretary of State 2009). The committee subsequently accepted the four *tier one* requests on March 3, 2009 (SC/9608).

The P3 repeated the same arguing process for the five FDLR *tier two* names, deleting those with little substance and adding other well-documented names in reaction to newly reported violations (US Permanent Mission to the UN 2009c). France agreed to designate Gaston Iyamuremye ("Second Vice President of FDLR"), Emmanuel Ruzindana ("FDLR Political Commissioner," US State Department 2008d), and Juma Ngilinshuti ("FDLR external relations commissioner," S/2008/43, para. 40). The UK and US regarded these three individuals as suitable targets, subject to "receipt of more information." In contrast, there was little support for Apollinaire Hakizimana ("FDLR Defense Commissioner"), and Leodomir Mugaragu ("FOCA Chief of Staff") (US State Department 2008d). Subsequently, the P3 agreed that more information was needed on all candidates in order to submit individually successful proposals (US Permanent Mission to the UN 2009c). Because little information could be gathered for the lower ranked Hakizimana, Ruzindana and Ngilinshuti (for instance, the Group of Experts reports contained no evidence for violations, S/2008/43, S/2008/772, S/2008/773), the P3 dropped these individuals entirely. Conversely, the proposal on Iyamuremye was bolstered with Group of Experts reports proving his position as second vice-president of FDLR and core member of the "FDLR military high command" (S/2009/603, para. 91, Annex 16–17). The case of Mugaragu was relatively uncomplicated, since it was well-established that he was FOCA Chief of Staff, the FDLR's armed wing (S/2009/603, para. 91, Annex 16–17; International Crisis Group 2009, p. 34), so the requests could be augmented with evidence from "open-source and official reporting" (SC/10099).

Furthermore, the P3 prepared a listing request for two additional names based on new Group of Experts evidence. Félicien Nsanzubukire, 1st FDLR battalion leader would be implicated for arms embargo violations, citing a Group of Experts report (S/2009/603, paras. 70–71). Felicien Zimurinda, former Congrès national pour la défense du peuple (CNDP) member now integrated into FARDC, would be designated as a result of his responsibility for deliberate attacks against civilians (S/2010/596, paras. 135–136; S/2009/603), and as a "notorious perpetrator" of recruiting child soldiers (S/2010/596, paras. 135–136; CAC report S/2010/369, para. 65). The P3 co-designated the four individual requests, which the committee then adopted on December 1, 2010 (SC/10099).

A third listing initiative on February 12, 2010, again by Rwanda, reflects the tendency of committee members to scrutinize each suggestion and reject proposals below a certain threshold, making sure that every request relies on at least two sources of information. Building upon a Group of Experts report, which cited FDLR sanctions violations but without calling for listings (S/2009/603), Rwanda on this occasion requested the sanctioning of one individual who supported RUD-Urunana, a FDLR splinter group, and four FDLR supporters

(S/2010/93). The five requests could not succeed for a number of reasons. First, three of the requests completely lacked sufficient identifying information. Second, all five requests failed to provide at least two sources of information and solely built on the Group of Expert reports that the Group itself had not intended to be used for the purpose of sanctions designations. Furthermore, for at least two individuals the initiative relied only on outdated or singular events. For instance, the request to add Lt. Col. Nizeyimana was founded on allegations of activities in 1994 (death of Belgian soldiers), 2001 (leader of a small rebel group), 2004 (RUD liaison officer), and an incident of recruitment based on two unidentified interviews (S/2010/93, pp. 3–4). Above all, Rwanda undermined its own listing request by making its submission in the form of a public letter, which gave sanctions targets more than enough time for assets flight. Holds have been placed on these names for further information, but to date none of them have been listed (SCR Forecast May 2010).

A fourth initiative launched in late 2010, when Uganda proposed listing Jamil Mukulu associated with the Allied Democratic Forces (ADF) (SCR Forecast February 2011; What's in Blue 2011b), shows that even small states can place successful requests if they conform to the criteria and evidentiary threshold. ADF is a Uganda-focused rebel group with Islamist tendencies operating in DRC. Several P5 members placed a hold on this request (What's in Blue 2011b). On October 13, 2011, after P3 members had collected more evidence, the committee listed Jamil Mukulu based on his position as "the military leader of the Allied Democratic Forces (ADF), a foreign armed group operating in the DRC that impedes the disarmament, (…) repatriation or resettlement (…), as described in paragraph 4 (b) of resolution 1857 (2008)" and based on information from "multiple sources" (SC/10410, SCR Forecast November 2011).

A fifth initiative, the Mayi Mayi listing of November 28, 2011, shows that even designations based on disputed designation criteria of human rights violations can be successful, if states are able to make a strong case. Sanctioning human rights violators in Eastern DRC proved difficult because perpetrators' identities are rarely reliably reported in the quality needed (S/2009/253, para. 87; SCR Forecast November 2009). For that reason, there were disputes among committee members regarding the requirement for a suitable listing criterion. Following a P3 initiative, the committee listed Ntabo Ntaberi Sheka, the "Commander-in-Chief of the political branch of the Mayi Mayi Sheka" as a "political leader of a Congolese armed group" (SC/10461). The committee justified its decision by quoting his responsibility for the "series of attacks in Walikale territory" resulting in mass violation of children's rights (UN Permanent Missions of France, UK and US, 2011). Margot Wallström, the UN SRSG on Sexual Violence in Conflict, had advocated for Council action on such violations in the DRC, including this well-documented mass rape (Worsnip 2011), which the Council had also previously condemned in a presidential press statement (SC/10016).

In conclusion, this episode shows that the DRC sanctions regime's listing process prompted rule-based governance. At Council level, decision criteria to address the situation in DRC were relatively consistent. At committee level, powerful members could meaningfully use designation criteria and informal rules as focal points to solve problems of diverging interests among themselves (hypothesis 1). Thereby, the listing process and P3 prescreening of potential listing candidates followed both formal and informal rules. Individuals needed to be either high-level political or military leaders of an armed group or otherwise directly related to one of the Council listing criteria. A request also had to be accompanied by evidence, usually from two sources, and sufficient identifying information. Moreover, the individual's sanctionable behavior had to be recent. In effect, members consistently sorted out listing proposals that fell below recognized standards. Yet, the committee accepted well-documented listing proposals even if they originated from less powerful states.

Rwanda in the DRC Committee: The limits of committee governance

The episode of Rwanda's 2013–2014 Council tenure demonstrates how Council members anticipated that a relatively weak state, albeit with high stakes in the conflict could cause committee deadlock, but illustrates Council's efforts to sidestep such potential deadlocks. Rwanda was elected as a Security Council member in October 2012 replacing South Africa, in line with the African rotational system (Security Council Report 2012a, pp. 6–7). Rwanda's election coincidentally commenced as Eastern Congo experienced yet another escalation of violence, this time associated with the Rwandan-backed Mouvement du 23 Mars (M23), which quickly advanced its area of influence in Eastern Congo and captured the provincial capital Goma in late 2012 (Carayannis 2013, pp. 196–197).

Council members interested in a properly functioning DRC sanctions regime were concerned about Rwanda's tenure because of its long involvement in the DRC civil war, and consequently also because Rwanda had high stakes in the DRC sanctions regime. Earlier, a Group of Experts' report had revealed how much Rwanda and to a lesser extent Uganda were involved in Eastern DRC. A 2012 report accused Rwanda of violating the sanctions regime, providing direct assistance, recruiting for and providing arms to M23, direct incursions of Rwandan military forces into Congolese territory as well as violating the assets freeze and travel ban of sanctioned individuals (S/2012/348.Add1). A subsequent report outlined similar and additional Rwandan violations. It even established a direct chain of command from the Rwandan Defense Minister James Kabarebe to M23 (S/2012/843). Rwanda repeatedly denied the charges and accused the Group of Experts of misrepresenting Rwanda's role (Rwanda Ministry of Foreign Affairs and Cooperation 2012).

For other members it was immediately obvious that Rwanda's election posed "the prospect of division and deadlock" in the committee (Smith 2012). Rwanda as an incoming committee member would be in a privileged position "to halt ongoing investigation and protect its officials from UN sanctions" (Manrique Gil 2012, p. 5), and furthermore would do everything to deflect criticism from its own role. Western diplomats acknowledged that achieving "unanimity among the 15 Council members on Congo's rebellion would be difficult with Rwanda in the room" (Smith 2012). Since the committee operates on a consensus basis, listing proposals including those relating to Rwandan individuals, publishing unfavorable Group of Experts reports, acting on the reports' contents, or re-appointing Group of Experts members would be much more difficult, if not impossible, during Rwanda's tenure (Smith 2012; Security Council Report 2012b).

Proactive Council members devised a two-tier strategy for dealing with a prospective deadlock: additional designations before Rwanda began its tenure, and negotiating procedures that would restrict the discretion of committee members to behave arbitrarily. As a first reaction, some Council members sought to list M23 together with its political and military leaders. To achieve that, France, the UK and US (S/PV.6866), together with six co-sponsors, crafted a M23 insurgency resolution, which built on five press statements (SC/10819, SC/10736, SC/10709, SC/10702, SC/10675), and a Presidential statement (S/PRST/2012/22). The Council unanimously adopted this draft as resolution 2076 (2012) on November 20, 2012.

Despite its focus on the M23 rebellion, all rules and procedures conform to the consistency thesis of committee governance. The Council expressed concern "that M23 commanders Innocent Kaina and Baudouin Ngaruye are engaging in activities for which the Committee (…) may designate individuals" (para. 7). Furthermore, the Council directed the committee "to review, as a matter of urgency, their activities and those of any other individuals who meet the criteria for designation" (paras. 7, 8) set out in resolution 1857 (2008, para. 4). Moreover, the Council recalled that external supporters of M23 as well as sanctions violators may also be eligible sanctions targets, and that UN member states should provide suitable proposals (para. 8). In addition, the Council expressed its concern about "external support" for M23 without specifically naming Rwanda or Uganda (para. 4). The first French draft initially included an annex imposing sanctions on two M23 individuals. However, this was not included in the final resolution because some members requested more time for a "thorough vetting of the two individuals" (Security Council Report 2012b).

These rules paved the way for the committee to adopt several last-minute decisions before Rwanda joined the Council on January 1, 2013. This required significant investment on behalf of designating states: They quickly had to assemble well-reasoned listing proposals despite lacking intelligence information from Eastern Congo (interview with UN member state official, New York, December 2013). The committee listed a first M23 military leader, Sultani Makenga, on November 13, 2012 (SC/10812). On November 30, 2012, the committee designated Baudoin Ngaruye, another M23 military leader, and Innocent Kaina, a sector commander of M23 (SC/10842). Finally, on December 31, 2012 the committee sanctioned two other individuals, Eric Badege, a M23 military commander, and Jean-Marie Runiga, a political leader of M23, as well as two entities: the M23 itself and the FDLR (SC/10876). All listed individuals clearly conformed to the designation criteria as military or political leaders of a non-state armed group. Justifications for the listings drew extensively on the Group of Expert's evidence, which Rwanda strongly contested, as well as civil society reports, internal M23 documents and press coverage (SC/10812; SC/10842; SC/10876). In its narrative for listing M23, the committee even emphasized that the Rwandan Defense Forces had provided "general military supplies" to M23 (SC/10876), something Rwanda would have prevented at all costs.

In a next step before the membership cycle's turn, the Council amended the procedure on publication of Group of Experts' reports, whose findings Rwanda strongly contested. Anticipating that Rwanda would likely block future Group of Experts' reports, the Council removed entirely all committee members' discretion to obstruct the publication of such reports. The earlier procedure, in which Council asked the Group "to report to the Council in writing, through the Committee" (resolution 2021 (2011), para. 4), in practice required the committee to adopt a consensus decision when forwarding the report to the Council, after which it would become a public Council document. Instead, on November 28, 2012, the Council adopted a French drafted resolution 2078 (2012), which stipulated that the Group of Experts should submit "(…) a written final report before December 13, 2013, (…) and further requests that, after a discussion with the Committee, the Group of Experts submit *to the Council its final report upon termination of the Group's mandate*" (resolution 2078 (2012), para. 5, emphasis added). Thus, regardless of what resulted from the committee's discussion, the report would be submitted to the Council as a public document.

The proactive Council members also adopted further decisions relating to the Group of Experts in anticipation of Rwandan obstruction. On November 12, after one month of consideration, the committee transferred the latest Group of Experts report to the Council for publication (see S/2012/843). In this context, the committee adopted an unusual press release (SC/10872) that drew UN member states' attention to two aspects of the report: Primarily, the committee called upon rebel groups including M23 to stop recruitment of children, to release all child soldiers and to cease any recruitment of minors. The committee also called upon exporters, industries and consumers of natural resources from Eastern DRC to invest in traceability and due diligence "in order to halt cross-border smuggling." In addition, proactive committee members pushed for the Group of Experts' early reappointment because they anticipated Rwanda's objection (SCR Forecast February 2013). Thus, the committee adopted the new Group of Experts' configuration, which the Secretary-General appointed three days before the turn of the year (S/2012/967, S/2013/1). It is very likely that Rwanda as a committee member would have prevented or delayed all three aspects (Carayannis 2016, p. 674).

The change of Council composition provides evidence that proactive Council members' rationale was in reality well-founded since Rwanda immediately undermined the committee's work (What's in Blue 2013a). At Council level, Rwanda blocked or significantly delayed consensus-based presidential press statements and presidential statements (What's in Blue 2013b; What's in Blue

2013c; SCR Forecast October 2013). In a particularly contentious case of an M23 attack on UN peacekeepers, which killed one peacekeeper and wounded several others, Rwanda claimed that the Western-drafted statement was "unbalanced and unfairly targeted the M23 while ignoring attacks by the Congolese army." This is remarkable considering that the Council always condemned such attacks. Rwanda blocked several drafts until the sponsors introduced more "balanced" language, calling upon *all* belligerents to cease violence (Charbonneau 2013; SC/11108). Rwanda also voiced serious concerns over a draft resolution extending the DRC sanctions regime and its Group of Experts, in particular references to the Group together with its latest report, the external links of M23 and possible regrouping of M23 (What's in Blue 2014a). Yet, Rwanda finally decided to support the resolution (2136 (2014); SCR Forecast March 2014; S/PV.7107). Similar haggling commenced over language used in the MONUSCO re-authorization resolution 2147 (2014) (What's in Blue 2014b).

At committee level, Rwanda also blocked additional M23 designations, even though powerful committee members had proposed them. In August 2013, Rwanda blocked a US-French proposal to list Vianney Kazarama, a M23 military spokesperson, and Erick Mboneza, an M23 commander. Rwanda was the only committee member to oppose the request arguing that it was based on "very poor" evidence, even though it was supported by several evidentiary sources including Group of Expert reports (Charbonneau 2013). The designating states could have sidelined Rwanda through a Council resolution, but ultimately decided against referring the issue to the Council (SCR Forecast October 2013; S/2013/747, para. 47). Yet, Rwanda took no issue with the designation of the Allied Democratic Forces (SC/11459), which originated in Uganda and operated the Uganda-DRC border area, based on the group's abuse of child soldiers, killing, maiming, together with sexual violence against women and children, as well as attacks against MONUSCO peacekeepers, all designation criteria of resolution 2078 (2012) (Lederer 2014).

When the Group of Experts submitted its final report to the committee and accordingly to the Council at the end of the Group's tenure (S/2014/42), Rwanda could no longer block the report from becoming public, because the committee was no longer competent enough to decide upon its publication. The report again highlighted Rwanda's support for M23, recruitment of rebel fighters, arms transfers to the DRC and even direct military involvement (S/2014/42, paras. 28–31). During consideration of the Group's report in a committee meeting, Rwanda denied these accusations, dispelled the evidence and objected to all recommendations, including those without connection to Rwanda. In that regard, Rwanda was scathing in its criticism that the Group of Experts had submitted the report directly to the Council and thereby published it "without a prior decision of the Committee" (What's in Blue 2014a). However, other committee members, who had intentionally changed the procedure to that effect, rejected this claim citing resolution 2078 (2012) (What's in Blue 2014a).

Despite Rwanda's improving cooperation in the wake of M23's military defeat in late 2013, many members expected that the end of Rwanda's tenure would "allow for greater consensus in the Council and the DRC Sanctions Committee" (Security Council Report 2015) and a return to the previous rule-based committee practice. Accordingly, in February 2015 and again in October 2016, the committee completely overhauled this list, updating identifiers and justifications (SC/11772, SC/12553, SC/12559). This would certainly have been more difficult with Rwanda as a committee member. On February 1, 2018, based on designation criteria covering human rights violations, the committee listed four individuals, all of whom had often appeared in previous Group of Experts reports for having committed atrocities (SC/13194): Lucien Nzabamwita, FDLR military leader for supporting a designated entity (S/2014/42, para. 101), Guidon Mwissa, NDC-R leader for the abuse of child soldiers, human rights abuses, illegal taxation of gold mining to buy weapons despite the arms embargo (S/2015/797, para. 93, S/2016/466, pp. 102, S/2016/1162, para. 70, S/2017/1091, para. 72), Muhindo Mundos, FARDC commander for providing support to the ADF, which conducted human rights violations (S/2016/466, paras. 198–204), and Gedeon Mutanga, Bakata Katanga militia commander, involved in serious human rights violations and war crimes (S/2013/433, para. 83, S/2014/42, paras. 47–57).

In sum, Rwanda's Council tenure highlights that sanctions committees are indeed threatened by deadlock, even when caused by relatively small states, and that there are limits to rule-based committee governance. Under the restrictive consensus procedure, as long as Rwanda preferred non-agreement over agreement, it had little interest in rule adherence. At the same time, proactive members were not at the mercy of a dissenting member. Instead, members interested in a working sanctions regime strategically restricted the discretion of committee members and adopted several decisions immediately before Rwanda became a member.

Concluding thoughts

The DRC Sanctions Committee provides a confirmatory case for the committee governance thesis. Council members shared a common interest in creating and maintaining a sanctions regime alongside a sizable peacekeeping mission as a substitute for military adventures. However, among the proactive P3 there was a political conflict regarding how to implement the sanctions regime. These members faced a coordination problem because France, sympathetic to the DRC government, and the UK, which tended to support its former colonies Rwanda and Uganda, disagreed over the designation of individuals and entities.

The DRC Sanctions Committee provides confirmatory evidence for the effects of rule-making. Regarding listing, initially the committee could not process listing requests in the absence of procedural criteria, and accordingly used the externally produced guidelines of the Côte d'Ivoire Committee as a focal point. These rules were consistent and guided the committee listing process in subsequent rule-application. In a second case episode concerning the listing of individuals and entities, Council adopted consistent decision criteria to address the civil war in DRC by means of targeted sanctions.

The DRC Sanctions Committee case provides confirmatory evidence for hypothesis 1, according to which committee members facing a stream of separate decision proposals are expected to abide by given criteria, rules and procedures, even if these rules contradict situation-specific preferences of some committee members. Within the DRC Sanctions Committee, two episodes support the presumption that decision criteria and procedures were decisive in explaining committee decision-making as well as the content of decisions taken. Even powerful members acceded to the dropping of decision requests, where no reliable and up-to-date information from at least two sources could be assembled. Decision requests that fulfilled the informational requirements were successfully presented, even if they stemmed from seemingly less powerful states. As a result, the criteria served as a filter for determining substantiated from unsubstantiated requests. Accordingly, while requests usually came in sets, members discussed and weighed the merits of each proposed individual or entity separately against established formal and informal committee standards. In fact, member states invested significant resources over substantial periods of time in assembling convincing listing proposals based on more than one source of information. Effectively, all successfully submitted decision requests match the decision criteria, whereas the proponents dropped below-threshold requests.

Rwanda's Council membership illustrates that the effects of committee governance do not occur, if at least one committee member favors stalemate over a coordinated solution. Because rule-based solutions are in fact situated outside the win-set of one single committee member, Rwanda cannot be bound by substantive rules because deadlock is Rwanda's preferred outcome. Essentially, Rwanda had not originally consented to sanctions as it had not been a Council member when sanctions were imposed. However, the episode of Rwanda's tenure also shows that proactive member states have opportunities to cope with an uncompromising committee member through restricting the discretion of individual committee members to block decisions, for instance on Group of Experts' reports, and adopting early implementation decisions.

Apart from the Rwanda case episode, the alternative power politics explanation cannot convincingly explain observed decision-making patterns; this holds that decision-making and the content of decisions taken can be sufficiently well explained by the constellation of interests among powerful members. At Council level, it is not evident that powerful members pushed for or even achieved provisions that would have one-sidedly favored any of the members, but rather one observes quite consistent criteria. At committee level, there are no package deals to be seen.

The DRC Sanctions Committee complements the analysis of committee governance with a case that has gained less attention, public scrutiny and due process criticism than the Al-Qaida/Taliban sanctions regime or other country-specific regimes. While this made data generation more demanding, the DRC sanctions regime enriches the analysis through controlling for alternative empirical explanations drawn from targeted sanctions regimes; the due process criticism usually associated with the occurrence of a densely regulated form of decision-making cannot be observed here.

Note

1 As of August 2005, other committees' guidelines were much older or non-existent: Sierra Leone (November 10, 2004), Al-Qaida/Taliban (April 10, 2003), Iraq (June 11, 2003), Liberia (March 16 2004 and August 31, 2004). No guidelines: Sudan, Rwanda, and Somalia.

7 The Sudan

How the committee failed to implement targeted sanctions

Following the onset of a brutal civil war in the Sudanese province of Darfur during early 2003, after months of the Western members' protracted struggles with China and Russia, the Security Council eventually imposed an arms embargo in July 2004 and targeted sanctions in March 2005. This conflict had cost the lives of tens of thousands before the Council even considered Darfur. The Darfur conflict is among the most atrocious and deadliest conflicts since the end of the Cold War, causing an estimated 300,000 lives to be lost, massive displacement, grave human rights violations, attacks on civilians and a severe humanitarian crisis. The infamous pro-government Janjaweed militias had been fighting a brutal counter-insurgency in Darfur. This conflict triggered a massive outcry among human rights advocates and the Western media. Usually, permanent members have some common interest in an operational committee in other sanctions regimes. By contrast, on this occasion they clashed over UN Charter principles of state sovereignty and non-intervention in Darfur. Driven by domestic and geopolitical factors as well as fallout from the US intervention in Iraq, China and Russia fiercely contested the Western claim that the government of Sudan was responsible for genocide having taken place.

Committee governance did not work in the Sudan sanctions regime. Council members began by delegating the usual tasks dealing with case issues to the same states in a sanctions committee, namely "identifying specific persons against whom the sanctions could be targeted" (SCR Forecast November 2005b). The committee would then normally draw up a list of individuals who are seen as impeding the peace process; here this would specifically include those responsible for destabilizing Darfur, committing atrocities and violating the arms embargo, all of which would lead to assets freezes and travel bans. However, unlike the situation in other sanctions regimes, even though Council members created some rules, committee members neither followed any of these, nor did they create other informal rules. Indeed, at an early stage it "[became] clear [that] the Sanctions Committee itself [was] incapable of taking action because of paralyzing internal splits" (Prendergast 2007, p. 12). Since the sanctions committee was unable to designate individuals, committee members referred this issue back to the Council, which then sanctioned four individuals in resolution 1672 (2006). While Council members took sweeping decisions on peacekeeping and referred Darfur to the International Criminal Court (ICC), to date the committee has yet to take action on sanctioning any individuals. As a consequence, this sanctions regime remains an example of poor sanctions management, inadequate enforcement, and insufficient reaction to frequently reported sanctions violations. In other words, the sanctions regime has resulted in hardly any impact.

This chapter traces and explores why transferring tasks, which elsewhere have led to functioning sanctions regimes, has not triggered similar effects in the Sudan Sanctions Committee. How can we account for this marked variance? Why did China and Russia agree to a sanctions regime, even though they have vehemently opposed sanctions on Sudan? Why did committee members refer decisions back to the Council? How does it affect the nature of the listings, when the Council itself decides about aspects typically dealt with in a committee? The committee governance thesis helps us to explore these critical issues, account for why rules leave the committee unaffected and what the members can do about it.

The Sudan sanctions regime is a challenging, but intriguing case for the committee governance framework, which makes it possible for us to study issues arising in the process of sanctions listing. In reality, even though several members demanded and presented listing requests, on this occasion none of them was adopted by the sanctions committee. Here, creating rules is not very effective in avoiding committee stalemate as imposing sanctions on Sudan can be rejected by one or more of the Council's permanent members. The transfer of tasks to a sanctions committee did not lead its members to follow rules because every Council member can block any request within the committee confines. The committee governance thesis posits that focal points, such as rules or precedents, create an impact only if committee members have to coordinate in choosing among different solutions. As a result, it is not a question of explaining a stalemate, but rather why skeptics allow the transference of decisions to a committee even though they wanted to avoid sanctions being imposed on Sudan. To be specific about my aim in this chapter, I do not intend to recount the complete story of the Council's conflict with Sudan sanctions. Rather, I seek to evaluate the scope conditions of the key variables.

The next section traces the Sudan sanctions regime's political origins, how the great power struggle over sanctions on Sudan arose, and what this means for the book's thesis. Thereafter, to shed light on the hypotheses' limits, I explore why committee members have not followed rules, as they have in other sanctions regimes, and how proactive states approach decision-making in the shadow of fundamental conflict over sanctions. In a first episode, I study the negotiations about whether or not sanctions should be imposed on Sudan as well as the motives of China and Russia in agreeing to a sanctions regime that they oppose so fiercely. In a second episode, I examine how the great power conflict over sanctions leads to a deadlock in the sanctions committee. Then, I demonstrate how proactive members try to resolve the stalemate and following the failure of rule-making, why these members submit a listing proposal to the Council. In a last episode, I show that proactive members no longer submit formal requests because they expect to fail in the light of great powers' protracted conflict.

The political origins of the Sudan sanctions regime

A deadly war in Darfur broke out when two rebel groups, the Justice and Equality Movement (JEM) and the Sudanese Liberation Army (SLA), attacked the Sudanese Armed Forces (SAF) as well as government facilities in a fight against what they perceived to be the political and economic marginalization of African tribes (on the conflict's roots, Cockett 2010, pp. 170–184). The Al-Bashir government and government-supported Janjaweed militias responded with a brutal counter-insurgency campaign, aerial bombardments and Janjaweed land operations resulting in death, massive displacement and starvation (Flint and Waal 2009, pp. 116–149). Initially, the Darfur conflict did not draw any attention outside Sudan. However, late in 2003 UN officials started to express serious concern about an unfolding humanitarian crisis in Dafur with widespread atrocities against civilians, women and children. Major Western news outlets and human rights activists began demanding a strong response to the severe humanitarian crisis, including an arms embargo and targeted sanctions (Hamilton 2011, pp. 27–53). The Security Council hesitantly imposed an arms embargo (resolution 1556 (2004)) in July 2004. In March 2005, despite Chinese hesitance the Western powers pushed the Council to add a travel ban and assets freeze on listed individuals (resolution 1591 (2005)), and established a Panel of Experts to monitor sanction implementation.

In contrast to other sanctions regimes, the permanent Council members had irreconcilable positions on Sudan sanctions. Initially, Western members had little interest in bringing Darfur to the Council. The US and UK were orchestrating the Comprehensive Peace Agreement (CPA) between Sudan and the SPLM; they feared, therefore, that pressure on Khartoum might jeopardize this deal (Cockett 2010, pp. 175–180), or create the risk of losing Sudanese counter-terrorism cooperation (Prendergast 2007, pp. 2–4; differently Stedjan and Thomas-Jensen 2010, pp. 164–165). The US and UK were also keen to register a diplomatic success after Iraq (Williams and Bellamy 2005, pp. 34–35). However, the CPA signing in January 2005 relieved the West from accommodating Sudan (Cockett 2010, pp. 223–224); this was a breakthrough peace deal ending the Second Sudanese Civil War, thus paving the way for South Sudanese independence. Nevertheless, the dire humanitarian situation in Darfur and mounting reports about large-scale atrocities, a massive civil society campaign pressured Western leaders to take action (Stedjan and Thomas-Jensen 2010, pp. 158–160). Regarding counter-terrorism, the US had offered to remove Sudan from its list of states sponsoring terrorism, but lost its room to maneuver due to immense domestic pressure (Cockett 2010, p. 180). The UK had distinct stakes in pushing the concept of responsibility to protect and was facing a public outcry at home (Williams 2010, pp. 201–203). France, as a former colonial power of Sudan's neighbors Chad and CAR with strong ties to Francophone Africa, wanted to uphold stability in the region (Charbonneau 2010, pp. 221–224).

Driven by these factors, the P3 were looking for a feasible policy option, not too costly, but promising visible action: sanctions. The military and political resources spent on the war in Iraq had practically removed an intervention or no-fly zone from the menu (Bolton 2007, pp. 348–361). Yet, the P3 agreed not only that a more robust peacekeeping mission should be established, but also that the perpetrators should be brought to account. However, the Bush administration favored a special hybrid-tribunal and opposed the ICC, which France and the UK staunchly supported (Schabas 2010, pp. 138–141). Hence, the sanctions avenue provided a reasonable policy option for the P3. Sanctions would mirror visible action and respond to domestic pressures. The US, UK and France had no major economic interests in Sudan that would make sanctions unattractive (see Table 7.1, Williams 2010, pp. 202–203). Accordingly, the P3 became the driving force on Darfur (Bosco 2009, p. 246). The UK and US sponsored early sanctions resolutions, often accompanied by France and other states including Argentina, Germany, Japan and Spain (see Table 7.2).

However, China and Russia had something very different in mind. While China fiercely opposed sanctions, maintaining an "anti-sanctions line" throughout (Taylor 2010, p. 184; Holslag 2008, pp. 74–82), it was proactive in convincing the Sudanese leadership to accept the UN/AU peacekeeping mission. China had growing economic ties with Sudan and was the only sizable trading partner among the P5. More precisely, Sudan was the fifth largest supplier of oil to China. Even shortly after imposing sanctions, China increased its trade volume by more than 150 percent compared with the pre-sanctions era (see Table 7.1, Wuthnow 2013, pp. 95–96). Russia largely followed the Chinese lead but had its own motives. It had lucrative oil deals with Sudan and did not want to risk jeopardizing the fulfillment of these contracts and related financial transactions by imposing sanctions. According to the SIPRI Arms Transfers Database, both China and Russia had continually provided arms to the regime in Khartoum from 2000 to 2010 (Stockholm International Peace Research Institute 2018). China was also a key supplier of conventional arms to Sudan, making up 7 percent of Chinese exports. Moreover, China provided 90 percent of small arms sales to

Table 7.1 P5 and EU trade volume with Sudan in billion US$, 2000–2010

Year	*2000*	*2002*	*2004*	*2006*	*2008*	*2010*	*2006–2010 % change*
China	0.89	1.55	2.52	3.35	8.20	8.62	157
France	0.10	0.08	0.12	0.34	0.23	0.18	–47
Russia	0.01	0.02	0.15	0.11	0.12	0.18	65
United Kingdom	0.15	0.17	0.24	0.30	0.27	0.23	–23
United States	0.02	0.01	0.07	0.08	0.15	0.13	51
EU-28	0.67	0.80	1.39	2.11	2.05	1.54	–27
Total	**1.84**	**2.63**	**4.49**	**6.29**	**11.02**	**10.88**	**73**

Source: UN Comtrade Database.

Note
Total trade volume combines import and export. Data by respective state (reporter) to Sudan (partner).

Sudan and had also supplied heavy weapons including fighter jets, helicopters, tanks and armored vehicles (Wuthnow 2013, pp. 95–96; Wezeman 2007, p. 3). Furthermore, purely as a matter of principle both China and Russia rejected sanctions as illegitimate outside intervention in Sudan, doubted that sanctions solved the Darfur conflict, and therefore strongly supported the Al-Bashir government (Williams and Bellamy 2005, pp. 32–33; Happaerts 2009, p. 108). As a result, China and Russia have consistently abstained (five times and three times, respectively) on resolutions threatening, imposing or strengthening sanctions (see Table 7.2). In several statements after Council voting, China and Russia have made clear that they strongly oppose imposing sanctions on Sudan (S/PV.5015, S/PV.5040). For instance, China raised "serious reservations" against proposed sanctions measures and reinforced its policy by stating that "China's position against sanctions remains unchanged" (China, S/PV.5040).

Because the Western powers' interests clash with those of China and Russia, I do not expect to find a committee governance effect in the Sudan sanctions regime. The great powers have no common interest and accordingly are not in a coordination situation. Because committee listing decisions require consensus, the West depends on Chinese cooperation, but this is not so in reverse. China has no interest in a cooperative solution because it prefers the status quo (deadlock). China can undermine the sanctions regime and precisely by doing that achieve its preference. The P5 do not disagree about "which targets," but rather

Table 7.2 Selected resolutions Sudan sanctions regime 2004–2006

Date	*Resolution*	*Subject*	*Sponsors*	*Abstentions*
July 30, 2004	1556	Sanctions	Chile, France, Germany, Romania, Spain, UK, US	**China**, Pakistan
September 18, 2004	1564	Accountability, sanctions threat	Germany, Romania, Spain, UK, US	Algeria, **China**, Pakistan, **Russia**
November 19, 2004	1574	Sudan–South Sudan peace deal		None
March 29, 2005	1591	Sanctions	US	Algeria, **China**, **Russia**
March 31, 2005	1593	ICC referral	UK	Algeria, Brazil, **China**, **USA**
April 25, 2006	1672	Sanctions	Argentina, Denmark, France, Japan, Peru, Slovakia, UK, US	**China**, Qatar, **Russia**

Source: author's illustration.

Note
Sponsors, see S/2004/611; S/2004/74; S/2005/206; S/2006/255.

about the existence of "targets at all." Rules and precedents are likely to be irrelevant because they offer solutions that are beyond what committee members can agree on collectively ("win set"). Some committee members already achieve their most preferred outcome and cannot improve their payoffs through compromise. Because committee stalemate is probable, one would expect that permanent members seek to compensate other members through Council package deals.

The creation of the Sudan sanctions regime

The early phase from conflict onset to creation of the sanctions committee shows that Security Council members had no common interest in Sudan. The group of sanctions supporters pushed for a credible sanctions threat and creation of a targeted sanctions regime against conflict parties. The group which was critical of sanctions imposition undermined these efforts and watered down resolutions by threatening to use their vetoes. While the proactive states finally managed to create a sanctions regime, the four rounds of preceding bargaining over a resolution imposing sanctions had taken its toll. Consequently, skeptical members preferred to avoid tough measures and retain control of future decisions, while at the same time trying to minimize reputational costs in light of a looming humanitarian crisis.

The phase leading to resolution 1591 (2005) clearly demonstrates Council divisions in regard to Sudan sanctions. The Council had a first closed meeting on Darfur in April 2004 (SC/8050) and issued a presidential statement in May (S/PRST/2004/18) demanding that the ceasefire agreement be upheld along with the disarmament of Janjaweed militias. Resolution 1547 (2004) was then adopted in June, with a repeat of the Council's request. Responding to Sudanese intransigence, the US circulated a first sanctions resolution draft on June 30, suggesting the imposition of a travel ban coupled with an arms embargo applying solely to Janjaweed militia members. This draft foresaw a threat to imposing sanctions on those responsible for atrocities in Darfur, including the Sudanese government (Marquis and Lacey 2004). A newly created sanctions committee would need to select the specific sanctions targets (Lederer 2004a). Meanwhile, on July 3, following Kofi Annan's diplomatic initiative, Sudan made several concessions including disarming the Janjaweed and improving humanitarian access in a UN-Sudan joint communiqué (MacKinnon 2010, p. 74).

However, this joint communiqué played into the hands of China, Russia and Pakistan, which all rejected moving forward on sanctions and demanded that Sudan be given more time. The US had to drop the travel ban as well as the sanctions committee, and reframed the arms embargo as applying to all armed groups, including the Janjaweed and rebel militias. Lastly, the revised draft expressed the Council's intention to consider imposing sanctions on the government should it not comply within 30 days (Lynch 2004a). Despite this revision, the US was still running into stiff resistance from seven Council members (Hoge 2004a), including China and Russia, which even objected to using the term "sanctions" and urged that Sudan be given more time to comply with the joint communiqué (Lederer 2004b). After intense negotiations, the US decided to revise the draft further and substituted the threat of sanctions with: "to consider further actions, including measures as provided for in Article 41 (…) on the Government of Sudan" (resolution 1556 (2004), para. 6; Hoge 2004a). On July 30, 2004, with China and Pakistan abstaining, the Council imposed an arms embargo on "non-governmental entities and individuals, including the Janjaweed" restricted to Darfur (resolution 1556 (2004), paras. 7–9).

The statements after the vote show how much Council members disagreed. The sponsors Chile, France, Germany, Romania, Spain, the UK, and US all favored a clear sanctions threat and saw the main responsibility as resting with the Sudanese leadership (S/PV.5015). Western governments regarded the Council resolution as representing a final opportunity for Sudan to avoid sanctions (France, Germany, UK, S/PV.5015, pp. 5, 7, 9). The US claimed that "the Government of Sudan has left us no choice. (…) Sudan must know that serious measures – international sanctions – are looming" (S/PV.5015, pp. 3–4). To the contrary, Algeria, Brazil, China, Pakistan, and Russia emphasized that there was no automaticity toward sanctions (S/PV.5015). China found it deplorable that the "draft resolution (…) still includes mandatory measures against the Sudanese Government (…) [which] cannot be helpful in resolving the situation in Darfur and may even further complicate it (…). We can therefore only abstain in the voting" (S/PV.5015, pp. 2–3). Russia lauded the point that "the resolution does not foresee possible further Security Council action with regard to Darfur" (S/PV.5015, p. 7).

In the face of Sudanese non-compliance, the Chinese delegation acquiesced by accepting the resolution, mindful that key elements had been watered down (Ahmed 2010, p. 7). Because the arms ban applied only to non-governmental militias in Darfur, no threat was posed to China's arms exports to the Sudan government (Holslag 2008, p. 82). China also demanded that no sanctions committee should monitor the arms embargo, without which even proponents doubted that it could be effective (Lynch 2004a). The skeptics prevented other direct targeted sanctions on pro-government Janjaweed, and a sanctions threat, which pro tem precluded forceful measures (Hoge 2004a).

In late August 2004, when Special Representative of the Secretary-General Jan Pronk reported that Sudan had not complied with key Council demands and had not started to disarm the Janjaweed (S/2004/703, S/PV.5027), the proactive states again pushed for sanctions (MacKinnon 2010, pp. 74–75). On September 8, 2004, the US circulated a new draft resolution, which suggested that an International Commission of Inquiry should be created to investigate human rights violations in Darfur and determine whether or not genocide had occurred. The draft also contained a threat of oil sector sanctions. Since proponents had little confidence in the prospects of a tougher resolution being adopted, the draft foresaw neither targeted sanctions nor a sanctions committee (Hoge 2004b; Federal News Service 2004, p. 15). Nevertheless, China, Russia, Algeria and Pakistan strongly opposed the sanctions threat. China even announced that it would use its veto unless the language were altered (Hoge 2004c). Consequently, the US revised its draft four times to achieve consensus. The sanctions threat was softened from "shall take" to "shall consider" (Hoge 2004c) making the sanctions threat "more conditional and less automatic." Moreover, the drafters included language to acknowledge that the Council "welcomes" steps by the Sudanese government to refrain from obstructing aid (Hoge 2004d). Finally, resolution 1564 (2004), co-sponsored by Romania, Spain and the UK, established the International Commission of Inquiry (para. 12). Concerning sanctions, the Council "shall consider taking additional measures as contemplated in Article 41 (…), such as actions to affect Sudan's petroleum sector and the Government of Sudan or individual members of the Government of Sudan (…)" (resolution 1564 (2004), para. 14). Algeria, China, Pakistan, and Russia abstained.

Again, statements made after the resolution's adoption exemplify the clash of interests. The sanctions supporters, including the US, UK, France and Germany, outlined that although they had to compromise, sanctions were vital in countering Sudan's potential lack of compliance. The US delegate claimed that "if the Government of the Sudan continues to persecute its people and does not cooperate fully (…), the Council will, indeed, have to consider sanctions (…)" (S/PV.5040, p. 5). Yet, Russia was "convinced that threatening sanctions is far from the best method of inducing Khartoum to fully implement its obligations" (Russia, S/PV.5040, p. 4). China complained that

> [t]he Sudanese Government has shown its sincerity in trying to resolve the problem (…). For those reasons, the Chinese delegation has serious reservations about the resolution just adopted. (…) China's position against sanctions remains unchanged. It has been our consistent view that, instead of helping to solve complicated problems, sanctions may make them even more complicated.
>
> (S/PV.5040, pp. 4–5)

China decided to abstain because the drafters had grudgingly respected its red lines. The resolution did not alter the arms embargo. However, the revised draft included positive language on Sudan's behavior and threats to impose biting sanctions were watered down. In fact, another resolution would now be needed to impose tougher sanctions, which China would then have the power to veto (MacKinnon 2010, p. 75). As a result, "since a key element of the Council's work at present is support for the African Union in extending its deployment in Darfur (…) the Chinese delegation refrained from blocking the adoption of the draft resolution (…)" (China, S/PV.5040, p. 5).

When the Council held a meeting in Nairobi to support the North-South negotiations over a peace deal in November 2004, sanctions supporters expressed their desire to adopt a consensus resolution; however, the Darfur conflict was again contentious (Lacey 2004). Accordingly, the initial UK draft called for "further urgent action" lest there be Sudanese non-compliance. The draft did not foresee any tightened sanctions or a sanctions committee (Lederer 2004c). China, Russia, Algeria and Pakistan immediately demanded that all references to Darfur should be dropped, arguing that such language could compromise negotiations (Farley 2004). The US recognized that "[i]t would clearly be extremely difficult to get a resolution that actually imposes sanctions (…) adopted" (Lynch 2004b) and a split vote would undermine Council's support for the peace deal. Reluctantly, the drafters altered the provisions on Darfur (Lederer 2004c). Hence, in resolution 1574 (2004), the Council expressed that it was "deeply concerned by the situation in Sudan," called for a cessation of violence as well as compliance with international humanitarian law, and threatened "to take appropriate action against any party failing to fulfil its commitments." Strikingly, skeptical states did not even mention Darfur in their statements, while proponents restated that sanctions were still an option (China, Russia, UK, France, US, S/PV.5082).

A new window of opportunity emerged in January 2005 once a North-South peace deal was in place. This coincided with the International Commission of Inquiry's final report, which found that all conflict parties had committed serious war crimes and crimes against humanity; it recommended that Darfur should be referred to the ICC, but stopped short of finding that genocide had occurred (Cassese *et al.* 2005, p. 630). In Darfur, all conflict parties continued fighting and completely ignored the Council's demands to end violence (e.g., S/2005/68). A lack of oversight over the arms embargo in the absence of a sanctions committee seriously impeded its effectiveness (S/2005/56). All these developments created an urgent need to deal with three issues: (1) creating a peacekeeping operation to implement the CPA, (2) imposing of sanctions as well as (3) holding perpetrators accountable (MacKinnon 2010, p. 77).

On February 14, 2005, the US circulated a package draft resolution creating a peacekeeping operation, strengthening sanctions, and suggesting trying perpetrators through "internationally accepted means." To secure adoption of the proposals' consensual sections, the US later circulated three separate draft resolutions (Lederer 2005b). On peacekeeping, the Council unanimously adopted resolution 1590 (2005) and authorized a peace support operation, transforming UNAMIS into the UNMIS operation (MacKinnon 2010, p. 77). Following a French-British initiative, departing from the strong US preference for a hybrid court, which had received little support (US Embassy Paris 2005a), the Council referred Darfur to the ICC. This resulted from the abstentions not just of Algeria, Brazil and China, but also the US, despite its introducing provisions on financing, recognizing bilateral immunity agreements and limiting ICC jurisdiction over foreign personnel (resolution 1593 (2005)).

Regarding the sanctions track, the US draft envisaged not only targeted sanctions, including an assets freeze and a travel ban on those impeding the peace process, threatening the stability of Darfur or violating human rights, but also a new sanctions committee which would determine targets. The arms embargo to the Sudanese government would also be extended so that transferring military assets into Darfur would become subject to committee approval. Additionally, the US draft proposed restricting military flights in Darfur and threatened further sanctions including "actions relating to Sudan's petroleum sector" (Linton 2005). Finally, the draft would establish a Panel of Experts to identify individuals for sanctions (CNN 2005). Predictably, the drafters ran into stiff opposition from China, Russia and Algeria. China stressed that they "(…) have difficulties with the whole concept of sanctions" (Lederer 2005a) and would veto a resolution which violated their core interests (Holslag *et al.* 2007, p. 50).

In what followed, the P5 bargained over the scope of targeted sanctions, the arms embargo, the sanctions committee's role and the consequences of non-compliance. Skeptical states demanded that their agreement to targeted sanctions should lead to a new sanctions committee, which would be responsible for any designations and therefore give them full control over the committee's implementing of targeted sanctions (Holslag *et al.* 2007, p. 50). The assets freeze should also be dropped. However, proactive states refused to accept anything less than targeted sanctions and a broadening of the arms embargo in Darfur for the Sudanese government. Resolution drafters merely watered down the consequences of non-compliance and deleted the threat of an oil embargo (Leopold 2005a; MacAskill 2005). Eventually, on March 29, after China, Russia and Algeria had decided to abstain, the Security Council imposed targeted sanctions including travel bans and assets freezes on individuals, who should be determined by a new sanctions committee. In addition, the Council extended the arms embargo to all belligerents in Darfur and subjected to prior committee approval the Sudanese government's arms transfers to Darfur. Likewise, the Council created a four-member Panel of Experts for a period of six months (resolution 1591 (2005), paras. 3, 7).

After the vote, Russia and China clarified that they stood ready to undermine the effective implementation of sanctions. China noted that it had "serious reservations about the resolution" and reminded the Council that "China has always taken a cautious approach to the issue of sanctions and we abstained on both resolutions 1556 (2004) and 1564 (2004). (…)" (S/PV.5153, pp. 4–5). Russia in turn was "convinced that the potential of political and diplomatic measures to defuse the conflict in Darfur has by no means been exhausted" and that the Council needed "to draw up an effective mechanism to assist the parties to quickly resume the negotiating process [which] (…) [s]anctions against the Sudanese Government are hardly likely to promote." Sanctions should be reviewed "as quickly as possible" (S/PV.5153, p. 4). In other words, sanctions on Sudan were counterproductive and impeded a political solution. On the very next day, China publicly declared its opposition to UN sanctions on Sudan (Associated Press International 2005).

Why did China and Russia acquiesce on resolution 1591 (2005) even though they opposed sanctions on Sudan? On the one hand, abstention is fully in line with the policy goal of deadlock and the resolution respected their primary interest. In fact, both ruled out the threat of an oil embargo or other economic sanctions that would have threatened their economic interests (Human Rights First 2008, p. 18). In addition, they maintained that they would still be allowed to continue arms exports to the Sudanese government without violating the arms embargo, because Sudan would be responsible for sanctioned arms transfers to Darfur (Wezeman 2007, p. 6; both have since used this loophole, Lewis 2009). Concerning targeted sanctions, their insistence on creating a sanctions committee would allow them to block any committee decisions. Without the committee issuing designations, the targeted sanctions would remain ineffective because the resolution did not determine any targets (Holslag 2008, p. 81). On the other hand, abstaining would avoid further antagonization of the West through obstructionism (Wuthnow 2010, p. 71; Taylor 2010, pp. 187–188). A Council veto would have been difficult to sustain as sanctions would be the logical next step. Not even China challenged the magnitude of this crisis nor all belligerents' failure to comply with the Council's demands (S/PV.5153). Transferring political conflict over Darfur into the sanctions committee was an ideal way of deflecting international pressure away from the Council. At the same time, abstaining on resolution 1591 (2006) minimized the negative impact on a strategic partnership with African nations. Yet, China gave immediate assurances to the Sudanese government that it would block the implementation of sanctions (Holslag *et al.* 2007, p. 46).

Resolution 1591 (2005) provided committee members with a clear set of rules, no different to those contained in other sanctions resolutions. Included was a first set of listing criteria: individuals

> (…) who impede the peace process, constitute a threat to stability in Darfur and the region, commit violations of international humanitarian or human rights law or other atrocities, violate the (…) [arms embargo], or are responsible for offensive military overflights (…).
>
> (Para. 3c)

The Council requested the committee "to designate those individuals subject to the measures," albeit without suggesting a specific listing procedure, and also to establish guidelines as needed for implementation. It also mandated the committee to monitor targeted sanctions and the arms embargo, decide about sanctions exemptions, report to the Council at regular intervals, and assess reports both from the Panel of Experts as well as member states reports (para. 3a).

This early phase shows that although Russia and China had finally acceded to the establishment of a Sudan sanctions regime, they were reluctant to see sanctions imposed on Sudan. While minimizing the diplomatic fallout, skeptical members had little interest in seriously implementing sanctions on Sudan. In essence, the political conflict inherent to imposing sanctions on Sudan was transferred from the Council to the consensus-based Sudan Sanctions Committee. This marked the beginning of an intense phase of protracted committee negotiations on how to proceed with the Darfur crisis in the face of continuing atrocities and the humanitarian disaster there. Beyond the committee governance thesis' scope conditions, the Sudan case leads us to expect a "non-resolvable" committee stalemate in the next episode; committee members are not coordinating about equally plausible solutions to single-case listing requests, but instead continue fighting about whether or not to implement sanctions against Sudan.

Down the committee route

This episode shows that committee stalemate can indeed be a viable outcome from collective decision-making, although Council members effectively transferred tasks to themselves within the sanctions committee. In the Sudan case, committee governance was absent because the basic conditions, namely committee members' common interests, were also absent. The sanctions regime was not merely symbolic, since the P3 had repeatedly requested listings and invested considerable resources in the cause. However, whatever developed within committee, China and Russia had a clear policy goal of producing deadlock. Because both the P5 and elected members have the power to withhold consensus, albeit three committee members' opposed genuine implementation, delegation to the committee rendered any outcomes doomed to stalemate. Efforts to resolve a deadlock with additional rules were also bound to fail because they could simply be voted down by sanctions skeptics. As a result, China and Russia largely blocked the committee and undermined the division of labor between Council and committee.

Immediately after the imposition of sanctions, China and Russia began to sabotage the committee's work and "used procedural machinations to ensure that the committee did not begin its work" (Prendergast and Sullivan 2008, pp. 6–7). For instance, they declined several candidates for the Panel of Experts, questioned the candidates' experience or political views on Sudan and delayed their appointment for three months (Leopold 2005b; S/2006/543, para. 6). Throughout 2005, none of the committee members pursued listing requests (Couturier 2005), because even sanctions proponents hoped that the Abuja Peace Process for Darfur would lead to a peace deal between warring parties. However, progress was slow and previous accords such as the N'Djamena Ceasefire Agreement had been instantly, grossly and repeatedly violated (Nathan 2007, p. 248). Moreover, the conflict parties continued fighting and committing large-scale violations of international humanitarian law against civilians (S/2005/378, S/2005/650, S/2005/719, S/2005/825), a fact that even the divided Council accepted (S/PRST/2005/48, S/PRST/2005/67). Thus, before the US, UK and France started to consider designating individuals in late 2005 (US Embassy Paris 2005c), "[t]he sanctions committee (…) [was] still inoperative, with no agreement on guidelines and therefore no capacity to target sanctions against individuals" (SCR Forecast November 2005b). The Council merely extended the expert body's mandate (resolution 1651 (2005)).

Culmination of the first Panel of Experts' mandate cycle by December 30, 2005 provided a window of opportunity to consider pursuing sanctions. The Panel report contained 13 recommendations to improve the sanctions regime (S/2006/250). Most importantly, it contained a list of individuals attached in a confidential annex who, in the view of the panel, fulfilled the listing criteria of resolution 1591 (2005). The annex named 17 individuals, including the Sudanese interior minister, the defense minister together with the director of national security and intelligence services. Furthermore, the annex listed "several Sudanese military and police commanders, two Janjaweed militia leaders and five rebel commanders" (Human Rights Watch 2006; Turner 2006). The annex also named "five other people against whom the panel is considering recommending sanctions, including President Omar Hassan al-Bashir of Sudan and President Idriss Deby of Chad" (Lynch 2006a) as well as "two top commanders of the rebel Sudan Liberation Army (SLA)" (Human Rights Watch 2006). Yet, UN member states still had to make formal designations.

In January 2006, a coalition of committee members (Denmark, France, Greece, Japan, the UK, and US) initiated discussions on listings despite the expected Chinese, Qatari and Russian objections (Lederer 2006b). The US started to gather and corroborate information in the confidential list, requesting its embassies to cross-check and assemble additional information for potential requests (US Embassy Khartoum 2006a; US Embassy The Hague 2006). Meanwhile in committee, sanctions proponents "ran into enormous difficulties, especially from China" (Bolton 2007, p. 352). First, the Arab member Qatar had joined forces with China to produce a serious delay in publication of the Panel's report, usually a routine matter, because they disagreed with its conclusions (Lederer 2006a). The committee Chair, frustrated about the lack of progress, stressed that the committee "did not even get to the point of discussing its list, and other lists, of people who might be subject to sanctions (…)" (Lederer 2006b). However, the committee finally submitted the report to Council for publication in late January 2006 (S/2006/543, para. 17), even though in substance it had not been altered (SCR Update Report No. 3 2006). Second, sanctions skeptics delayed the adoption of committee guidelines, hence the committee lacked a set of concrete procedures. Resolution 1591 (2005) did not establish the exact procedure and timeframe under which the committee could designate individuals or take other decisions. Aware of this, China, Qatar and Russia insisted that first "the sanctions committee [should] establish criteria to determine who should be subject to sanctions (…)" (Lederer 2006b). Thereafter, China and Qatar put up continual procedural objections during committee meetings (Goldberg 2006). Throughout February, committee discussions concerning possible listings were ongoing; however, without an agreement on committee guidelines, the committee would not be able to list any targets (SCR Forecast March 2006b).

The committee finally agreed on committee guidelines on March 23, 2006 "[f]ollowing extensive discussions on the subject" (S/2006/543, para. 20). According to the guidelines, "[t]he Committee will decide on the designation of an individual (…) on the basis of the criteria contained in (…) [resolution 1591 (2005)]." Thereby, "the Committee will consider information provided by Member States, the Secretary-General, the High Commissioner for Human Rights, the Panel of Experts (…) and other relevant sources" (committee guidelines, para. 7a). As with other sanctions regimes, a designation should "be accompanied by, to the greatest extent possible, a narrative description of the information that justifies how that individual fits within the criteria (...) of resolution 1591 (2005)" (para. 7b). It should include "relevant, specific and up-to-date" identifying information such as "name, date of birth, place of birth, nationality, aliases, residence, passport or travel document number, professional or functional title" (para. 7c). The committee will decide by consensus (para. 25) in a written "no-objection procedure" within a timeframe of two working days (para. 26).

Despite breaking the deadlock on procedures, the P5 were still sharply divided over Sudan sanctions. On the one hand, the P3 and others (Argentina, Denmark, Ghana, Greece, Japan, Peru, and Slovakia) now pushed for additional sanctions to uphold Council credibility and incentivize conflict parties to opt for a peaceful settlement (US Permanent Mission to the UN 2006b). On the other hand, China and Russia strongly opposed increasing pressure on Sudan arguing that sanctions would undermine the cooperation of Sudan vis-à-vis the UN (Lynch 2006a). In private P5 consultations, China made clear that it opposed any further pressure on Sudan in the form of sanctions designations or possible extension of the arms embargo to the entire territory of Sudan (US Embassy Moscow 2006a).

On March 1, 2006, more than a year after the Council had imposed targeted sanctions, fighting against a looming defeat of any single proposal in committee, the UK changed its strategy and proposed a complete, but considerably shorter listing package to the committee. In fact the UK "had taken pains to draw up a 'balanced' list of up to eight leaders from both sides," including a number of senior government officials (Penketh 2006; MacAskill 2006). This listing package containing a set of individuals enabled committee members to bargain over the proposal's content. However, several committee members including China, Russia, Qatar and even the US raised objections to the UK's proposal partly on grounds of "insufficient evidence to implicate some senior Sudanese officials" (Lynch 2006b). Additionally, the SRSG on Sudan, Jan Pronk, realizing that a package deal was a potential solution, openly made the suggestion to "designate individuals from the middle of the list of names, rather than those at either extreme, in order to demonstrate greater flexibility and realism" (US Permanent Mission to the UN 2006b).

To placate China, Russia and Qatar within the committee, the UK and US together further trimmed down the list to four individuals and garnered support from other committee members. On April 13, 2006, the Chairman following a joint designation by Argentina, Denmark, France, Japan, Peru, Slovakia, the UK and US circulated a shorter list of four individuals as a "balanced package" (Lederer 2006d). The proposal now deliberately included "individuals from all sides, but refrains from naming high officials" (Agence France Presse 2006a; SCR Forecast April 2006). The US noted that the proposal merely resembled a "down payment on what we expect will be additional sanctions" (Lederer 2006c). Within the timeframe of two working days, China and Russia placed a hold on the listing request (Hoge 2006b). According to the Chinese ambassador, "[i]n the sanctions committee meeting, he had joined others in requesting clarifications on the inclusion of individuals on the sanctions list" (Security Council Press Release 2006). While China and Russia did not principally rule out that those individuals could be sanctioned, they criticized the timing, stated that sanctions would undermine the cooperation of conflict parties and requested more time to discuss the request (Lederer 2006e). The proposed designation was taken up again at committee consultations on April 19, 2006 (S/2006/1045, para. 14), with no change of positions. It became clear that the committee was seriously deadlocked, and any listing initiative would fail to win the support of sanctions skeptics.

From the perspective of committee governance, this episode of committee decision-making between 2005 and early 2006 illustrates that, even though the Council had transferred aspects such as listing individuals and entities to the identical group of states in committee, decision-making fell victim to stalemate. This left sanctions proponents with the option to submit packages of listing requests, but to no avail. Skeptical members kept preferring deadlock and rejected all initiatives to implement the sanctions regime by way of sanctions designations. It points to the limits of committee governance: Its effects seem to occur only if the overall sanctions implementation is in the interests of all committee members, irrespective of disagreements on the specifics.

Bypassing the committee: The prelude to resolution 1672 (2006)

In the third episode, member states resolved committee deadlock by referring the issue back to the Council. At this stage, Council members faced two alternatives to avoid stalemate. First, they could seek to negotiate criteria and rules, with the aim of fixing focal points that would indicate on which requests to compromise. However, since rule-making efforts ran into resistance from China and Russia, sanctions proponents instead sought to resolve the deadlock by adopting a Council package resolution.

To move forward on the blocked listing proposal, the P3 started by attempting to set decision criteria for the committee. With respect to procedures, France suggested dropping the consensus practice. Instead, as in the United Nations Compensation Commission (Becker *et al.* 2018), it favored a majoritarian voting system without veto, which it had advocated since the early 2000s' sanctions reform process (Sievers and Daws 2014, p. 530). In US–French consultations on committee stalemate, the French diplomat "clarified, that designations are best taken by consensus at the committee level; however, "as a matter of doctrine," the principle of consensus should not become a straitjacket, and a sanctions committee should be allowed to overcome the obstacle of a hold, as in the Chinese/Russian hold over Sudanese names, through a simple procedural vote, without requiring recourse to Security Council deliberations" (US Embassy Paris 2006a). However, during the negotiations about committee rules, sanctions skeptics objected to the French position, precisely because the consensus rule played into their hands. As a result, "France's reservations against the consensus rule" (SCR Forecast April 2006) could not be accommodated and the guidelines instead used the standard language that "if (…) consensus still cannot be reached, the matter may be submitted to the Security Council" (guidelines, para. 25(c)).

With respect to substantive criteria, "refusing to succumb to the stall tactics that have become standard operating procedures for the Chinese, Russian and Qatari delegations" (US Permanent Mission to the UN 2006d), the P3 tried to change the designation criteria. Meanwhile, the Darfur Peace Agreement (DPA) had been signed on May 5, 2006, but to no avail since both the JEM and a SLA splinter group immediately discredited it (Traub 2010, p. 17). Still, the US submitted a draft resolution endorsing the DPA and preparing for transition to an AU-UN peacekeeping mission (Wadhams 2006a). The draft also included new listing criteria and tasked the committee with sanctioning any individual or group that violated or undermined the DPA, including Sudan or the Janjaweed (Holslag 2008, pp. 81–82; Wadhams 2006b). However, China and Russia dismissed any change on the sanctions track. In US-Chinese consultations, China "indicate[d] its strong preference for unanimity and provided a veritable roadmap of what it needed to secure this outcome: omission of a reference to UNSCR 1591 (2005) (…) on which China had abstained" (US Permanent Mission to the UN 2006d). To secure the peacekeeping transition under a Chinese veto threat, "[a]fter three rounds of working-level negotiations and an eleventh-hour Ambassadorial exchange" (US Permanent Mission to the UN 2006d), the P5 agreed to a softer wording. So instead of breaking the deadlock through rules, the Council "expresse[d] its intention to consider taking, (…) strong and effective measures, such as a travel ban and assets freeze, against any individual or group that violates or attempts to block the implementation" of the DPA (resolution 1679 (2006), para. 1, emphasis removed). In addition, the Council no longer directed the committee to designate violators (Wadhams 2006c). Since any language directed toward the committee was deleted, the Chinese immediately supported the draft resolution, which "(…) had a domino effect on the other dissenters, with Russia and Qatar ultimately voting in favor" (US Permanent Mission to the UN 2006d). The following resolution 1706 (2006) simply reiterated this intention (para. 14).

Since rule-making had proven unsuccessful and the listing proposals failed in committee, the proactive states altered course and suggested listing individuals by means of a Council resolution (Sievers and Daws 2014, p. 530). The P3 no longer expected that the Council could solve the deadlock with rules (US Embassy Paris 2006a). In fact, it was costlier to negotiate over rules than to bypass the committee simply because China, Russia and Qatar maintained that they opposed sanctions on Sudan (Lederer 2006e). Hence, on April 18, 2006, the US presented a draft resolution with the same four individuals as before to the Council in the form of a sanctions package (Lynch 2006b). The US strategy to table the requests as a draft resolution was intended "to circumvent the opposition from Russia and China with the hope that the two countries would not veto the text" (Aziakou 2006a). While the US asked other countries to support a sanctions resolution instead of continuing discussions in the committee (US Embassy Paris 2006a; US Embassy Tokyo 2006), there was no change of positions. Although it remained unclear whether or not China and Russia would veto the draft, the US was "hopeful that it will pass" and noted that they "haven't heard the 'v' word" (Aziakou 2006b).

To secure the resolution's passage, it had to be put into an even larger package deal. A compromise was established to couple the resolution with a presidential statement supporting the Abuja peace process (S/PRST/2006/17) upon the insistence of African members and "thereby sending a signal that the sanctions were not aimed at pressuring the talks per se, but in response to the ongoing violations of human rights and of the ceasefire" (SCR Forecast May 2006b); thereafter, the Council adopted the resolution on April 25, 2006. China, Russia, and Qatar abstained, as expected. Resolution 1672 (2006) implemented sanctions on four individuals, namely, Gaffar Elhassan (Western Military Region Commander, Sudanese Armed Forces), Sheikh Musa Hilal (Janjaweed), Adam Shant (SLA Commander), Gabril Badri (National Movement for Reform and Development Field Commander). The US hailed the news that "[u]ltimately, on April 25, we prevailed, but imposed sanctions on fewer individuals than we wanted" (Bolton 2007, p. 352). Conversely, China, Qatar and Russia were critical that "this resolution might have a negative impact on the prospects for concluding a peace agreement" (Russia, S/PV.5423, 2), demanding that proactive states should rather have provided "supplementary material" and that going to the Council instead of the committee "is at variance with the Council's practice of many years' standing" (China, S/PV.5423, p. 3).

The puzzling Chinese acquiescence to sanctioning the four individuals can be explained by two factors. First, the stakes had already been considerably lowered from the original confidential annex with 17 individuals to 4 mid-level individuals, 2 of which were Darfur rebels, while only 2 were affiliated with the Sudanese government. Accordingly, the Chinese and Russian abstention "indicates that neither may be willing to veto as long as proposals do not target the highest-ranking Sudanese officials" (US Permanent Mission to the UN 2006c). In addition, "[n]one of the four had significant assets in foreign banks or indulged in foreign travel, so the impact of these sanctions was more symbolic than real" (Prendergast and Sullivan 2008, p. 7). Second, China wanted to avoid being isolated. In bilateral US-Chinese consultations, a Chinese diplomat explained that "China decided to abstain (…), because going against a majority of the Council's members would have been 'unthinkable,' (…)." Further he acknowledged that China had changed its tactics since April 17, when China, Russia, and Qatar blocked the [committee listing request] (…), but reiterated that China's fundamental opposition to sanctions had not changed. "Once Russia and Qatar decided to abstain, Ambassador Wang (Guangya) decided it was better to abstain than veto" (US Embassy Khartoum 2006b).

Still, the adoption of sanctions targets via Council resolution created implementation issues because in contrast to a committee listing, which would have required minimal identifying information, there were no such requirements for the Council. Without a certain quality of identifiers, enforcing a travel ban and identifying individual's assets is difficult. As the committee Chair noted, the resolution "had not included sufficient identifying elements on the designated persons, despite the relevant provisions of the [committee] guidelines. There were fears that that might create problems for implementation of the targeted measures" (Press Release Briefing of 1591 Committee Chair; S/PV.5601). Indeed, even French officials mentioned "the inadequacy of identifiers in enforcing the travel ban and asset freeze" (S/2006/795, para. 119). Consequently, the Panel of Experts recommended increasing the amount of identifying information for effective implementation (S/2006/795, para. 120). In response, the committee sent a note verbale to all member states requesting additional information; however, not a single response was received (S/2006/1045, para. 19; S/2007/584, para. 154). Subsequently, when the Panel of Experts provided further identifying information (S/2006/795, paras. 115–123, S/2007/584, paras. 142–157), the committee amended its sanctions list (SC/9093, SC/10938, SC/11112; S/2007/779, para. 26).

Two conclusions can be drawn from this third case episode. From the perspective of committee governance, it shows that Council members perceive rule-making as a practical option in overcoming committee deadlock. However, skeptical members derailed rule-making efforts, both on majority voting as well as decision criteria. Although the Council has been more active on Sudan since 2012, the discussions have yet to be translated into significant changes, and in any event those decisions adopted were mostly vague declarations of intent.[1] For instance, the Council requested the committee "to respond effectively to any reports of non-compliance, (…) including by engaging with all relevant parties" (resolution 2035 (2012), para. 14) omitting potential new listings. The episode also demonstrates that, if rule-making fails, a Council package resolution under majority voting provides a viable alternative. Circumventing the committee and thereby disregarding the division of labor between Council and committee, proved successful because sanctions opponents would have to veto a resolution publicly, the content of which was relatively minor.

A committee without consensus

The fourth episode demonstrates that two permanent members' opposition to sanctions on Sudan led to a sustained stalemate of sanctions implementation. Proactive members no longer considered rule-making as a viable strategy since previous efforts remained unsuccessful. Instead, they sought to overcome deadlock through package deals. Within the committee, the US, UK and France actively spearheaded listing requests in several instances, mostly with China, Russia and the Arab member opposing sanctions. Because sanctions proponents were no longer willing to risk the failure of their proposals within Council, the committee was largely stalemated. All further listing attempts have proven futile. In practice, the sanctions regime has been largely dormant as there were only four sanctioned individuals and ultimately the sanctions have remained unenforced.

While again committee members had two alternative ways of solving the stalemate, namely rule-making or package deal, they no longer believed that the former was viable. There is no indication that any member tried to change committee rules to break the logjam. In fact, the committee made only a symbolic change to its internal guidelines. On the first occasion, when the Council introduced the Focal Point for Delisting procedure (resolution 1730 (2006)) to circumvent governments that were unwilling or unable to forward delisting petitions to any committee, it directed all committees to revise their guidelines accordingly, albeit without issuing a deadline. Despite this window of opportunity, the amended guidelines of December 2007, more than a year after the Council's directive, incorporated only the Focal Point for Delisting procedure (see Chapter 3).[2] For Sudan, it is insignificant due to the list's brevity. The fact that neither individuals nor any governments have asked for delistings or humanitarian exemptions *verify* that, in violation of international law, the sanctions have not been implemented (S/2017/1125, para 182). On the second occasion, in late 2013 following an initiative from the Chair, the committee guidelines were to be updated for three reasons. First, they were to be brought into line with the latest standard procedures. Second, the now-standard rules were to be implemented extending the no-objection procedure from two to five working days for listings. The Sudan Sanctions Committee was the only active committee that had a shorter than five days no-objection procedure.[3] Third, the remaining guidelines were to be harmonized into now-standard language. While all this followed a general trend to increase transparency (S/2006/997, para. 16a) and as the Sudan Committee lagged the most, changes were merely symbolic rather than contentious and agreed without even a single committee meeting (S/2013/788). The updated guidelines incorporated a five working days no-objection procedure, restricting holds for a maximum of six months, restricting outgoing members' holds, and harmonized information requirements for new listings as well as notifications (paras. 2c, 4, 5, 10). Even skeptical members could easily agree to these changes since they would have few practical consequences.

Concerning sanctions measures, the sanctions opponents clearly signaled that they would undermine every effort to strengthen the sanctions regime, particularly any geographical extension of the arms embargo or the enforcement of a no-fly zone (Happaerts 2009, pp. 108–110; Wuthnow 2013, pp. 99–101). Even when faced with compelling evidence that Chinese weapons were used in Darfur, China maintained that "its weapons sales to Khartoum are legitimate, since the embargo covers only the territory of Darfur, not all of Sudan," so that it was not China but Khartoum that violated the sanctions regime (Rice 2009a).

The P3, encouraged by Council resolution 1672 (2006) sanctioning four individuals (US Permanent Mission to the UN 2006c), strived for new sanctions packages. The P3 held off on sanctions until early 2007, so as not to provoke outright Sudanese rejection of "rehatting" the AMIS into the UNAMID peacekeeping mission, haggling over whether or not Khartoum's "consent" to peacekeeping was required (resolution 1706 (2006), with China, Russia, and Qatar abstaining, Wuthnow 2013, pp. 98–99). However, following Khartoum's continued refusal to consent to a UN mission, the P3 held talks over a strategy to present a new sanctions "package" (Lynch 2007). In February 2007, the UK and US met to decide on "[p]ossible next steps," which included additional sanctions targets, extending the arms embargo to all of Sudan, and imposing a no-fly zone over Darfur (US Embassy London 2007). In addition, France, the UK and US exchanged lists of possible targets. The US proposed designation of three individuals: The Head of Sudanese Military Intelligence and Security, a JEM leader and the State Minister for Humanitarian Affairs, whereas the UK suggested nine names comprising the SAF Western Military Commander, the Former SAF Western Military Commander, the SAF Air-force Commander, the State Minister for Humanitarian Affairs, the current and the former SLM spokesperson, another rebel leader, the leader of the Liberation and Justice Movement, and the Janjaweed leader (US Permanent Mission to the UN 2007c; US Embassy Khartoum 2007). The UK was well aware that China and Russia would oppose the US proposed high-ranking Military Intelligence Head and noted that this listing would endanger UK-Sudanese counter-terrorism cooperation (US Permanent Mission to the UN 2007e). Thus, the UK

> proposed to present the names (…) as an opening position, and use the threat of submitting the names to the Sudan Sanctions Committee to induce China and Russia to pressure Sudan to deliver 1) an immediate improvement in humanitarian situation (…), 2) an end to violations of the arms embargo and to offensive overflights, and 3) complete cooperation on the Heavy Support Package [for the peacekeeping mission].
>
> (US Permanent Mission to the UN 2007c)

The French delegation was skeptical about the US list, partly because the ranks included were too senior, and partly because it did not want to complicate ICC proceedings, preferring to designate "intermediate-level" individuals and "criminal field commanders" (US Permanent Mission to the UN 2007d; US Embassy Paris 2007). As an alternative suggestion, on March 15 the French circulated a list among the P3 with five potential targets of intermediate rank. The individuals included the Former Governor of North Darfur and Major General in the SAF, a Janjaweed militiaman involved in the attacks of April 2005 and April 2006, the Former SLA chief of staff, and two G-19 commanders. The latter four names had also appeared in the Panel of Experts confidential annexes (US Permanent Mission to the UN 2007i).

Meanwhile, during sanctions committee meetings and P5 consultations, despite support from many committee members on new sanctions measures and new designations (Casert 2007), China and Russia as well as Qatar, South Africa and Indonesia stressed that additional sanctions and designations would be a "mistake" (US Permanent Mission to the UN 2007e; US Permanent Mission to the UN 2007f). During P5 consultations, China issued a direct veto threat and warned that the US "should not bother to table a sanctions resolution, as Beijing had already decided it 'could not be allowed to pass' (…) and explicitly rejected sanctions as a threat to the political process and further dialogue with Khartoum" (US Permanent Mission to the UN 2007g). During two informal committee meetings in May 2007 discussing results of the latest Panel of Experts report, which had suggested extending the arms embargo and listing new individuals, among others China, Russia, Qatar and Indonesia objected to all recommendations. Belgium, France, Slovakia, UK, and the US realized that any listing initiative in the committee would be futile. The US diplomat was highly critical about the Italian Chair's "commitment to gain consensus on every issue, no matter how anodyne, [which] has the effect of facilitating the obstructionism of Committee members sympathetic to Khartoum" (US Permanent Mission to the UN 2007j). Now even the Panel of Experts, "[n]oting that the Committee was constrained by the consensus rule" urged UK and US diplomats "to force a vote in the Council on new names and sanctions measures" (US Permanent Mission to the UN 2007h).

However, the US did not raise the matter to the Security Council for a number of reasons. First, the US had received an explicit veto threat from China and other Council members including Russia, none of which supported new sanctions measures or additional designations. Second, even the P3 had different views on whom to designate and while such issues could have been resolved, for the moment it no longer represented a unified coalition. Even some Western allies including Belgium, Germany, Italy, and Peru hesitated (US Embassy Rome 2007). Third, the UN Secretary-General had requested that his diplomatic initiatives should not be undermined. Fourth, as the US administration quickly wanted to send a visible sign of "doing something" instead of rallying support within the Council, with only "remote" prospects of succeeding (Abramowitz and Lynch 2007), it was considered that a domestic listing would counter pressures for action and be more cost-effective. Accordingly, the US unilaterally designated three individuals and 31 government-run Sudanese companies on May 29, 2007 (Abramowitz and Lynch 2007).

In late 2007, Qatar suddenly signaled its intention to designate rebels opposed to Khartoum, which called the P3 into action. During a committee meeting, Qatar requested other delegations' opinions on listing "JEM leader Khalil Ibrahim and SLM faction leader Abdelwahid el-Nur for their failure to attend the UN/AU-led Darfur mediation talks." Qatar argued "that Ibrahim's and Abdelwahid's absence at the talks constituted an impediment to the peace process per paragraph 3 (c) of resolution 1591." This offer received initial support. Qatar even suggested circumventing the sanctions committee and submitting a Council resolution "to raise the profile of the designations" (Khalizad 2007a). While the sanctions proponents welcomed such suggestions and realized that "Qatar's unprecedented call for Committee action may represent a unique opportunity for Council action on sanctions (…), while also offering us the leverage to press for a broader list of targets," the US insisted that listings should also include the Sudanese government, which Qatar objected to (Khalizad 2007a). Internally, the P3 agreed that they "should be prepared with a counterproposal" to the Qatari initiative (US Permanent Mission to the UN 2007m). Ultimately, the Qataris did not follow through and the initiative subsided (SCR Forecast December 2007b). However, it shows that committee members might argue about the applicability of sanctions on a certain group of individuals, provided that they had a common interest in making targeted sanctions work effectively.

When the committee discussed the Panel of Experts' final report in November 2007, the dynamics among committee members remained unchanged. The panel suggested designating five individuals, extending the arms embargo and imposing sanctions on jet fuel and six cargo airlines for violations of Council resolutions (S/2007/584, pp. 6–8). Within the committee, China "objected to any further discussion" about whether or not the arms embargo should be strengthened. China and Qatar also opposed aviation sanctions, while Russia provided a reminder that only member states, and not the Panel can make formal listing requests. In essence, "[c]onforming to predictable positions, China and Russia opposed all of the Panel's substantive proposals, and Qatar and Indonesia attempted to block even the most basic recommendations (…), such as sending follow-up letters to states" that have failed to respond to Panel information requests (Khalizad 2007b).

In response, the US ambassador sent an intriguing cable to Washington:

> [T]he Committee is not empowered to adopt new sanctions measures–only the Council can do this (…). Though the Committee did not agree to endorse any of the Panel's substantive recommendations to the Council, the Council may consider these recommendations at any time on the initiative of a Council member. We should not read too much into positions taken in the Committee adverse to ours as consensus rules allow members a cost-free veto on any issue–no votes are taken and deliberations are not public. Elevating an issue for Council discussion or vote makes adverse positions more difficult to sustain. We should keep this avenue in mind if there is interest in enacting any of the recommendations.
>
> (Khalizad 2007b)

This demonstrates that member states perceive the Council and committee as distinct bodies, despite identical membership, where only the Council is considered as having the competence to amend sanctions measures. It also illustrates that delegating to a consensus-based committee does indeed create a situation prone to deadlock, which member states could resolve through Council action. The comment also shows that members consider a Council veto to be costlier than withholding consensus in the committee.

In early 2008, the P3 began a new sanctions initiative as a means of forcing Khartoum into giving its consent for UNAMID deployment, while China still opposed any sanctions (US Permanent Mission to the UN 2008a). In May 2008, the US forged a new sanctions list of four individuals, including identifiers and evidentiary packages, and sought P5 reactions (US State Department 2008b). The UK supported the list. France supported three names, but challenged the inclusion of Daoussa Déby, the Chadian president's half-brother (S/2007/584, para. 124), because this would undermine Chad-EU cooperation on the EUFOR mission. In turn, the US offered to support "one or two" Chadian rebels to win French support for Déby (US State Department 2008e). Russia informally pledged "not to obstruct (…) efforts to sanction any of the four" (Khalizad 2008b). However, China was opposed and reasoned that

> [f]irst, (…) the imposition of sanctions could affect the Government of Sudan's "fragile" acceptance of the deployment of [UNAMID] (…). Second, sanctioning the four individuals could affect the Sudanese Government's willingness to participate in political negotiations (…). Third, "technically speaking," China remains unconvinced that the information (…) makes a case for sanctioning the four individuals. Fourth, noting that China abstained on UNSCR 1591, (…) China continues to be skeptical of the utility of sanctions in solving the Darfur crisis.
>
> (US Embassy Beijing 2011)

China explicitly cautioned about the measure's prudence and urged "the United States to 'think twice' about adding the four names" (US Embassy Beijing 2008). Yet, the US would not back down and assembled a package coupled with a threat to use a public Council vote to win Chinese acquiescence within the committee. A US cable outlined the strategy. The US hoped that China "may calculate that their national interests are better served by not opposing any of the four names in committee." Furthermore, US diplomats should explicitly threaten a Council referral, arguing that

> Committee consensus would be quicker and generate far less media attention (…). If consensus is not reached, we will be compelled to pursue imposition of sanctions on these individuals through a vote in the Security Council, as was done in 2006.
>
> (US State Department 2008b)

Early in September 2008, the US called a final P3 meeting to discuss the proposal (US State Department 2008e). However, the US realized that the French and the British no longer supported the proposal. France believed that "new sanctions would derail ongoing mediation and dialogue efforts underway involving Chad, Sudan and the various rebel movements (…)." The French also cautioned that a committee proposal might severely backfire. Because the committee considered requests separately, "Sudan's friends" might use the Sudan Sanctions Committee's procedures to ensure that the Committee only approves sanctioning the anti-government rebel, Khalil Ibrahim, while rejecting the other three names. (…) If this were done, (…) Sudan would win a propaganda victory." The US acknowledged that "[t]he Committee approves or rejects names individually, not on a slate – therefore, Libya and/or China could theoretically place holds on all the names except Ibrahim" (US Permanent Mission to the UN 2008b). Finally, the UK had concerns because "the timing of this proposal – with the ICC issue looming and just before the UN General Assembly ministerial week – was poor" (US Permanent Mission to the UN 2008b).

Lacking P3 support and facing a likely failure, the US Permanent Mission advised the State Department against any further action:

> In light (*sic*!) France's position (…), the UK's lack of enthusiasm and China's near-certain opposition (…), USUN recommends holding off temporarily on this initiative (…). If we propose new names for sanctions without P3 support, we run a high risk of public failure. (…) [F]orcing a Council vote on our proposed names (…) would worsen an already tense atmosphere in the Council.
>
> (US Permanent Mission to the UN 2008b)

As the committee again disagreed on Panel recommendations in late 2008 (US Permanent Mission to the UN 2008d), the P3 deliberated as to how they could apply pressure on Sudan apart from the use of sanctions designations, but without success. Such measures would have included media briefings "when China or Russia block a proposal," summoning Sudanese and Chadian ambassadors "for direct questioning," inviting "UN/AU/EU officials" as well as national experts to "highlight SCR violations," and urging NGOs to submit reports to the committee (US State Department 2008f). In December 2008, the P3 orchestrated a situation where Belgium issued a request to invite the Sudanese and Chadian ambassadors, while Human Rights First offered to brief the committee on human rights violations. However, Russia and China fiercely objected even to "soft measures" so that the Chair could "simply 'remind' the Perm Reps [of Sudan and Chad] that they could address the committee if they so chose," which they simply refused (US State Department 2008g).

Chinese and Russian intransigence has effectively cemented the present committee stalemate. First, although the P3 strongly prefer and heavily invest in listings proposals, they do not submit them because they no longer expect to succeed. Second, while sanctions regimes provide for delisting procedures and humanitarian exemptions, neither have resulted from decision problems, and nor has any state used them (S/2013/79, paras. 140–149; S/2017/1125, para. 182). Third, while the committee implemented symbolic recommendations such as entering an Interpol Special Notice Agreement in 2012 (S/2012/978, para. 15), updating the listing information in 2013 (SC/10938, SC/11112, SC/11436), and issuing narrative summaries for the four listed individuals in 2014, it incorporated none of the substantive recommendations, despite receiving the names of violators (S/2007/584, S/2011/111, para. 208; S/2013/79, para. 16). Fourth, skeptical states have seriously delayed or blocked Panel of Experts appointments and reports (for instance, What's in Blue 2011a, for report see S/2011/111). Fifth, the Panel of Experts did not perceive rule-making as a viable option and even asked proactive states to circumvent the committee. Sixthly, all sanctions measures remained non-implemented, while the panel extensively documented systematic violations of the arms embargo and the targeted sanctions (most recently, S/2015/31, S/2016/805, S/2017/1125).

In conclusion, this fourth episode illustrates the committee governance thesis' limitations. It shows that proactive members no longer believed that either rule-making or a Council resolution would yield successful outcomes, although these actors invested significantly into devising a strategy to overcome the skeptics' stalemate. Sanctions opponents over the years achieved their desired policy goal, namely to avoid any further pressure against Sudan. Overall, as a result of the preference constellation and the lack of implementation decisions, the sanctions regime has become totally ineffective.

Concluding thoughts

The Sudan sanctions regime represents a challenging case and illustrates the limitations of the committee governance framework. The Sudan case operates according to the logic of power politics and displays its expected effects. At least one permanent Council member first rejects the imposition of sanctions on Sudan and later undermines implementation, pursuing a policy of deadlock. The effects of committee governance occur only if members have to coordinate among several plausible options, for instance on designating individuals. Only in this constellation will focal points, such as rules or precedents, become influential. Accordingly, the sanctions regime follows entirely the logic of bargaining over package deals, though some lessons about committee governance can also be distilled.

Four conclusions for the committee governance framework can be drawn from this case. First, transferring tasks to a sanctions committee does not inevitably prompt rule-based governance, even if the Council has delegated tasks to the committee, because every member possesses the ability to block committee decisions. The appointed Sudan Sanctions Committee has failed to designate any individuals and entities subject to targeted sanctions due to the veto position of three committee members. The preference constellation is also visible in the few committee listing proposals. Committee members do not even discuss the merits of listing proposals, but rather reject listings out of principle. This stage shows that the committee can indeed be subject to deadlock. This finding does not contradict a theory of committee governance, because the committee can indeed fall prey to looming stalemate, despite the Council explicitly assigning the performance of tasks to the committee. Quite to the contrary, committee governance in the Security Council is clearly designed to leave room for political decisions, because Council members delegate to themselves, not to independent agents.

Second, the committee discussion leading up to Council resolution 1672 (2006) shows that proactive members principally consider rule-making as a viable option to overcome stalemate. However, as some members prefer inaction over action, committee members do not find themselves in a coordination situation where focal points would provide opportunities to overcome committee stalemate. Regulating committee decision-making does not work, if one member pursues deadlock as a policy goal and can simply reject any unfavorable set of rules. Accordingly, skeptical members objected to all efforts for changing procedural (e.g., the consensus requirement) and substantive rules (e.g., listing criteria). At the same time, Chinese and Russian opposition to a change in procedure indicates that rules would indeed endanger achieving their interest in committee deadlock.

Third, Council decision-making without recourse to a committee yields decisions characterized by power-politics. This has two aspects. On the one hand, proactive members view bargaining over the contents of a Council resolution, which combines listing requests to a package, as a principle and constantly available route to circumventing committee stalemate. In this case proactive members elevated the listing request to Council, because skeptical members blocked their proposals within the committee, calculating that a public Council vote would incentivize opposing members not to veto the resolution containing designations. On the other hand, the draft of what became resolution 1672 (2006) reflected a balanced package that traded-off two rebel commanders with two mid-level Sudanese officials. Hence, the decision taken by and large mirrored the interest constellation among powerful Council members.

Fourth, conforming to the committee governance thesis, Council members perceive Council and committee as distinct arenas, despite the identical membership. After resolution 1672 (2006), the proactive members again sought to overcome committee stalemate by suggesting packages of names, but faced resistance from China and Russia. However, this time even the US had to accept that according to established procedures the committee treats requests separately, which favored Chinese and Russian obstructionism. As a result, facing the likely failure of a Council draft resolution designating a second package of individuals, the proactive members refrained from putting the draft to a vote. As a consequence, even proactive members no longer submitted formal listing requests to the Council expecting a likely Chinese veto, while the committee remained in logjam. In fact, the sanctions regime is entirely ineffective as there are only four listed individuals and the sanctions measures remain unenforced.

Notes

1 Resolution 1779 (2007) included two Panel of Experts changes, to coordinate with UNAMID and to assess arms embargo violations (para. 3). Resolution 1945 (2010) clarified that arms embargo exemptions require committee approval and that exporting states should ensure end-user documentation (paras. 9, 10). On listing criteria, sanctions also applied to entities (resolution 2035 (2012), para. 3) and individuals and entities which "plan, sponsor or participate in attacks against UNAMID (…) may (…) meet the designation criteria" (resolution 2091 (2013), para. 8). Resolutions 2138 (2014), 2200 (2015) and 2265 (2016) further express intent.

2 A lexical search of *Security Council Report* forecasts, *Lexis Nexis*, *Panel of Experts reports* and *Wikileaks* has not yielded any attempts to create committee rules.

3 The inactive 1518/Iraq Sanctions Committee (three days) and the 1636/Lebanon Sanctions Committee (no defined timeframe) are exceptions, see Security Council Report 2013, pp. Annex.

8 The West vs. Iran

Sanctions in the context of nuclear non-proliferation

The non-proliferation dispute surrounding Iran's nuclear program emerged in August 2002 when information surfaced that Iran has constructed secret nuclear facilities in Natanz and Arak. Back in the 1960s, Iran had initiated a nuclear program and built a first research reactor, for which the country had Western assistance. At that time, though, Iran also committed itself to peaceful use of nuclear technologies and ratified the Non-proliferation Treaty in 1968. Since then, Iran continues to be legally bound not to acquire nuclear weapons, to adopt an IAEA safeguards agreement for verification of compliance concluded in 1974, and to allow IAEA inspections to confirm whether or not Iran has declared items correctly and if necessary to investigate what was not declared. However, in 2002 the news raised suspicion that Iran might secretively be pursuing enrichment with the aim of acquiring nuclear weapons capability. Since Iran had not declared the Natanz and Arak facilities, it had violated its obligations and the IAEA, therefore, began to investigate (Wuthnow 2013, pp. 77–78), later reporting that Iran had violated the safeguards agreement, insufficiently cooperated, and had developed new centrifuge enrichment technologies (GOV/2004/83, para. 107). Hence, a military motive behind Iran's nuclear program seemed plausible. IAEA Director-General ElBaradei concluded that "(…) Iran had failed in a number of instances over an extended period of time to meet its obligations" including reporting on processing nuclear material and declaring nuclear facilities (GOV/2005/67, para. 4; GOV/2006/15; GOV/2006/27). After three years of unsuccessful French, German and British diplomacy (known as the EU-3) and continued Iranian defiance, the IAEA Board of Governors referred Iran to the Security Council (GOV/2006/14).

In 2006, the Security Council demanded that Iran halted its enrichment-related and reprocessing activities, and fully cooperated with the IAEA. With the four following resolutions, the Security Council imposed far-reaching, detailed and stringent sanctions in the face of Iranian defiance: Targeted sanctions on individuals and entities (travel ban, assets freeze), commodity sanctions on nuclear material, equipment and technology, dual-use goods and ballistic-missile related goods, import and export embargoes on arms, financial restrictions and a cargo interdiction regime. The Iran sanctions regime had the third-largest sanctions list after the Al-Qaida and Taliban regimes and is in many ways similar to that imposed on North Korea, as for instance, the frequent designation via Council resolutions. With conclusion of the P5+1–Iran nuclear deal in July 2015, the Council partially suspended the sanctions regime (Joint Comprehensive Plan of Action, resolution 2231 (2015)).

So far, the literature has considered Iran sanctions regime mostly from the perspective of foreign policy or sanctions effectiveness, but has failed to understand the regime's dynamics. At the outset, from 2006 to 2010 sanctions proponents favored holding the Iran sanctions case at Council level, churning out four detailed sanctions packages within this period. As soon as they transferred decisions to the committee, they established a system of divided labor. So how exactly did this transfer of decisions by the Council to the same group of states in the committee affect the decision-making dynamics and quality of decisions? The concept of committee governance helps us to delve into these issues and account for why power matters in the Council, but rules matter at committee level.

The Iran sanctions regime makes it possible to contrast the committee governance thesis with an alternative setup without committee, but still within the same setting. Indeed, the Iran case demonstrates that Council members have two equally plausible options for pursuing a sanctions regime, but both come with distinct consequences. While Council decision-making operates according to the logic of package deals, committee decision-making requires the submission of well-reasoned listing proposals that satisfy a high evidence threshold. In addition, within the Iran sanctions regime we can compare decision-making on individual targeted sanctions and the granting of exemptions, with regulatory governance on proliferation-related items subject to export control. It is also a regime vested with great power interest, where finding the effect of committee governance would strengthen our confidence in the mechanism.

In the next section, I describe the Iran sanctions regime's political origins, the interests among permanent members and what this means for committee governance. In the second section, I carefully dissect the bargaining process over the four Council resolutions which imposed a complex web of sanctions measures up until 2010, without recourse to a committee. In the third section, I compare how the Council affected decision-making by referring sanctions violators' designations to the committee. The fourth section explores an alternate route for overcoming coordination problems in sanctions regimes: In the field of proliferation and ballistic missile related commodity sanctions, the Council used Nuclear Suppliers Group and the Missile Technology Control Regime export trigger lists as external focal points. Finally, the last section discusses key findings in light of the committee governance thesis.

The political origins of the Iran sanctions regime

In reaction to the Iranian nuclear program, the Security Council demanded that Iran should cease all enrichment-related and reprocessing activities and resume its cooperation with IAEA inspectors (resolution 1696 (2005)). By resolution

1737 (2006), the Council imposed an assets freeze, commodity sanctions on proliferation-related materials and items related to ballistic-missile programs and provided a first list of sanctions targets and lists of embargoed items. The sanctions regime was modified and tightened through subsequent resolutions introducing an embargo on imports from Iran (resolution 1747 (2007)) and exports to the country of certain conventional arms (resolution 1929 (2010)), as well as a travel ban on listed individuals (resolution 1803 (2008)). The Council also adopted subsidiary measures including provision of a legal basis for unilateral and regional financial sanctions together with cargo inspections. The Council created a sanctions committee to monitor sanctions implementation, add or remove individuals and entities from its sanctions list, along with determining additional nuclear and ballistic missile-related goods. In 2010, the Council established a Panel of Experts (resolution 1929 (2010)), which it extended up until it was dissolved in 2015 with the entry into force of the Iran nuclear deal.

On the one hand, the P5+1 shared a common interest in preventing Iran from gaining nuclear weapons. While Western powers perceived a "nuclearized" Iran as a direct threat to their security and that of Israel as well as a potential danger to regional stability, China and Russia also had a strong interest in non-proliferation. Both have repeatedly stressed their concerns about Iran's nuclear program (S/PV.5500, S/PV.5612). China was worried about continued non-compliance with IAEA and the destabilizing effects of a "nuclearized" Iran (Wuthnow 2013, p. 75). Russia "(…) did not want 'under any circumstance' to see the emergence of a nuclear Iran (…). Not only would it upset the stability of the Gulf, but it would fatally compromise the nonproliferation regime." In fact, Russia perceived Iran's behavior as "incomprehensible" (US Embassy Moscow 2007).

On the other hand, P5+1 interests also clashed, in particular on how much and what type of pressure the Council should exert on Iran and accordingly, how strict the sanctions regime should be. The Bush administration was a staunch supporter of UN sanctions for what it considered a rouge regime seeking nuclear weapons and exporting terrorism that needed to be forced into compliance by maximizing pressure. The US, having subjected Iran to sanctions since the Islamic Revolution, had almost negligible trade relations (0.2 percent, see Table 8.1), and hence, the economic costs would also be marginal. When the Council imposed sanctions in 2006, among Iran's major trading partners was the EU, with large trade shares held by Italy (6 percent), Germany and France (each 5 percent). While generally in favor of sanctions, these countries were wary about the economic impact; consequently they initially preferred diplomacy, and also championed more generous sanctions exemptions at a later stage. The UK held only a small trade share (1 percent) and hence supported a tougher stance. Overall, the P3 had a strong interest in legally-binding sanctions (see e.g., US, UK, France S/PV.5500). These powers sought to prevent Iran from obtaining nuclear-weapons capability and invested significant diplomatic resources to this cause.

It is worth noting here that Germany had a special role. The country had participated in negotiating all major sanctions resolutions since 2006, despite not

Table 8.1 P5+1 and EU trade volume with Iran in billion US$, 2002–2012

Year	*2000*	*2002*	*2004*	*2006*	*2008*	*2010*	*2012*	*2006–2012 % change*
China	2.5	3.7	7.0	14.4	27.8	29.4	36.5	152
Russia	0.7	0.8	2.0	2.1	3.7	3.6	2.3	9
France	1.8	2.2	4.6	5.4	6.2	3.5	1.3	–77
United Kingdom	0.51	1.2	0.89	0.94	0.90	0.75	0.35	–63
United States	0.19	0.19	0.24	0.25	0.79	0.31	0.26	6
Germany	2.0	2.4	4.9	5.7	6.6	6.3	3.8	–34
EU-28	12.8	13.2	25.1	32.3	37.6	34.2	16.7	–48
Total	**20.4**	**23.7**	**44.8**	**61.1**	**83.5**	**78.1**	**61.2**	**0**

Source: UN Comtrade Database.

Note
Total trade volume combines import and export. Data by relevant state (reporter) to Iran (partner).

being a permanent member. This even included highly secretive P5 deliberations in forming the so-called P5+1 group (i.e., P5 plus Germany, also referred to as E3+3 or EU3+3). This is mainly attributed to Germany's economic relations with Iran and its leading role in EU foreign policy so that it effectively became "the sixth permanent member" just for the specific case of Iran (Sauer 2009, pp. 119–121). Thus, all Iran sanctions resolutions have been drafted by the EU-3, except for resolution 1929 (2010) sponsored by EU-3 and the US (S/2006/589; S/2006/1010; S/2007/170; S/2008/141; S/2010/283).

In contrast to the Western members, Russia and China were cautious. Russia (2 percent) had little interest in Iran's natural oil and gas, but was Iran's largest supplier of nuclear technologies, including construction of the Bushehr reactor and supplying uranium (Anthony *et al.* 2007, pp. 60–63). China (12 percent) was about to become Iran's single most important trading partner and had a strong interest in accessing Iranian oil and gas reserves to satisfy its growing energy consumption, but also re-exported refined petroleum. In particular, China was keen on avoiding trade sanctions on natural resources and goods as it frequently exchanged resources for goods (Kleine-Ahlbrandt and Small 2008, p. 41; Wuthnow 2013, p. 75). As a consequence, Russia and China were skeptical about sanctions being an effective means of solving the nuclear crisis (Wuthnow 2013, pp. 75–76; SCR Forecast May 2006a; SCR Forecast June 2006b). In essence, China warned that sanctions could "lead to complications" (China, S/PV.5500) and that "diplomatic efforts (…) should be strengthened" (China, S/PV.5612). Both countries were determined to prevent an automatic shift toward military intervention (S/PV.5500, pp. 5–6).

Accordingly, the P5+1 were in a coordination situation. While all P5+1 were interested in a "non-nuclearized" Iran, they disagreed about how to achieve their objective. The US advocated sanctions the most vocally, while the EU-3 favored sanctions after expediting the negotiations track for economic interests (Bolton 2007, pp. 130–164). Russia and China instead preferred a cautious approach, not impacting on what they considered to be legitimate trade relations. Although members shared an interest in preventing Iran from gaining nuclear weapons, they assessed in different ways if and how sanctions should be applied. Adding further complication, the strong economic interests involved required significant bargaining over the scope of sanctions measures. In this constellation, the P5+1 principally had two ways of solving the coordination problem. Either the proactive members could pursue a larger package deal entirely at Council level, including the sanctions measures combined with lists of embargoed items and sanctions designations. In this case, the outcomes are expected to reflect entirely the interest constellation among powerful members. Alternatively, proactive members could transfer the task of determining these implementation decisions to a sanctions committee. In this case, due to diverging interests among committee members, I would expect to observe the effects of committee governance triggering rule-based governance.

Despite Council-centric decision-making on Iran sanctions in the sanctions regime's initial stages, the Council provided formal decision criteria for the committee with respect to individual targeted sanctions and commodity sanctions. The Council determined that those individuals and entities

> engaged in, directly associated with or providing support for Iran's proliferation sensitive nuclear activities or the development of nuclear weapon delivery systems, or by persons or entities acting on their behalf or at their direction, or by entities owned or controlled by them, including through illicit means (…),
>
> (resolution 1737 (2006), para. 12)

are eligible for listing. Since the travel ban was initially voluntary, the Council provided for exemptions to the assets freeze only for particular expenses (para. 13). Concerning the list of non-proliferation related items, the Council stipulated that the committee should determine "any additional items, materials, equipment, goods and technology, (…), which could contribute to enrichment-related, or reprocessing, or heavy water-related activities, or to the development of nuclear weapon delivery systems" (para. 3d).

Down the Council route: Imposing rounds of sanctions packages

From 2006 to 2010, the sanctions regime followed the logic of grand politicized bargaining in the Council chamber and, as mentioned earlier, not in a committee, although the Council had created a committee in 2006 (resolution 1737 (2006)). Sanctions supporters deliberately kept Iran sanctions within the confines of the Council to escalate sanctions with detailed resolutions, combining new sanctions measures and implementing them at the same time. Subsequent sanctions resolutions complemented earlier resolutions with additional or strengthened measures without sunset clauses. Altogether, sanctions proponents achieved the adoption of remarkably biting sanctions in four resolutions combined with the third largest sanctions list in just four years of Council negotiations (1737 (2006), 1747 (2007), 1803 (2008) and 1929 (2010)).

The Iranian nuclear conflict posed great challenges for Council members. While the P5 agreed that "Iran's unwillingness to comply (…) is unreasonable and constitutes a serious problem for the international community," they disagreed about how the Council should react (SCR Forecast May 2006a; SCR Forecast June 2006b). Sanctions supporters wished to impose tough sanctions early on, but the skeptics preferred measures tailored to the proliferation of nuclear weapons and delivery systems, vowing to oppose any measures that would negatively affect their business interests (SCR Forecast November 2006). This created an unstable P5 consensus on a "dual-track" approach consisting of small but incremental up-scaling of sanctions and the offer of a negotiation package (SCR Forecast May 2006a). However, Iran repeatedly derailed the fragile P5 consensus by initially acceding to a settlement or ceasing enrichment, only to withdraw from commitments shortly thereafter; this situation had prevented IAEA referral to the Council for almost three years (Bolton 2007, pp. 130–164).

Until 2010, the P3 and Germany preferred to pursue progress on the Iran sanctions regime entirely in the Council chamber. Even after resolution 1737 (2006), Council members preferred not to activate the new Iran sanctions committee. On the one hand, Council resolutions had the advantage of fixing P5 consensus at a given point in time and used a window of opportunity for designating additional targets named in a resolution annex. As part of Council negotiations, therefore, the P5+1 negotiated all measures and targets at the same time. In practice, Council negotiations resembled a bargaining logic involving significant trade-offs. This could mean, for instance, that negotiators dropped one entry from the list but achieved some additional sanctions measure in return. Or a sanctions measure could be dropped in return for a larger list of targets. In that respect, diplomats could trade off measures and targets to compensate a skeptical member for painful compromises. Consequently, the Council negotiated sanctions targets as a comprehensive package and not as single, separate requests (as in a committee). Thus, additionally designations did not need to fit in with listing requirements (two separate interviews with UN member state officials, New York, December 2013).

On the other hand, sanctions proponents feared that their efforts might be derailed or delayed in a committee, even though they did not anticipate outright stalemate (US Permanent Mission to the UN 2007a). Russian delegates told the US that they intended to prevent the sanctions regime from taking on a "life of (…) [its] own which could injure Russian interests" (US Embassy Moscow 2006c) and China was hesitant to move beyond resolution 1737 (2006) (US Embassy Beijing 2007a). Because the committee could easily fall prey to changing interests under consensus, leaving it to the committee would have made listing prospects uncertain. The P3's concerns seem to have been immediately confirmed as skeptical members sought to delay substantive committee work by haggling over procedures. A US diplomat concluded that "[a]s in the North Korea Sanctions Committee, we expect extensive and unconstructive edits from Russia and China to constrain the Committee's substantive work" (US Permanent Mission to the UN 2007a). After six months and several almost weekly informal meetings, the committee finally adopted its guidelines (S/2007/780, para. 6).

Enhancing sanctions within the Council (as opposed to a sanctions committee) followed the logic of power politics deals. The resolutions accumulated several aspects, for instance targeted sanctions *and* a list of individuals into a single package. Powerful members invested significantly into the negotiations to bring the resolution's language closer toward their preferred position. While rules did not become a source of influence, powerful members did not accept any unfavorable language unless other members compensated for these aspects in some way. Consequently, the resolutions reflected interests that had been traded off among powerful members. Over the years, sanctions proponents repeated the logic of package deals four times within the Security Council (see Table 8.2).

Table 8.2 Iran sanctions resolutions 2006–2010

Date	*Resolution*	*Sanctions measures*	*Annexes*
December 23, 2006	1737	Assets freeze Commodity sanctions: MTCR list, NSG Part 1 (nuclear material, equipment and technology)	12 individuals 10 entities
March 24, 2007	1747	Embargo on Iranian arms exports	15 individuals 13 entities
March 3, 2008	1803	Travel ban Extended commodity sanctions: NSG Part 2 (dual-use) Cargo interdiction	13 individuals (AF) 12 entities (AF) 5 individuals of res. 1737 and 1747 (TB)
June 9, 2010	1929	Arms embargo on Iranian arms procurement Strengthened cargo interdiction	All previously listed individuals subject to AF and TB 1 individual 40 entities

Source: author's illustration.

Notes
"AF" translates "assets freeze." "TB" translates "travel ban." "NSG" translates "Nuclear Suppliers Group." "MTCR" translates "Missile Technology Control Regime."

As a prelude to sanctions, after inconclusive EU3–Iran negotiations, the Council first haggled over a watered-down presidential statement demanding Iranian compliance with IAEA Board of Governors resolutions and requested the IAEA Director-General to report on compliance (PRST/2006/15; Hoge 2006a). While the P3+1 favored the application of strong pressure on Iran by means of a legally-binding Chapter VII resolution, Russia and China preferred the use of incremental steps (SCR Forecast March 2006a). After the IAEA had submitted its report with negative conclusions, the UK and France circulated a first draft resolution. Only after Iran had rejected yet another P5+1 negotiation package, did Russia and China accept that the Council should take cautious further measures and accordingly the Council adopted a resolution in July 2006. This resolution demanded Iran's suspension of its nuclear weapons program and full collaboration with the IAEA. In the event of non-compliance, once the IAEA had issued its report, Council threatened that it would impose "appropriate measures under Article 41 of Chapter VII" (resolution 1696 (2006)), thus ruling out military intervention (SCR Forecast August 2006).

In August 2006, when the IAEA again found Iran non-compliant, the P3+1 immediately brought up sanctions among the P5. While the US favored tough sanctions, Russia and China were skeptical, with the UK and France between those two positions (Wuthnow 2013, p. 78). For instance, US cables reveal that "China agrees Iran needs to be penalized for its behavior but the penalty should fit the crime" (US Embassy Beijing 2006a). This led to a "long, complicated, sensitive" negotiation in which the P5 carved out the sanctions measures, the targets and the consequences of non-compliance (Gootman 2006).

To impose sanctions on Iran, the EU3 and the US discussed a new draft resolution on October 22, 2006 and circulated it among the P5+1 two days later. The draft suggested an embargo on "items, materials, equipment, goods and technology which could contribute to Iran's nuclear and ballistic missile programmes," including those set out in NSG and MTCR lists, together with the provision of technical, financial assistance as well as training for Iran's nuclear and ballistic missile related activities (leaked draft, Japan Economic Newswire 2006, paras. 4–5). The draft exempted items for constructing the Bushehr nuclear reactor (para. 14), but not the nuclear fuel subject to Council approval. The draft also included a travel ban as well as assets freezes on individuals and entities involved in such programs named in a resolution annex (paras. 7, 9), sanctions exemptions for targeted sanctions (paras. 8, 10–12); a sanctions committee was also created for follow-up decisions on targeted sanctions together with other items (para. 16) and further sanctions were threatened for non-compliance (para. 22) (Burkhardt 2006; Aziakou 2006c).

Russia and China argued that "the current draft is too broad" and that "[t]he focus of the resolution's demands should be narrowed to preventing Iran from receiving assistance that would help with sensitive elements of a nuclear fuel cycle." Hence, the resolution's annex and the "measures, such as a travel ban and assets freeze, go beyond what was agreed to by Foreign Ministers" (Bolton 2006c). Russia suggested instead "a phased approach" starting with measures on proliferation only (Lederer 2006f). Concerning Bushehr, Russia was opposed to being singled out and insisted on a general exemption because "[i]f an item were deemed safe for Bushehr, then certainly it would be safe for other peaceful projects as well." China added that "[a]ny UNSC action should leave room for a diplomatic solution. Sanctions have a role but they are not the objective" (Bolton 2006c).

In response to Russian and Chinese objections, on November 30 the EU3 dropped references to the Bushehr reactor and instead included an exemption for light-water reactors (US Embassy Moscow 2006b; Cooper 2006), but still Russia and China balked. Hence, on December 7 the EU3 circulated a revised draft. This draft lowered the scope of dual-use sanctions so that only "nuclear material, equipment and technology" (NSG Part 1) but not "dual-use" items (NSG Part 2) would be banned. The draft also exempted the MTCR list for short-range Unmanned Aerial Vehicles. The text maintained targeted sanctions and an annex of 12 persons and 11 entities (Agence France Presse 2006c), but exempted travel in the framework of cooperating with the IAEA. Moreover, the IAEA should report on compliance within 60 days, not 30 days. Finally, sanctions would be immediately lifted once compliance had been confirmed (SCR Update Report No. 4 2006). While Russia and China now agreed to limited proliferation-sensitive sanctions, they still objected to non-proliferation financing sanctions, the assets freeze and the travel ban, on which the US insisted (Lederer 2006g; US Embassy Beijing 2006b). A contentious issue was how sanctions targets would be selected. Whereas the EU3 and the US wanted to include these in a resolution annex, Russia advocated delegation of the task to a sanctions committee (SCR Update Report No. 4 2006). To win Russian and Chinese support, the drafters dropped the travel ban, which now only called upon member states to "exercise vigilance" in the travel of 12 individuals and demands committee notification, but retained the assets freeze and the annex (Aziakou 2006d). Another last-minute trade-off neatly illustrates the logic of Council bargaining without committee. To accommodate Russian concerns about the assets freeze, the P3 and Russia made a "deal struck in New York whereby Russia agreed to support the resolution in exchange for dropping AIO from UNSCR 1737's list of sanctions entities" (US Embassy London 2006). On December 23, 2006, the Council adopted its first round of sanctions as a nine-page comprehensive package with one annex detailing the sanctions targets. Resolution 1737 (2006) imposed an assets freeze on 12 individuals and 10 entities, imposed commodity sanctions on nuclear proliferation and ballistic missile related items; furthermore the resolution created a committee to monitor implementation and adopt further decisions as required.

Following resolution 1737 (2006), the Western powers retained this initiative in the Council until 2012.[1] When the IAEA Director-General reported Iranian non-compliance in February 2007 (GOV/2007/08), the P3+1 sought to strengthen measures and add targets via a Council "package approach" (UK, in Lederer 2007a), although Russia and China remained skeptical to new sanctions. A few days later, the P5+1 discussed potential resolution elements to be added onto existing measures (Wagner 2007). Sanctions supporters proposed an embargo on arms exports to and imports from Iran, banning transactions, assistance and training "to entities involved in Iran's nuclear and missile programs," prohibiting "grants, loans and credits" to public institutions in Iran, limiting export credits, a mandatory travel ban and an expanded range of targets, including the Revolutionary Guard Corps (Aziakou 2007; Olson 2007). To accommodate Russian and Chinese concerns, sanctions supporters dropped the travel ban and export credit restrictions. Regarding the arms embargo, only the export of arms by Iran was censured, while the import ban was made voluntary and applied only to seven categories of heavy weapons including battle tanks, together with artillery and combat aircraft. In return, Russia and China agreed to expand the list of targets. However, the assets freeze on Revolutionary Guard Corps was also amended to name 3 specific entities and 7 key members of the Revolutionary Guard Corps, among the 15 individuals and 13 entities in the annex (Lederer 2007a; Lederer 2007b). With this second sanctions round, the Council adopted a package deal with two annexes on March 24, 2007. Resolution 1747 (2007) imposed a ban on Iranian arms exports and added the 15 individuals and 13 entities as subject to the assets freeze. US Ambassador Wolff neatly summarized the Council negotiation: "It's a package approach, and so there are things that we're very pleased about, and things that we're less pleased about and likewise for probably every delegation involved" (Lederer 2007a).

Faced with an unchanged constellation, the sanctions supporters kept initiatives at Council level. When the IAEA Director-General once more reported that Iran had failed to comply (GOV/2007/22), the EU3 and the US considered a third sanctions round. Yet, interests remained unaltered and spanned between "the US and the Europeans pushing for significant additional measures and Russia and China preferring small increments" (SCR Forecast May 2007). For months, Iran unraveled the shaky P5 consensus by announcing that it would allow inspections. In September 2007, the P5+1 foreign ministers agreed to pursue a third sanctions round should the IAEA and the EU foreign policy chief report negatively on Iranian compliance and EU-Iran negotiations (SCR Forecast December 2007a). After negotiations with Iran had failed, the P5+1 agreed on the need for a third resolution adding onto existing measures, but disagreed on the scope of the "incremental increase," because China and Russia remained reluctant to impose economic sanctions (SCR Forecast January 2008).

In December 2007, the EU3 and US proposed first draft elements to strengthen existing measures: an arms embargo on arms exports to Iran, an enlarged list of sanctionable items, a travel ban on all listed individuals, an expanded sanctions list including the Revolutionary Guard Corps, the Quds Force and three Iranian banks (Wright 2007). Whereas China rejected any sanctions affecting its trade interests as well as the type and number of targets, Russia also opposed sanctions on Iranian banks (Lederer 2007c). In a first negotiation round, the P3 dropped the arms embargo and two Iranian banks (Wright 2007). Unable to reach agreement, the diplomats referred discussions to foreign ministers, who agreed to a package on January 22. The package included Chinese and

Russian concessions, mainly on financial and economic sanctions. The P3 also had to delete the Revolutionary Guard Corps and the Quds Force (Wright and Lynch 2008; Agence France Presse 2008a). On February 1, 2008, the P5+1 circulated a draft resolution to the Council based on agreed elements: voluntary travel ban for 13 individuals (Annex I), legally-binding travel ban on individuals listed in Annex II (i.e., the five individuals listed in 1737 (2006) and 1747 (2007)), 13 individuals and 12 entities subject to assets freeze (Annex I and III). This draft also extended the commodity sanctions to NSG Part 2 dual-use items (except for light-water reactors), calls to "exercise vigilance" in granting export credits to Iran together with activities by Iranian banks, and provides for cargo inspections (SCR Update Report No. 2 2008). Following the logic of give-and-take bargaining subsuming sanctions measures *and* targets, the Council adopted resolution 1803 (2008) on March 3, 2008.

While Council action was sidelined due to a new, but unsuccessful diplomatic initiative, including a new P5+1 proposal and an US offer for direct talks, the EU3 and the US again pushed for tougher sanctions in mid-2009. In light of Iranian defiance (IAEA reports GOV/2009/74, GOV/2010/10), even Russia was getting "fed up" with Iranian behavior. Russia accepted that a new resolution was required "to put pressure on Iran," while at the same time remaining cautious about economic sanctions (US Embassy Moscow 2010). China remained the most hesitant among the P5 (US Embassy Beijing 2010). As in the three rounds before, the drafters decided to negotiate a new Council package to include new sanctions designations, hence still without recourse to the committee.

The US took the lead on supplementing previous sanctions and circulated draft elements among the P5+1 in early 2010 (US Permanent Mission to the UN 2010). These elements included new sanctions designations, including the Revolutionary Guards Corps and "any individuals and entities acting on their behalf or at their direction." The elements suggested complementing the Iranian arms export embargo with an arms import embargo, an embargo against "Iranian state-owned air and shipping lines" subject to committee approval, an embargo on insurance services for Iranian transport companies, and an embargo on the purchase and sale of Iranian bonds. Finally, all previously listed individuals would be subject to mandatory travel bans and assets freezes (Crawford *et al.* 2010; Lederer 2010a).

Since China opposed anything that could threaten its interest in the Iranian oil sector, namely the insurance of oil transports and financial investments, the US revised the draft transforming the aviation and shipping embargo into a cargo interdiction regime similar to the DPRK sanctions. The US also dropped the insurance embargo and subjected the issuance of bonds to Iran solely to a notification requirement (Crawford *et al.* 2010). Further, the US softened financial sanctions, dropped any reference to Iranian energy sector investments and merely called upon states to "exercise vigilance" in entering into new trade commitments with Iran, including granting export credits, guarantees or insurance" (Lederer 2010b). In a US-Russian deal, to allow Russia the sale of S-300 anti-aircraft batteries to Iran, the US restricted the arms embargo to seven heavy weapons categories (excluding ground-to-air missiles), and agreed domestically to delist four Russian entities implicated in transferring sensitive technologies to Iran (Baker and Sanger 2010). Tough last-minute bargaining ensued over the annex's scope. All previously listed individuals would be subject to both travel bans and assets freezes, with the new list including only 1 individual and 40 entities. However, on Russian and Chinese insistence the US dropped all banks (including the Iranian Central Bank), except for the First East Export Bank (MacFarquhar *et al.* 2010; Lederer 2010c).

On June 9, 2010, the Council adopted its fourth sanctions round as an 18-page package with 4 annexes. Resolution 1929 (2010) included the subjecting of all previously listed individuals and entities to travel bans and assets freezes, as well as designating an additional 40 entities and 1 individual, among those 15 Revolutionary Guard Corps entities (Annex II) and three Islamic Republic of Iran Shipping Lines entities (IRISL, Annex III). Furthermore, the resolution added an arms embargo to prevent the sale of conventional arms to Iran, authorized (voluntary) domestic cargo inspections and (voluntary) cargo inspections on the high seas with flag state consent, together with the (voluntary) tightening of sanctions on the Iranian financial sector. In addition, the Council created a Panel of Experts. Ever since resolution 1929 (2010), due to the nuclear deal negotiations, all subsequent resolutions simply extended the mandate of the Panel of Experts until conclusion of the 2015 nuclear deal (resolutions 1984 (2011), 2049 (2012), 2105 (2013), 2159 (2014)).

The power-politics on Iran sanctions, which followed the logic of package resolutions, trade-offs and linkages, resulted in inadequate regulation. It demonstrates that bargaining is not suitable for providing well-reasoned designations required for effective implementation. In contrast to committee governance, the Council did not satisfy listing standards and acceptability controls were absent. Designations in the first three resolution's annexes, for instance, had few or no identifiers and provided only names and functions. Although the individuals mostly held top-level positions in nuclear and ballistic-missile programs, implementation suffered. US cables show that when prompted by Taiwan, the US admitted that "[o]f the 40 designated individuals (…) the United States government has identifier information for 17" and that the US "(…) has only been able to designate 16 individuals thus far because we do not want to designate the wrong person" (Secretary of State 2008b). German authorities complained that "UNSC 1737 Annex would be more helpful if it provided more information about the entities and persons, such as addresses and dates of birth" (US Embassy Berlin 2007). In addition, most listings did not contain any justification, which contributed to court proceedings which annulled EU implementation (S/2013/331, para. 151; Eckert and Biersteker 2012, pp. 30–33). Only in December 2014 was the list finally updated, albeit still often lacking basic identifiers.

This episode from 2006 to 2010 shows that despite the two options to implement sanctions, Council members deliberately negotiated at Council level and imposed far-reaching sanctions measures together with a considerable list of targets in four sanctions resolutions. Council decisions resembled large packages, including annexes detailing targets to accommodate diverging P5 interests and required extensive negotiations. The designations resembled the logic of bargaining. These packages were not problem-adequate and impeded implementation. However, as the next section demonstrates, the same Council members attempted to designate additional individuals and entities within the committee after 2010.

The committee route: Substantive criteria and independent evidence determine committee designations

The 2012–2013 committee designations episode makes possible a comparison between Council and committee decision-making, showing that, in contrast to the Council's bargaining outcomes, committee governance prompts rules' adherence by powerful members. A systematic analysis of all listing initiatives on sanctions violations demonstrates that the mode of committee interaction did not rely on bargaining power but on the supply of convincing arguments as to why a request was warranted against the designation criteria. Anticipating a committee deadlock, sanctions proponents negotiated a Council directive to the committee so that the latter would designate sanctions violators, and the committee subsequently developed an (albeit high) evidence-threshold by precedent. Even reluctant powerful members accepted well-founded requests, while they rejected less-documented requests. There is no evidence for the alternative explanation that decisions merely resemble package deals. Since late 2013 and after the election of the Rouhani government, sanctions proponents refrained from further committee initiatives so as not to hamper negotiating a P5+1-Iran nuclear deal (SCR Forecast June 2014; SCR Forecast December 2014). Significantly, the Panel of Experts also no longer made substantive recommendations that might have derailed the negotiations before it was dissolved (S/2015/401, S/2014/394).

Until the Council adopted resolution 1929 (2010) and despite repeated violations of the arms exports embargo, the committee received no listing proposals.[2] Before 2012, the committee was mainly involved not only with discussing internal rules and implementation reports, but also with serving as a conduit for IAEA. In this phase, the committee rarely met (see annual reports S/2007/780, S/2008/839, S/2009/688). The first clear violation of the arms exports embargo was discovered when Cyprus seized a consignment of ammunition aboard the Islamic Republic of Iran Shipping Lines (IRISL) chartered cargo "motor vessel" (M/V) Monchegorsk in February 2009 (S/2009/688, para. 20). However, internal US cables show that even the US did not consider designations. Instead, as a first step the US sought to establish the case as a clear Iranian sanctions violation by means of a low-key committee decision. Accordingly, the US proposed first sending letters to Iran and Syria requesting explanations and second having the committee issue a note verbale to all UN member states, later adopted as Implementation Assistance Notice, which determined that IRISL arms shipments had violated resolution 1747 (2007) (US Permanent Mission to the UN 2009a).

The IRISL-chartered container ship M/V Hansa India case, which "involved virtually identical circumstances," led the committee to issue another Implementation Assistance Notice in January 2010 (S/2009/688, paras. 19–25). Before the Council imposed a fourth round of sanctions, including targeted sanctions on IRISL, the committee took no further action on sanctions violations.

With the adoption of resolution 1929 (2010), sanctions supporters changed their strategy and used committee governance to pursue new listings in reaction to Iranian sanctions violations. First, because the four Council resolutions had considerably tightened sanctions measures, the proactive states no longer intended to negotiate a new sanctions resolution (SCR Forecast March 2011; SCR Forecast June 2012). In anticipation of a committee deadlock, the sanctions proponents did not simply seek a one-time Council package deal in resolution 1929 (2010), but rather sought to adopt a general, less-ambiguous rule on committee designations to react to Iranian sanctions violations. The US deliberately included language on sanctions violators in the designation criteria to lower the threshold for a committee listing (interview with UN member state official, New York, December 2013). Consequently, since sanctions proponents now concentrated on small-scale implementation, it was reasonable to seek additional designations within the committee first and only if that failed, revert to the Council.

The adopted rule was more precise, explicitly provided a committee mandate to impose targeted sanctions on sanctions violators and did not favor any of the powerful members. The Council straightly

> [d]irects the Committee to respond effectively to violations of the measures decided in resolutions 1737 (2006), 1747 (2007), 1803 (2008) and this resolution, and recalls that the Committee may designate individuals and entities who have assisted designated persons or entities in evading sanctions of, or in violating the provisions of, these resolutions.
>
> (Resolution 1929 (2010), para. 26)

The committee amended its guidelines and acknowledged that it "will decide on the designation of individuals and entities" (previously: "the committee shall receive (…) proposals for additions to [the list]," see guidelines April 2008, para. 13), laid out detailed requirements concerning identifiers and reaffirmed that each proposal should be accompanied with a "narrative description" on how the individual or entity fits the decision criteria (guidelines August 2011, paras. 20–25), namely being

> engaged in, directly associated with or providing support for Iran's proliferation sensitive nuclear activities or for the development of nuclear weapon delivery systems or (…) acting on behalf of such individuals and entities (…), assist designated persons or entities in evading sanctions or in violating (…) Security Council resolutions 1737 (2006), 1747 (2007), 1803 (2008) or 1929 (2010).
>
> (Para. 22)

In addition, the consensus no-objection procedure was extended from five to 10 working days (paras. 15, 21).

Second, sanctions proponents strongly advocated for establishing a Panel of Experts. Having a Panel of Experts proved useful for sanctions supporters because it independently investigated violations, regularly submitted reports to the committee and suggested potential designations (interview with UN member state official, New York, December 2013). The Panel of Experts comprised eight members, while the P5+1 consistently had one national on the panel (S/2010/576, S/2011/4, S/2011/405, S/2012/521, S/2013/375, S/2013/615, S/2014/464, S/2015/78). The Council instructed the Panel to "gather, examine and analyse information (…) regarding the implementation of the measures (…), in particular incidents of non-compliance (…)," make recommendations and provide a final report before the termination of its mandate, subject to re-authorization after one year (resolution 1929 (2010), para. 29). The Panel had no formal decision function and while it worked under the direction of the sanctions committee, the Panel as a collective could freely decide about its reports' contents. Committee members could, but did not have to, pick up recommendations and evidence and turn them into formal requests.

Committee members faced a coordination situation: The P5 had collectively established the sanctions regime and had an interest in maintaining it to prevent the proliferation of nuclear weapons. Simultaneously, their interests diverged strongly. The P3 favored additional designations in response to violations, whereas Russia and China made clear that they opposed new sanctions and preferred negotiations (SCR Forecast December 2011; SCR Forecast June 2012). In a Council debate on Iran sanctions in June 2011, the US, France and UK advocated the prompt designation of individuals and entities responsible for sanctions violations (S/PV.6563, pp. 3–4, 6–7), whereas Russia opposed the contents and conclusions of violation reports calling the information "[u]nverified and politicized" (S/PV.6563, p. 5). Russia was particularly determined to ensure that the committee "acted in a balanced and objective manner and has not overstepped its mandate" and cautioned that the "Panel [of Experts] must work impartially and independently and be guided (…) only by reliable and objective information" (S/PV.6888, p. 4). China, added that it was "a firm supporter of diplomatic solutions, and is not in favour of putting excessive pressure or imposing new sanctions on Iran" (S/PV.6888, p. 12).

In contrast to the Council, which adopted sanctions measures *and* designations in packages, the Iran sanctions committee designations followed criteria and rules. Overall, in nine alleged sanctions violation cases the new Panel of Experts confronted the committee with reports detailing the cases' circumstances and investigating responsible individuals or entities for designations (see Table 8.3). Only for the five recommendations with strongest evidence stemming from three violations incidents, did committee members request designations, and the committee subsequently granted all five requests despite the objections of powerful members. For the remaining incidents, the Panel drew no definite conclusions as to whether or not the violations had taken place. In the KAL Cargo

Table 8.3 Panel investigations and committee response 2012–2013

Report	*Case*	*Recommendation*	*Committee decision*
May 2011	M/V Hansa India	Incident reported before resolution 1929 (2010)	
	Francop (Israel)	Incident reported before resolution 1929 (2010)	
	Everest (Nigeria)	Committee "should designate" two individuals and one entity	Committee listing
		Committee "should consider, in view of information be received from Member States, the designation" of one entity	No listing request
	M/S Finland (Italy)	Incident constituted a violation, but no recommendations	
	KAL Cargo (Republic of Korea)	Incident did not constitute a violation, because item did not fall under embargo (dual-use)	
	STX Patraikos (Singapore)	Investigation ongoing, no recommendations	
June 2012	Safir/Rasad launch	Inconclusive, disputed whether or not case constituted a violation, no recommendation	
	Yas Air (Turkey)	Committee should designate one entity	Committee listing
	Kilis (Turkey)	Committee should designate one entity	Committee listing
		Panel "draws the attention of the Security Council and the Committee" to one entity	No listing request

Source: Panel of Experts Iran (2011); S/2012/395; SC/10615; SC/10871.

(Republic of Korea) case, the Panel concluded that the discovered item (rolls of phosphor bronze wire mesh) "does not fall under the list of items" subject to sanctions (Panel of Experts Iran 2011, 70). In the STX Patraikos (Singapore) case, the Panel noted that there "are commercial applications for fine aluminium powder" but that "most likely end-use is solid propellant for missiles," but stopped short of recommending committee action (Panel of Experts Iran 2011, 75). Concerning the Safir/Rasad launch, the Panel claimed that the "Safir space launch vehicle itself was not designed to carry a nuclear weapon" and three Panel members concluded that the case did not constitute a violation (S/2012/395, para. 36).

The scope of evidence in the first Panel of Experts report in May 2011 explains the listing outcomes, while package deals are unlikely. Above all, the Panel asserted that "(…) Iran's circumvention of sanctions across all areas, (…) is wilful and continuing" (Panel of Experts Iran 2011, para. 5). Pro-active Western powers lauded the Panel for its revelations, but Russia blocked its publication and China also fiercely rejected its content (Agence France Presse 2011b). The report was leaked (Panel of Experts Iran 2011). The Panel investigated six incidents of arms and proliferation-related embargo violations, only two of which the Panel pursued further since two cases were prior to its establishment, one investigation was ongoing and for one case, the Panel concluded that it did not constitute a violation (Panel of Experts Iran 2011, para. 34).

Both the cases which were investigated further concerned violations of the arms exports embargo from Iran, but differed in their evidential weight. In the less-substantiated "Finland case," Italian authorities had discovered a concealed shipment of 200 sacks of T4 explosives onboard the cargo "motor ship" (M/S) Finland at an Italian port. However, the only source of evidence was the bill of lading, which stated that the shipment was from an Iranian company to a Syrian company. Although the Panel perceived the *Finland incident* as a violation, it did not recommend designating responsible individuals or entities. In the much stronger "Everest case," Nigerian authorities seized a shipment of 240 tons of ammunition hidden in 13 containers onboard the cargo vessel M/V Everest in the port of Lagos, Nigeria. In the wake of the seizure, two Iranian citizens, who had accompanied the cargo, fled to the Iranian embassy. This prompted the Iranian foreign minister to negotiate their repatriation. The foreign minister even "acknowledged that the arms originated in Iran." Accordingly, the Panel concluded that "as confirmed by the Iranian Foreign Minister and confirmed by documentary evidence" the shipment was a violation of the arms embargo. Concerning designations, on the one hand, the Panel recommended that "[t]he Security Council should designate" the two individuals directly involved (Ali Tabatabaei and Azim Aghajani) as well as the entity Behineh Trading of Tehran, which had "played the role of freight forwarder in Iran (…), made contact with the agent of shipping line (*sic*!), (…) provided stuffed containers [and] (…) also provided a false declaration of their contents." On the other hand, the Panel having less evidence recommended only that "[t]he Security Council should consider (…) the designation of" one entity (International General Trading and

Construction), because it had provided unspecified "support" to an individual implicated in the case (Panel of Experts Iran 2011, 3, 60–61).

Even Russia was forced to adhere to rules although it objected to further sanctions, if the cases are bolstered with strong evidence and clearly fit to Council designation criteria. While no member acted on the less substantiated recommendation, the UK transformed the panel listing recommendations for two individuals and one entity with strong evidence into formal requests (SCR Forecast June 2012). Because the committee was unambiguously directed to act upon violations and the evidence in the Everest case was strong, independent and even confirmed by the Iranian foreign minister, Russia gave in and the committee added Ali Tabatabaei, Azim Aghajani and Behineh Trading in April 2012 (SC/10615). In this context, based on direct Council language on sanctions violations, the committee could designate sanctions violators in well-documented cases. Since there were no immediate substantive committee decisions taken on other matters, a package deal to compensate skeptical members seemed unlikely.

These two cases set a precedent and enabled proactive members to place subsequent committee designations based on similarly strong evidence, despite Russian and Chinese hesitance. In its June 2012 report, the Panel investigated embargo violations and again made differentiated listing recommendations (S/2012/395). In the "Yas Air case," Turkish authorities interdicted an Iranian Yas Air operated Ilyushin-76 aircraft en route from Iran to Syria and seized 19 boxes with assault rifles, machine guns, mortar shells and ammunition. Turkey had reported the interdiction with detailed cargo inventory and the Panel had inspected and confirmed the sanctions violation on site (paras. 33–34, 102–103, 156). In the "Kilis (Turkey) case," Turkish authorities seized a truck from Iran bound for Syria at the Turkish-Syrian border loaded with gunpowder, propelling charges, detonators, solid rockets, and 1,700 kg of explosives. The panel established that documents accompanying the shipment "including an invoice issued by the consignor of the shipment, SAD Import Export Company (…) further established the nature, origin and destination" (paras. 37–38, 104–106). The case involved another entity (Chemical Industries and Development of Materials Group), the alleged producer of propelling charges, while not being the direct violator (para. 229). Now, the panel again differentiated between Yas Air and the SAD Import Export Company, both supported with strong evidence, together with the Chemical Industries and Development of Materials Group, with less substantiated evidence. The panel "(…) in accordance with existing practice" recommended designating "Yas Air, for the transport of prohibited arms (…) and SAD Import Export Company, for its role as a trading agent of prohibited arms." Furthermore, the panel asserted that "[b]oth recommended designations are supported by strong documentary and factual evidence" (para. 248). However, the panel merely "[drew] attention" to the Chemical Industries and Development of Materials Group (para. 249). The sanctions proponents submitted only two listing requests for Yas Air and SAD Import Export Company, which Russia let pass in December 2012 (SC/10871). Shortly thereafter, the US domestically listed the Chemical Industries and Development of Materials Group

(Gladstone 2012), which shows that the US could not assemble a case withholding arguments of inadmissibility against the committee standard. As the committee took no other immediate substantive committee decisions, a compensating package deal was unlikely.

Another alleged sanctions violation case shows that the committee's evidentiary threshold was extremely high and that sanctions opponents would block requests if they could base their objections on Council criteria. When Iran launched ballistic "Shahab 1 and 3, Zelzal, Fateh-110 and Tondar" missiles during its "Great Prophet 7" military exercise in July 2012, the Panel asserted that these tests "constituted a violation (…) of paragraph 9 of resolution 1929 (2010)." The Panel, though, did not recommend any listing (S/2013/331, paras. 82–86, S/2012/395, Annex VIII). Whereas the P3 demanded new designations or at least that the committee should officially recognize the violation, Russia and China objected (S/PV.6999, S/PV.7028, SCR Forecast July 2013). Russia, referring to a provision in resolution 1929 (2010) that "Iran shall not undertake any activity related to ballistic missiles *capable of delivering nuclear weapons*" (para. 9, emphasis added), argued that the tested missiles were not designed for nuclear warheads, thus would not be subject to sanctions and hence no sanctions violation had taken place (interview with UN member state official, December 2013). Indeed, the missiles launched were developed in the 80s and 90s, long before Iran's nuclear ambitions came into being. Following this line of argument, Russia blocked any decision ranging from a common committee statement (S/PV.6999, p. 2), implementation assistance notices or any listings (SCR Forecast December 2014).

Since 2012, the Panel of Experts has only once recommended pursuance of additional designations (S/2013/331, paras. 18–22, 130, for 2014 see S/2014/394, for 2015 see S/2015/401), in this case one entity (Pentane Chemistry Industries), which allegedly was used as front company in a partly successful attempt to procure valves for the Arak heavy-water reactor on behalf of the Modern Industries Technique Company (MITEC). However, MITEC was already listed in the annex of resolution 1929 (2010), Pentane Chemistry Industry had been subject to US domestic sanctions in 2012, and four responsible individuals were sentenced in a German court in 2013 (Oberlandesgericht Hamburg 2013). There is no evidence that any member proposed a designation in this case. In addition, Pentane Chemistry Industry had been previously acquitted of an embargo violation in a different case (Panel of Experts Iran 2011, pp. 14–15; Lynch 2013).

In the late 2013 final listing initiative, the US sought to use the Iran sanctions committee to list a Syrian pro-government militiaman implicated as the benefactor of an alleged Iranian weapons transfer and assistance; he had previously been listed under US sanctions (SCR Forecast December 2013). However, since the Panel of Experts noted that "[g]iven the deteriorating security situation in the Syria Arab Republic, there is no possibility of gathering evidence that would confirm or deny these allegations" (S/2015/401, para. 32), Russia placed a hold on the request (SCR Forecast March 2015). Since reinvigorated efforts by the

P5+1 in late 2013 on negotiating what became the Iranian nuclear deal, the committee had essentially been in "waiting mode" and no further committee listing initiatives had been made (SCR Forecast December 2014).

The 2012–2013 episode shows that in contrast to the Council, the Iran sanctions committee operates in the logic of committee governance in line with hypothesis 1. The variance in Panel of Experts recommendations demonstrates that the degree of case evidence seems decisive for explaining outcomes. Successful listings had to suffice a high evidentiary threshold, whereas below-threshold proposals had little chance of succeeding. In the Everest, Yas Air and Kilis incidents, the proponents were successful because they combined unambiguous evidence with a clear committee mandate to list sanctions violators. Whereas skeptical members refrained from blocking strong cases, they avoided less clear-cut cases. Committee members tend to accept only water-tight listing proposals because reluctant members will dismiss those requests which expose the slightest uncertainty. Deliberately making sanctions violations an explicit committee mandate has hampered rejecting substantiated requests for political reasons (two separate interviews with UN member state officials, New York, December 2013).

The alternative route: Rule-based governance through opting for NSG and MTCR lists of proliferation-related items

This episode shows that the Council decided about lists of items prohibited from export to Iran following rule-based governance, albeit in unexpected ways. While the task presented a tremendous challenge to Council members because they had to decide which items contribute to a nuclear weapons or ballistic missile program and therefore should be banned from trade with Iran, members disagreed chiefly over sanctions' strictness. Instead of deciding on prohibited items lists or delegating the task to committee, the Council availed itself of external focal points, namely export trigger lists developed by two transgovernmental networks, to solve the coordination problem. Due to the task's complexity, Council members had to revert to networks of export control specialists to decide about the lists' contents. However, because these networks specialize on technical details, one-sided political interference is difficult. Generally speaking, this transformed the Council's rationale toward focusing on grand political issues, for instance whether commodity sanctions should be imposed at all, when this should be the case and which sections of existing lists should be applicable.

An effective non-proliferation export control regime poses a regulatory problem: Which objects do, and which objects do not, fall under the category of "all items, materials, equipment, goods and technology which could contribute to Iran's enrichment-related, reprocessing or heavy water-related activities, or to the development of nuclear weapon delivery systems" (resolution 1737 (2007), para. 3)? There are not many nuclear weapons states, which shows that developing nuclear warheads and delivery systems is challenging. It requires designing or acquiring a multitude of technologies. Thus, preventing proliferation demands strict export controls on an abundant range of items. Exporters face additional hurdles: First, many goods are inherently dual-use. For example, a turbofan engine can power a nuclear cruise missile but also a small civilian airliner. Second, exporters need to control so-called "below threshold items," which could be manufactured into dual-use items. Third, export control must be constantly revised to cover technological progress. Whereas failing to list an item, which could contribute to a nuclear weapons program, would undermine the export control's effectiveness, adding an unjustified item could hamper legitimate trade relations. Hence, to take these decisions, Council members had good reasons to resort to technological expertise of the Nuclear Suppliers Group (NSG) and the Missile Technology Control Regime (MTCR).

Both the NSG and MTCR are transgovernmental networks of domestic mid-level regulators (Slaughter and Hale 2011). Canada, France, Japan, Soviet Union, United Kingdom, United States and West Germany established the NSG in 1974 as a network of nuclear technology suppliers coordinating national export licensing, responding to India's first nuclear weapons test (Nuclear Suppliers Group 2015a, pp. 1–3). In 1987, G7 members created the MTCR to prevent delivery systems proliferation (Missile Technology Control Regime 2015). The MTCR comprises 35 members, 25 of which are Western, 2 Latin American, 6 East European, 1 Asian and 1 African. Aside from India, all MTCR members are also NSG members, of which there are 48 in total (Nuclear Suppliers Group 2015b). Among the P5, only China is an NSG, but not MTCR member. However, China, not least because it wanted to avoid other suppliers' sanctions, pledged to adhere to MTCR guidelines and applied for membership in 2004 (Eilstrup-Sangiovanni 2009, pp. 220–221). The NSG and MTCR networks operate on the basis of consensus, but without secretariats or formal legally-binding treaties. Accordingly, domestic regulators make export decisions solely in accordance with domestic law (Lipson 2006, p. 187).

For their members, the NSG and MTCR transgovernmental networks provide distinct advantages over formal organizations. An uncoordinated system of export control is inadequate to address collective action problems associated with proliferation under conditions of globalized trade and technological progress (Lipson 2006, pp. 184–186). Only few states can supply nuclear technologies or delivery systems and these states share a preference for preventing transfers that may contribute to proliferation while trading these technologies among each other. Because such clubs usually control large market shares, spoilers can be excluded for setting strict standards initially and later might be compelled to accede to these standards or face exclusion from privileges such as access to technologies (Anthony *et al.* 2007, pp. 16–18). Because numerous potential dual-use items and the technical nature of export control expose states to uncertainties about technological advances, there is a high dependency on regulatory experts with a high degree of specialization. Moreover, transgovernmental networks are flexible, responsive to changes and entirely informal. In contrast to formal treaties or organizations, agreements can be made at low transaction and sovereignty costs and staffing with experts, not diplomats, enhances efficiency (Slaughter and Hale 2011, p. 343).

The major products of the two transgovernmental networks are three export control trigger lists of proliferation and ballistic missile related goods. The NSG adopts Part 1 and Part 2 as annexes to its NSG Guidelines (together about 120 pages). The former first introduced in 1978 contains "items that are especially designed or prepared for nuclear use" including nuclear fuel, nuclear reactors and parts, equipment for reprocessing, nuclear fuel rods fabrication, isotopes separation and heavy-water production. The latter governs the export of "nuclear related dual-use items and technologies," items that have contributed to nuclear weapons development, but also have non-nuclear uses. This list was first issued in 1992 in reaction to Iraqi attempts to acquire non-regulated dual-use items (Nuclear Suppliers Group 2015b). The technical MTCR Equipment, Software and Technology Annex (about 75 pages) enumerates "a broad range of equipment and technology, both military and dual-use, that are relevant to missile development, production, and operation." It contains two sections: Category I items consist of complete rocket or other delivery systems or major sub-parts, whereas Category II items consist of dual-use missile related equipment or parts. While MTCR members should handle Category I items with the greatest of restraint, they have more flexibility on Category II items (Missile Technology Control Regime 2015).

Decision-making in transgovernmental non-proliferation networks reduces opportunities for political interference on behalf of special interest cases such as Iran. To strengthen export controls effectively in the face of growing proliferation threats, trigger lists must be as comprehensive as possible. Domestic mid-level officials with relevant portfolios in foreign affairs, trade, defense, customs, as well as nuclear or ballistic missiles experts elaborate trigger lists within technical committees, which are later adopted by annual plenary meetings of state representatives (Lipson 2006, pp. 187–191). Because the item lists have to be applicable to all goods that could contribute to nuclear weapons and delivery systems proliferation, regulators deliberating about such lists have to sort out extreme positions based on specifics of the Iran conflict. Representatives negotiate under a significant "veil of uncertainty" because they cannot know their interests in cases that have not emerged yet (e.g., Iran prior to 2002, earlier Libya, Syria, Iraq). The endeavor's extremely technical nature incentivizes consistent rule-making to the disadvantage of power politics. Bargaining processes are not suited to clarifying validity claims and would hardly solve the regulatory problem at hand (e.g., Gehring and Ruffing 2008, p. 126). Even more so, bargaining provides no suitable approach in cases with high uncertainty, such as where there is no clear distinction between acceptable and unacceptable activities, as is the case with nuclear and ballistic missile export control (Eilstrup-Sangiovanni 2009, pp. 218–222). In addition, technical experts as negotiators in export control policy operate quite autonomously from their governments and foreign policy concerns vis-à-vis Iran (Lipson 2006, p. 184). For those reasons, political intervention in technical export control is difficult (see Gehring 2004, p. 682).

The preexisting NSG and MTCR items lists provided a useful focal point for solving the Council's coordination problem. Instead of deciding about the technical details of export control vis-à-vis Iran, the Council simply accepted readily-available NSG and MTCR lists of goods and subjected listed items to a mandatory trade embargo. The committee, in turn, was only responsible for determining "as may be necessary additional items" (resolution 1737 (2006)). Because Council members intended to avoid engaging in technical discussions, they naturally focused on the broader political questions, and hence the Council's technical lists remained unaffected by special interests on Iran. Consequently, the Council retreated to determining, which sections of the lists were authoritative, in particular every time the NSG and MTCR updated the items lists due to technical innovation (interview with UN member state official, New York, December 2013). Despite political interference being likely in the Council, the division of labor between the Council and the two regulatory networks constrained its members due to the technical nature.

Accordingly, Council members did not haggle over technical details and disputed only the timing of imposing broad trigger lists sections (e.g., Russia's insistence on light-water reactors and its fuel supply). Nonetheless, the dynamics of sanctions rounds led to a strategy of escalating the number of broad categories of items as determined by NSG and MTCR lists. Accordingly, in resolution 1737 (2006), the Council determined items on the NSG Part 1 list as embargoed items except for complete light-water reactors and components including low-enriched nuclear fuel (resolution 1737 (2006), para. 3ab), while NSG Part 2 dual-use expert controls was left to a state's discretion (para. 4). Concerning ballistic missile items, the Council adopted an embargo on MTCR annex items (S/2006/815), except for complete unmanned aerial vehicle systems with more than 300 km range (para. 3c). Finally, the Council exempted "such items or assistance (…) for food, agricultural, medical or other humanitarian purposes" upon consensus committee decision (para. 9). In resolution 1803 (2008), the Council made NSG Part 2 list authoritative (S/2006/814), while maintaining the dual-use items for "exclusive use in light-water reactors" exceptions (para. 8a). Concerning the MTCR list, the Council removed the exemption for unmanned aerial vehicles (para. 8b, S/2006/815). In resolution 1929 (2010, para. 13), the Council replaced existing lists with the updated versions of NSG and MTCR lists (INFCIRC/254/Rev.9/Part 1, INFCIRC/254/Rev.7/Part 2 and S/2010/263). In March 2013, the Iran sanctions committee again updated the items lists with new NSG and MTCR list versions (SC/10928, NSG Rev.11/Part 1 and Rev.8/Part 2; MTCR S/2012/947).

So why did the Council not leave the task of determining embargoed goods to the committee? First, the export trigger lists were readily available. Since creation of the transgovernmental networks, such lists had been developed and adapted to changing circumstances. Simultaneously, since major nuclear and ballistic missile technologies producers adopted them by consensus, potential exporters can easily and quickly implement them. Second, determining such goods within the confines of Council sanctions committees would be costly.

Since sanctions committees are staffed with lower-rank generalists, and there is no powerful secretariat or other expert body available, the "complexities of defining what 'proliferation sensitive' items are, (...) could lead to very significant challenges for the Committee" (SCR Update Report No. 4 2006). According to people involved, the issue is of such a technical nature that it is impossible for diplomats to negotiate within the Council framework (interview with UN member state officials, New York, December 2013). Third, when the Iran nuclear conflict surfaced, the sanctions supporters could appeal to these lists because they had not been generated to sanction Iran. Thus, their content is relatively independent of any conflict scenario, which makes the lists particularly appealing as focal points (interview with UN sanctions expert, Washington DC, December 2013). Fourth, the Council members had previously adopted these lists within the context of the DPRK sanctions regime, which served as a useful precedent (resolution 1718 (2006, para. 8), and increased pressure to argue why one item would be sanctionable in the DPRK case but not in Iran despite their similarity.

This episode shows that external focal points provide a rule-based alternative to coordinate the selection of proliferation-related items subject to a trade embargo. Instead of making a Council package deal or implementing export control separately at committee level, the Council readily accepted NSG and MTCR produced export trigger lists. The technical nature made bargaining over lists unattractive and restricted the Council to deciding about whether those items should be sanctioned at all and when this should be the case. Essentially, this left skeptical Council members with a take-it or leave-it option also because P5 members had accepted these lists in NSG and MTCR fora, where such lists had been developed long before the Iran conflict emerged. Remarkably, it also shows that focal points can emanate from outside the confines of the Security Council.

Concluding thoughts

The Iran sanctions committee is a confirmatory case for my committee governance thesis and exhibits several fascinating facets of the theme. Being certainly one of the most contested sanctions regimes, even though the permanent members shared an interest in preventing a "nuclearized" Iran, they frequently clashed on how much sanctions should be imposed. The US was the most vocal in advocating sanctions and the UK and France also favored sanctions, albeit to a lesser extent. However, China and Russia were reluctant, especially when sanctions touched their economic interests in Iran. Whereas the proactive members sought to overcome looming committee stalemate by taking a Council-centered approach, in a second stage, as expected, the divergence of interests among the permanent members prompted rule-based governance. For this reason, and others, the Iran sanctions regime is in many ways similar to the one imposed on the DPRK.

The Iran sanctions regime presents several intriguing results. First, the Iran sanctions regime shows that Council members do not have to delegate to a committee. However, without committee the Council-centered process leads to power politics and grand package resolutions. The early phase confirms the baseline expectation that decisions taken without a committee will mirror grand package resolutions, the contents of which reflect the constellation of interests among powerful Council members. In this stage, proactive members deliberately chose to impose sanctions measures *and* define a set of designations to which those sanctions were applicable simultaneously in a Council package resolution. This strategy was repeated four times, increasingly strengthening sanctions measures and expanding the list of targets over time. Council decisions did not adhere to any kind of substantive decision criteria, which created implementation issues. This suggests that bargaining might not be a suitable means to produce problem-adequate decisions. In this regard, the DPRK sanctions regime is quite similar, where members also preferred a Council-centered approach combining sanctions measures with longer lists of targets in a resolution annex.

Second, in contrast to the Council-centered approach, Council members referred the task to designate additional individuals to a sanctions committee in later stages, created the effects of rule-based committee governance even against the interests of powerful committee members. A committee episode clearly exhibits the effects of rule-making. An anticipated committee stalemate prompted sanctions supporters to have the Council direct the committee to designate sanctions violators and establish a Panel of Experts to make committee designations more likely to succeed. This rule is consistent and does not favor any powerful member.

Third, the Iran sanctions committee confirms hypothesis 1 according to which committee members, who face a stream of separate proposals, abide by criteria and rules, even if these contradict what some members might favor in a specific case. The episode of listing decisions demonstrates that after the Council had provided substantive criteria on listing sanctions violators, the documented embargo violations brought in front of the committee prompted even highly skeptical permanent members to accept well-documented decision proposals, while rejecting below threshold requests.

Fourth, the case of commodity sanctions on proliferation-related items shows that the Security Council can also use external focal points to solve a coordination problem on non-proliferation related commodity sanctions. The Council completely relied on NSG and MTCR provided export trigger lists as knowledge-based solutions to regulating export control. In this case, the technical nature of defining which items are subject to trade restrictions and which are not, provided incentives to adopt given NSG and MTCR lists of proliferation-related items. Because NSG and MTCR were autonomous from the conflict at hand, special interests were difficult to introduce. At Council level, members focus on larger political questions of whether and when such sanctions should be applied, and which larger sections of lists should be authoritative. Bargaining over the contents of such lists is unattractive so that Council members refrained from negotiating about the lists' content. As a result, referring to NSG/MTCR lists provided a rule-based solution to deciding about non-proliferation commodity sanctions.

The Iran sanctions regime complements the analysis of committee governance in Council sanctions regimes and makes possible the comparison of members deciding in the Council to the same members deciding in a subsequent committee stage. As the concept of committee governance suggests, the Council-centered approach yields power politics, while delegation to a committee creates rule-based decisions. The Iran case also shows that committee governance occurs both in targeted sanctions as well as proliferation-related commodity sanctions and hence irrespective of the sanctions type applied. The alternative explanation, which holds that decision-making in the committee stage can be explained by the constellation of interests among powerful members cannot convincingly account for the observed committee patterns.

Notes

1 Text-based searches in *LexisNexis*, *Security Council Report* and *WikiLeaks* revealed no committee activities.

2 Before resolution 1929 (2010), the committee received one sanctions violations report in 2007 and three in 2009 (Panel of Experts Iran 2011, para. 34). The author conducted text-based searches in *WikiLeaks*, *LexisNexis* and *Security Council Report* publications to assess whether any state had submitted a listing request.

9 Conclusion

What can we learn from committee governance in the Security Council?

This book has developed a novel Security Council committee governance concept and, based on five intriguing sanctions regimes as well as a multitude of data sources, explored how and with what consequences delegating tasks to a committee affects the logic of decision-making among Council members. Security Council sanctions governance demonstrates a remarkable design for introducing formal and informal rules to a setting shaped by strong national interests and power politics. The findings reveal that committee governance prompts decision-making based on criteria, rules and evidence. This effect can be attributed to separating rule-making and subsequently implemented sanctions based on such rules. I find emerging patterns of rule-based governance across four considerably different Council sanctions regimes, while the Sudan sanctions regime illustrates the mechanism's limitations. The findings exemplify that committee governance works even for "high politics" security institutions such as the Security Council, in which the same group of members decides about all key aspects.

The comparative design of in-depth case studies provides for empirical results which are robust across a range of political constellations, sanctions measures and decision contents (see Table 9.1). Their effect is rooted in the comparable decision situation across sanctions regimes, namely to decide about many similar single cases over time. The rule-based nature of committee decision-making is not just observable with regard to the Al-Qaida/Taliban Sanctions Committee that has attracted so much attention in the literature. Significantly, the effect is equally observable in the trade embargo sanctions regime on Iraq and thus, does not result from collective learning. This particular sanctions regime shows that the effect occurred in the early phase, before vocal critique on the humanitarian consequences of comprehensive sanctions had set in. The same applies to the Iran sanctions regime that imposes targeted sanctions against individuals involved in the Iranian nuclear program, but also non-proliferation related dual-use commodity sanctions. Similarly, committee governance also affected decision-making in the DRC sanctions regime, where the conflict of interest lies not between the Western powers and China and Russia, but between the three Western permanent members. Rule-based governance is also independent of powerful members' capacity to act within committee. While the US was able to

Table 9.1 Summary of episodes in case studies

Regime	*Episode*	*Committee task*	*Source*	*Mechanism*
Iraq	I	Waive goods (foodstuffs)	Deadlock	Rule-based (precedents)
	II	Waive goods (general)	Threat of deadlock	Rule-based (precedents)
	III	Grant flights	Threat of deadlock	Rule-based (rules/precedent)
AQ/Taliban	I	List individuals/entities	Threat of deadlock	Laissez-faire
	II	List individuals/entities	Laissez-faire	Rule-based (rules)
	III	Delist individuals/entities	Deadlock	Rule-based (rules)
	IV	Delist individuals/entities (Taliban)	Deadlock	Rule-based (rules)
	V	Delist individuals/entities (Ombudsperson)	Rule-based	Rule-based (rules)
DRC	I	List individuals/entities	Deadlock	Rule-based (rules/precedent)
	II	List individuals/entities	Threat of deadlock	Rule-based (rules)
	III	List individuals/entities	Deadlock	Deadlock (committee)
Sudan	I	Sanctions (Council)		Power politics (Council)
	II	List individuals/entities	Deadlock	Deadlock (Committee)
	III	List individuals/entities	Deadlock	Power politics (Council)
	IV	List individuals/entities	Deadlock	Deadlock (Committee)
Iran	I	List individuals/entities		Power politics (Council)
	II	List individuals/entities	Threat of deadlock	Rule-based (rules)
	III	List "dual-use" goods	Threat of deadlock	Rule-based (precedents)

Source: author's illustration.

veto exemption decisions in some cases (Iraq), it depended on other members' consent to designate individuals in others (AQT, DRC, Iran).

These results show that the Security Council can be transformed from an exclusive forum for great power politics into a more complex organization that decides according to abstract rules within the scope of its sanctions regimes. While the effects of committee governance are certainly not intended, they are not at odds with great power interests, insofar as rule adherence on the whole promises to result in creating workable committees, which implement sanctions purposefully. The findings illustrate that delegating tasks to a committee significantly shapes incentives even for the same group of states and leads Council members to behave in ways that they would otherwise have been unlikely to choose. While UN member states have to accept politically motivated sanctions decisions in the Council, sanctions committees provide a more reliable and rule-oriented mechanism that promises to yield increasingly rule-based, consistent and thus more predictable decisions.

Implementing decisions in a committee alters incentives for Council members and leads to remarkably consistent rules, even though powerful members might strongly disagree on a particular rule's implication for specific single cases. In all the episodes studied, rules were adopted favoring neither the permanent members nor any other parties. For instance, the Al-Qaida/Taliban sanctions regime's second episode shows that Council members will adopt abstract listing criteria for individuals and entities subject to targeted sanctions, even though the powerful members have diverging interests on specific single cases. For instance, in the Iraq aviation sanctions episode, while the US and the UK strongly objected to granting Sudanese requests for political reasons, when negotiating rules even such powerful members had to represent a consistent position that exempted certain types of flights (i.e., humanitarian flights), irrespective of which country had requested the exemption. In the DRC sanctions regime, the Council adopted consistent designation criteria, which applied to all state applicants equally, even though the France and the UK had strong interests in different types of requests later in committee.

Rule-based governance can occur in two ways. First, the Council may intend to forge rule-based governance at the expense of power politics, by providing clear criteria and procedures for committee decision-making, as it did in the Iran and Al-Qaida cases. These cases emphasize that Council members may credibly commit themselves to previously elaborated rules even without retreating from the decision process, if they have a collective interest in rule-based decisions. Second, a tendency toward rule-based governance also occurs when powerful member states intend not to be bound by rules. In the Iraq sanctions regime powerful member states understood that their decision in an exceptional case would provide a precedent for subsequent cases and lead to the evolution of rules. While the US and UK refused to consider cases as precedents and formalize precedent-based rules, they could not avoid rule-based governance, simply because committees need rules to solve numerous contentious cases.

Rule-making and rule-application do not have to be separated between Council and committee. To the contrary, rule-making effects can also occur when the committee elaborates rules subject to the same constraints. Thus, the Council can also explicitly or implicitly delegate rule-making to committee. For instance, the delisting episode within the Al-Qaida/Taliban sanctions regime, where the Security Council has frequently directed its committee to make rules, exemplifies that committees effectively separate the consideration of rules from their implementation. Similarly, in the DRC regime the Council directed the committee to promulgate guidelines within a strict timeframe. Such Council directives have also frequently occurred in the DPRK sanctions regime and are difficult to understand unless one pays due attention to committee governance. In the absence of Council guidance, the Iraq Committee frequently derived rules from precedents in the humanitarian exemptions episode after the Gulf War. Committee members often considered the consequences of a single-case decision on a similar future request. In other words, elaborating rules naturally precedes decisions about single cases. Similarly, a first case serving as precedent guides decision-making through all later cases of a similar type. Hence, the committee governance effect is independent of the separation between Council and committee, but is in practice caused by separating rule-making and rule-application systematically.

The analysis of five Security Council sanctions committees confirms this study's hypothesis 1: If a committee of states processes separate decision proposals of limited scope, committee members abide by given criteria and rules, even if these rules contradict the preferences of some members. One aspect of this is that states tend to align their proposals to criteria or previous precedents insofar as they know such rules and are capable of substantiating requests. Within the Iraq sanctions regime, while some states have simply forwarded all requests received from exporting companies to the committee, other states have submitted primarily only rule-conforming requests and were thus more successful. Accordingly, those states that performed some quality control fared substantially better. Within the DRC Sanctions Committee, proactive states out-sorted non-conforming designation requests to avoid rejections by other members. In the Iran committee listing episode, proactive members submitted those listing requests that were equipped with the strongest evidence and conformed best to established rules, thereby increasing the likelihood of committee approval.

Across all cases, committees considered proposals separately, not in packages. During the second stage of the Al-Qaida/Taliban sanctions regime, the committee considered proposed designations on individuals and entities suspected of being associated with transnational terrorism as entirely separate issues. The DRC listing episode shows that even though states consider decision requests in sets, the merits of each request was assessed separately. Processing exemption requests from the Iraq trade embargo shows that the committee treated every decision request on its own merits. Even the Sudan sanctions regime demonstrates that procedures effectively preclude adding single cases to packages in committee. This is remarkable because powerful members explicitly aimed at forging such a package deal.

There is considerable evidence demonstrating that in a committee setting members applied the same criteria to every request and, therefore, accepted requests that were rule-conforming, but rejected those that were rule-violating. The Al-Qaida/Taliban Committee listing episode revealed that existing criteria and procedures enabled members to scrutinize and, if necessary, block requests which did not conform to established rules. Similarly, the amended Taliban delisting rules allowed proactive members to submit requests that Russia eventually accepted. As regards Iranian sanctions violators, the committee accepted those requests that fulfilled a high standard of evidence, while proactive members avoided submitting requests which fell below this evidence threshold. In the second DRC listing episode, proactive members consistently out-sorted listing proposals that fell below the established standards. Nevertheless, the committee accepted well-documented designation requests even if they originated from less powerful states.

The empirical analysis confirms this study's hypothesis 2: Committee members abide by rules derived from precedents, even if such rules contradict the situation-specific preferences of some committee members. If formal rules are absent or ambiguous, committee members frequently resorted to earlier and similar cases as precedents to avoid deadlock. Based on the original Iraq Sanctions Committee files, I was able to show that the committee's rule-adherence emerged spontaneously as committee members used precedents to overcome deadlocks. A large-N analysis of committee decisions confirms rule-based committee practice based on previous precedents, despite the US and UK explicitly rejecting the constraints of being bound by rules emerging from precedent. Indeed, committee members perceive formal rules and precedents as equivalents. As with formal rules, committee members even accepted that precedents also bind non-permanent committee members, who had not been members when the precedent was initially set. The Iraq foodstuffs episode underscores the binding nature of precedents; this was so despite powerful members explicitly rejecting the idea that allowing one shipment to proceed would set a precedent for other shipments of the same kind.

Overall, even the powerful permanent members adhered to rules. In other words, rules and precedents bind powerful committee members, less powerful members and other UN member states equally. Permanent members accepted committee decisions despite disagreeing on substances in single cases. This could be observed even in key single cases insofar as stalemate was the only, albeit unattractive, alternative. In the Iraq sanctions regime's first episode, the US and UK gave in to a series of rule-conforming requests to ship foodstuffs to Iraq, although they vehemently opposed such requests because they came from India, Palestine, Yemen and other states opposed to sanctions. Committee governance enabled even Sudan to use formal and informal rules to force the US and UK to accept rule-conforming requests with the objective of considerably expanding flight approvals by committee practice. In the Iran sanctions regime,

Russia accepted listing requests for sanctions violators with compelling evidence despite opposing designations, because the requests conformed to established rules. In the Taliban delisting episode, Russia reluctantly accepted such delisting requests after the Taliban sanctions regime had been separated from that of Al-Qaida, despite its long-standing opposition to delisting any Taliban members.

Security Council committee governance does indeed prompt rule-based sanctions decisions. Across the board, a request's quality has always been decisive in determining its fate at the committee stage. This finding is robust over all case studies, given the presence of a more or less pronounced shared interest of all permanent members in the sanctions regime's operation. In the Al-Qaida/Taliban sanctions regime, the increasingly regulating committee procedures ensured that members sorted out unwarranted listing proposals and accepted the delisting of individuals that no longer met designation criteria. In the DRC sanctions regime, Western members applied a system of mutual control to ascertain that decisions conform to established rules, while dropping those requests which fell short of standards. In the Iraq Sanctions Committee, exemptions from the trade embargo consistently follow acceptable and unacceptable categories of goods determined by precedent. In the Iran sanctions regime, despite high evidence thresholds, proactive members could place successful listing requests that conformed to designation criteria and were bolstered by significant evidence, even though skeptical members objected to additional designations.

As regards the Ombudsperson, two conclusions can be drawn. On the one hand, comparing the Ombudsperson episode to a time before the Council had created this post shows that the separation of rule-making and rule-application was already driving committee members toward rule adherence. Hence, the Ombudsperson as an agent provides additional incentives for rule adherence as non-conforming listing decisions can quickly be overturned. The Taliban episode underscores the view that committee governance effects provide incentives to abide by rule-based governance, even for highly skeptical members and in the absence of an Ombudsperson. Beyond the Al-Qaida/Taliban case, episodes from other sanctions regimes show that in general terms committee governance prompts rule-based governance, with or without the presence of an Ombudsperson. Hence, from a theoretical perspective, the Ombudsperson can foster rule-based governance, hardly surprising given the position's strong agenda-setting role. On the other hand, without an Ombudsperson mechanism committee governance relies upon the committee members' willingness to scrutinize requests and consequently bears the constant risk of committee vetoes and stalemate. Hence, the Ombudsperson mechanism may be better understood as an additional safeguard for rule-based governance.

Three findings can be reconciled with the committee governance model but also point to its limitations. First, the analysis highlights a necessary precondition for the mechanism: Council members share a more or less pronounced common interest in the sanctions regime's functionality. In other words, the effects of committee governance occur only if members prefer coordination over stalemate. In the Sudan sanctions regime, the committee did not designate any individuals and entities due to the veto position of a few committee members. In the DRC sanctions regime, the non-permanent member Rwanda completely blocked additional committee listings during its Council tenure. Accordingly, the Council competency in delegating to committee does not always result in rule-based governance, because even relatively minor members can produce committee stalemate. In both cases, China and Rwanda respectively have obstructed the committee's work by withholding consensus on any requests. Nevertheless, both cases show that committee members could give fresh impetus to the committee's work through rule-making, for instance by abandoning the consensus requirement in favor of a majority threshold. While it failed in the Sudan case, because the Chinese delegation deliberately chose the option of stalemate, it is reasonable to assume that it might work if a non-permanent member caused the stalemate.

Second, rule-based governance neither implies nor requires the absence of conflict. Quite to the contrary, moderate conflict is necessary for motivating Council members to scrutinize proposals and enforce rules. In many cases, rule-based governance has evolved in the shadow of testing circumstances. In the Iraq sanctions regime, for instance, the US and UK advocated a restrictive approach to humanitarian deliveries, while nonaligned countries favored flexibility. The DRC Committee operated in full awareness of distinct interests expressed by France and the UK. Cleavages are conducive to rule-based governance, because they force members to identify rules and criteria as focal points. However, the first Al-Qaida/Taliban episode follows a fateful logic. Particularly in the wake of 9/11, this committee listed numerous individuals and entities without leading to stalemate. Thereby, the committee members took a laissez-faire approach with designations which were simply accepted across the board, regardless of their merits, evidence and origin. From a theoretical perspective, this finding highlights that the extent of rule adherence by committee members is based on a conflict of interests among Council members within the sanctions regime and their willingness to challenge non-conforming decisions. Indeed, this mutual system of control was also observed in other sanctions regimes. For instance, the US and UK exercised control over other committee members in the Iraq sanctions regime. Equally, Russia and China observed a high level of scrutiny within the Iran sanctions regime. Furthermore, in the DRC sanctions regime, a conflict of interests emerged even among Western permanent members. However, too much conflict will lead to stalemate, as the Sudan sanctions regime demonstrates.

Third and finally, the results demonstrate that Council resolutions and delegation to committee are two principled mechanisms with which to implement a sanctions regime, each of them generating significant implications. The Iran sanctions regime shows that delegation to a committee led to rule-based decisions, which is not the case when such a system is absent. The Council initially listed individuals and entities implicated in the Iranian nuclear program, but only in 2012 delegated this task to committee. As expected the Council traded off designations with other contents and accumulated many complex regime aspects into a draft resolution. Designations followed neither criteria nor rules. In 2012 the committee took over the listing task from the Council, which yielded rule-based governance in an entirely different way from previous Council packages. Both avenues are equally plausible and there is no automaticity in delegation. Council designations alternating with committee designations can also be observed, for instance in the DPRK sanctions regime. Actors may choose the avenue that they perceive as leading to the largest payoffs, depending on circumstances. However, the Sudan and Iran episodes illustrate that Council designations seem quite difficult to implement, because they lack identifiers and justification.

The alternative explanation, according to which Security Council decisions mirror the interest constellation among powerful members, cannot explain the observed patterns convincingly. The logic of power politics applies to decision-making without committee, as initially was the situation in the Iran sanctions regime, for instance, where the P3+1 preferred Council package resolutions over a committee process. However, in all cases studied, the alternative explanation fails to account for rule-based governance observed in committee. The Iraq flight exemption episode, for example, shows that even powerful members will not reject unfavorable but rule-conforming requests by less powerful states. Likewise, the Iran committee episode showed that reluctant powerful members would accept well-founded requests even though they objected to additional listings. In none of the cases studied did I find any evidence that committee members were pursuing package deals successfully. Indeed, the Sudan sanctions regime goes so far as to provide counter-evidence: A strategy of package deals failed at committee level, even when the members explicitly aimed at such packages, because the committee's no-objection procedure precluded submitting decisions in packages.

Committee member behavior is also difficult to explain by "individual agency" of the committee Chair. An agenda-setter who can pre-select proposals may change the preference constellation among members. However, committees operate without an agenda-setter under the "no-objection" procedure, which grants de facto veto rights to all members. In addition, the chairing delegation has quite limited autonomy, though it may be more autonomous in other areas such as sanctions monitoring. Additionally, "loyalties" cannot readily explain the findings; loyalties are evident when certain members demonstrate behavior which is governed by their closeness to others who are more powerful or important. Loyalty-driven committees would take inconsistent rather than rule-based decisions. Yet, Chapter 4 on Iraq shows that the both the US and UK frequently accepted decisions that vocally, at least, they opposed and could have blocked. Hence, if the most powerful states cannot mobilize loyalties to their advantage in cases important to them, we have little reason to believe that loyalties affect committee governance significantly. Moreover, the patterns are difficult to explain by socialization, which presumes that new members gradually become accustomed to existing shared norms or organizational culture. The Council, a high-politics institution with a high turnover even among P5 diplomats, is an unfavorable environment for socialization. The diplomatic service is strictly hierarchical, and members enjoy little autonomy. While member states are represented in Council and committee by different personnel with the inevitable specialization of individuals, it would be far-fetched to assume that members might be tempted away from their own leadership. Decision-making according to the "logic of appropriateness," in turn, presumes internalization of what the committee may find collectively appropriate. It assumes largely habitual and norm-driven behavior. In the Iraq Committee, continuing conflict between the UK and US as well as their opponents about appropriate decisions shows that collective choices were not driven by collectively internalized norms. Finally, the findings cannot be reconciled with the US' continued drafting of most Council resolutions, which thereby skews committee decisions in its favor. My argument is not that committee governance is directed against powerful members. Quite to the contrary, committee governance will generally reflect their objectives. However, the findings suggest that such governance comes with constrains that even powerful members cannot escape.

The alternative "due process" explanation is placed within a broader context. According to this view the increasing regulation of Council sanctions regimes can primarily be traced back to the systematic infringement of basic due process rights in the Al-Qaida/Taliban sanctions regime. On the one hand, these approaches explain increasing regulation within the Al-Qaida/Taliban sanctions regime, primarily as a result of pressure from states, activists, and courts. On the other hand, they ascribe effects to the far-reaching review and agenda-setting functions of an independent Ombudsperson, which applies only to the Al-Qaida sanctions regime, and conclude that having such a mechanism is indispensable for rule-based governance. However, the empirical analysis provides evidence that the observed effect of rule-based decision-making occurs equally without external pressure and in sanctions regimes that are not equipped with Ombudsperson-like bodies. This is particularly true for the Iraq sanctions regime, which administered a trade embargo. In that sense, the empirical analysis offers a broader perspective for explaining decision-making in Council sanctions regimes and thereby confirms practitioners' observations that committee governance in the realm of sanctions regimes is a decisive step toward Council adopting a legal-regulatory approach.

The Security Council as an international organization

What does the comparative analysis of five sanctions regimes imply for our conceptual understanding of the Security Council, and indeed the workings of international organizations broadly? As concerns the former, a prevailing forum perspective is insufficient for explaining its decision-making and decisions' contents from the perspective of separating rule-making from rule-application. At the same time, the committee governance concept provides a fruitful approach for analyzing decision-making processes, which rely on divided labor. Institutional theory, complemented with organizational theory elements, offers a meaningful lens through which to assess the Security Council's workings systematically. The concept directs our focus toward how the Security Council's specific institutional setup affects decision-making and ultimately the decisions taken. Going beyond the scope and singularities of the sanctions regimes' design, the concepts shows that committee governance constraints make up a decisive factor in explaining Council decisions. This is true even though the organization is a high politics and intergovernmental body providing wide-ranging prerogatives for great powers. Committee governance opens a new perspective for exploring states' rationales behind their decisions in intergovernmental security institutions, which constrain actors from applying their material and institutional power in all instances. In fact, the causal model goes beyond neorealist and institutionalist concepts of security institutions, according to which the field of international security eschews the impact of institutionalized cooperation, observed by rational institutionalism for other low politics fields.

What does this imply for the role and workings of IOs in IR theory? Modern regulatory theory argues that delegating to an independent agent is necessary for the credible commitment of member states to their long-term interests. By contrast, committee governance demonstrates that these members can be implicitly committed to rule-based governance even though they control all decisions. In other words, states do not have to be excluded from decision-making to ensure that their long-term objectives are achieved. Indeed, an institutional setup where the organization and its committee constitute the same group of members is prevalent in IOs and widely acceptable for their members; delegating tasks to an independent agent, such as a strong secretariat, would limit member's discretion and touch upon great power prerogatives. Nonetheless, it can also be seen that this institutional setup of committee governance does not insulate decision-making entirely from political interference and constantly bears the risk of deadlocks.

The ongoing debate about the role and workings of IOs has to accommodate the fundamental sources of organizational effects and thereby has to reach beyond the prevailing focus on agents and bureaucratic actors. This conclusion is based on the finding that even in circumstances where an organization assigns tasks to two bodies comprising the same membership in different settings, decisions are significantly affected despite the absence of independent agents and bureaucratic actors. Focusing on how decision processes are structured stems from the primary function of organizations and is capable of systematically grasping the factors influencing its members' behavior. My IO concept incorporates agent effects, but eschews a conceptual reduction to this single factor alone which may even lead to the misperception that if a strong secretariat is absent, the organization as such does affect decision-making. Notably, the committee governance concept incorporates organization theory elements without departing from the fundamental assumptions of rational institutionalism, and is therefore firmly grounded in mainstream IR scholarship.

Applying this concept to an organization considered least prone to committee governance effects suggests that the mechanism points to a universal phenomenon within IOs. Even though one cannot easily carry conclusions drawn from one organization to others, it is reasonable to assume that if committee governance affects Security Council decision-making, it is also likely to affect decision-making within other IOs, for instance granting projects in the World Bank or listing endangered species in the CITES regime. In other words, if the mechanism is present in "high politics" institutions, then it should also be present in "low politics" institutions that are regarded as more accessible for rule-based governance. In addition, because the Security Council has a comparatively simple structure, the findings should also be transferable to other, more complex organizations. Selecting a setting with a low a priori likelihood of confirming the mechanism has certainly provided a strong test for the committee governance concept.

The model specifies how committee governance can influence organizational decisions and is likely to prompt rule-based decision-making in any (international) organization meeting the following conditions: (1) The mechanism occurs if a group of actors separate rule-making from rule-application; (2) This effect is independent of specific content provided that the single cases appear in a stream of separate decisions; (3) The effect is also independent of the decision-making organs' composition (e.g., experts or member states); (4) The effect even occurs if the same group of actors controls both rule-making and rule-implementation and, therefore, does not presuppose the existence of independent agents; (5) The effect is independent of whether actors seek to bind themselves to their long-term interests or simply separate the functions to reduce their workload. Above all, the precondition is that all members prefer the institution's functionality over stalemate.

Policy implications

What does committee governance mean for Security Council sanctions management in practice? First, the Security Council should systematically employ the built-in effects of referring a stream of implementation decisions to its sanctions committees because it prompts rule-based governance and promises to make Council sanctions decisions more predictable. These decisions could include, for instance, designating individuals and entities to sanctions lists or determining a list of dual-use items restricted from export to a target country. In effect, this provides for increasingly problem-adequate decisions, because they are increasingly based on evidence and information. If committee decision-making embedded in Council sanctions regimes can bind even the powerful permanent members to their long-term interests in rule-based governance, this has enormous implications for the Council's sanctions policy. The Security Council can deliberately design its sanctions regimes so as to produce decisions that promise to realize in practice its political objectives within a conflict. While this effect, as we have seen, depends on Council members sharing a collective interest for any given case, it does not rely on consensus in the committee. Consequently, the Council can facilitate procedures that, for instance, provide incentives for listed individuals to change their behavior. Reducing the Council's workload, while simultaneously keeping committee decisions under tight Council member control, was initially the key motivation in creating committees and delegating tasks to them. However, the effects of committee governance will also increase the legitimacy of the Council's sanctions decisions vis-à-vis non-Council member states if they are based on sound, transparent and efficient procedures.

Second, the Security Council should whenever possible separate rule-making from the application of rules to single-cases. The Security Council has a powerful governance instrument for guiding the committee stage, when it takes its role as rule-maker seriously and provides criteria, rules and procedures. Thereby, rules can markedly change committee members' incentives and either provide for or constrain discretion, as well as possibly removing other options entirely. In fact, rules incentivize committee members to decide consistently and strive to realize their interests by submitting criteria-based requests instead of bluntly exercising power, which is more likely to create stalemate. Council members can also delegate rule-making to committee, without undermining the division of rule-making and rule-application. In the cases studied, virtually every committee was involved in rule-making alongside the Council and thereby complemented Council rules. Even more so, member states frequently used the interplay between Council and committee. For instance, in the Al-Qaida/Taliban case, the Council often directed the committee to clarify criteria and procedures. In the Iraq case, the committee deliberately referred an unsolvable issue to the Council for guidance. These cases demonstrate that Council and committee can and should actively develop criteria and rules as problems emerge or requests confront committee members with previously unexpected issues, resulting from too much discretion, too little discretion, or a complete absence of guidance on unforeseen developments.

Third, the findings suggest that the committee consensus principle does not inhibit, as is often claimed, but instead enables rule-based governance in practice. While decisions may take more time and require more effort, the Council will benefit from decisions that better reflect the Council's collective interest in a given case. As opposed to a majoritarian voting system, where minorities can be outvoted, consensus puts all committee members on an equal footing, irrespective of their power. No matter how much stake you have in a case at hand, all committee members' acquiescence is required for decisions to be taken. However, the need for consensus can also carry a looming danger of deadlock on implementation. Nevertheless, because stalemate is unattractive, and packages which satisfy the needs all 15 members are difficult to forge, consensus creates a demand for criteria and rules. It is likely that packages become more attractive in a majoritarian voting system as some members can be outvoted. As a result, it seems that maintaining the consensus principle is totally within the Council's interests.

Fourth, single-case implementation decisions should rigorously follow the established criteria, rules and procedures. The cases studied here highlight that the Council-committee constellation prompts some form of implicit commitment from committee members to the established rules, and this includes the permanent members. Conversely, arm-twisting and bargaining over single cases would create deadlocks, which in the long run are detrimental to a sanctions regime's effectiveness. In practice, the findings suggest that even powerful members have an interest in upholding and following formal and informal rules, even if they have contradictory interests on a specific case; giving in on one case may secure the committee's functioning in many other cases. Significantly though, results demonstrate that committee members in any event do already follow decision criteria and evidentiary standards. Hence, they could in fact openly commit themselves to these rules and, in doing so, contribute to establishing an increasingly predictable, transparent and legitimate form of sanctions governance. Noticeably, Council members could do this without losing political control over any of their decisions.

Fifth, criteria, rules and procedures should be made widely accessible. For instance, the DRC regime shows that states, which are unacquainted with decision criteria as well as the kind and amount of evidence necessary to submit successful requests, can significantly add to a committee workload. While Council resolutions and formal committee procedures might be public, many informal rules, often including evidentiary requirements, are mostly inaccessible to outside members. As a best practice example, the Al-Qaida/Taliban Sanctions Committee went to great lengths in codifying and publishing its decision criteria for its committee guidelines, fact sheets and standardized forms to guide submission of requests. Being more transparent about their procedures and criteria, sanctions committees could on the one hand reduce the number of obviously unjustified requests which had plagued some committees, increase the number of requests that have a reasonable chance of being accepted, and show designated individuals what they would need to do to be delisted. On the other hand, this at the same time has increased the legitimacy of Council sanctions regimes as their rules are now publicly accessible.

Sixthly, the Council should increasingly make use of external information as produced by Council-mandated Panels of Experts in as much as these bodies provide solutions to coordination problems at committee stage. The Iran sanctions regime illustrates that Panel of Experts' suggestions for designations solved a committee decision problem, precisely because these suggestions and accompanying evidence did not originate from any of the great powers. Similarly, the usage of external Nuclear Suppliers Group and Missile Technology Control Regime export trigger lists provided a means of coordinating behavior, because these lists were not created in the context of the Iranian nuclear crisis. Of course, the Council should not simply ignore other expedient Panels of Expert recommendations, for instance on imposing new sanctions measures, but these will remain as political questions, on which Council members need to decide, subject to the political climate in the Council.

In sum, to achieve a practice that is aligned to rules, the Council does not have to be less politicized, as is often assumed or demanded, precisely because the separation of rule-making and rule-application can ensure that the Council's decisions are rule-based while guaranteeing the member states' rights to take political decisions. In other words, it is astonishing to observe that a deliberately political organ is capable of taking fact-based technical decisions despite being composed of the world's most powerful states that often have clashing interests. When decisions are indeed increasingly oriented by impersonal rules, the Council can ensure that the "right" individuals are sanctioned and accordingly, minimize or even totally avoid potential humanitarian consequences. Indeed, the effect is not entirely intended and while reducing the Council's workload is the ultimate motive, the effect stems from delegating implementation to a committee, regardless of its membership.

References

Abbott, K.W., and Snidal, D., 1998. Why States Act through Formal International Organizations. *Journal of Conflict Resolution*, 42, 1, 3–32.

Abramowitz, M., and Lynch, C., 2007. President Imposes New Sanctions on Sudan. Some Say Action Is Too Little, Too Late. *Washington Post*, May 30, A3.

Agence France Presse, 2003. *Three Chechen Groups Added to UN Security Council al-Qaeda Sanctions List*. United Nations: Agence France Presse, March 5.

Agence France Presse, 2005. *UN Security Council Expands DRCongo Arms Embargo*. United Nations: Agence France Presse, April 18.

Agence France Presse, 2006a. *US, Britain Circulate List of Sudanese Targeted for Sanctions over Darfur Violence*. United Nations: Agence France Presse, April 12.

Agence France Presse, 2006b. *Great Lakes Countries List Rebel Chiefs to Face Sanctions*. Kigali: Agence France Presse, May 27.

Agence France Presse, 2006c. *List of Iranian Entities or Individuals That Could Face UN Sanctions*. United Nations: Agence France Presse, December 11.

Agence France Presse, 2008a. *Elements of New UN Sanctions Package Agreed by Six Major Powers*. United Nations: Agence France Presse, January 25.

Agence France Presse, 2008b. *Armed Rebels in DRCongo Ordered to Disarm or Face UN Sanctions*. United Nations: Agence France Presse, March 13.

Agence France Presse, 2011a. *Afghans Want Taliban Dropped from UN List*. Kabul: Agence France Presse, June 07.

Agence France Presse, 2011b. *Iran in "Alarming" Breaches of UN Sanctions, Envoys*. United Nations: Agence France Presse, June 23.

Ahmed, G.K., 2010. *The Chinese Stance on the Darfur Conflict*. Johannesburg: South African Institute of International Affairs.

Alter, K.J., 2006. Delegation to International Courts and the Limits of Re-Contracting Political Power. *In*: D.G. Hawkins *et al*., eds., *Delegation and Agency in International Organizations*. Cambridge, MA: Cambridge University Press, 312–338.

Alter, K.J., 2008. Delegating to International Courts: Self-Binding vs. Other-Binding Delegation. *Law and Contemporary Problems*, 71, 1, 37–76.

Annan, K., 2012. *Interventions. A Life in War and Peace*. New York: Penguin Press.

Anthony, I., Ahlström, C., and Fedchenko, V., 2007. *Reforming Nuclear Export Controls. The Future of the Nuclear Suppliers Group*. Oxford: Oxford University Press.

Armed Conflict Location & Event Data Project, 2014. *Rebel Groups of the DRC and Attacks on Civilians* [online]. Available from: www.crisis.acleddata.com/rebel-groups-of-the-drc-and-attacks-on-civilians/.

Associated Press International, 2005. *China Opposes U.N. Sanctions against Sudan*. Beijing: Associated Press International, March 31.

Axelrod, R.M., 1984. *The Evolution of Cooperation*. New York: Basic Books.

Axelrod, R.M., and Keohane, R.O., 1985. Achieving Cooperation under Anarchy. Strategies and Institutions. *World Politics*, 38, 01, 226–254.

Aziakou, G., 2006a. *US Proposes Sanctions against Sudan Officials*. United Nations: South African Press Association – AFP, April 19.

Aziakou, G., 2006b. *Security Council Set to Take up US Draft on Sudan Sanctions Tuesday*. United Nations: Agence France Presse, April 24.

Aziakou, G., 2006c. *UN Powers Unveil Iran Sanctions Draft*. United Nations: Agence France Presse, October 25.

Aziakou, G., 2006d. *Security Council Set to Vote Friday on Iran Sanctions*. United Nations: Agence France Presse, December 21.

Aziakou, G., 2007. *China, Russia Voice New Reservations about Tighter UN Sanctions on Iran*. United Nations: Agence France Presse, March 9.

Baker, P., and Sanger, D.E., 2010. U.S. Makes Concessions to Russia after Gaining its Support on Iran Sanctions. *New York Times*, May 22, A6.

Ballmann, A., Epstein, D., and O'Halloran, S., 2002. Delegation, Comitology, and the Separation of Powers in the European Union. *International Organization*, 56, 3, 551–574.

Barnett, M.N., and Finnemore, M., 1999. The Politics, Power, and Pathologies of International Organizations. *International Organization*, 53, 4, 699–732.

Barnett, M.N., and Finnemore, M., 2004. *Rules for the World. International Organizations in Global Politics*. Ithaca, NY: Cornell University Press.

BBC, 2005. *DR Congo Election Hostages Freed*: BBC News, November 3.

BBC, 2012. *Saudi Dissident Faqih Removed from UN Sanctions List*. BBC News, July 3.

Beach, D., and Pedersen, R.B., 2013. *Process-Tracing Methods. Foundations and Guidelines*. Ann Arbor, MI: University of Michigan Press.

Becker, M., Dörfler, T., and Gehring, T., 2018. Credible Commitment without Independent Regulatory Agent. Evidence from the Security Council's United Nations Compensation Commission. *Regulation & Governance*.

Biermann, F., and Siebenhüner, B., eds., 2009. *Managers of Global Change. The Influence of International Environmental Bureaucracies*. Cambridge, MA: MIT Press.

Biermann, F., and Siebenhüner, B., 2013. Problem Solving by International Bureaucracies. The Influence of International Secretariats on World Politics. *In*: B. Reinalda, ed., *Routledge Handbook of International Organization*. Milton Park, Abingdon, Oxon: Routledge, 149–161.

Biersteker, T.J., 2004. Counter-Terrorism Measures Undertaken under UN Security Council Auspices. *In*: A.J.K. Bailes and I. Frommelt, eds., *Business and Security. Public-Private Sector Relationships in a New Security Environment*. Solna, Sweden, Oxford, New York: SIPRI; Oxford University Press, 59–75.

Biersteker, T.J. *et al*., 2005. Consensus from the Bottom Up? Assessing the Influence of the Sanctions Reform Processes. *In*: P. Wallensteen and C. Staibano, eds., *International Sanctions. Between Words and Wars in the Global System*. London, New York: Frank Cass, 15–30.

Biersteker, T.J., 2010. Targeted Sanctions and Individual Human Rights. *International Journal*, 65, 1, 85–103.

Biersteker, T.J., and Eckert, S.E., 2006. *Strengthening Targeted Sanctions through Fair and Clear Procedures*. Providence, RI: Brown University.

Biersteker, T.J., and Eckert, S.E., 2009. *Addressing Challenges to Targeted Sanctions: An Update of the "Watson Report."* Providence, RI: Watson Institute for International Studies, Brown University.

Biersteker, T.J., Eckert, S.E., and Romaniuk, P., 2008. International Initiatives to Combat the Financing of Terrorism. *In*: T.J. Biersteker and S.E. Eckert, eds., *Countering the Financing of Terrorism*. London, New York: Routledge, 234–259.

Biersteker, T.J., Eckert, S.E., and Tourinho, M., eds., 2016a. *Targeted Sanctions. The Impacts and Effectiveness of United Nations Action*. Cambridge: Cambridge University Press.

Biersteker, T.J., Tourinho, M., and Eckert, S.E., 2016b. The Effectiveness of United Nations Targeted Sanctions. *In*: T.J. Biersteker, S.E. Eckert, and M. Tourinho, eds., *Targeted Sanctions. The Impacts and Effectiveness of United Nations Action*. Cambridge: Cambridge University Press, 220–248.

Bolton, J.R., 2006a. DRC Sanctions: UK Proposes Revised List of Names, 06USUNNEW YORK1041_a, May 23.

Bolton, J.R., 2006b. DRC Sanctions: Committee Chair Calls for More Names, 06USUN NEWYORK1228_a, June 16.

Bolton, J.R., 2006c. UNSC/Iran: November 3rd Meeting P5 Plus One, 06USUNNEW YORK2123_a, November 6.

Bolton, J.R., 2007. *Surrender Is Not an Option. Defending America at the United Nations and Abroad*. 1st ed. New York: Threshold Editions.

Bosco, D.L., 2009. *Five to Rule Them All. The UN Security Council and the Making of the Modern World*. Oxford: Oxford University Press.

Boucher, A.J., and Holt, V.K., 2009. *Targeting Spoilers. The Role of United Nations Panel of Experts*. Washington, DC: Stimson Center.

Boucher, R., 1990. *State Department Regular Briefing*. Washington, DC.

Boulden, J., 2008. The Security Council and Terrorism. *In*: A.V. Lowe *et al*., eds., *The United Nations Security Council and War. The Evolution of Thought and Practice since 1945*. Oxford, New York: Oxford University Press, 608–623.

Boustany, N., 2002. Swedes Appeal for Access to Money. *Washington Post*, January 23, A13.

Brennan, G., and Buchanan, J.M., 1985. *The Reason of Rules. Constitutional Political Economy*. Cambridge: Cambridge University Press.

Brown, R.L., 2010. Measuring Delegation. *The Review of International Organizations*, 5, 2, 141–175.

Brzoska, M., 2003. From Dumb to Smart? Recent Reforms of UN Sanctions. *Global Governance*, 9, 519–535.

Burkhardt, P., 2006. *Key Security Council Nations at Odds over U.N. Resolution Imposing Sanctions on Iran*. United Nations: The Associated Press, October 27.

Buzan, B., and Albert, M., 2010. Differentiation: A Sociological Approach to International Relations Theory. *European Journal of International Relations*, 16, 3, 315–337.

Carayannis, T., 2013. The Democratic Republic of the Congo, 1996–2012. *In*: J. Boulden, ed., *Responding to Conflict in Africa. The United Nations and Regional Organizations*. New York: Palgrave Macmillan, 177–202.

Carayannis, T., 2016. The Democratic Republic of the Congo. *In*: S.V. Einsiedel, D.M. Malone, and B. Stagno Ugarte, eds., *The UN Security Council in the Twenty-First Century*. Boulder, CO: Lynne Rienner Publishers, 661–680.

Carisch, E., 2014. *Congo's Golden Web*. Johannesburg: South Africa Resrouce Watch.

Carisch, E., and Rickard-Martin, L., 2011. *Global Threats and the Role of United Nations Sanctions*. New York: FES.

Carter, D.B., and Stone, R.W., 2015. Democracy and Multilateralism. The Case of Vote Buying in the UN General Assembly. *International Organization*, 69, 1, 1–33.

Casert, R., 2007. *EU Wants Tougher Action on the Darfur Crisis but Sees Limited Options*. Brussels: Associated Press International, March 26.

Cassese, A. *et al.*, 2005. *Report of the International Commission of Inquiry on Darfur to the United Nations Secretary-General. Pursuant to Security Council Resolution 1564 of September 18, 2004*. Geneva.

Cassimon, D., Engelen, P.-J., and Reyntjens, F., 2013. Rwanda's Involvement in Eastern DRC: A Criminal Real Options Approach. *Crime, Law and Social Change*, 59, 1, 39–62.

Charbonneau, B., 2010. France. *In*: D.R. Black and P.D. Williams, eds., *The International Politics of Mass Atrocities. The Case of Darfur*. London, New York: Routledge, 213–231.

Charbonneau, L., 2012a. *U.N. Confirms Saudi Dissident, His Group off al Qaeda List*. United Nations: Reuters, July 2.

Charbonneau, L., 2012b. *Saudi Man Dropped from U.N. al Qaeda Sanctions List*. United Nations: Reuters, October 5.

Charbonneau, L., 2013. *Rwanda Blocks Proposed U.N. Sanctions for Two Congo Rebels*. United Nations: Reuters, August 28.

CNN, 2005. *U.S. Proposes 10,000 U.N. Peacekeepers for Sudan*. United Nations: CNN, February 14.

Cockett, R., 2010. *Sudan. Darfur and the Failure of an African State*. New Haven: Yale University Press.

Coen, D., and Thatcher, M., 2008. Network Governance and Multi-Level Delegation: European Networks of Regulatory Agencies. *Journal of Public Policy*, 28, 01, 49–71.

Coleman, J.S., 1974. *Power and the Structure of Society*. New York: Norton.

Coleman, J.S., 1988. *Markets, Morals and the Law*. Cambridge: Cambridge University Press.

Comras, V.D., 2010. *Flawed Diplomacy. The United Nations & the War on Terrorism*. Dulles, VA: Potomac Books Inc.

Conlon, P., 1995a. Die Fragwürdige Sanktionspraxis der UNO. *Aussenpolitik*, 46, 4, 327–338.

Conlon, P., 1995b. Lessons from Iraq: The Functions of the Iraq Sanctions Committee as a Source of Sanctions Implementation Authority and Practice. *Virginia Journal of International Law*, 35, 3, 633–668.

Conlon, P., 1996a. Legal Problems at the Centre of United Nations Sanctions. *Nordic Journal of International Law*, 65, 73–90.

Conlon, P., 1996b. The Humanitarian Mitigation of UN Sanctions. *In*: *German Yearbook of International Law*. Berlin: Duncker & Humblot, 249–284.

Conlon, P., 2000. *United Nations Sanctions Management. A Case Study of the Iraq Sanctions Committee, 1990–1994*. Ardsley, NY: Transnational Publishers.

Contessi, N.P., 2010. Multilateralism, Intervention and Norm Contestation: China's Stance on Darfur in the UN Security Council. *Security Dialogue*, 41, 3, 323–344.

Cooley, A., and Spruyt, H., 2009. *Contracting States. Sovereign Transfers in International Relations*. Princeton: Princeton University Press.

Cooper, H., 2006. Draft Resolution on Iran Drops Threat of Sanctions. *The International Herald Tribune*, November 30, A4.

Cortright, D., 2009. *Patterns of Implementation. Do Listing Practices Impede Compliance with UN Sanctions? A Critical Assessment*. Sanctions & Security Research Program.

Cortright, D. *et al.*, 2010. *Integrating UN Sanctions for Peace and Security*. Goshen, IN: Fourth Freedom Forum & Kroc Institute for International Peace Studies.

Couturier, H., 2005. *US Miffed by UN Failure to Stop Darfur Violence*. United Nations: Agence France Presse, October 11.

Cramér, P., 2003. Recent Swedish Experiences with Targeted UN Sanctions: The Erosion of Trust in the Security Council. *In*: E. De Wet and A. Nollkaemper, eds., *Review of the Security Council by Member States*. Antwerp: Intersentia, 85–107.

Crawford, D., Boudreaux, J.L., and Solomon, J., 2010. U.S. Softens Sanctions Plan Against Iran. *The Wall Street Journal*, March 25, A1.

Curtis, D., 2013. China and the Insecurity of Development in the Democratic Republic of the Congo (DRC). *International Peacekeeping*, 20, 5, 551–569.

Deutsche Presse Agentur, 2005. *U.N. Security Council Team Urges DR Congo to Disarm Militias*. Entebbe, Uganda: Deutsche Presse Agentur, November 9.

DeYoung, K., 2002. U.S. and China Ask U.N. to List Separatists as Terror Group. *Washington Post*, September 11, A13.

Dörfler, T., and Gehring, T., 2015. Wie internationale Organisationen durch die Strukturierung von Entscheidungsprozessen Autonomie gewinnen. Der Weltsicherheitsrat und seine Sanktionsausschüsse als System funktionaler Differenzierung. *In*: E.d. Conceição-Heldt, M. Koch, and A. Liese, eds., *Internationale Organisationen. Autonomie, Politisierung, interorganisationale Beziehungen und Wandel*. Baden-Baden: Nomos Verlagsgesellschaft, 54–80.

Doxey, M., 2000. United Nations Sanctions: Lessons of Experience. *Diplomacy & Statecraft*, 11, 1, 1–18.

Doyle, J., 2004. Irish Diplomacy on the UN Security Council 2001–2: Foreign Policy-Making in the Light of Day. *Irish Studies in International Affairs*, 15, 1, 73–101.

Doyle, L., 1990. Crisis in the Gulf: UN Races to Avert Starvation in Kuwait; Sanctions Committee Responds to Indian Plea to Lift Embargo on Food and Medical Aid for Stranded Foreigners. *The Independent*, September 12, 8.

Dreher, A., Sturm, J.-E., and Vreeland, J.R., 2009. Development Aid and International Politics. Does Membership on the UN Security Council Influence World Bank Decisions? *Journal of Development Economics*, 88, 1, 1–18.

Dreher, A., Sturm, J.-E., and Vreeland, J.R., 2015. Politics and IMF Conditionality. *Journal of Conflict Resolution*, 59, 1, 120–148.

Easton, D., 1965. *A Systems Analysis of Political Life*. Chicago, IL: University of Chicago Press.

Eckert, S.E., and Biersteker, T.J., 2012. *Due Process and Targeted Sanctions. An Update of the "Watson Report."* Providence, RI: Watson Institute for International Studies, Brown University.

Eckholm, E., 2002. U.S. Labeling of Group in China as Terrorist is Criticized. *New York Times*, September 13, A6.

Eilstrup-Sangiovanni, M., 2009. Varieties of Cooperation. Government Networks in International Security. *In*: M. Kahler, ed., *Networked Politics. Agency, Power, and Governance*. Ithaca, NY: Cornell University Press, 194–227.

Einsiedel, S.V., Malone, D.M., and Stagno Ugarte, B., 2016. Conclusion. *In*: S.V. Einsiedel, D.M. Malone, and B. Stagno Ugarte, eds., *The UN Security Council in the Twenty-First Century*. Boulder, Colorado: Lynne Rienner Publishers, 827–876.

Elsig, M., and Pollack, M.A., 2014. Agents, Trustees, and International Courts. The Politics of Judicial Appointment at the World Trade Organization. *European Journal of International Relations*, 20, 2, 391–415.

Elster, J., 1989. *The Cement of Society. A Study of Social Order*. 1st ed. Cambridge: Cambridge University Press.

Eriksson, M., 2010. Unintended Consequences of Targeted Sanctions. *In*: C. Daase and C. Friesendorf, eds., *Rethinking Security Governance. The Problem of Unintended Consequences*. London, New York: Routledge, 157–175.

Farley, M., 2004. Security Council Votes to Provide Aid After End to Sudan Civil War. The U.N. Resolution Is Aimed at Nudging the Nation's Warring Sides to Abide by a Newly Signed Pact and Finalize a Peace Agreement by Dec. 31. *Los Angeles Times*, November 20.

Farrall, J.M., 2007. *United Nations Sanctions and the Rule of Law*. Cambridge, MA, New York, Melbourne, Madrid, Cape Town, Singapore, Sao Paulo, Delhi: Cambridge University Press.

Farrall, J.M., 2009. Should the United Nations Security Council Leave it to the Experts? The Governance and Accountability of UN Sanctions Monitoring. *In*: J.M. Farrall and K. Rubenstein, eds., *Sanctions, Accountability and Governance in a Globalised World:* Cambridge University Press, 191–214.

Farrall, J.M., and Charlesworth, H., eds., 2016. *Strengthening the Rule of Law through the UN Security Council*. London, New York: Routledge.

Federal News Service, 2004. *Hearing of the Senate Foreign Relations Committee*. Washington, DC: Federal News Service, September 9.

Feinäugle, C.A., 2010. The UN Security Council Al-Qaida and Taliban Sanctions Committee: Emerging Principles of International Institutional Law for the Protection of Individuals? *In*: A. von Bogdandy *et al*., eds., *The Exercise of Public Authority by International Institutions. Advancing International Institutional Law*. Heidelberg, New York: Springer, 101–131.

Flint, J., and Waal, A. de, 2009. *Darfur. A New History of a Long War*. 2nd ed. London: Zed Books.

Franchino, F., 2002. Efficiency or Credibility? Testing the Two Logics of Delegation to the European Commission. *Journal of European Public Policy*, 9, 5, 677–694.

Garrett, G., and Weingast, B.R., 1993. Ideas, Interests, and Institutions: Constructing the European Community's Internal Market. *In*: J. Goldstein and R.O. Keohane, eds., *Ideas and Foreign Policy. Beliefs, Institutions, and Political Change*. Ithaca, NY: Cornell University Press.

Gegout, C., 2009. The West, Realism and Intervention in the Democratic Republic of Congo (1996–2006). *International Peacekeeping*, 16, 2, 231–244.

Gehring, T., 2002. *Die Europäische Union als komplexe internationale Organisation. Wie durch Kommunikation und Entscheidung soziale Ordnung entsteht*. 1st ed. Baden-Baden: Nomos Verlagsgesellschaft.

Gehring, T., 2003. Communicative Rationality in European Governance? Interests and Communicative Action in Functionally Differentiated Single Market Regulation. *In*: E.O. Eriksen, C. Joerges, and J. Neyer, eds., *European Governance, Deliberation and the Quest for Democratization*. Oslo: Arena and EUI, 57–140.

Gehring, T., 2004. The Consequences of Delegation to Independent Agencies: Separation of Powers, Discursive Governance and the Regulation of Telecommunications in Germany. *European Journal of Political Research*, 43, 4, 677–698.

Gehring, T., 2009. Die Autonomie Internationaler Organisationen: Lehren aus der systemtheoretischen Organisationstheorie. *In*: K. Dingwerth, D. Kerwer, and A. Nölke, eds., *Die Organisierte Welt: Internationale Beziehungen und Organisationsforschung*. Baden-Baden: Nomos Verlagsgesellschaft, 60–95.

Gehring, T., and Dörfler, T., 2013. Division of Labor and Rule-based Decisionmaking within the UN Security Council: The Al-Qaeda/Taliban Sanctions Regime. *Global Governance*, 19, 4, 567–587.

Gehring, T., and Kerler, M., 2008. Institutional Stimulation of Deliberative Decision-Making. Division of Labour, Deliberative Legitimacy and Technical Regulation in the European Single Market. *Journal of Common Market Studies*, 46, 5, 1001–1023.

Gehring, T., and Plocher, I., 2009. Making an Administrative Trustee Agent Accountable: Reason-Based Decision Making within the Kyoto Protocol's Clean Development Mechanism. *International Studies Quarterly*, 53, 3, 669–693.

Gehring, T., and Ruffing, E., 2008. When Arguments Prevail Over Power: The CITES Procedure for the Listing of Endangered Species. *Global Environmental Politics*, 8, 2, 123–148.

George, A.L., and Bennett, A., 2005. *Case Studies and Theory Development in the Social Sciences*. Cambridge, MA: MIT Press.

Gerhardt, M.J., 2005. The Limited Path Dependency of Precedent. *Journal of Constitutional Law*, 7, 4, 905–1000.

Gerring, J., 2004. What Is a Case Study and What Is It Good for? *American Political Science Review*, 98, 02, 341–354.

Gladstone, R., 2012. U.S. Acts with Europe to Strengthen Iran Penalties. *New York Times*, December 22, A9.

Goldberg, M.L., 2006. The Test. *The American Prospect*, February 17.

Gootman, E., 2006. Security Council Approves Sanctions Against Iran Over Nuclear Program. *New York Times*, December 24, A1.

Gordon, J., 2010. *Invisible War. The United States and the Iraq Sanctions*. Cambridge, MA, London: Harvard University Press.

Gowlland-Debbas, V., 1990. *Collective Responses to Illegal Acts in International Law*. Dordrecht, Geneva: Martinus Nijhoff Publishers.

Graham-Brown, S., 1999. *Sanctioning Saddam. The Politics of Intervention in Iraq*. London: I.B. Tauris in association with MERIP.

Gross Stein, J., 1989. Getting to the Table: Processes of International Prenegotiation. *International Journal*, 44, 2, 231–236.

Gutherie, P., 2005. Security Council Sanctions and the Protection of Individual Rights. *NYU Annual Survey of American Law*, 60, 3, 491–542.

Haftel, Y.Z., and Thompson, A., 2006. The Independence of International Organizations: Concept and Applications. *Journal of Conflict Resolution*, 50, 2, 253–275.

Hall, C., Doyle, L., and Dowden, R., 1990. Khamenei Denounces US; Washington Backs down over Block on Food and Medicine to Iraq as Iran's Spiritual Leader Calls Fight a Holy War. *The Independent*, September 13, A1.

Hamilton, R., 2011. *Fighting for Darfur. Public Action and the Struggle to Stop Genocide*. 1st ed. New York: Palgrave Macmillan.

Happaerts, S., 2009. Dealing with Darfur: The UN Security Council Enters A Complex Battleground. *In*: J. Wouters, E. Drieskens, and S. Biscop, eds., *Belgium in the UN Security Council. Reflections on the 2007–2008 Membership*. Antwerpen: Intersentia, 103–113.

Hawkins, D.G. *et al.*, 2006. Delegation under Anarchy: States, International Organizations, and Principal-Agent Theory. *In*: D.G. Hawkins *et al.*, eds., *Delegation and Agency in International Organizations*. Cambridge, MA: Cambridge University Press, 3–38.

Heupel, M., 2009. Multilateral Sanctions against Terror Suspects and the Violation of Due Process Standards. *International Affairs*, 85, 2, 307–321.

Heupel, M., 2013. With Power Comes Responsibility. Human Rights Protection in United Nations Sanctions Policy. *European Journal of International Relations*, 19, 4, 1–24.

Hoffmann, J., 2008. Terrorism Blacklisting: Putting European Human Rights Guarantees to the Test. *Constellations*, 15, 4, 543–560.

Hoge, W., 2004a. U.S. Alters Sudan Resolution to Attract U.N. Votes. *New York Times*, July 30, A7.

Hoge, W., 2004b. U.S. Urges Security Council to Take Tougher Stance on Sudan. *New York Times*, September 9, A5.

Hoge, W., 2004c. U.S. Proposes A Softer Threat on Sudan's Oil. *New York Times*, September 15, A13.

Hoge, W., 2004d. Authority Is Approved for Sanctions Against Sudan. *New York Times*, September 19, A12.

Hoge, W., 2006a. U.N. Council Urges Iran to Halt Atom Activity. *New York Times*, March 30, A6.

Hoge, W., 2006b. U.S. Envoy to Expose 4 Sudanese in U.N. Debate About Darfur. *New York Times*, April 18, A12.

Holslag, J. *et al.*, 2007. *China's Resources and Energy Policy in Sub-Saharan Africa. Report for the Development Committee of the European Parliament*. Brussels.

Holslag, J., 2008. China's Diplomatic Manoeuvring on the Question of Darfur. *Journal of Contemporary China*, 17, 54, 71–84.

Holslag, J., 2009. China's True Intentions in Congo. *Harvard International Review* [online]. Available from: http://hir.harvard.edu/article/?a=2604.

Hooghe, L., and Marks, G., 2015. Delegation and Pooling in International Organizations. *The Review of International Organizations*, 10, 3, 305–328.

Hovell, D., 2016. *The Power of Process. The Value of Due Process in Security Council Sanctions Decision-Making*. Oxford, New York: Oxford University Press.

Human Rights First, 2008. *Investing in Tragedy. China's Money, Arms, and Politics in Sudan*. New York, Washington, DC: Human Rights First.

Human Rights Watch, 2006. *U.N.: Leaked Names Highlight Sudan's Failure to Protect. Strong U.N. Force, Sanctions Needed to Combat Continuing Attacks in Darfur*. Washington, DC: Human Rights Watch.

Hurd, I., 2007. *After Anarchy. Legitimacy and Power in the United Nations Security Council*. Princeton, NJ: Princeton University Press.

Huth, P.K., Croco, S.E., and Appel, B.J., 2013. Bringing Law to the Table: Legal Claims, Focal Points, and the Settlement of Territorial Disputes since 1945. *American Journal of Political Science*, 57, 1, 90–103.

International Crisis Group, 2009. *Congo: A Comprehensive Strategy to Disarm the FDLR*. Washington, DC: International Crisis Group.

Japan Economic Newswire, 2006. *Text of Original Draft Sanctions Resolution on Iran*. New York: Japan Economic Newswire, October 26.

Joerges, C., 2006. 'Deliberative Political Processes' Revisited. What Have We Learnt About the Legitimacy of Supranational Decision-Making. *Journal of Common Market Studies*, 44, 4, 779–802.

Joerges, C., and Neyer, J., 2001. Transforming Strategic Interaction into Deliberative Problem-Solving: European Comitology in the Foodstuffs Sector. *Journal of European Public Policy*, 4, 4, 609–625.

Johnson, T., and Urpelainen, J., 2014. International Bureaucrats and the Formation of Intergovernmental Organizations. Institutional Design Discretion Sweetens the Pot. *International Organization*, 68, 01, 177–209.

Johnstone, I., 1994. *Aftermath of the Gulf War: An Assessment of UN Action*. Boulder, CO, London: Lynne Rienner Publishers.

Kanetake, M., 2008. Enhancing Community Accountability of the Security Council through Pluralistic Structure: The Case of the 1267 Committee. *In*: A. von Bogdandy, R. Wolfrum, and C. Philipp, eds., *Max Planck Yearbook of United Nations Law*. Leiden, Biggleswade: Brill, 113–175.

Kaul, H.-P., 1996. Die Sanktionsausschüsse des Sicherheitsrats. *Vereinte Nationen*, 44, 3, 96–103.

Keohane, R.O., 1984. *After Hegemony. Cooperation and Discord in the World Political Economy*. 1st ed. Princeton, NJ: Princeton University Press.

Keohane, R.O., and Martin, L.L., 2003. Institutional Theory as a Research Program. *In*: C. Elman and M.F. Elman, eds., *Progress in International Relations Theory. Appraising the Field*. Cambridge, MA: MIT Press, 71–107.

Kerler, M., 2010. *Gutes Regieren in Internationalen Organisationen*. 1st ed. Baden-Baden, Bamberg: Nomos Verlagsgesellschaft.

Khalizad, Z., 2007a. UN/Sudan Sanctions: Qatar Calls for Sanctions on Rebels, 07USUNNEWYORK1004_a, November 12.

Khalizad, Z., 2007b. UN/Sudan Sanctions: China, Russia Indonesia Reject Strengthening Arms Embargo, Qatar Seeks Rebel Sanctions, 07USUNNEWYORK1058_a, November 21.

Khalizad, Z., 2008a. UN/1267 Sanctions: Belgians Request U.S. Reconsider Case to Delist Sayadi and Vinck, 08USUNNEWYORK209_a, March 6.

Khalizad, Z., 2008b. UN/Sudan Sanctions: French Reaction to USG-Proposed Designations, 08USUNNEWYORK486_a, June 3.

Kingsbury, B., Krisch, N., and Stewart, R.B., 2005. The Emergence of Global Administrative Law. *Law and Contemporary Problems*, 68, 3–4, 15–62.

Kleine-Ahlbrandt, S., and Small, A., 2008. China's New Dictatorship Diplomacy: Is Beijing Parting with Pariahs? *Foreign Affairs*, 87, 1, 38–56.

Koch, M., 2009. Autonomization of IGOs. *International Political Sociology*, 3, 4, 431–448.

Koremenos, B., Lipson, C., and Snidal, D., 2001. The Rational Design of International Institutions. *International Organization*, 55, 4, 761–799.

Koskenniemi, M., 1991. Le Comité des Sanctions Créé par la Résolution 661 (1990) du Conseil de Sécurité. *Annuaire français de droit international*, 37, 119–137.

Krisch, N., 2004. The Rise and Fall of Collective Security: Terrorism, US Hegemony, and the Plight of the Security Council. *In*: C. Walter *et al*., eds., *Terrorism as a Challenge for National and International Law: Security versus Liberty?* Berlin: Springer, 879–907.

Krisch, N., 2008. The Security Council and Great Powers. *In*: A.V. Lowe *et al*., eds., *The United Nations Security Council and War. The Evolution of Thought and Practice since 1945*. Oxford, New York: Oxford University Press, 133–153.

Kuziemko, I., and Werker, E., 2006. How Much Is a Seat on the Security Council Worth? Foreign Aid and Bribery at the United Nations. *Journal of Political Economy*, 114, 5, 905–930.

Lacey, M., 2004. U.N. Council, in Nairobi, Again Warns Sudan. *New York Times*, November 19, A7.

Lederer, E.M., 2002. *Swedish Legal Expert Urges U.N. to Protect Rights of Those Linked to al-Qaida*. United Nations: The Associated Press, February 12.

Lederer, E.M., 2004a. *U.S. Calls for U.N. Sanctions on Arab Militias in Western Sudan Blamed for Humanitarian Crisis*. United Nations: Associated Press International, June 30.

Lederer, E.M., 2004b. *U.S. Threatens Sanctions against Sudan if it Doesn't Quickly Rein in Militias in Western Darfur*. United Nations: The Associated Press, July 22.

Lederer, E.M., 2004c. *Security Council Heads to Nairobi for Rare Meeting in Field to Promote Peace in Sudan*. United Nations: Associated Press International, November 16.

Lederer, E.M., 2005a. *Security Council to Extend U.N. Political Mission in Sudan for a Crimes*. United Nations: Associated Press International, March 9.

Lederer, E.M., 2005b. *U.S. Circulates Three Sudan Resolutions on Peacekeepers, Sanctions and Punishment for Atrocities*. United Nations: The Associated Press, March 23.

Lederer, E.M., 2006a. *U.N. Panel Recommends Sanctions against Individuals from Sudanese Government and Rebel Groups Blocking Peace in Darfur*. United Nations: Associated Press International, January 11.

Lederer, E.M., 2006b. *Security Council Deeply Divided over Sanctions against Sudanese*. United Nations: The Associated Press, February 28.

Lederer, E.M., 2006c. *Britain and U.S. Calls for Sanctions against Four Sudanese over Darfur*. United Nations: Associated Press International, April 12.

Lederer, E.M., 2006d. *Blog: Behind the Scenes at the U.N.* United Nations: Associated Press Online, April 15.

Lederer, E.M., 2006e. *In Blow to Britain and U.S., Russia and China Will Oppose Sanctions against Sudanese Blocking Peace in Darfur*. United Nations: Associated Press International, April 17.

Lederer, E.M., 2006f. *Russia Locked in Disagreement with U.S., Europe over Sanctions against Iran*. United Nations: The Associated Press, November 16.

Lederer, E.M., 2006g. *Six Key Countries Make Progress on Iran Sanctions Resolution*. United Nations: The Associated Press, December 14.

Lederer, E.M., 2007a. *Major Powers Move Closer to Agreement on New Sanctions against Iran*. United Nations: Associated Press International, March 13.

Lederer, E.M., 2007b. *6 World Powers Agree to New U.N. Sanctions against Iran*. United Nations: The Associated Press, March 15.

Lederer, E.M., 2007c. *China Wants Sanctions and New Diplomatic Effort on Iran*. United Nations: Associated Press International, December 13.

Lederer, E.M., 2010a. *6 Powers Meet Again on Iran Sanctions*. United Nations: Associated Press International, April 15.

Lederer, E.M., 2010b. *China Wants Changes to Iran Sanctions Proposal*. United Nations: Associated Press International, April 21.

Lederer, E.M., 2010c. *US Gets China, Russia on Board for Iran Sanctions*. United Nations: The Associated Press, May 19.

Lederer, E.M., 2011. *UN Separates al-Qaida and Taliban Sanctions*. United Nations: Associated Press Online, June 17.

Lederer, E.M., 2014. *UN Sanctions ADF Rebel Group Fighting in Congo*. United Nations: Associated Press International, July 1.

Leopold, E., 2005a. *Annan Calls Emergency Sudan Session of UN Council*. United Nations: Alertnet, March 7.

Leopold, E., 2005b. *UN Delays Sudan Sanctions by Three Months*. United Nations: Reuters, July 7.

Levy, J., 2010. Counterfactuals and Case Studies. *In*: J.M. Box-Steffensmeier, H.E. Brady, and D. Collier, eds., *The Oxford Handbook of Political Methodology*. Oxford, New York: Oxford University Press, 627–644.

Lewis, M., 2009. *Skirting the Law. Sudan's Post-CPA Arms Flows*. Geneva: Small Arms Survey.

Lewis, P., 1991. U.N. Survey Calls Iraq's War Damage Near-Apocalyptic. *New York Times*, March 22, A6.

Linton, L., 2005. *Draft U.N. Resolution Would Send Peacekeepers to Sudan*. United Nations: Associated Press International, February 14.

Lipson, M., 2006. Transgovernmental Networks and Nonproliferation. *International Journal*, 61, 1, 179–198.

Lynch, C., 2002. U.S. Seeks to Take 6 Names off U.N. Sanctions List. Administration Was Criticized for Offering Little Proof That Individuals, Groups Aided al Qaeda. *The Washington Post*, August 22, A13.

Lynch, C., 2004a. U.S. Seeks U.N. Pressure on Sudan. *Washington Post*, July 23, A25.

Lynch, C., 2004b. U.S. Urges Aid to Spur Peace in Sudan. *Washington Post*, November 15, A21.

Lynch, C., 2006a. Sanctions against Sudanese Officials Sought over Darfur. *Washington Post*, February 23, A20.

Lynch, C., 2006b. U.S. Seeks U.N. Sanctions against Four in Sudan. *Washington Post*, April 19, A11.

Lynch, C., 2007. Sudan Backs away from U.N. Plan. Bashir Reneging on November Agreement: Sanctions, "No-Fly" Zone Possible. *Washington Post*, March 14, A12.

Lynch, C., 2013. Hidden Report Reveals how Iran Dodges Nuclear Watchdogs. *Foreign Policy*, June 18.

MacAskill, E., 2005. Britain Backs UN Sanctions after Losing Patience in Sudan Crisis. *Guardian*, March 8, A2.

MacAskill, E., 2006. Sudan Leaders Face UN Sanctions. *The Guardian*, March 1, 18.

MacFarquhar, N., Landler, M., and Sanger, D.E., 2010. U.N. Approves New Sanctions to Deter Iran. *New York Times*, June 10, A1.

MacKinnon, M.G., 2010. The United Nations Security Council. *In*: D.R. Black and P.D. Williams, eds., *The International Politics of Mass Atrocities. The Case of Darfur*. London, New York: Routledge, 71–99.

Majone, G., 2001. Two Logics of Delegation: Agency and Fiduciary Relations in EU Governance. *European Union Politics*, 2, 1, 103–122.

Malone, D.M., 2006. *The International Struggle over Iraq. Politics in the UN Security Council, 1980–2005*. Oxford: Oxford University Press.

Malone, D.M., and Chitalkar, P., 2016. Iraq. *In*: S.v. Einsiedel, D.M. Malone, and B. Stagno Ugarte, eds., *The UN Security Council in the Twenty-First Century*. Boulder, CO: Lynne Rienner Publishers, 551–568.

Manrique Gil, M., 2012. *The M23 and Eastern D.R. Congo: An Intractable Problem or an Opportunity to Engage?* Brussels, Strasbourg: European Parliament.

March, J.G., and Olsen, J.P., 1989. *Rediscovering Institutions: The Organizational Basis of Politics*. New York: Simon & Schuster.

Marquis, C., and Lacey, M., 2004. Powell and Annan See Hints of Disaster in Sudan. *New York Times*, June 30, A1.

Martin, L.L., and Simmons, B.A., 2013. International Organizations and Institutions. *In*: B.A. Simmons, T. Risse-Kappen, and W. Carlsnaes, eds., *Handbook of International Relations*. London, Thousand Oaks, CA: SAGE Publications, 326–351.

McCubbins, M.D., and Schwartz, T., 1984. Congressional Oversight Overlooked: Police Patrols versus Fire Alarms. *American Journal of Political Science*, 28, 1, 165–179.

McKibben, H.E., and Western, S.D., 2014. Levels of Linkage. Across-Agreement versus Within-Agreement Explanations of Consensus Formation among States. *International Studies Quarterly*, 58, 1, 44–54.

Mehta, J., Starmer, C., and Sugden, R., 1994. The Nature of Salience: An Experimental Investigation of Pure Coordination Games. *The American Economic Review*, 84, 3, 658–673.

Miller, E., 2003. The Use of Targeted Sanctions in the Fight against International Terrorism – What about Human Rights? *Proceedings of the Annual Meeting (American Society of International Law)*, 97, 46–51.

Missile Technology Control Regime, 2015. *The Missile Technology Control Regime* [online]. Available from: www.mtcr.info/english/index.html [accessed April 17, 2015].

Monusco, 2018. *The Active and Illegal Foreign Armed Groups Operating on the Soil of the DR Congo* [online]. Available from: https://monusco.unmissions.org/en/foreign-armed-groups.

Moravcsik, A.M., 1998. *The Choice for Europe. Social Purpose and State Power from Messina to Maastricht*. Ithaca, NY: Cornell Univ. Press.

Nathan, L., 2007. The Making and Unmaking of the Darfur Peace Agreement. *In*: A. de Waal, ed., *War in Darfur and the Search for Peace*. Cambridge, MA: Global Equity Initiative Harvard University, 245–266.

Nielson, D.L., and Tierney, M.J., 2003. Delegation to International Organizations: Agency Theory and World Bank Environmental Reform. *International Organization*, 57, 2, 241–276.

Nordland, R., 2011. Afghans Want Sanctions Lifted on Taliban Figures. *New York Times*, June 5, A16.

Nuclear Suppliers Group, 2015a. *The Nuclear Suppliers Group: Its Origins, Role and Activities*. Vienna.

Nuclear Suppliers Group, 2015b. *Nuclear Suppliers Group* [online]. Nuclear Suppliers Group. Available from: www.nuclearsuppliersgroup.org/en/ [accessed April 17, 2015].

Oberlandesgericht Hamburg, 2013. Judgement of August, 11, (3–1/13).

Odell, J., 2013. Negotiation and Bargaining. *In*: B.A. Simmons, T. Risse-Kappen, and W. Carlsnaes, eds., *Handbook of International Relations*. London, Thousand Oaks, CA: SAGE Publications, 379–400.

Olson, A., 2007. *Major Powers Struggle to Agree on New Sanctions against Iran*. United Nations: Associated Press International, March 9.

Panel of Experts Iran, 2011. *Panel of Experts Established Pursuant to Resolution 1929 (2010). Final Report*. Acton, ACT, Australia.

Paulus, A., 2012. Article 29. *In*: B. Simma *et al*., eds., *The Charter of the United Nations: A Commentary*. Oxford: Oxford University Press, 983–1027.

Penketh, A., 2006. Britain Pushes for Travel Ban on Leaders to Curb Killing in Darfur. *The Independent*, March 1, 22.

Peters, A., 2012. Article 24. *In*: B. Simma *et al*., eds., *The Charter of the United Nations: A Commentary*. Oxford: Oxford University Press, 761–786.

Pollack, M.A., 1997. Delegation, Agency, and Agenda Setting in the European Community. *International Organization*, 51, 1, 99–134.

Pollack, M.A., 2003. *The Engines of European Integration. Delegation, Agency, and Agenda Setting in the EU*. Oxford: Oxford University Press.

Prendergast, J., 2007. *The Answer to Darfur. How to Resolve the World's Hottest War*. Washington, DC.

Prendergast, J., and Sullivan, D., 2008. *Irresolution. The U.N. Security Council on Darfur*. Washington, DC: Enough Project.

Prost, K., 2012a. Fair Process and the Security Council: A Case for the Office of the Ombudsperson. *In*: Salinas de Frías, Ana, K. Samuel, and N.D. White, eds., *Counter-Terrorism. International Law and Practice*. Oxford, New York: Oxford University Press, 409–423.

Prost, K., 2012b. *The Office of the Ombudsperson. A Case for Fair Process* [online]. Available from: http://regnet.anu.edu.au/research/publications/2788/working-paper-no-43-office-ombudsperson-case-fair-process.

Prost, K., and Wilmshurst, E., 2013. *UN Sanctions, Human Rights and the Ombudsperson*. London: Chatham House.

Prunier, G., 2009. *From Genocide to Continental War. The "Congolese" Conflict and the Crisis of Contemporary Africa*. London: Hurst.

Quaglia, L., Francesco, F. de, and Radaelli, C.M., 2008. Committee Governance and Socialization in the European Union. *Journal of European Public Policy*, 15, 1, 155–166.

Rawls, J., 1971. *A Theory of Justice*. 22nd ed. Cambridge, MA: Belknap Press of Harvard University Press.

Reinalda, B., 2013. International Organizations as a Field of Research since 1910. *In*: B. Reinalda, ed., *Routledge Handbook of International Organization*. Milton Park, Abingdon, Oxon: Routledge, 1–23.

Rice, S., 2009a. Sudan/Sanctions: Expert Brief on Violations and Poor Cooperation with UN Agencies, 09USUNNEWYORK695_a, July 16.

Rice, S., 2009b. Saving the Al-Qaeda/Taliban Sanctions Regime, 09USUNNEWYORK 818_a, September 4.

Riechmann, D., 2011. *UN Could Split Afghan Taliban, al-Qaida Black List*. Kabul: The Associated Press, June 7.

Ringe, N., 2005. Policy Preference Formation in Legislative Politics: Structures, Actors, and Focal Points. *American Journal of Political Science*, 49, 4, 731–745.

Risse, T., 2000. "Let's Argue!": Communicative Action in World Politics. *International Organization*, 54, 1, 1–39.

Rittberger, V., Zangl, B., and Kruck, A., 2012. *International Organization*. 2nd ed. Basingstoke: Palgrave Macmillan.

Romaniuk, P., 2010. *Multilateral Counter-Terrorism. The Global Politics of Cooperation and Contestation*. Milton Park, Abingdon, Oxon, New York: Routledge.

Rosand, E., 2004. The Security Council's Efforts to Monitor the Implementation of Al Qaeda/Taliban Sanctions. *The American Journal of International Law*, 98, 4, 745–763.

Rosand, E., 2010. The UN Response to the Evolving Threat of Global Terrorism: Institutional Reform, Rivalry, or Renewal? *In*: P.G. Danchin and H. Fischer, eds., *United Nations Reform and the New Collective Security*. Cambridge: Cambridge University Press.

Rowe, T., 1992. Aid-Dependent Sudan to Sell Beef to Iraq. *Washington Post*, October 6.

Rwanda Ministry of Foreign Affairs and Cooperation, 2012. *Rwanda's Response to the Allegations Contained in the Addendum to the UN Group of Experts Interim Report*. Kigali.

Salton, H., 2017. *Dangerous Diplomacy. Bureaucracy, Power Politics, and the Role of the UN Secretariat in Rwanda.* 1st ed. Oxford, United Kingdom: Oxford University Press.

Sartori, G., 1987. *The Theory of Democracy Revisited.* Chatham, NJ: Chatham House Publishers.

Sauer, T., 2009. The Unbearable Lightness of UN Security Council Resolutions: The Case of Iran. *In*: J. Wouters, E. Drieskens, and S. Biscop, eds., *Belgium in the UN Security Council. Reflections on the 2007–2008 Membership.* Antwerpen: Intersentia, 115–126.

Schabas, W.A., 2010. The International Criminal Court. *In*: D.R. Black and P.D. Williams, eds., *The International Politics of Mass Atrocities. The Case of Darfur.* London, New York: Routledge, 134–154.

Schaefer, G.F., 1996. Committees in the EC Policy Process: A First Step towards Developing a Conceptual Framework. *In*: R.H. Pedler and G.F. Schaefer, eds., *Shaping European Law and Policy. The Role of Committees and Comitology in the Political Process.* Maastricht, 3–23.

Scharf, M.P., and Dorosin, J.L., 1993. Interpreting UN Sanctions: The Rulings and Role of the Yugoslavia Sanctions Committee. *Brooklyn Journal of International Law*, 19, 1, 771–827.

Scharpf, F.W., 1997. *Games Real Actors Play. Actor-Centered Institutionalism in Policy Research.* New York: Westview Press.

Schelling, T.C., 1960. *The Strategy of Conflict.* Cambridge, MA: Harvard University Press.

Schimmelfennig, F., 2001. The Community Trap: Liberal Norms, Rhetorical Action, and the Eastern Enlargement of the European Union. *International Organization*, 55, 1, 47–80.

Schmemann, S., 2002. A Nation Challenged: Sanctions and Fallout. Swedes Take up the Cause of 3 on U.S. Terror List. *New York Times*, January 26, A9.

Schneider, C.J., 2011. Weak States and Institutionalized Bargaining Power in International Organizations. *International Studies Quarterly*, 55, 2, 331–355.

Schorlemer, S. von, 2003. Human Rights: Substantive and Institutional Implications of the War Against Terrorism. *European Journal of International Law*, 14, 2, 265–282.

Schweid, B., 1993. *Sudan Added to Terrorist List.* Washington, DC: The Associated Press, August 18.

SCR Forecast November, 2005a. *Democratic Republic of the Congo.* New York: Security Council Report, 2005.

SCR Forecast November, 2005b. *Sudan/Darfur.* New York: Security Council Report, 2005.

SCR Forecast March, 2006a. *Iran.* New York: Security Council Report, 2006.

SCR Forecast March, 2006b. *Sudan/Darfur.* New York: Security Council Report, 2006.

SCR Forecast April, 2006. *Sudan/Darfur.* New York: Security Council Report, 2006.

SCR Forecast May, 2006a. *Iran.* New York: Security Council Report, 2006.

SCR Forecast May, 2006b. *Sudan/Darfur.* New York: Security Council Report, 2006.

SCR Forecast June, 2006a. *Democratic Republic of the Congo.* New York: Security Council Report, 2006.

SCR Forecast June, 2006b. *Iran.* New York: Security Council Report, 2006.

SCR Forecast July, 2006. *Democratic Republic of the Congo.* New York: Security Council Report, 2006.

SCR Forecast August, 2006. *Iran.* New York: Security Council Report, 2006.

SCR Forecast September, 2006. *Democratic Republic of the Congo*. New York: Security Council Report, 2006.
SCR Forecast November, 2006. *Iran*. New York: Security Council Report, 2006.
SCR Forecast December, 2006. *Democratic Republic of the Congo*. New York: Security Council Report, 2006.
SCR Forecast May, 2007. *Iran*. New York: Security Council Report, 2007.
SCR Forecast December, 2007a. *Iran*. New York: Security Council Report, 2007.
SCR Forecast December, 2007b. *Sudan/Darfur*. New York: Security Council Report, 2007.
SCR Forecast January, 2008. *Iran*. New York: Security Council Report, 2008.
SCR Forecast November, 2009. *Democratic Republic of the Congo*. New York: Security Council Report, 2009.
SCR Forecast May, 2010. *Democratic Republic of the Congo*. New York: Security Council Report, 2010.
SCR Forecast February, 2011. *Democratic Republic of the Congo*. New York: Security Council Report, 2011.
SCR Forecast March, 2011. *Iran*. New York: Security Council Report, 2011.
SCR Forecast June, 2011. *SCR Forecast June. Counter-Terrorism: 1267 Committee*. New York: Security Council Report, May 31.
SCR Forecast November, 2011. *Democratic Republic of the Congo*. New York: Security Council Report, 2011.
SCR Forecast December, 2011. *Iran*. New York: Security Council Report, 2011.
SCR Forecast June, 2012. *Iran*. New York: Security Council Report, 2012.
SCR Forecast February, 2013. *Democratic Republic of the Congo*. New York: Security Council Report, 2013.
SCR Forecast July, 2013. *Iran*. New York: Security Council Report, 2013.
SCR Forecast October, 2013. *Democratic Republic of the Congo*. New York: Security Council Report, 2013.
SCR Forecast December, 2013. *Iran*. New York: Security Council Report, 2013.
SCR Forecast March, 2014. *Democratic Republic of the Congo*. New York: Security Council Report, 2014.
SCR Forecast June, 2014. *Iran*. New York: Security Council Report, 2014.
SCR Forecast December, 2014. *Iran*. New York: Security Council Report, 2014.
SCR Forecast March, 2015. *Iran*. New York: Security Council Report, 2015.
SCR Forecast May, 2018. *Counter-Terrorism*. New York: Security Council Report, 2018.
SCR Update Report, 2005. *Democratic Republic of the Congo*. New York: Security Council Report, 2005.
SCR Update Report No. 3, 2006. *Sudan/Darfur*. New York: Security Council Report, January 13.
SCR Update Report No. 4, 2006. *Iran*. New York: Security Council Report, 2006.
SCR Update Report No. 2, 2008. *Iran*. New York: Security Council Report, 2008.
Sebenius, J.K., 1983. Negotiation Arithmetic: Adding and Subtracting Issues and Parties. *International Organization*, 37, 2, 281–316.
Secretary of State, 2008a. UN 1267: Requesting Assistance to Resolve Longstanding USG Holds on Libyan Terrorist Sanctions Requests, 08STATE97379_a, September 11.
Secretary of State, 2008b. Response to Taiwan's Request for Identifier Information on Iranian UNSCR Designated Individuals, 08STATE127254_a, December 3.
Secretary of State, 2009. UNSC DRC Sanctions Committee – Designation of FDLR Leaders, 09STATE16194_a, February 21.

Security Council Press Release, 2006. *Security Council Imposes Travel, Financial Sanctions on 4 Sudanese, Adopting Resolution 1672 (2006) by 12-0-3. 5423rd Meeting (PM)*. United Nations.

Security Council Report, 2005. *Update Report No.1 Côte d'Ivoire*. New York: Security Council Report, December 1.

Security Council Report, 2006. *Monthly Forecast July*. New York: Security Council Report, July 29.

Security Council Report, 2012a. *Security Council Elections 2012*. New York: Security Council Report.

Security Council Report, 2012b. *Council Activities on the Democratic Republic of the Congo*. New York: Security Council Report, November 20.

Security Council Report, 2013. *UN Sanctions*. New York: Security Council Report.

Security Council Report, 2014. *Security Council Elections 2014*. New York: Security Council Report.

Security Council Report, 2015. *SCR Forecast January*. *The Democratic Republic of the Congo*: Security Council Report, 2015.

Security Council Report, 2016. *Human Rights and the Security Council – An Evolving Role*. New York: Security Council Report.

Sievers, L., and Daws, S., 2014. *The Procedure of the UN Security Council*. 4th ed. Oxford: Oxford University Press.

Simmons, B.A., and Danner, A., 2010. Credible Commitments and the International Criminal Court. *International Organization*, 64, 2, 225.

Simons, G.L., 1996. *The Scourging of Iraq. Sanctions, Law and Natural Justice*. Basingstoke: Macmillan.

Singer, D.J., 1987. Reconstructing the Correlates of War Dataset on Material Capabilities of States, 1816–1985. *International Interactions*, 14, 115–132.

Slaughter, A.-M., and Hale, T.N., 2011. Transgovernmental Networks. *In*: M. Bevir, ed., *The SAGE Handbook of Governance*. London: SAGE Publications, 342–351.

Smith, D., 2012. Rwanda joins UN Security Council despite Damning Congo Report. *Guardian*, October 18.

Snidal, D., 1985. Coordination versus Prisoners' Dilemma: Implications for International Cooperation and Regimes. *American Political Science Review*, 79, 4, 923–942.

Soderlund, W.C., 2012. *Africa's Deadliest Conflict. Media Coverage of the Humanitarian Disaster in the Congo and the United Nations Response, 1997–2008*. Waterloo, ON: Wilfrid Laurier University Press.

Stedjan, S., and Thomas-Jensen, C., 2010. The United States. *In*: D.R. Black and P.D. Williams, eds., *The International Politics of Mass Atrocities. The Case of Darfur*. London, New York: Routledge, 157–175.

Stein, A.A., 1982. Coordination and Collaboration: Regimes in an Anarchic World. *International Organization*, 36, 2, 299–324.

Stockholm International Peace Research Institute, 2018. *SIPRI Arms Transfers Database* [online]. Stockholm International Peace Research Institute. Available from: www.sipri.org/databases/armstransfers [accessed April 18, 2018].

Stone, R.W., 2011. *Controlling Institutions. International Organizations and the Global Economy*. 1st ed. Cambridge: Cambridge University Press.

Stone Sweet, A., and Sandholtz, W., 2004. Law, Politics, and International Governance. *In*: C. Reus-Smit, ed., *The Politics of International Law*. Cambridge: Cambridge University Press, 238–271.

Sugden, R., 1989. Spontaneous Order. *Journal of Economic Perspectives*, 3, 4, 85–97.

Sugden, R., and Zamarrón, I.E., 2006. Finding the Key. The Riddle of Focal Points. *Journal of Economic Psychology*, 27, 5, 609–621.

Sullivan, G., and Goede, M. de, 2013. Between Law and the Exception. The UN 1267 Ombudsperson as a Hybrid Model of Legal Expertise. *Leiden Journal of International Law*, 26, 4, 833–854.

Taylor, I., 2010. The People's Republic of China. *In*: D.R. Black and P.D. Williams, eds., *The International Politics of Mass Atrocities. The Case of Darfur*. London, New York: Routledge, 176–194.

Thompson, A., 2006. Coercion Through IOs: The Security Council and the Logic of Information Transmission. *International Organization*, 60, 1, 1–34.

Thompson, A., 2009. *Channels of Power. The UN Security Council and U.S. Statecraft in Iraq*. Ithaca: Cornell University Press.

Traub, J., 2010. *Unwilling and Unable: The Failed Response to the Atrocities in Darfur*. New York: Global Centre for the Responsibility to Protect.

Tsebelis, G., 2000. Veto Players and Institutional Analysis. *Governance*, 13, 4, 441–474.

Turner, M., 2006. Sudan Ministers Named in Leaked UN Darfur List. *Financial Times*, February 22.

Turner, T., 2013. *Congo*. 1st ed. Cambridge: Polity Press.

Tzanakopoulos, A., 2011. *Disobeying the Security Council. Countermeasures against Wrongful Sanctions*. Oxford: Oxford University Press.

UN Permanent Missions of France, UK and US, 2011. *Press Release from the Permanent Missions to the United Nations of France, the United Kingdom, and the United States on the Designation for Sanctions of an Armed Group Leader in the DRC*. New York: UN.

US Embassy Beijing, 2006a. PRC supports UNSC Action on Iran; Differs on Scope, 06BEIJING23933_a, November 20.

US Embassy Beijing, 2006b. Corrected Copy: PRC/Iran: Beijing Responds to Demarche on UK-French Draft Resolution, 06BEIJING24499_a, December 13.

US Embassy Beijing, 2007a. A/S Silverberg and AFM Cui Discuss Burma, Haiti, Iran, UNSC Reform, Sudan and Human Rights, 07BEIJING617_a, January 26.

US Embassy Beijing, 2007b. Democratic Republic of Congo Sanctions Demarche Delivered to China, 07BEIJING1839_a, March 19.

US Embassy Beijing, 2008. China Opposes Four Sudan-Related Designations, 08BEIJING2201_a, June 6.

US Embassy Beijing, 2010. PRC/Iran: Beijing Continues to Call for Patience, 10BEIJING293_a, February 4.

US Embassy Beijing, 2011. China Urged to Reconsider Four Sudan-related Designations, 08BEIJING2277_a, June 11.

US Embassy Berlin, 2007. German Government Actions to Implement UNSCR 1737 Sanctions on Iran, 07BERLIN34_a, January 5.

US Embassy Kabul, 2009. UN 1267 Al Qaeda/Taliban Sanctions Team Briefs Embassy on Delisting Strategy, 09KABUL1520_a, June 14.

US Embassy Khartoum, 2006a. Sudan – Response to Demarche on Gathering Information for Individuals under UNSCR 1591, 06KHARTOUM235_a, January 30.

US Embassy Khartoum, 2006b. Sudan/China: UNSC Vote on Darfur Shows Limits of Friendship, 06KHARTOUM996_a, April 26.

US Embassy Khartoum, 2007. Response to Request: UK-Proposed Individuals for Designation Under UNSCR 1591, 07KHARTOUM363_a, March 8.

US Embassy Kinshasa, 2005a. UN/DRC Sanctions List, 05KINSHASA1429_a, September 7.

US Embassy Kinshasa, 2005b. China's Influence in Africa: Expanding in the DRC, 05KINSHASA1614_a, September 29.
US Embassy London, 2006. Demarche on UNSC Action on Iran: HMG in Full Agreement, but Pessimistic on Moving Russia, China, 06LONDON8073_a, November 22.
US Embassy London, 2007. Darfur: UK Mulling Tougher Measures, 07LONDON438_a, February 2.
US Embassy London, 2008. DRC Sanctions: UK Appreciates Information, Keen to Move Forward, 08LONDON2196_a, August 27.
US Embassy London, 2009. DRC/Sanctions: UK Prefers Previous Approach and Statements of Case, 09LONDON124_a, January 16.
US Embassy Moscow, 2006a. P-5 Hold Consultations March 2 in Moscow, 06MOSCOW3362_a, 03.31.
US Embassy Moscow, 2006b. MFA on UNSC Action on Iran, 06MOSCOW12783_a, December 4.
US Embassy Moscow, 2006c. Russia and Iran: After the Sanctions Resolution, 06MOSCOW12171_a, December 29.
US Embassy Moscow, 2007. HIRC Chairman Lantos Meeting with Russian Security Council Secretary Ivanov, 07MOSCOW753_a, February 21.
US Embassy Moscow, 2008. Russia Concerned with UNSCR 1267 Delisting of Taliban, 08MOSCOW1817_a, June 25.
US Embassy Moscow, 2010. U/S Burns' Moscow Meetings, 10MOSCOW144_a, January 22.
US Embassy Paris, 2005a. Darfur Accountability: Amb. Prosper's Discussion with French MFA, 05PARIS1039_a, February 17.
US Embassy Paris, 2005b. France Will Review Their Position on Language in the UNSCR 1267 Successor Resolution, 05PARIS5157_a, July 26.
US Embassy Paris, 2005c. PDAS Volker Hears French Views on Africa, 05PARIS 6938_a, October 11.
US Embassy Paris, 2006a. Sudan Sanctions Demarche Elicits MFA Remarks on UNSC Procedures, 06PARIS2587_a, April 19.
US Embassy Paris, 2006b. French Comment on U.S. Proposal Regarding the 1267 Committee, 06PARIS3382_a, May 19.
US Embassy Paris, 2007. France/Darfur: Alignment on HSP, Divergence on Sanctions Designations, 07PARIS1062_a, March 19.
US Embassy Paris, 2008. France Agrees with USG Approach on Rwandan FDLR Sanctions, 08PARIS1100_a, June 10.
US Embassy Rome, 2007. Darfur: Italy Agrees Pressure Needed, but Wants Time for Dialogue, 07ROME903_a, April 30.
US Embassy The Hague, 2006. Netherlands/Sudan: Gathering Information for Individuals under UNSCR 1591, 06THEHAGUE207_a, January 31.
US Embassy Tokyo, 2006. Sudan Sanctions: Japan Supports U.S. Efforts, 06TOKYO 2182_a, April 21.
US Permanent Mission to the UN, 2006a. UNSC/Sanctions: China's ETLO/SHAT Designation Request, 06USUNNEWYORK340_a, February 23.
US Permanent Mission to the UN, 2006b. A Step Closer to Transition: With UNSCR 1663 Passage, SYG Can Reach out to NATO, 06USUNNEWYORK618_a, March 28.
US Permanent Mission to the UN, 2006c. UNSC/Sudan: Council Adopts Sanctions Resolution and Abuja PRST in Package Deal, 06USUNNEWYORK890_a, April 28.

US Permanent Mission to the UN, 2006d. Darfur Resolution Passes Unanimously with Some Chinese Help, 06USUNNEWYORK1017_a, May 18.

US Permanent Mission to the UN, 2007a. UNSC Iran Sanctions Committee First Meeting, 07USUNNEWYORK66_a, January 26.

US Permanent Mission to the UN, 2007b. Making Taliban Sanctions Relevant, 07USUNNEWYORK173_a, March 2.

US Permanent Mission to the UN, 2007c. UN/Sudan: UK and French Reactions to US Sanctions Targets, 07USUNNEWYORK166_a, March 2.

US Permanent Mission to the UN, 2007d. UN/Sudan Sanctions: French Reactions to US Names for Sanctions, 07USUNNEWYORK194_a, March 12.

US Permanent Mission to the UN, 2007e. UN/Sudan Sanctions: Initial Markers on Possible Sanctions Laid Down in Committee Meeting, UK Ready to Table Names, 07USUNNEWYORK197_a, March 12.

US Permanent Mission to the UN, 2007f. UN/Sudan Sanctions: P5 Ambassadors Discuss Sudan Sanctions, 07USUNNEWYORK198_a, March 12.

US Permanent Mission to the UN, 2007g. UNSC/Darfur: Members Disappointed with Bashir Response but Little Appetite for Sanctions, 07USUNNEWYORK227_a, March 21.

US Permanent Mission to the UN, 2007h. UN/Sudan Sanctions: Committee Meets with Experts Panel to Discuss Embargo Violations, 07USUNNEWYORK282_a, April 11.

US Permanent Mission to the UN, 2007i. UN/Sudan Sanctionos: French Seek US Reaction on Proposed Sanctions Targets, 07USUNNEWYORK305_a, April 19.

US Permanent Mission to the UN, 2007j. UN/Sudan Sanctions: Committee Discusses Strengthening the Embargo, 07USUNNEWYORK385_a, May 17.

US Permanent Mission to the UN, 2007k. UN/DRC Sanctions: Unanimous Council Support for Renewed Sanctions in DRC, 07USUNNEWYORK619_a, July 27.

US Permanent Mission to the UN, 2007l. UN/1267 Sanctions: Russians Unyielding on Removing Holds on Afghan De-Listing Requests, 07USUNNEWYORK1024_a, November 15.

US Permanent Mission to the UN, 2007m. UN/Sudan Sanctions: London Considering Alternatives to Qatar's Sanctions Proposal, 07USUNNEWYORK1055_a, November 21.

US Permanent Mission to the UN, 2008a. P5 Discussion Shows Continued Divisions on Darfur, 08USUNNEWYORK74_a, January 23.

US Permanent Mission to the UN, 2008b. UN/Sudan Sanctions: U.S. Isolated on New Names, 08USUNNEWYORK809_a, September 08.

US Permanent Mission to the UN, 2008c. UN/DRC Sanctions: Moving on Second Group of FDLR Targets, 08USUNNEWYORK908_a, March 10.

US Permanent Mission to the UN, 2008d. UN/Sudan Sanctions: Committee Divided on Expert Recommendations, 08USUNNEWYORK1051_a, November 10.

US Permanent Mission to the UN, 2009a. Iran/Cyprus: Next Steps on Monchegorsk, 09USUNNEWYORK103_a, February 10.

US Permanent Mission to the UN, 2009b. 1267 Committee Launches Work on Major New Tasks, 09USUNNEWYORK185_a, February 27.

US Permanent Mission to the UN, 2009c. DRC: Moving on Second Batch of FDLR Designations, 09USUNNEWYORK267_a, March 16.

US Permanent Mission to the UN, 2010. USUN and Turkish Missions Exchange Views on Issues before Security Council, 10USUNNEWYORK95_a, February 20.

US State Department, 2008a. USUN Place Hold on Rwandan FDLR Submission and Request Information, 08STATE60880_a, June 5.

US State Department, 2008b. Sudan/Chad – Urge Support for Designating 4 Individuals under targeted Sanctions, 08STATE61842_a, June 09.

US State Department, 2008c. FDLR Information Request for UN Sanctions in DRC Committee, 08STATE86006_a, August 11.

US State Department, 2008d. Information Sharing for UN Sanctions in DRC Committee, 08STATE90905_a, August 23.

US State Department, 2008e. USUN Instruction: Call P-3 Meeting Regarding Sudan Sanctions, 08STATE94825_a, September 4.

US State Department, 2008f. USUN Guidance: UKUN Sudan Sanctions Non-Paper, 08STATE119781_a, November 11.

US State Department, 2008g. Sudan: Sanctions Committee Splits on Proposals, 08USUNNEWYORK1134_a, December 4.

US State Department, 2009. 4 Names to Be Added to UNSC DRC Sanctions Committee's List, 09STATE3354_a, January 13.

van Walsum, P., 2004. The Iraq Sanctions Committee. *In*: D.M. Malone, ed., *The UN Security Council: From the Cold War to the 21st Century*. Boulder, CO: Lynne Rienner Publishers, 181–193.

van Woudenberg, A., 2005. *The Curse of Gold. Democratic Republic of Congo*. New York: Human Rights Watch.

Voeten, E., 2001. Outside Options and the Logic of Security Council Action. *American Political Science Review*, 95, 4, 845–858.

Voeten, E., 2005. The Political Origins of the UN Security Council's Ability to Legitimize the Use of Force. *International Organization*, 59, 3, 527–557.

Vreeland, J.R., and Dreher, A., 2014. *Political Economy of the United Nations Security Council. Money and Influence*. Cambridge: Cambridge University Press.

Wadhams, N., 2005a. *Europe and America Clash over Refining U.N. Terrorism Sanctions*. United Nations: Associated Press International, July 20.

Wadhams, N., 2005b. *U.S. Aims to Strengthen Terror Sanctions*. United Nations: The Associated Press, July 29.

Wadhams, N., 2006a. *U.S. Circulates Draft Resolution on Sudan Peacekeeping Transfer*. United Nations: Associated Press International, May 8.

Wadhams, N., 2006b. *U.S. Runs into Trouble with Tough Sudan Resolution*. United Nations: Associated Press International, May 12.

Wadhams, N., 2006c. *Security Council Passes Resolution to Speed U.N. Peacekeeping Force in Darfur*. United Nations: Associated Press International, May 16.

Wagner, T., 2007. *Major Powers Begin Work on New Iran Nuclear Resolution, Still Seeking Diplomatic Solution*. London: Associated Press International, February 27.

Ward, C.A., 2005. The Counter-Terrorism Committee. *In*: P. Wallensteen and C. Staibano, eds., *International Sanctions. Between Words and Wars in the Global System*. London, New York: Frank Cass, 167–180.

Wezeman, P.D., 2007. *United Nations Arms Embargoes. Their Impact on Arms Flows and Target Behavior. Case Study: Darfur, Sudan, 2004–2006*. Stockholm.

What's in Blue, 2011a. *Insights on Sudan Sanctions Committee*. New York: Security Council Report, March 10.

What's in Blue, 2011b. *Democratic Republic of the Congo Sanctions Committee*. New York: Security Council Report, July 12.

What's in Blue, 2013a. *Democratic Republic of the Congo*. New York: Security Council Report, February 4.

What's in Blue, 2013b. *High-Level Debate on the Democratic Republic of the Congo.* New York: Security Council Report, July 24.

What's in Blue, 2013c. *Democratic Republic of the Congo.* New York: Security Council Report, September 11.

What's in Blue, 2014a. *Democratic Republic of the Congo.* New York: Security Council Report, January 29.

What's in Blue, 2014b. *Democratic Republic of the Congo.* New York: Security Council Report, March 26.

What's in Blue, 2014c. *Adoption of a Resolution Reviewing Al-Qaida Sanctions.* New York: Security Council Report, June 16.

Williams, P.D., 2010. The United Kingdom. *In*: D.R. Black and P.D. Williams, eds., *The International Politics of Mass Atrocities. The Case of Darfur.* London, New York: Routledge, 195–212.

Williams, P.D., and Bellamy, A.J., 2005. The Responsibility to Protect and the Crisis in Darfur. *Security Dialogue*, 36, 1, 27–47.

Worsnip, P., 2011. *UN Committee Sanctions Congo Militia Chief.* United Nations: Reuters, November 29.

Wright, R., 2007. New U.N. Iran Resolution Considered; Draft Measure Would Impose New Sanctions on Military Unit, Bank. *Washington Post*, December 11, A17.

Wright, R., and Lynch, C., 2008. U.N. Imposes New Sanctions on Iran; Administration Must Settle for Watered-Down Resolution. *Washington Post*, March 4, A15.

Wuthnow, J., 2010. China and the Processes of Cooperation in UN Security Council Deliberations. *The Chinese Journal of International Politics*, 3, 1, 55–77.

Wuthnow, J., 2013. *Chinese Diplomacy and the UN Security Council. Beyond the Veto.* New York: Routledge.

Young, O.R., 1989. The Politics of International Regime Formation: Managing Natural Resources and the Environment. *International Organization*, 43, 3, 349–375.

Young, O.R., 1994. *International Governance. Protecting the Environment in a Stateless Society.* Ithaca, NY: Cornell University Press.

Index

Page numbers in **bold** denote tables, those in *italics* denote figures.

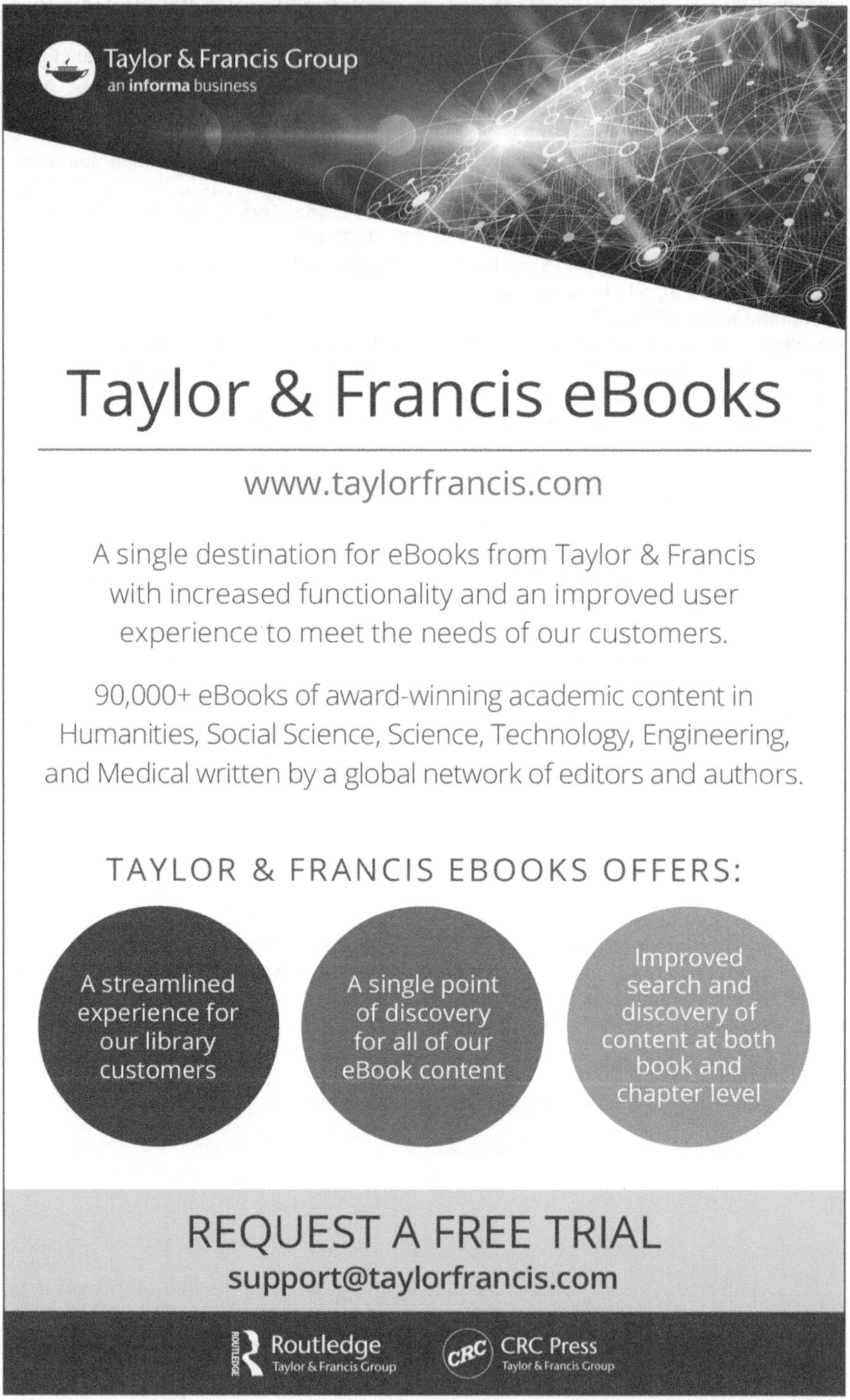
Taylor & Francis Group
an informa business
Taylor & Francis eBooks
www.taylorfrancis.com
A single destination for eBooks from Taylor & Francis with increased functionality and an improved user experience to meet the needs of our customers.
90,000+ eBooks of award-winning academic content in Humanities, Social Science, Science, Technology, Engineering, and Medical written by a global network of editors and authors.
TAYLOR & FRANCIS EBOOKS OFFERS:
A streamlined experience for our library customers
A single point of discovery for all of our eBook content
Improved search and discovery of content at both book and chapter level
REQUEST A FREE TRIAL
support@taylorfrancis.com
Routledge
Taylor & Francis Group
CRC Press
Taylor & Francis Group